Learning Processing

A Beginner's Guide to Programming Images, Animation, and Interaction

Learning Processing

A Beginner's Guide to Programming Images, Animation, and Interaction

Second Edition

Daniel Shiffman

AMSTERDAM • BOSTON • HEIDELBERG • LONDON
NEW YORK • OXFORD • PARIS • SAN DIEGO
SAN FRANCISCO • SINGAPORE • SYDNEY • TOKYO

Morgan Kaufmann Publishers is an imprint of Elsevier

Morgan Kaufmann Publishers is an imprint of Elsevier
30 Corporate Drive, Suite 400, Burlington, MA 01803, USA

Library of Congress Cataloging-in-Publication Data

A catalog record for this book is available from the Library of Congress.

ISBN: 978-0-12-394443-6

For information on all Morgan Kaufmann publications, visit our website at *www.mkp.com* or *www.books.elsevier.com*

Printed in the United States of America.

In memoriam

Red Burns was born in 1925 in Ottawa, Canada. In 1971, after having already led several full lives, she founded the Alternate Media Center at New York University. The center later became the Interactive Telecommunications Program (ITP) where she served as chair from 1982 until 2010. I met Red in 2001, when she introduced the program to me in what was likely her 20th year of student orientation. I was rather terrified of Red, but it didn't last. I quickly discovered her warmth, and over the next twelve years I was incredibly lucky to experience her fierce intelligence, five-word e-mails, and unwavering protectiveness of humanity over technology. People were always at the center of her thinking, and the tools (like the one taught in this book) were just a means for expression and communication. The ideas in this book were born from her mentorship and friendship. As the ITP saying goes, "Red Burns Changed My Life."

http://itp.nyu.edu/redburns/

Table of Contents

Acknowledgments ix
Introduction xi

Lesson 1: The Beginning
    Chapter 1: Pixels 3
    Chapter 2: Processing 19
    Chapter 3: Interaction 33

Lesson 2: Everything You Need to Know
    Chapter 4: Variables 49
    Chapter 5: Conditionals 67
    Chapter 6: Loops 93

Lesson 3: Organization
    Chapter 7: Functions 117
    Chapter 8: Objects 139

Lesson 4: More of the Same
    Chapter 9: Arrays 163

Lesson 5: Putting It All Together
    Chapter 10: Algorithms 189
    Chapter 11: Debugging 219
    Chapter 12: Libraries 225

Lesson 6: The World Revolves Around You
    Chapter 13: Mathematics 233
    Chapter 14: Translation and Rotation (in 3D!) 265

Lesson 7: Pixels Under a Microscope
    Chapter 15: Images 301
    Chapter 16: Video 329

Lesson 8: The Outside World
    Chapter 17: Text 361
    Chapter 18: Data Input 383
    Chapter 19: Data Streams 427

Lesson 9: Making Noise
    Chapter 20: Sound 453
    Chapter 21: Exporting 473

Lesson 10: Beyond Processing
    Chapter 22: Advanced Object-Oriented Programming 487
    Chapter 23: Java 503

Common Errors 523
Index 535

Acknowledgments

In the fall of 2001, I wandered into the Interactive Telecommunications Program in the Tisch School of the Arts at New York University, having not written a line of code since the early 1980s, when I'd done some experimenting in BASIC on an AppleII+. There, in a first semester course entitled "Introduction to Computational Media," I discovered programming. ITP has been my home ever since. Without the inspiration and support of the department, this book would never have been written.

Red Burns, the department's founder, encouraged and championed me for my first ten years at ITP. Sadly, she passed away in August 2013; this book is dedicated to her legacy. Dan O'Sullivan was the first to suggest that I try a course in Processing, giving me a reason to start putting together programming tutorials. Shawn Van Every sat next to me in the office throughout the majority of the writing of this book's first edition, providing helpful suggestions, code, and a great deal of moral support along the way. Tom Igoe's work with physical computing provided inspiration for this book, and he was particularly helpful as a resource while putting together examples on network and serial communication. And it was Clay Shirky who I can thank for stopping me in the hall one day to tell me I should write a book in the first place. Clay also provided a great deal of feedback on early drafts of the first edition.

All of my fellow computational media teachers at ITP have provided helpful suggestions and feedback along the way: Danny Rozin (the inspiration behind Chapters 15 and 16), Mimi Yin, Lauren McCarthy (whose innovative work developing p5.js has opened my eyes up to the world of JavaScript and the web), Amit Pitaru (who helped in particular with the first edition's chapter on sound), Nancy Lewis, James Tu, Mark Napier, Chris Kairalla, Luke Dubois, Roopa Vasudevan, Matt Parker, Heather Dewey-Hagborg, and Jim Moore (who was my teacher for that first semester course!). My gratitude goes to the following ITP full-time faculty members for continuously offering their insight and fortitude throughout the writing of this book: Marianne Petit, Nancy Hechinger, Marina Zurkow, Katherine Dillon, Eric Rosenthal, Gabe Barcia-Colombo, and Benedetta Piantella Simeonidis. And my full appreciation goes to the rest of the faculty and staff at ITP who have made this possible: George Agudow, Edward Gordon, Midori Yasuda, Rob Ryan, John Duane, Marlon Evans, Tony Tseng, Matthew Berger, Karl Ward, and Megan Demarest.

The students of ITP, too numerous to mention, have been an amazing source of feedback, having used much of the material in this book in trial runs for various courses. I have stacks of pages with notes scrawled in the margins, as well as a vast archive of email exchanges with corrections, comments, and generous words of encouragement, all of which were integral to the development of this book's ideas.

I'm also indebted to the energetic and supportive community of Processing programmers and artists. I'd probably be out of a job if it weren't for Casey Reas and Ben Fry who created Processing, to say the least. I've learned half of what I know simply from reading through the Processing source code; the elegant simplicity of the Processing language, website, and IDE has made programming accessible and fun for me and all of my students. I've received advice, suggestions, and comments from many Processing programmers including Andres Colubri, Scott Murray, Florian Jennet, Elie Zananiri, Scott Garner, Manindra Mohanara, Jer Thorp, Marius Watz, Robert Hodgin, Golan Levin, Tom Carden, Karsten Schmidt, Ariel Malka, Burak Arikan, and Ira Greenberg. The following teachers were also helpful in test-driving early versions of the first edition in their courses: Hector Rodriguez, Keith Lam, Liubo Borissov, Rick Giles, Amit Pitaru, David Maccarella, Jeff Gray, and Toshitaka Amaoka.

Peter Kirn and Douglas Edric Stanley provided extraordinarily detailed comments and feedback during the first edition's technical review process; the book is a great deal better than it would have been without their efforts. Demetrie Tyler did a tremendous job working on the original visual design of the cover and interior of the book. And a thanks to David Hindman, who helped me organize the original screenshots and diagrams. My thanks to Rich Hauck who developed the website for the first edition.

I'd also like to thank everyone at Morgan Kaufmann/Elsevier who worked on producing the first edition: Gregory Chalson, Tiffany Gasbarrini, Jeff Freeland, Danielle Monroe, Matthew Cater, Michele Cronin, Denise Penrose, and Mary James.

For the second edition, I am incredibly grateful to everyone at Morgan Kaufmann/Elsevier and O'Reilly who were supportive of my choice in using the Atlas publishing platform (https://atlas.oreilly.com/) to create this book.

Using Atlas allowed me to have a more fluid process and involve lots of contributors with feedback and advice. Wilm Thoben, Seth Kranzler, and Jason Sigal all provided sound feedback and edits on Chapter 20: Sound. Mark Sawula, Yong Bakos, and Kasper Kasperman read PDFs as they were generated and gave excellent critique and feedback. J. David Eisenberg acted as a de-facto technical editor, offering numerous and terrific suggestions for improving explanations and examples. A special thanks goes to Johanna Hedva who copy-edited almost the entire book during elaborate layout transformations. In addition, several key content changes exist because of her keen eye.

From Elsevier, Todd Green went above and beyond in working out the details of the complex collaboration with O'Reilly and Atlas. Thanks also to Charlie Kent and Debbie Clark for their help in facilitating production details. I'd like to say, in general, that the Atlas platform and the team at O'Reilly are terrific to work with: This book has all sorts of strange layout quirks, and it's amazing that the entire end product is generated from an HTML file using CSS and XSLT for layout. Thanks to Andrew Odewahn, Rune Madsen, Sanders Kleinfeld, Dan Fauxsmith, and Adam Zaremba for giving me early access to Atlas and teaching me its magic. Thanks to Rebecca Demarest for her help and advice with illustrations, and Ron Bilodeau for his feats of CSS. Last, but the opposite of least, I'd like to thank Kristen Brown who listened thoughtfully to every, single, tiny detail I asked about and applied the exact skills I lacked, knowing how to prioritize and keep a schedule to make sure this book actually met its deadline. You can see the scale of her contribution in this book's Github repo's pulse.

Excluding merges, **6 authors** have pushed **1,299 commits** to master and **1,299 commits** to all branches. On master, **476 files** have changed and there have been **213,930 additions** and **7 deletions**.

Most importantly, I'd like to thank my wife, Aliki Caloyeras; my children, Elias and Olympia; my parents, Doris and Bernard Shiffman; and my brother, Jonathan Shiffman, for their moral support, advice, and encouragement, not only in the second edition of this book, but in everything else.

Introduction

What is this book?

This book tells a story. It is a story of liberation, of taking the first steps toward understanding the foundations of computing, writing your own code, and creating your own media without the bonds of existing software tools. This story is not reserved for computer scientists and engineers. This story is for you.

Who is this book for?

This book is for the beginner. If you have never written a line of code in your life, you're in the right place. No assumptions are made, and the fundamentals of programming are covered slowly, one by one, in the first nine chapters of this book. You do not need any background knowledge besides the basics of operating a computer — turning it on, browsing the web, launching an application, that sort of thing.

Because this book uses Processing (more on Processing in a moment), it's especially good for someone studying or working in a visual field, such as graphic design, painting, sculpture, architecture, film, video, illustration, web design, and so on. If you're in one of these fields (at least one that involves using a computer), you're probably well-versed in a particular software package, possibly more than one, such as Photoshop, Illustrator, AutoCAD, Maya, After Effects, and so on. The point of this book is to release you, at least in part, from the confines of existing tools. What can you make, what can you design, if, instead of using someone else's tools, you create your own?

If you already have some programming experience but are interested in learning about Processing, this book could also be useful. The early chapters will provide you with a quick refresher (and solid foundation) for the more advanced topics found in the second half of the book.

What is Processing?

Let's say you're taking Computer Science 101, perhaps taught using the Java programming language. Here is the output of the first example program demonstrated in class:

Traditionally, programmers are taught the basics via command line output:

1. TEXT IN → You write your code as text.
2. TEXT OUT → Your code produces text output on the command line.
3. TEXT INTERACTION → The user can enter text on the command line to interact with the program.

The output "Hello, World!" of this example program is an old joke, a programmer's convention in which the text output of the first program you learn to write in any given language says "Hello, World!" It first appeared in a 1974 Bell Laboratories memorandum by Brian Kernighan entitled, "Programming in C: A Tutorial."

The strength of learning with Processing is its emphasis on a more intuitive and visually responsive environment, one that is more conducive to artists and designers learning programming.

1. TEXT IN → You write your code as text.
2. VISUALS OUT → Your code produces visuals in a window.
3. MOUSE INTERACTION → The user can interact with those visuals via the mouse (and more as you will see in this book!).

Processing's "Hello, World!" might look something like this:

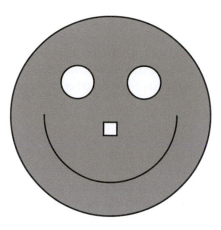

Hello, Shapes!

Though quite friendly looking, it's nothing spectacular (both of these first programs leave out #3: interaction), but neither is "Hello, World!" However, the focus — learning through immediate visual feedback — is quite different.

Processing is not the first language to follow this paradigm. In 1967, the Logo programming language was developed by Daniel G. Bobrow, Wally Feurzeig, and Seymour Papert. With Logo, a programmer writes instructions to direct a turtle around the screen, producing shapes and designs. John Maeda's Design By Numbers (1999) introduced computation to visual designers and artists with a simple, easy-to-use syntax.

While both of these languages are wonderful for their simplicity and innovation, their capabilities are limited.

Processing, a direct descendent of Logo and Design by Numbers, was born in 2001 in the Aesthetics and Computation research group at the Massachusetts Institute of Technology Media Lab. It is an open source initiative by Casey Reas and Benjamin Fry, who developed Processing as graduate students studying with John Maeda.

> *Processing is an open source programming language and environment for people who want to program images, animation, and sound. It is used by students, artists, designers, architects, researchers, and hobbyists for learning, prototyping, and production. It is created to teach the fundamentals of computer programming within a visual context and to serve as a software sketchbook and professional production tool. Processing is developed by artists and designers as an alternative to proprietary software tools in the same domain.*
>
> *—www.processing.org*

To sum up, Processing is awesome. First of all, it's free. It doesn't cost a dime. Secondly, because Processing is built on top of the Java programming language (this is explored further in the last chapter of this book), it is a fully functional language without some of the limitations of Logo or Design by Numbers. There is very little you can't do with Processing. Finally, Processing is open source. For the most part, this will not be a crucial detail of the story of this book. Nevertheless, as you move beyond the beginning stages, this philosophical principle will prove invaluable. It's the reason that such an amazing community of developers, teachers, and artists come together to share work, contribute ideas, and expand the features of Processing.

A quick surf-through of the processing.org website reveals this vibrant and creative community. There, code is shared in an open exchange of ideas and artwork among beginners and experts alike. While the site contains a complete reference, as well as a plethora of examples to get you started, it does not have a step-by-step tutorial for the true beginner. This book is designed to give you a jump-start on joining and contributing to this community by methodically walking you through the fundamentals of programming as well as exploring some advanced topics.

In 2012, The Processing Foundation (a non-profit 501(c)(3) corporation) was founded to formalize the goals and ideals behind the Processing software — to "empower people of all interests and backgrounds to learn how to program, so as to facilitate a sophisticated way of thinking about and creating media at a time when such knowledge is crucial." To that end, the Foundation supports several software environments with different languages including Processing (Java), p5.js (JavaScript), and Processing.py (Python). While this book focuses on the Java side of things, I would highly recommend you investigate these other frameworks (especially p5.js, if you're interested in building work for the web). I also maintain p5.js versions of all of this book's examples, which you can find at *http://learningprocessing.com*.

It's important to realize that, although without Processing this book might not exist, this book is not a Processing book per se. The intention here is to teach you programming. I'm choosing to use Processing as the learning environment, but the focus is on the core computational concepts, which will carry you forward in your digital life as you explore other languages and environments.

But shouldn't I be learning _____ ?

You know you want to. Fill in that blank. You heard that the next big thing is that programming language and environment Flibideeflobidee. Sure it sounds made-up, but that friend of yours will not stop talking about how awesome it is. How it makes everything soooo easy. How what used to take you a whole day to program can be done in five minutes. And it works on a Mac. And a PC! And a toaster oven! And you can program your pets to speak with it. In Japanese!

Here's the thing. That magical language that solves all your problems does not exist. No language is perfect, and Processing comes with its fair share of limitations and flaws. Processing, however, is an excellent place to start (and stay). This book teaches you the fundamentals of programming so that you can apply them throughout your life, whether you use Processing, Java, JavaScript, C, Python, or some other language.

It's true that for some projects, other languages and environments can be better. But Processing is really darn good for a lot of stuff, especially media-related and screen-based work. A common misconception is that Processing is just for fiddling around; this is not the case. People (myself included) are out there using Processing from day number one to day number 365 of their project. It's used for web applications, art projects in museums and galleries, and exhibits and installations in public spaces. For example, I've used Processing for a real-time graphics video wall system that can display content on a 120-by-12 foot (yes, feet!) screen in the lobby of InterActive Corps's New York City headquarters.

Not only is Processing great for actually doing stuff, but for learning, it's terrific. It's free and open source. It's simple. It's visual. It's fun. It's object-oriented (I'll get to this later). And it works on Macs, PCs, and Linux machines (no talking dogs though, sorry).

One drawback to Processing is its incompatibility with the web. In 2001, when Processing was first invented, Java applets were a primary means of publishing real-time graphics projects to web pages. In 2015, however, Java applets are an almost entirely defunct technology. The Processing Foundation's p5.js project (*http://p5js.org*) led by Lauren McCarthy is a great alternative. This and other options are addressed a bit more in Chapter 21.

All in all, I would suggest that you stop worrying about what it is you should be using and focus on learning the fundamentals with Processing. That knowledge will take you above and beyond this book to any language you want to tackle.

Write in this book!

Let's say you are a novelist. Or a screenwriter. Is the only time you spend writing the time spent sitting and typing at a computer? Or (gasp) a typewriter? Most likely, this is not the case. Perhaps ideas swirl around in your mind as you lie in bed at night. Or maybe you like to sit on a bench in the park, feed the pigeons, and play out dialogue in your head. And one late night, at the local pub, you find yourself scrawling out a brilliant plot twist on a napkin.

Well, writing software, programming, and creating code is no different. It's really easy to forget this since the work itself is so inherently tied to the computer. But you must find time to let your mind wander, think about logic, and brainstorm ideas away from the chair, the desk, and the computer. Personally, I do all my best programming while jogging.

Sure, the actual typing on the computer part is pretty important. I mean, you will not end up with a life-changing, working application just by lying out by the pool. But thinking that you always need to be hunched over the glare of an LCD screen will not be enough.

Writing all over this book is a step in the right direction, ensuring that you will practice thinking through code away from the keyboard. I have included many exercises in the book that incorporate a fill-in-the-blanks approach. (All of these fill-in-the-blanks exercises have answers on the book's website, *http://learningprocessing.com*, so you can check your work.) Use these pages! When an idea inspires you, make a note and write it down. Think of the book as a workbook and sketchbook for your computational ideas. (You can of course use your own sketchbook, too.)

I would suggest you spend half your time reading this book away from the computer and the other half, side by side with your machine, experimenting with example code along the way.

How should I read this book?

It's best to read this book in order. Chapter 1, Chapter 2, Chapter 3, and so on. You can get a bit more relaxed about this after the end of Chapter 9, but in the beginning it is pretty important.

The book is designed to teach you programming in a linear fashion. A more advanced text might operate more like a reference where you read bits and pieces here and there, moving back and forth throughout the book. But here, the first half of the book is dedicated to making one example and building the features of that example one step at a time (more on this in a moment). In addition, the fundamental elements of computer programming are presented in a particular order, one that comes from several years of trial and error with a group of patient and wonderful students in New York University's Interactive Telecommunications Program (ITP) at the Tisch School of the Arts (*http://itp.nyu.edu*).

The chapters of the book (23 total) are grouped into lessons (10 total). The first nine chapters introduce computer graphics, and cover the fundamental principles behind computer programming. Chapters 10 through 12 take a break from learning new material to examine how larger projects are developed with an incremental approach. Chapters 13 through 23 expand on the basics and offer a selection of more advanced topics ranging from 3D, to incorporating live video, to data visualization.

The lessons are offered as a means of dividing the book into digestible chunks. The end of a lesson marks a spot at which I suggest you take a break from reading and attempt to incorporate that lesson's chapters into a project. Suggestions for these projects are offered, but they are really just that: suggestions.

Is this a textbook?

This book is designed to be used either as a textbook for an introductory level programming course or for self-instruction.

I should mention that the structure of this book comes directly out of the course "Introduction to Computational Media" at ITP. Without the help of my fellow teachers of this class and hundreds of students (I wish I could name them all here), this book would not exist.

To be honest, though, I am including a bit more material than can be taught in a beginner-level, one-semester course. Out of the 23 chapters, I probably cover about 18 of them in detail in my class (but make reference to everything in the book at some point). Nevertheless, whether or not you're reading the book for a course or learning on your own, it's reasonable that you could consume the book in a period of a few months. Sure, you can read it faster than that, but in terms of actually writing code and developing projects that incorporate all the material here, you will need a fairly significant amount of time. As tempting as it is to call this book *Learn to Program with 10 Lessons in 10 Days!*, it's just not realistic.

Here is an example of how the material could play out in a 14 week course.

Week 1	Lesson 1: Chapters 1–3
Week 2	Lesson 2: Chapters 4–6
Week 3	Lesson 3: Chapters 7–8
Week 4	Lesson 4: Chapter 9
Week 5	Lesson 5: Chapters 10–11
Week 6	Midterm! (Also, continue Lesson 5: Chapter 12)
Week 7	Lesson 6: Chapters 13–14
Week 8	Lesson 7: Chapters 15–16
Week 9	Lesson 8: Chapters 17–19
Week 10	Lesson 9: Chapters 20–21
Week 11	Lesson 10: Chapters 22–23
Week 12	Final Project Workshop
Week 13	Final Project Workshop
Week 14	Final Project Presentations

Will this be on the test?

A book will only take you so far. The real key is practice, practice, practice. Pretend you're 10 years old and taking violin lessons. Your teacher would tell you to practice every day. And that would seem perfectly reasonable to you. Do the exercises in this book. Practice every day if you can.

Sometimes when you're learning, it can be difficult to come up with your own ideas. These exercises are there so that you do not have to. However, if you have an idea for something you want to develop, you should feel free to twist and tweak the exercises to fit with what you're doing.

A lot of the exercises are little drills that can be answered in a few minutes. Some are a bit harder and might require up to an hour. Along the way, however, it's good to stop and work on a project that takes longer: a few hours, a day, or a week. As I just mentioned, this is what the lesson structure is for. I suggest that in between each lesson, you take a break from reading and work on making something in Processing. A page with project suggestions is provided for each lesson.

The answers to all of the exercises can be found on this book's website. Speaking of which....

Do you have a website?

The website for this book is: *http://learningprocessing.com.*

There you will find the following things:

- Answers to all exercises in the book
- Downloadable versions of all the code in the book
- Companion video lessons to all of the book's content
- Online versions of the examples (running via p5.js) in the book
- Additional tips and tutorials beyond material in the book
- Questions and comments page

Since many of the examples in this book use color and are animated, the black-and-white, static screenshots provided in the pages here will not give you the whole picture. As you're reading, you can refer to the website to view the examples running in your browser (using p5.js), as well as download them to run locally on your computer.

The source code of all of the book's examples and related examples can also be found in the Learning Processing github repository (*https://github.com/shiffman/LearningProcessing/*). I use github issues (*https://github.com/shiffman/LearningProcessing/issues*) as a system for tracking errors in the book, so please contribute there if you find any content or source code mistakes. You'll find some slight variations between the examples here in the book and what is online, but the core concepts will remain. (For example, the examples here are shown at 200-by-200 pixels to fit in the book's layout, but the online examples are a bit larger.)

This book's website is not a substitute for the amazing resource that is the official Processing website: *http://processing.org*. There, you will find the Processing reference, many more examples, and a lively forum.

Take It One Step at a Time

The Philosophy of Incremental Development

There is one more thing I should discuss before you embark on this journey. It's an important driving force behind the way I learned to program and will contribute greatly to the style of this book. As coined by a former professor of mine, it's called the "philosophy of incremental development." Or perhaps, more simply, the "one-step-at-a-time approach."

Whether you're a total novice or a coder with years of experience, with any programming project, it's crucial not to fall into the trap of trying to do too much all at once. Your dream might be to create the über Processing program that, say, uses Perlin noise to procedurally generate textures for 3D vertex shapes that evolve via the artificial intelligence of a neural network that crawls the web mining for today's news stories, displaying the text of these stories onscreen in colors taken from a live video feed of a viewer in front of the screen who can control the interface with live microphone input by singing.

There is nothing wrong with having grand visions, but the most important favor you can do for yourself is to learn how to break those visions into small parts and attack each piece slowly, one at a time. The previous example is a bit silly; nevertheless, if you were to sit down and attempt to program its features all at once, I'm pretty sure you would end up using a cold compress to treat your pounding headache.

To demonstrate, let's simplify and say that you aspire to program the game *Space Invaders* (see: *http:// en.wikipedia.org/wiki/Space_Invaders*). While this is not explicitly a game programming book, the skills to accomplish this goal will be found here. Following this newfound philosophy, however, you know you need to develop one step at a time, breaking down the problem of programming *Space Invaders* into small parts. Here is my quick attempt:

1. Program the spaceship.

2. Program the invaders.

3. Program the scoring system.

I divided the program into three steps! Nevertheless, I'm not at all finished. The key is to divide the problem into the *smallest pieces possible*, to the point of absurdity, if necessary. You will learn to scale back into larger chunks when the time comes, but for now, the pieces should be so small that they seem ridiculously oversimplified. After all, if the idea of developing a complex game such as *Space Invaders* seems overwhelming, this feeling will go away if you leave yourself with a list of steps to follow, each one simple and easy.

With that in mind, I'm going to try a little harder, breaking Step 1 from above down into smaller parts. The idea here is that I would write six programs, the first being the simplest: *display a triangle*. With each step, I add a small improvement: *move the triangle*. As the program gets more and more advanced, eventually I'll be finished.

1. Program the spaceship.
   a. Draw a triangle onscreen. The triangle will be the spaceship.
   b. Position the triangle at the bottom of the screen.
   c. Position the triangle slightly to the right of where it was before.
   d. Animate the triangle so that it moves from position left to right.
   e. Animate the triangle from left to right only when the right-arrow key is pressed.
   f. Animate the triangle right to left when the left-arrow key is pressed.

Of course, this is only a small fraction of all of the steps needed for a full *Space Invaders* game, but it demonstrates a vital way of thinking. The benefits of this approach are not simply that it makes programming easier (which it does), but that it also makes *debugging* easier.

Debugging[1] refers to the process of finding defects in a computer program and fixing them so that the program behaves properly. You have probably heard about bugs in, say, the Windows operating system: miniscule, arcane errors deep in the code. For us, a bug is a much simpler concept: a mistake. Each time you try to program something, it's very likely that *something* will not work as you expected, if at all. So if

---

[1] The term "debugging" comes from the apocryphal story of a moth getting stuck in the relay circuits of one of computer scientist Grace Murray Hopper's computers.

you start out trying to program everything all at once, it will be very hard to find these bugs. The one-step-at-a-time methodology, however, allows you to tackle these mistakes one at a time, squishing the bugs.

In addition, incremental development lends itself really well to *object-oriented programming*, a core principle of this book. Objects, which will be introduced in Chapter 8, will help you to develop projects in modular pieces as well as provide an excellent means for organizing (and sharing) code. Reusability will also be key. For example, if you have programmed a spaceship for *Space Invaders* and want to start working on asteroids, you can grab the parts you need (i.e., the moving spaceship code), and develop the new pieces around them.

Algorithms

When all is said and done, computer programming is all about writing *algorithms*. An algorithm is a sequential list of instructions that solves a particular problem. And the philosophy of incremental development (which is essentially an algorithm for you, the human being, to follow) is designed to make it easier for you to write an algorithm that implements your idea.

As an exercise, before you get to Chapter 1, try writing an algorithm for something you do on a daily basis, such as brushing your teeth. Make sure the instructions seem comically simple (as in, "Move the toothbrush one centimeter to the left.")

Imagine that you had to provide instructions on how to accomplish this task to someone entirely unfamiliar with toothbrushes, toothpaste, and teeth. That is how it is to write a program. A computer is nothing more than a machine that is brilliant at following precise instructions, but knows nothing about the world at large. And this is where you begin your journey, your story, your new life as a programmer. You begin with learning how to talk to your friend, the computer.

Exercise I-1: Introductory Exercise: Write instructions for brushing your teeth.

Some suggestions:

- Do you do different things based on conditions? How might you use the words "if" or "otherwise" in your instructions? (For example: if the water is too cold, increase the warm water. Otherwise, increase cold water.)

- Use the word "repeat" in your instructions. For example: Move the brush up and down. Repeat five times.

Also, note that I am starting with Step #0. In programming, one often counts starting from 0, so it's good to get used to this idea right off the bat!

How to brush your teeth by _____

Step 0. _____

Step 1. _____

Step 2. _____

Step 3. _____

Step 4. _____

Step 5. _____

Step 6. _____

Step 7. _____

Step 8. _____

Step 9. _____

Lesson One
The Beginning

Chapter 1

Chapter 2

Chapter 3

1 Pixels

A journey of a thousand miles begins with a single step.
—Lao-tzu

In this chapter:
- Specifying pixel coordinates
- Basic shapes: point, line, rectangle, ellipse
- Color: grayscale, RGB
- Color: alpha transparency

Note that you are not doing any programming yet in this chapter! You are just dipping your feet in the water and getting comfortable with the idea of creating onscreen graphics with text-based commands, that is, "code"!

1-1 Graph paper

This book will teach you how to program in the context of computational media, and it will use the development environment Processing (*http://www.processing.org*) as the basis for all discussion and examples. But before any of this becomes relevant or interesting, you must first channel your eighth-grade self, pull out a piece of graph paper, and draw a line. The shortest distance between two points is a good old fashioned line, and this is where you will begin, with two points on that graph paper.

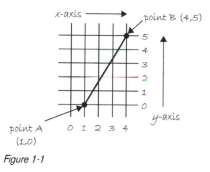

Figure 1-1

Figure 1-1 shows a line between point A (1,0) and point B (4,5). If you wanted to direct a friend of yours to draw that same line, you would say "draw a line from the point one-zero to the point four-five, please." Well, for the moment, imagine your friend was a computer and you wanted to instruct this digital pal to display that same line on its screen. The same command applies (only this time you can skip the pleasantries and you will be required to employ a precise formatting). Here, the instruction will look like this:

```
line(1, 0, 4, 5);
```

Congratulations, you have written your first line of computer code! I'll will get to the precise formatting of the above later, but for now, even without knowing too much, it should make a fair amount of sense. I am providing a *command* (which I will refer to as a *function*) named *line* for the machine to follow. In addition, I am specifying some *arguments* for how that line should be drawn, from point A (1,0) to point B (4,5). If you think of that line of code as a sentence, the *function* is a *verb* and the *arguments* are the *objects* of the sentence. The code sentence also ends with a semicolon instead of a period.

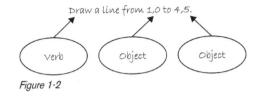

Figure 1-2

The key here is to realize that the computer screen is nothing more than a *fancier* piece of graph paper. Each pixel of the screen is a coordinate — two numbers, an x (horizontal) and a y (vertical) — that determine the location of a point in space. And it's your job to specify what shapes and colors should appear at these pixel coordinates.

Nevertheless, there is a catch here. The graph paper from eighth grade (*Cartesian coordinate system*) placed (0,0) in the center with the y-axis pointing up and the x-axis pointing to the right (in the positive direction, negative down and to the left). The coordinate system for pixels in a computer window, however, is reversed along the y-axis. (0,0) can be found at the top left with the positive direction to the right horizontally and down vertically. See Figure 1-3.

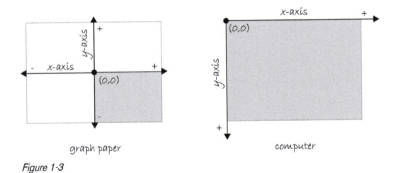

Figure 1-3

Exercise 1-1: Looking at how I wrote the instruction for line — `line(1, 0, 4, 5);` *— how would you guess you would write an instruction to draw a rectangle? A circle? A triangle? Write out the instructions in English and then translate it into code.*

English: _____

Code: _____

English: _____

Code: _____

English: _____

Code: _____

Come back later and see how your guesses matched up with how Processing actually works.

1-2 Simple shapes

The vast majority of the programming examples in this book will be visual in nature. You may ultimately learn to develop interactive games, algorithmic art pieces, animated logo designs, and (insert your own category here) with Processing, but at its core, each visual program will involve setting pixels. The simplest way to get started in understanding how this works is to learn to draw primitive shapes. This is not unlike how you learn to draw in elementary school, only here you do so with code instead of crayons.

I'll start with the four primitive shapes shown in Figure 1-4.

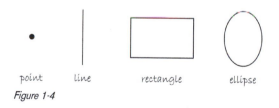

point   line   rectangle   ellipse

Figure 1-4

For each shape, ask yourself what information is required to specify the location and size (and later color) of that shape and learn how Processing expects to receive that information. In each of the diagrams below (Figure 1-5 through Figure 1-11), assume a window with a width of ten pixels and height of ten pixels. This isn't particularly realistic since when you really start coding you will most likely work with much larger windows (ten by ten pixels is barely a few millimeters of screen space). Nevertheless, for demonstration purposes, it's nice to work with smaller numbers in order to present the pixels as they might appear on graph paper (for now) to better illustrate the inner workings of each line of code.

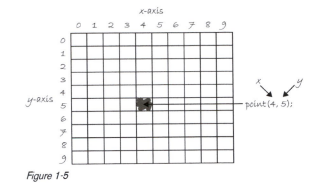

Figure 1-5

A point is the easiest of the shapes and a good place to start. To draw a point, you only need an (x,y) coordinate as shown in Figure 1-5. A line isn't terribly difficult either. A line requires two points, as shown in Figure 1-6.

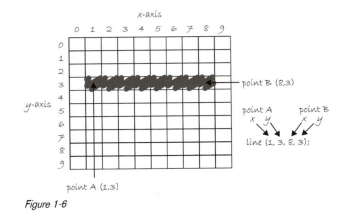

Figure 1-6

Once you arrive at drawing a rectangle, things become a bit more complicated. In Processing, a rectangle is specified by the coordinate for the top left corner of the rectangle, as well as its width and height (see Figure 1-7).

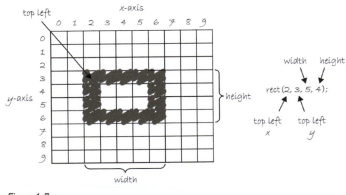

Figure 1-7

However, a second way to draw a rectangle involves specifying the centerpoint, along with width and height as shown in Figure 1-8. If you prefer this method, you first indicate that you want to use the

CENTER mode before the instruction for the rectangle itself. Note that Processing is case-sensitive. Incidentally, the default mode is CORNER, which is how I began as illustrated in Figure 1-7.

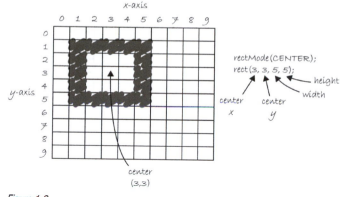

Figure 1-8

Finally, you can also draw a rectangle with two points (the top left corner and the bottom right corner). The mode here is CORNERS (see Figure 1-9).

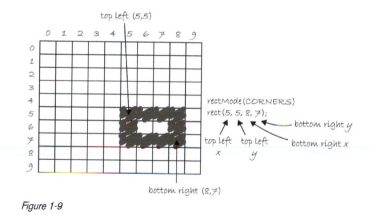

Figure 1-9

Once you have become comfortable with the concept of drawing a rectangle, an ellipse is a snap. In fact, it's identical to rect() with the difference being that an ellipse is drawn where the bounding box[1] (as shown in Figure 1-10) of the rectangle would be. The default mode for ellipse() is CENTER, rather than CORNER as with rect(). See Figure 1-11.

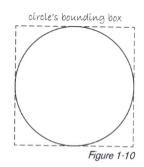

Figure 1-10

---

[1] A bounding box of a shape in computer graphics is the smallest rectangle that includes all the pixels of that shape. For example, the bounding box of a circle is shown in Figure 1-10.

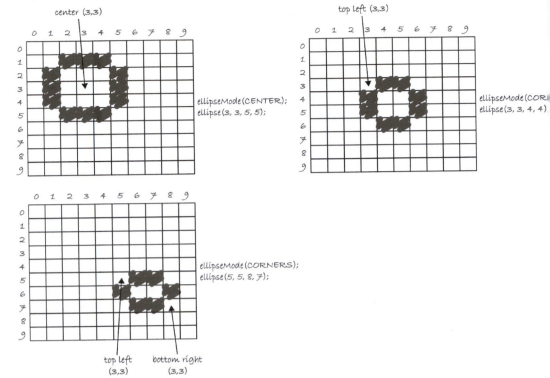

center (3,3)

ellipseMode(CENTER);
ellipse(3, 3, 5, 5);

top left (3,3)

ellipseMode(COR...
ellipse(3, 3, 4, 4)

ellipseMode(CORNERS);
ellipse(5, 5, 8, 7);

top left
(3,3)

bottom right
(3,3)

Figure 1-11

It's important to acknowledge that in Figure 1-11, the ellipses do not look particularly circular. Processing has a built-in methodology for selecting which pixels should be used to create a circular shape. Zoomed in like this, you get a bunch of squares in a circle-like pattern, but zoomed out on a computer screen, you get a nice round ellipse. Later, you will see that Processing gives you the power to develop your own algorithms for coloring in individual pixels (in fact, you can probably already imagine how you might do this using point() over and over again), but for now, it's best to let ellipse() do the hard work.

Certainly, point, line, ellipse, and rectangle are not the only shapes available in the Processing library of functions. In Chapter 2, you will see how the Processing reference provides a full list of available drawing functions along with documentation of the required arguments, sample syntax, and imagery. For now, as an exercise, you might try to imagine what arguments are required for some other shapes (Figure 1-12): triangle(), arc(), quad(), curve().

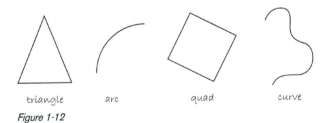

triangle   arc   quad   curve

Figure 1-12

Exercise 1-2: Using the blank graph below, draw the primitive shapes specified by the code.

```
line(0, 0, 9, 6);
point(0, 2);
point(0, 4);
rectMode(CORNER);
rect(5, 0, 4, 3);
ellipseMode(CENTER);
ellipse(3, 7, 4, 4);
```

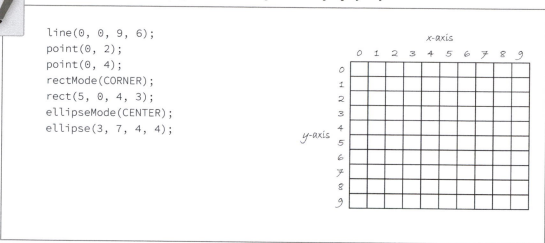

Exercise 1-3: Reverse engineer a list of primitive shape drawing instructions for the diagram below.

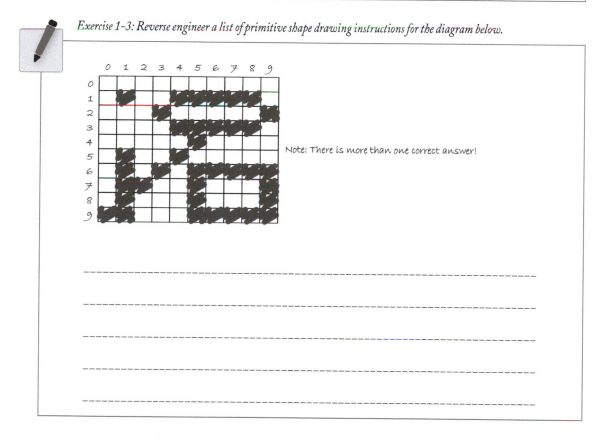

Note: There is more than one correct answer!

1-3 Grayscale color

As you learned in Section 1-2 on page 5, the primary building block for placing shapes onscreen is a pixel coordinate. You politely instructed the computer to draw a shape at a specific location with a specific size. Nevertheless, a fundamental element was missing — color.

In the digital world, precision is required. Saying "Hey, can you make that circle bluish-green?" will not do. Therefore, color is defined with a range of numbers. I'll start with the simplest case: *black and white* or *grayscale*. To specify a value for grayscale, use the following: 0 means black, 255 means white. In between, every other number — 50, 87, 162, 209, and so on — is a shade of gray ranging from black to white. See Figure 1-13.

Figure 1-13

Does 0–255 seem arbitrary to you?

Color for a given shape needs to be stored in the computer's memory. This memory is just a long sequence of 0's and 1's (a whole bunch of on or off switches.) Each one of these switches is a *bit*, eight of them together is a *byte*. Imagine if you had eight bits (one byte) in sequence — how many ways can you configure these switches? The answer is (and doing a little research into binary numbers will prove this point) 256 possibilities, or a range of numbers between 0 and 255. Processing will use eight bit color for the grayscale range and 24 bit for full color (eight bits for each of the red, green, and blue color components; see Section 1-4 on page 12).

Understanding how this range works, you can now move to setting specific grayscale colors for the shapes you drew in Section 1-2 on page 5. In Processing, every shape has a `stroke()` or a `fill()` or both. The `stroke()` specifies the color for the outline of the shape, and the `fill()` specifies the color for the interior of that shape. Lines and points can only have `stroke()`, for obvious reasons.

If you forget to specify a color, Processing will use black (0) for the `stroke()` and white (255) for the `fill()` by default. Note that I'm now using more realistic numbers for the pixel locations, assuming a larger window of size 200 × 200 pixels. See Figure 1-14.

```
rect(50, 40, 75, 100);
```

By adding the stroke() and fill() functions *before* the shape is drawn, you can set the color. It's much like instructing your friend to use a specific pen to draw on the graph paper. You would have to tell your friend *before* he or she starting drawing, not after.

There is also the function background(), which sets a background color for the window where shapes will be rendered.

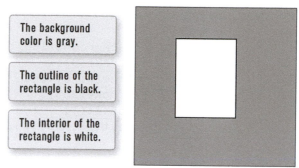

The background color is gray.

The outline of the rectangle is black.

The interior of the rectangle is white.

Figure 1-14

Example 1-1. Stroke and fill

```
background(255);
stroke(0);
fill(150);
rect(50, 50, 75, 100);
```

stroke() or fill() can be eliminated with the noStroke() or noFill() functions. Your instinct might be to say stroke(0) for no outline, however, it's important to remember that 0 is not "nothing," but rather denotes the color black. Also, remember not to eliminate both — with noStroke() and noFill(), nothing will appear!

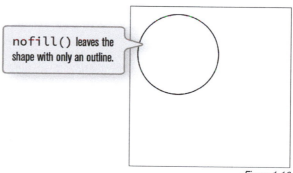

Figure 1-15

Example 1-2. noFill()

```
background(255);
stroke(0);
noFill();
ellipse(60, 60, 100, 100);
```

nofill() leaves the shape with only an outline.

When you draw a shape, Processing will always use the most recently specified stroke() and fill(), reading the code from top to bottom. See Figure 1-17.

Figure 1-16

```
background(150);
stroke(0);
line(0, 0, 200, 200);
stroke(255);
noFill();
rect(25, 25, 75, 75);
```

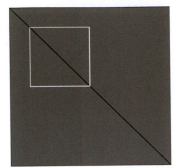

Figure 1-17

Exercise 1-4: Try to guess what the instructions would be for the following screenshot.

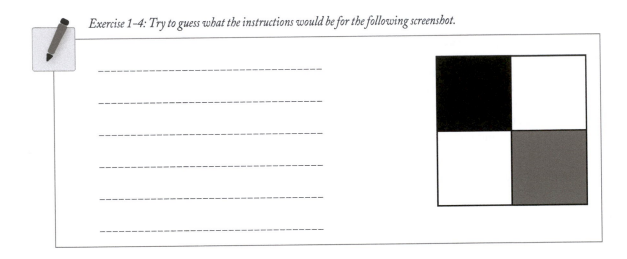

1-4 RGB color

A nostalgic look back at graph paper helped you to learn the fundamentals for pixel locations and size. Now that it's time to study the basics of digital color, here's another childhood memory to get you started. Remember finger painting? By mixing three "primary" colors, any color could be generated. Swirling all colors together resulted in a muddy brown. The more paint you added, the darker it got.

Digital colors are also constructed by mixing three primary colors, but it works differently from paint. First, the primaries are different: red, green, and blue (i.e., "RGB" color). And with color on the screen, you're mixing light, not paint, so the mixing rules are different as well.

- Red + green = yellow
- Red + blue = purple
- Green + blue = cyan (blue-green)
- Red + green + blue = white
- No colors = black

This assumes that the colors are all as bright as possible, but of course, you have a range of color available, so some red plus some green plus some blue equals gray, and a bit of red plus a bit of blue equals dark purple.

While this may take some getting used to, the more you program and experiment with RGB color, the more it will become instinctive, much like swirling colors with your fingers. And of course you can't say "Mix some red with a bit of blue"; you have to provide an exact amount. As with grayscale, the individual color elements are expressed as ranges from 0 (none of that color) to 255 (as much as possible), and they are listed in the order red, green, and blue. You will get the hang of RGB color mixing through experimentation, but next I will cover some code using some common colors.

Note that the print version of this book will only show you black and white versions of each Processing sketch, but all sketches can be seen online in full color at *http://learningprocessing.com*. You can also see a color version of the tutorial on the Processing website (*https://processing.org/tutorials/color/*).

Example 1-3. RGB color

```
background(255);
noStroke();

fill(255, 0, 0);          Bright red
ellipse(20, 20, 16, 16);

fill(127, 0, 0);          Dark red
ellipse(40, 20, 16, 16);

fill(255, 200, 200);      Pink (pale red).
ellipse(60, 20, 16, 16);
```

Figure 1-18

Processing also has a color selector to aid in choosing colors. Access this via "Tools" (from the menu bar) → "Color Selector." See Figure 1-19.

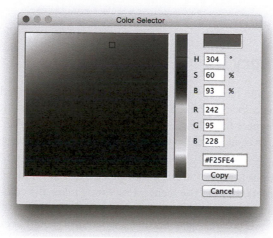

Figure 1-19

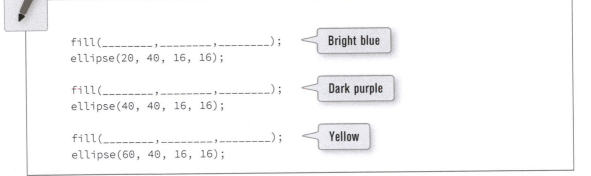

Exercise 1-5: Complete the following program. Guess what RGB values to use (you will be able to check your results in Processing after reading the next chapter). You could also use the color selector, shown in Figure 1-19.

```
fill(_____,_____,_____);        Bright blue
ellipse(20, 40, 16, 16);

fill(_____,_____,_____);        Dark purple
ellipse(40, 40, 16, 16);

fill(_____,_____,_____);        Yellow
ellipse(60, 40, 16, 16);
```

Exercise 1-6: What color will each of the following lines of code generate?

```
fill(0, 100, 0);          _____

fill(100);                _____

stroke(0, 0, 200);        _____

stroke(225);              _____

stroke(255, 255, 0);      _____

stroke(0, 255, 255);      _____

stroke(200, 50, 50);      _____
```

1-5 Color transparency

In addition to the red, green, and blue components of each color, there is an additional optional fourth component, referred to as the color's "alpha." Alpha means opacity and is particularly useful when you want to draw elements that appear partially see-through on top of one another. The alpha values for an image are sometimes referred to collectively as the "alpha channel" of an image.

It's important to realize that pixels are not literally transparent; this is simply a convenient illusion that is accomplished by blending colors. Behind the scenes, Processing takes the color numbers and adds a percentage of one to a percentage of another, creating the optical perception of blending. (If you're interested in programming "rose-colored" glasses, this is where you would begin.)

Alpha values also range from 0 to 255, with 0 being completely transparent (i.e., zero percent opaque) and 255 completely opaque (i.e., 100 percent opaque). Example 1-4 shows a code example that is displayed in Figure 1-20.

Example 1-4. Opacity

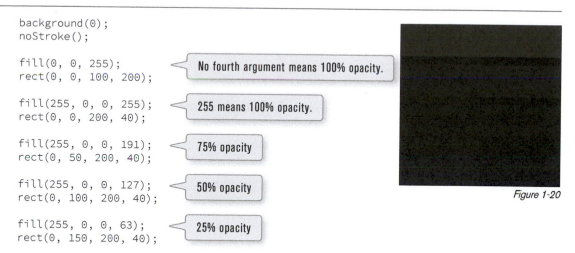

```
background(0);
noStroke();

fill(0, 0, 255);          No fourth argument means 100% opacity.
rect(0, 0, 100, 200);

fill(255, 0, 0, 255);     255 means 100% opacity.
rect(0, 0, 200, 40);

fill(255, 0, 0, 191);     75% opacity
rect(0, 50, 200, 40);

fill(255, 0, 0, 127);     50% opacity
rect(0, 100, 200, 40);

fill(255, 0, 0, 63);      25% opacity
rect(0, 150, 200, 40);
```

Figure 1-20

1-6 Custom color ranges

RGB color with ranges of 0 to 255 is not the only way you can handle color in Processing. Behind the scenes in the computer's memory, color is *always* talked about as a series of 24 bits (or 32 in the case of colors with an alpha). However, Processing will let you think about color any way you like, and translate any values into numbers the computer understands. For example, you might prefer to think of color as ranging from 0 to 100 (like a percentage). You can do this by specifying a custom colorMode().

```
colorMode(RGB, 100);      With colorMode() you can set your own color range.
```

The above function says: "OK, I want to think about color in terms of red, green, and blue. The range of RGB values will be from 0 to 100."

Although it's rarely convenient to do so, you can also have different ranges for each color component:

```
colorMode(RGB, 100, 500, 10, 255);
```

Now I am saying "Red values range from 0 to 100, green from 0 to 500, blue from 0 to 10, and alpha from 0 to 255."

Finally, while you will likely only need RGB color for all of your programming needs, you can also specify colors in the HSB (hue, saturation, and brightness) mode. While HSB values also default to a range of 0 to 255, a common set of ranges (with brief explanation) are as follows:

- **Hue** — The shade of color itself (red, blue, orange, etc.) ranging from 0 to 360 (think of 360° on a color "wheel").

- **Saturation** — The vibrancy of the color, 0 to 100 (think of 50%, 75%, etc.).

- **Brightness** — The, well, brightness of the color, 0 to 100.

Exercise 1-7: Design a creature using simple shapes and colors. Draw the creature by hand using only points, lines, rectangles, and ellipses. Then attempt to write the code for the creature, using the Processing commands covered in this chapter: point(), line(), rect(), ellipse(), stroke(), *and* fill(). *In the next chapter, you will have a chance to test your results by running your code in Processing.*

Example 1-5 shows my version of Zoog, with the outputs shown in Figure 1-21.

Example 1-5. Zoog

```
background(255);
ellipseMode(CENTER);
rectMode(CENTER);
stroke(0);
fill(150);
rect(100, 100, 20, 100);
fill(255);
ellipse(100, 70, 60, 60);
fill(0);
ellipse(81, 70, 16, 32);
ellipse(119, 70, 16, 32);
stroke(0);
line(90, 150, 80, 160);
line(110, 150, 120, 160);
```

Figure 1-21

The sample answer is my Processing-born being, named Zoog. Over the course of the first nine chapters of this book, I will follow the course of Zoog's childhood. The fundamentals of programming will be demonstrated as Zoog grows up. You will first learn to display Zoog, then to make an interactive Zoog and animated Zoog, and finally to duplicate Zoog in a world of many Zoogs.

I suggest you design your own "thing" (note that there is no need to limit yourself to a humanoid or creature-like form; any programmatic pattern will do) and recreate all of the examples throughout the first nine chapters with your own design. Most likely, this will require you to change only a small portion (the shape rendering part) of each example. This process, however, should help solidify your understanding of the basic elements required for computer programs — *variables, conditionals, loops, functions, objects,* and *arrays* — and prepare you for when Zoog matures, leaves the nest, and ventures off into the more advanced topics from Chapter 10 onwards in this book.

2 Processing

Computers in the future may weigh no more than 1.5 tons.
—*Popular Mechanics*, 1949

Take me to your leader.
—Zoog, 2008

In this chapter:
– Downloading and installing Processing
– The Processing interface
– The Processing *sketchbook*
– Writing code
– Errors
– The Processing reference
– The Run button
– Your first sketch

2-1 Processing to the rescue

Now that you have conquered the world of primitive shapes and RGB color, you are ready to implement this knowledge in a real-world programming scenario. Happily, the environment you are going to use is Processing, free and open source software developed by Ben Fry and Casey Reas at the MIT Media Lab in 2001. (See this book's introduction for more about Processing's history.)

Processing's core library of functions for drawing graphics to the screen will provide immediate visual feedback and clues as to what the code is doing. And since its programming language employs all the same principles, structures, and concepts of other languages (specifically Java), everything you learn with Processing is *real* programming. It's not some pretend language to help you get started; it has all the fundamentals and core concepts that all languages have.

After reading this book and learning to program, you might continue to use Processing in your academic or professional life as a prototyping or production tool. You might also take the knowledge acquired here and apply it to learning other languages and authoring environments. You may, in fact, discover that programming is not your cup of tea; nonetheless, learning the basics will help you become more adept in collaborations with other designers and programmers.

It may seem like overkill to emphasize the *why* with respect to Processing. After all, the focus of this book is primarily on learning the fundamentals of computer programming in the context of computer graphics and design. It is, however, important to take some time to ponder the reasons behind selecting a programming language for a book, a class, a homework assignment, a web application, a software suite, and so forth. After all, now that you are going to start calling yourself a computer programmer at cocktail parties, this question will come up over and over again: I need programming in order to accomplish _____ project; which language and environment should I use?

For me, there is no correct answer to this question. Any language that you feel excited to try is a great language. And for a first try, Processing is particularly well suited. Its simplicity is ideal for a beginner. At the end of this chapter, you will be up and running with your first computational design and ready to learn the fundamental concepts of programming. But simplicity is not where Processing ends. A trip through the Processing online exhibition (*http://processing.org/exhibition*) will uncover a wide variety of beautiful and innovative projects developed entirely with Processing. By the end of this book, you will have all the tools and knowledge you need to take your ideas and turn them into real world software projects like those found in the exhibition. Processing is great both for learning and for producing; there are very few other environments and languages you can say that about.

2-2 How do I get Processing?

For the most part, this book will assume that you have a basic working knowledge of how to operate your personal computer. The good news, of course, is that Processing is available for free download. Head to processing.org and visit the download page. This book is designed to work with the Processing 3.0 series, I suggest downloading the latest version on the top of the page. If you're a Windows user, you will see two options: "Windows 32-bit" and "Windows 64-bit." The distinction is related to your machine's processor. If you're not sure which version of Windows you're running you'll find the answer by clicking the Start button, right-clicking Computer, and then clicking Properties. For Mac OS X, there is only one download option. There are also Linux versions available. Operating systems and programs change, of course, so if this paragraph is obsolete or out of date, the download page on the site includes information regarding what you need.

The Processing software will arrive as a compressed file. Choose a nice directory to store the application (usually "C:\Program Files\" on Windows and in "Applications" on Mac), extract the files there, locate the Processing executable, and run it.

 Exercise 2-1: Download and install Processing.

2-3 The Processing application

The Processing development environment is a simplified environment for writing computer code, and it is just about as straightforward to use as simple text editing software (such as TextEdit or Notepad) combined with a media player. Each sketch (Processing programs are referred to as "sketches") has a name, a place where you can type code, and buttons for running sketches. See Figure 2-1. (At the time of this writing the version is Processing 3.0 alpha release 10 and so the version you download may look a little bit different.)

stop sketch

enable debugger

run sketch

current "mode"

sketch name

type code here

message area

Figure 2-1

To make sure everything is working, it's a good idea to try running one of the Processing examples. Go to File → Examples → (pick an example, suggested: Topics → Drawing → ContinuousLines) as shown in Figure 2-2.

Once you have opened the example, click the Run button as indicated in Figure 2-1. If a new window pops open running the example, you're all set! If this does not occur, visit the troubleshooting FAQ (*https://github.com/processing/processing/wiki/troubleshooting*) and look for "Processing won't start!" for possible solutions.

 Exercise 2-2: Open a sketch from the Processing examples and run it.

Processing programs can also be viewed full-screen (known as "Present mode" in Processing). This is available through the menu option: Sketch → Present (or by shift-clicking the Run button). Present will not make your sketch as big as the whole screen. If you want the sketch to cover your entire screen, you can use fullScreen() which I'll cover in more detail in the next section.

Under "Present," you'll also notice an option to "Tweak" your sketch, which will launch the program with a interface that allows you to tweak numbers on the fly. This can be useful for experimenting with the parameters of a sketch, from things as simple as the colors and dimensions of shapes to more complex elements of programs you'll learn about later in this book.

2-4 The sketchbook

Processing programs are informally referred to as *sketches*, in the spirit of quick graphics prototyping, and I will employ this term throughout the course of this book. The folder where you store your sketches is called your *sketchbook*. Technically speaking, when you run a sketch in Processing, it runs as an application on your computer. As you will see later in Chapter 21, Processing allows you to make platform-specific stand-alone applications from your sketches.

Once you have confirmed that the Processing examples work, you are ready to start creating your own sketches. Clicking the "new" button will generate a blank new sketch named by date. It's a good idea to "Save as" and create your own sketch name. (Note: Processing does not allow spaces or hyphens in sketch names, and your sketch name can't start with a digit.)

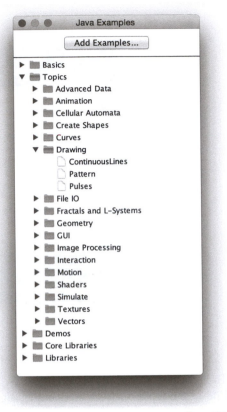

Figure 2-2

When you first ran Processing, a default "Processing" directory was created to store all sketches in the "My Documents" folder on Windows or in "Documents" on OS X. Although you can select any directory on your hard drive, this folder is the default. It's a pretty good folder to use, but it can be changed by opening the Processing preferences (which are available under the "File" menu).

Each Processing sketch consists of a folder (with the same name as your sketch) and a file with the extension "pde." If your Processing sketch is named *MyFirstProgram*, then you will have a folder named *MyFirstProgram* with a file *MyFirstProgram.pde* inside. This file is a plain text file that contains the source code. (Later you will see that Processing sketches can have multiple files with the "pde" extension, but for now, one will do.) Some sketches will also contain a folder called "data" where media elements used in the program, such as image files, sound clips, and so on, are stored.

Exercise 2-3: Type some instructions from Chapter 1 into a blank sketch. Note how certain words are colored. Run the sketch. Does it do what you thought it would?

2-5 Coding in Processing

It's finally time to start writing some code, using the elements discussed in Chapter 1. Let's go over some basic syntax rules. There are three kinds of statements you can write:

- Function calls
- Assignment operations
- Control structures

For now, every line of code will be a function call. See Figure 2-3. I will explore the other two categories in future chapters. Functions calls have a name, followed by a set of arguments enclosed in parentheses. Recalling Chapter 1, I used functions to describe how to draw shapes (I just called them "commands" or "instructions"). Thinking of a function call as a natural language sentence, the function name is the verb ("draw") and the arguments are the objects ("point 0,0") of the sentence. Each function call must always end with a semicolon. See Figure 2-4.

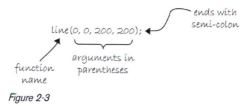

Figure 2-3

You have learned several functions already, including background(), stroke(), fill(), noFill(), noStroke(), point(), line(), rect(), ellipse(), rectMode(), and ellipseMode(). Processing will execute a sequence of functions one by one and finish by displaying the drawn result in a window. I forgot to mention one very important function in Chapter 1, however — size(). size() specifies the dimensions of the window you want to create and takes two arguments, width and height. If you want to show your sketch fullscreen, you can call fullScreen() instead of size(). Your sketch dimensions will match the resolution of your display. The size() or fullScreen() function should always be the first line of code in setup() and you can only have one of these in any given sketch.

```
void setup() {
```

> No code can go here before size()!

```
    size(320, 240);
}
```

> Opens a window of width 320 and height 240.

Here is `fullScreen()`.

```
void setup() {



    fullScreen();
}
```

> No code can go here before `fullScreen()`!

> Opens a fullscreen window.

Let's write a first example (see Figure 2-4).

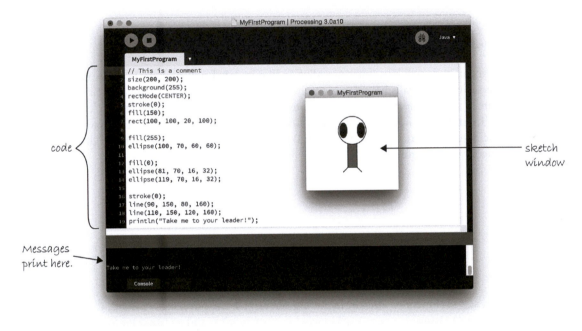

code

Messages print here.

sketch window

Figure 2-4

There are a few additional items to note.

- The Processing text editor will color known words (sometimes referred to as *reserved* words or *keywords*). These words, for example, are the drawing functions available in the Processing library, built-in variables (I will look closely at the concept of *variables* in Chapter 3) and constants, as well as certain words that are inherited from the Java programming language.

- Sometimes it's useful to display text information in the Processing message window (located at the bottom). This is accomplished using the `println()` function. The `println()` function takes one or more arguments, whatever you want to print to the message window. In this case (as shown in Figure 2-4) I'm printing the string of characters enclosed in quotes: "Take me to your leader!" (more about text in Chapter 17). This ability to print to the message window comes in handy when attempting to *debug* the values of variables. There's also a special button for debugging, the little insect in the top right, and I'll reference this again in Chapter 11.

- The number in the bottom left corner indicates what line number in the code is selected. You can also see the line numbers to the left of your code.

- You can write *comments* in your code. Comments are lines of text that Processing ignores when the program runs. You should use them as reminders of what the code means, a bug you intend to fix, a to-do list of items to be inserted, and so on. Comments on a single line are created with two forward slashes, **//**. Comments over multiple lines are marked by **/*** followed by the comments and ending with ***/**.

- Processing starts, by default, in what's known as "Java" mode. This is the core use of Processing where your code is written in the Java programming language. There are other modes, notably Python Mode, which allow you create Processing sketches in the Python programming language. You can explore these modes by clicking the mode button as indicated in Figure 2-4.

```
// This is a comment on one line.

/* This is a comment
that spans several
lines of code. */
```

A quick word about comments. You should get in the habit right now of writing comments in your code. Even though your sketches will be very simple and short at first, you should put comments in for everything. Code is very hard to read and understand without comments. You do not need to have a comment for every line of code, but the more you include, the easier a time you will have revising and reusing your code later. Comments also force you to understand how code works as you're programming. If you do not know what you're doing, how can you write a comment about it?

Comments will not always be included in the text here. This is because I find that, unlike in an actual program, code comments are hard to read in a book. Instead, this book will often use code "hints" for additional insight and explanations. If you look at the book's examples on the website, though, comments will always be included. So, I can't emphasize it enough: write comments!

```
// Draw a diagonal line starting at upper left
line(0, 0, 100, 100);
```
> A helpful comment about this code!

 Exercise 2-4: Create a blank sketch. Take your code from the end of Chapter 1 and type it in the Processing window. Add comments to describe what the code is doing. Add a `println()` *statement to display text in the message window. Save the sketch. Press the Run button. Does it work or do you get an error?*

2-6 Errors

The previous example only works because I did not make any errors or typos. Over the course of a programmer's life, this is quite a rare occurrence. Most of the time, your first push of the Run button will not be met with success. Let's examine what happens when you make a mistake in the code in Figure 2-5.

Figure 2-5 shows what happens when you have a typo — "elipse" instead of "ellipse" on line 9. Errors are noted in the code itself with a red squiggly line underneath where Processing believes the mistake to be. This particular message is fairly friendly, telling you that Processing has never heard of the function "elipse." This can easily be corrected by fixing the spelling. If there is an error in the code when the Run button is pressed, Processing will not open the sketch window, and will instead highlight the error message. Not all Processing error messages are so easy to understand, and I will continue to cover other errors throughout the course of this book. An appendix on common errors in Processing is also included at the end of the book.

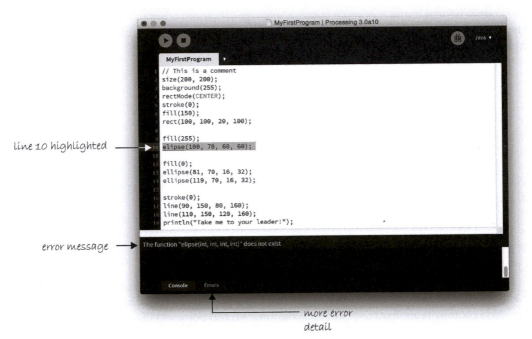

Figure 2-5

Processing is case sensitive!

Lower versus upper case matters. If you type `Ellipse` instead of `ellipse`, that will also be considered an error.

In this instance, there was only one error. If multiple errors occur, Processing will only alert you to the first one it finds when you press run. However, a complete list of errors can always be found in the errors console at the bottom as noted in Figure 2-5. Dealing with just one error at a time is much less stressful, however, so this further emphasizes the importance of incremental development discussed in the book's introduction. If you only implement one feature at a time, you can only make one mistake at a time.

Exercise 2-5: Try to make some errors happen on purpose. Are the error messages what you expect?

Exercise 2-6: Fix the errors in the following code.

```
size(200, 200;          ------------------------------------------

background();           ------------------------------------------

stroke 255;             ------------------------------------------

fill(150)               ------------------------------------------

rectMode(center);       ------------------------------------------

rect(100, 100, 50);     ------------------------------------------
```

2-7 The Processing reference

The functions I have demonstrated — ellipse(), line(), stroke(), and so on — are all part of *Processing*'s library. How do you know that "ellipse" isn't spelled "elipse," or that rect() takes four arguments (an x-coordinate, a y-coordinate, a width, and a height)? A lot of these details are intuitive, and this speaks to the strength of Processing as a beginner's programming language. Nevertheless, the only way to know for sure is by reading the online reference. While I will cover many of the elements from the reference throughout this book, it is by no means a substitute for the reference, and both will be required for you to learn Processing.

The reference for Processing can be found online at the official website (*processing.org*) under the "reference" link. There, you can browse all of the available functions by category or alphabetically. If you were to visit the page for ellipse(), for example, you would find the explanation shown in Figure 2-6.

As you can see, the reference page offers full documentation for the function rect(), including:

- **Name** — The name of the function.
- **Examples** — Example code (and visual result, if applicable).
- **Description** — A friendly description of what the function does.
- **Syntax** — Exact syntax of how to write the function.
- **Parameters** — These are the elements that go inside the parentheses. It tells you what kind of data you put in (a number, character, etc.) and what that element stands for. (This will become clearer as I explain more in future chapters.) These are also sometimes referred to as *arguments*.

- **Returns** — Sometimes a function sends something back to you when you call it (e.g., instead of asking a function to perform a task such as draw a circle, you could ask a function to add two numbers and *return* the answer to you). Again, this will become more clear later.

- **Related** — A list of functions often called in connection with the current function.

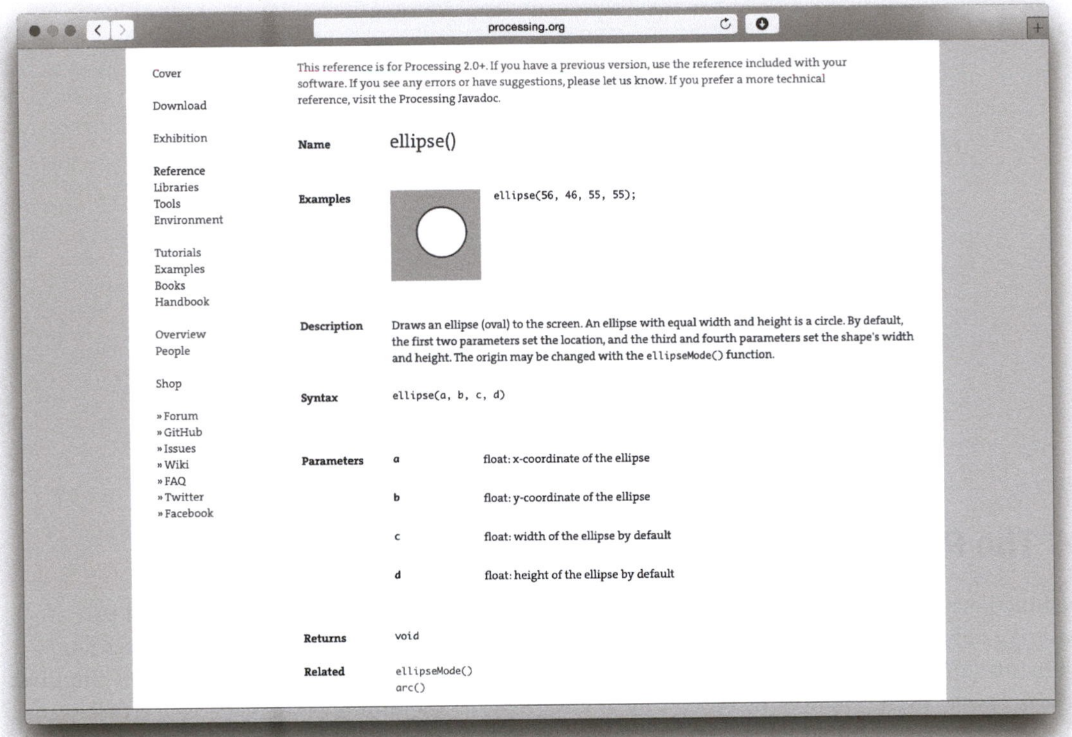

Figure 2-6

Processing also has a very handy "find in reference" option. Double-click on any keyword to select it and go to Help → Find in Reference (or select the keyword and hit Shift+Command+F (Mac) or Ctrl+Shift +F (PC)).

Exercise 2-7: Using the Processing reference, try writing a program that uses two functions I have not yet covered in this book. Stay within the "Shape" and "Color (setting)" categories.

Exercise 2-8: Using the reference, find a function that allows you to alter the thickness of a line. What arguments does the function take? Write example code that draws a line one pixel wide, then five pixels wide, then 10 pixels wide.

2-8 The Run button

One of the nice qualities of Processing is that all one has to do to run a program is press the Run button. The design is similar to a media "play" button you might find when *playing* animations, movies, music, and other forms of media. Processing programs output media in the form of real-time computer graphics, so why not just *play* them too?

Nevertheless, it's important to take a moment and consider the fact that what I am doing here is not the same as what happens when an audio or video plays. Processing programs start out as text, they are translated into machine code, and then executed to run. All of these steps happen in sequence when the Run button is pressed. Let's examine these steps one by one, relaxed in the knowledge that Processing handles the hard work for you.

1. **Translate to Java.** Processing is really Java (this will become more evident in a detailed discussion in Chapter 23). In order for your code to run on your machine, it must first be translated to Java code.

2. **Compile into Java byte code.** The Java code created in Step 1 is just another text file (with the .java extension instead of .pde). In order for the computer to understand it, it needs to be translated into machine language. This translation process is known as compilation. If you were programming in a different language, such as C, the code would compile directly into machine language specific to your operating system. In the case of Java, the code is compiled into a special machine language known as Java byte code. It can run on different platforms as long as the machine is running a "Java Virtual Machine." Although this extra layer can sometimes cause programs to run a bit slower than they might otherwise, being cross-platform is a great feature of Java. For more on how this works, visit the official Java website (*http://www.oracle.com/technetwork/java/index.html*) or consider picking up a book on Java programming (after you have finished with this one).

3. **Execution.** The compiled program ends up in a JAR file. A JAR is a Java archive file that contains compiled Java programs ("classes"), images, fonts, and other data files. The JAR file is executed by the Java Virtual Machine and is what causes the display window to appear.

2-9 Your first sketch

Now that you have downloaded and installed Processing, understand the basic menu and interface elements, and are familiar with the online reference, you are ready to start coding. As I briefly mentioned in Chapter 1, the first half of this book will follow one example that illustrates the foundational elements of programming: *variables*, *conditionals*, *loops*, *functions*, *objects*, and *arrays*. Other examples will be included along the way, but following just one will reveal how the basic elements behind computer programming build on each other.

The example will follow the story of our new friend Zoog, beginning with a static rendering with simple shapes. Zoog's development will include mouse interaction, motion, and cloning into a population of many Zoogs. While you are by no means required to complete every exercise of this book with your own alien form, it can be helpful to start with an idea and after each chapter, expand the functionality of your sketch with the programming concepts that are explored. If you're at a loss for an idea, then just draw your own little alien, name it Gooz, and get programming! See Figure 2-7.

Example 2-1. Zoog again

```
size(200, 200); // Set the size of the window
background(255); // Draw a white background

// Set ellipses and rects to CENTER mode
ellipseMode(CENTER);
rectMode(CENTER);

// Draw Zoog's body
stroke(0);
fill(150);
rect(100, 100, 20, 100);          Zoog's body

// Draw Zoog's head
fill(255);
ellipse(100, 70, 60, 60);         Zoog's head

// Draw Zoog's eyes
fill(0);
ellipse(81, 70, 16, 32);          Zoog's eyes
ellipse(119, 70, 16, 32);

// Draw Zoog's legs
stroke(0);
line(90, 150, 80, 160);           Zoog's legs
line(110, 150, 120, 160);
```

Figure 2-7

Let's pretend, just for a moment, that you find this Zoog design to be so astonishingly gorgeous that you just can't wait to see it displayed on your computer screen. (Yes, I am aware this may require a fairly significant suspension of disbelief.) To run any and all code examples found in this book, you have two choices:

- Retype the code manually.
- Visit the book's website (*http://learningprocessing.com*), find the example by its number, and copy/ paste (or download) the code.

Certainly option #2 is the easier and less time-consuming one, and I recommend you use the site as a resource for seeing sketches running in real time and for grabbing code examples. Nonetheless, as you start learning, there is real value in typing the code yourself. Your brain will sponge up the syntax and logic as you type, and you will learn a great deal by making mistakes along the way. Not to mention simply running the sketch after entering each new line of code will eliminate any mystery as to how the sketch works.

You will know best when you are ready for copy/paste. Keep track of your progress, and if you start running a lot of examples without feeling comfortable with how they work, try going back to manual typing.

Exercise 2-9: Using what you designed in Chapter 1, implement your own screen drawing, using only 2D primitive shapes — arc(), curve(), ellipse(), line(), point(), quad(), rect(), triangle() —*and basic color functions —* background(), colorMode(), fill(), noFill(), noStroke(), *and* stroke(). *Remember to use* size() *to specify the dimensions of your window or* fullScreen() *to have your sketch cover your entire display. Suggestion: Play the sketch after typing each new line of code. Correct any errors or typos along the way.*

3 Interaction

Always remember that this whole thing was started with a dream and a mouse.
—Walt Disney

The quality of the imagination is to flow and not to freeze.
—Ralph Waldo Emerson

In this chapter:
– The *flow* of a computer program
– The meaning behind `setup()` and `draw()`
– Mouse interaction
– Your first *dynamic* Processing sketch
– Handling events, such as mouse clicks and key presses

3-1 Go with the flow

If you have ever played a computer game, interacted with a digital art installation, or watched a screensaver at three in the morning, you have probably given very little thought to the fact that the software that runs these experiences happens over a *period of time.* The game starts, you find the secret treasure hidden in magical rainbow land, defeat the the scary monster who-zee-ma-whats-it, achieve a high score, and the game ends.

What I want to focus on in this chapter is that *flow* over time. A game begins with a set of initial conditions: you name your character, you start with a score of zero, and you start on level one. Let's think of this part as the program's *SETUP.* After these conditions are initialized, you begin to play the game. At every instant, the computer checks what you are doing with the mouse, calculates all the appropriate behaviors for the game characters, and updates the screen to render all the game graphics. This cycle of calculating and drawing happens over and over again, ideally 30 or more times per second for a smooth animation. Let's think of this part as the program's *DRAW.*

This concept is crucial to your ability to move beyond static designs (as in Chapter 2) with Processing.

1. Set starting conditions for the program one time.
2. Do something over and over and over and over (and over...) again until the program quits.

Consider how you might go about running a race.

1. Put on your sneakers and stretch. Just do this once, OK?
2. Put your right foot forward, then your left foot. Repeat this over and over as fast as you can.
3. After 26 miles, quit.

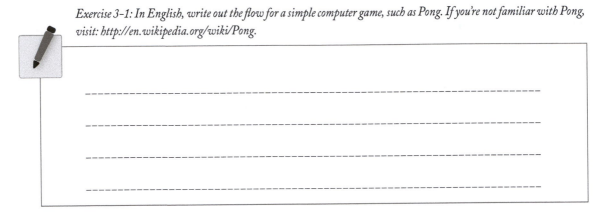

Exercise 3-1: In English, write out the flow for a simple computer game, such as Pong. If you're not familiar with Pong, visit: http://en.wikipedia.org/wiki/Pong.

3-2 Our good friends, `setup()` and `draw()`

Now that you are good and exhausted from running marathons in order to better learn programming, you can take this newfound knowledge and apply it to your first *dynamic* Processing sketch. Unlike Chapter 2's static examples, this program will draw to the screen continuously (i.e., until the user quits). This is accomplished by writing two "blocks of code": `setup()` and `draw()`. Technically speaking, `setup()` and `draw()` are functions. I will get into a longer discussion of writing your own functions in a later chapter; for now, you can understand them to be two sections where you write code.

What is a block of code?

A block of code is any code enclosed within curly brackets.

```
{
    A block of code
}
```

Blocks of code can be nested within each other, too.

```
{
    A block of code
    {
        A block inside a block of code
    }
}
```

This is an important construct as it allows you to separate and manage code as individual pieces of a larger puzzle. A programming convention is to indent the lines of code within each block to make the code more readable. Processing will do this for you via the menu option Edit → Auto-Format. Getting comfortable with organizing your code into blocks while more complex logic will prove crucial in future chapters. For now, you only need to look at two simple blocks: `setup()` and `draw()`.

Let's look at what will surely be strange-looking syntax for setup() and draw(). See Figure 3-1.

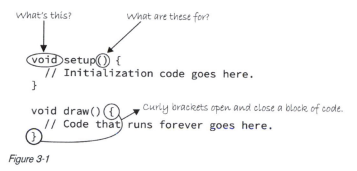

Figure 3-1

Admittedly, there is a lot of stuff in Figure 3-1 that you are not entirely ready to learn about. I have covered that the curly brackets indicate the beginning and end of a block of code, but why are there parentheses after "setup" and "draw"? Oh, and, my goodness, what is this "void" all about? It makes me feel sad inside! For now, you have to decide to feel comfortable with not knowing everything all at once, and that these important pieces of syntax will start to make sense in future chapters as more concepts are revealed.

For now, the key is to focus on how Figure 3-1's structures control the flow of a program. This is shown in Figure 3-2.

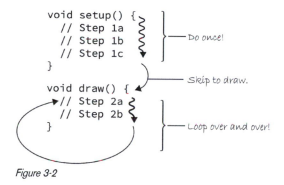

Figure 3-2

How does it work? When you run the program, it will follow the instructions precisely, executing the steps in setup() first, and then move on to the steps in draw(). The order ends up being something like:

1a, 1b, 1c, 2a, 2b, 2a, 2b, 2a, 2b, 2a, 2b, 2a, 2b, 2a, 2b...

Now, I can rewrite the Zoog example as a dynamic sketch. See Example 3-1.

Example 3-1. Zoog as dynamic sketch

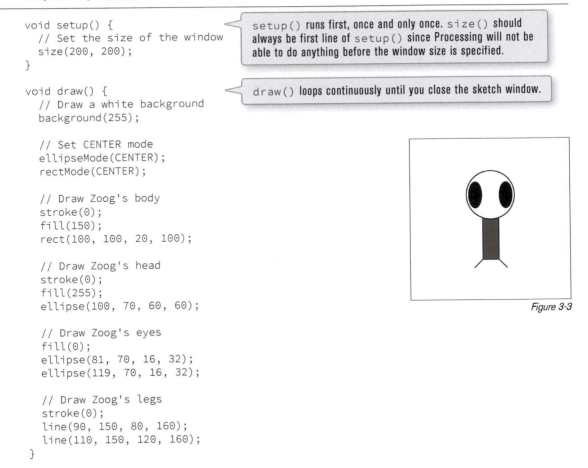

```
void setup() {
  // Set the size of the window
  size(200, 200);
}
```

> setup() runs first, once and only once. size() should always be first line of setup() since Processing will not be able to do anything before the window size is specified.

```
void draw() {
  // Draw a white background
  background(255);
```

> draw() loops continuously until you close the sketch window.

```
  // Set CENTER mode
  ellipseMode(CENTER);
  rectMode(CENTER);

  // Draw Zoog's body
  stroke(0);
  fill(150);
  rect(100, 100, 20, 100);

  // Draw Zoog's head
  stroke(0);
  fill(255);
  ellipse(100, 70, 60, 60);

  // Draw Zoog's eyes
  fill(0);
  ellipse(81, 70, 16, 32);
  ellipse(119, 70, 16, 32);

  // Draw Zoog's legs
  stroke(0);
  line(90, 150, 80, 160);
  line(110, 150, 120, 160);
}
```

Figure 3-3

Take the code from Example 3-1 and run it in Processing. Strange, right? You will notice that nothing in the window changes. This looks identical to a *static* sketch! What is going on? All this discussion for nothing?

Well, if you examine the code, you will notice that nothing in the draw() function *varies*. Each time through the loop, the program cycles through the code and executes the identical instructions. So, yes, the program is running over time redrawing the window, but it looks static since it draws the same thing each time!

Exercise 3-2: Redo the drawing you created at the end of Chapter 2 as a dynamic program. Even though it will look the same, feel good about your accomplishment!

3-3 Variation with the mouse

Consider this: What if, instead of typing a number into one of the drawing functions, you could type "the mouse's x location" or "the mouse's y location."

```
line(the mouse's x location, the mouse's y location, 100, 100);
```

In fact, you can, only instead of the more descriptive language, you must use the keywords mouseX and mouseY, indicating the horizontal or vertical position of the mouse cursor.

Example 3-2. mouseX *and* mouseY

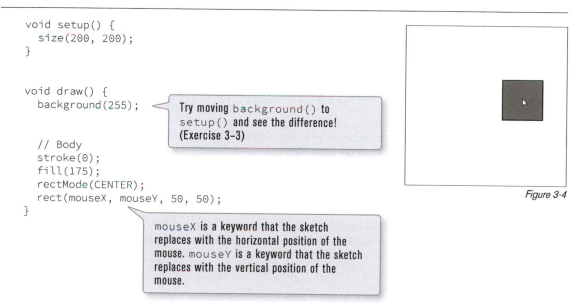

```
void setup() {
  size(200, 200);
}


void draw() {
  background(255);

  // Body
  stroke(0);
  fill(175);
  rectMode(CENTER);
  rect(mouseX, mouseY, 50, 50);
}
```

Try moving background() to setup() and see the difference! (Exercise 3–3)

mouseX is a keyword that the sketch replaces with the horizontal position of the mouse. mouseY is a keyword that the sketch replaces with the vertical position of the mouse.

Figure 3-4

Exercise 3-3: Explain why you see a trail of rectangles if you move `background()` *to* `setup()`, *leaving it out of* `draw()`.

An invisible line of code

If you are following the logic of `setup()` and `draw()` closely, you might arrive at an interesting question: *When does* Processing *actually display the shapes in the window? When do the new pixels appear?*

On first glance, one might assume the display is updated for every line of code that includes a drawing function. If this were the case, however, you would see the shapes appear onscreen one at a time. This would happen so fast that you would hardly notice each shape appearing individually. However, when the window is erased every time `background()` is called, a somewhat unfortunate and unpleasant result would occur: flicker.

Processing solves this problem by updating the window only at the end of every cycle through `draw()`. It's as if there were an invisible line of code that renders the window at the end of the `draw()` function.

```
void draw() {
    // All of your code
    // Update Display Window — invisible line of code you don't see
}
```

This process is known as *double-buffering* and, in a lower-level environment, you may find that you have to implement it yourself. Again, I'd like to take a moment to thank Processing for making our introduction to programming friendlier and simpler by taking care of this for you and me.

It should also be noted that any colors you have set with `stroke()` or `fill()` carry over from one cycle through `draw()` to the next.

I could push this idea a bit further and create an example where a more complex pattern (multiple shapes and colors) is controlled by mouseX and mouseY position. For example, I can rewrite Zoog to follow the mouse. Note that the center of Zoog's body is located at the exact location of the mouse (mouseX, mouseY), however, other parts of Zoog's body are drawn relative to the mouse. Zoog's head, for example, is located at (mouseX, mouseY-30). The following example only moves Zoog's body and head, as shown in Figure 3-5.

Example 3-3. Zoog as dynamic sketch with variation

```
void setup() {
  size(200, 200); // Set the size of the window
}

void draw() {
  background(255); // Draw a white background

  // Set ellipses and rects to CENTER mode
  ellipseMode(CENTER);
  rectMode(CENTER);

  // Draw Zoog's body
  stroke(0);
  fill(175);
  rect(mouseX, mouseY, 20, 100);

  // Draw Zoog's head
  stroke(0);
  fill(255);
  ellipse(mouseX, mouseY-30, 60, 60);

  // Draw Zoog's eyes
  fill(0);
  ellipse(81, 70, 16, 32);
  ellipse(119, 70, 16, 32);

  // Draw Zoog's legs
  stroke(0);
  line(90, 150, 80, 160);
  line(110, 150, 120, 160);
}
```

Figure 3-5

Zoog's body is drawn at the location (mouseX, mouseY).

Zoog's head is drawn above the body at the location (mouseX, mouseY-30).

Exercise 3-4: Complete Zoog so that the rest of its body moves with the mouse.

```
// Draw Zoog's eyes
fill(0);

ellipse(_____,_____, 16, 32);

ellipse(_____,_____, 16, 32);

// Draw Zoog's legs
stroke(0);

line(_____,_____,_____,_____);

line(_____,_____,_____,_____);
```

Exercise 3-5: Recode your design so that shapes respond to the mouse (by varying color and location).

In addition to mouseX and mouseY, you can also use pmouseX and pmouseY. These two keywords stand for the *previous* mouseX and mouseY locations, that is, where the mouse was the last time the sketch cycled through draw(). This allows for some interesting interaction possibilities. For example, let's consider what happens if you draw a line from the previous mouse location to the current mouse location, as illustrated in the diagram in Figure 3-6.

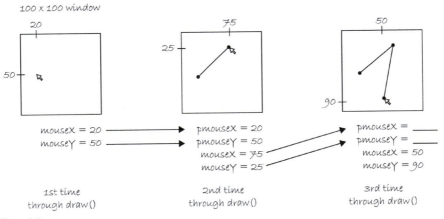

Figure 3-6

Exercise 3-6: Fill in the blank in Figure 3-6.

By connecting the previous mouse location to the current mouse location with a line each time through draw(), I am able to render a continuous line that follows the mouse. See Figure 3-7.

Example 3-4. Drawing a continuous line

```
void setup() {
  size(200, 200);
  background(255);
}

void draw() {
  stroke(0);
  line(pmouseX, pmouseY, mouseX, mouseY);
}
```

> Draw a line from previous mouse location to current mouse location.

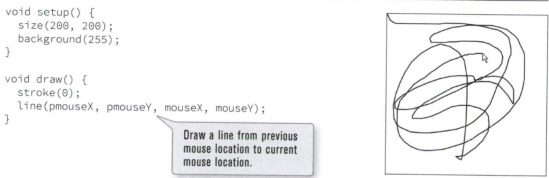

Figure 3-7

Exercise 3-7: Update Exercise 3-4 on page 40 so that the faster the user moves the mouse, the wider the drawn line. Hint: look up strokeWeight() *in the Processing reference (https://processing.org/reference/strokeWeight_.html).*

The formula for calculating the speed of the mouse's horizontal motion is the absolute value of the difference between mouseX and pmouseX. The absolute value of a number is defined as that number without its sign:

- The absolute value of -2 is 2.

- The absolute value of 2 is 2.

In Processing, you can get the absolute value of the number by placing it inside the abs() function, that is abs(-5) equals 5. The speed at which the mouse is moving is therefore:

```
float mouseSpeed = abs(mouseX - pmouseX);
```

Fill in the blank below and then try it out in Processing!

```
stroke(0);

_____(_____);
line(pmouseX, pmouseY, mouseX, mouseY);
```

3-4 Mouse clicks and key presses

You are well on your way to creating dynamic, interactive Processing sketches through the use the `setup()` and `draw()` framework and the `mouseX` and `mouseY` keywords. A crucial form of interaction, however, is missing — clicking the mouse!

In order to learn how to have something happen when the mouse is clicked, you need to return to the flow of the program. You know `setup()` happens once and `draw()` loops forever. When does a mouse click occur? Mouse presses (and key presses) are considered *events* in Processing. If you want something to happen (such as "the background color changes to red") when the mouse is clicked, you need to add a third block of code to handle this event.

This event "function" will tell the program what code to execute when an event occurs. As with `setup()`, the code will occur once and only once. That is, once and only once for each occurrence of the event. An event, such as a mouse click, can happen multiple times of course!

These are the two new functions you need:

- `mousePressed()` — Handles mouse clicks.
- `keyPressed()` — Handles key presses.

The following example uses both event functions, adding squares whenever the mouse is pressed and clearing the background whenever a key is pressed.

Example 3-5. `mousePressed()` **and** `keyPressed()`

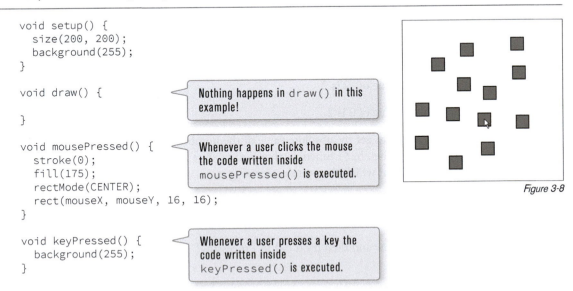

```
void setup() {
  size(200, 200);
  background(255);
}

void draw() {

}
```
> Nothing happens in `draw()` in this example!

```
void mousePressed() {
  stroke(0);
  fill(175);
  rectMode(CENTER);
  rect(mouseX, mouseY, 16, 16);
}
```
> Whenever a user clicks the mouse the code written inside `mousePressed()` is executed.

```
void keyPressed() {
  background(255);
}
```
> Whenever a user presses a key the code written inside `keyPressed()` is executed.

Figure 3-8

In Exercise 3-5 on page 40, I have four functions that describe the program's flow. The program starts in `setup()` where the size and background are initialized. It continues into `draw()`, looping endlessly. Since `draw()` contains no code, the window will remain blank. However, I have added two new functions: `mousePressed()` and `keyPressed()`. The code inside these functions sits and waits. When the user clicks the mouse (or presses a key), it springs into action, executing the enclosed block of instructions once and only once.

Exercise 3-8: Add `background(255);` *to the* `draw()` *function. Why does the program stop working?*

I am now ready to bring all of these elements together for Zoog.

- Zoog's entire body will follow the mouse.

- Zoog's eye color will be determined by mouse location.

- Zoog's legs will be drawn from the previous mouse location to the current mouse location.

- When the mouse is clicked, a message will be displayed in the message window: "Take me to your leader!"

Note the addition in Exercise 3-6 on page 41 of the function `frameRate()`. `frameRate()`, which requires a value of at least one, enforces the speed at which Processing will cycle through `draw()`. `frameRate(30)`, for example, means 30 frames per second, a traditional speed for computer animation. If you do not include `frameRate()`, Processing will attempt to run the sketch at 60 frames per second. Since computers run at different speeds, `frameRate()` is used to make sure that your sketch is consistent across multiple computers.

This frame rate is just a maximum, however. If your sketch has to draw one million rectangles, it may take a long time to finish the draw cycle and run at a slower speed.

Example 3-6. Interactive Zoog

```
void setup() {
  // Set the size of the window
  size(200, 200);
  frameRate(30);
}
```

> The frame rate is set to 30 frames per second.

```
void draw() {
  // Draw a white background
  background(255);

  // Set ellipses and rects to CENTER mode
  ellipseMode(CENTER);
  rectMode(CENTER);

  // Draw Zoog's body
  stroke(0);
  fill(175);
  rect(mouseX, mouseY, 20, 100);

  // Draw Zoog's head
  stroke(0);
  fill(255);
  ellipse(mouseX, mouseY-30, 60, 60);

  // Draw Zoog's eyes
  fill(mouseX, 0, mouseY);
  ellipse(mouseX-19, mouseY-30, 16, 32);
  ellipse(mouseX+19, mouseY-30, 16, 32);

  // Draw Zoog's legs
  stroke(0);
  line(mouseX-10, mouseY+50, pmouseX-10, pmouseY + 60);
  line(mouseX+10, mouseY+50, pmouseX+10, pmouseY + 60);
}

void mousePressed() {
  println("Take me to your leader!");
}
```

Figure 3-9

> The eye color is determined by the mouse location.

> The legs are drawn according to the mouse location and the previous mouse location.

Lesson One Project

(You may have completed much of this project already via the exercises in Chapter 1–Chapter 3. This project brings all of the elements together. You could either start from scratch with a new design or use elements from the exercises.)

1. Design a static screen drawing using RGB color and primitive shapes.

2. Make the static screen drawing dynamic by having it interact with the mouse. This might include shapes following the mouse, changing their size according to the mouse, changing their color according to the mouse, and so on.

Use the space provided below to sketch designs, notes, and pseudocode for your project.

Lesson Two

Everything You Need to Know

Chapter 4
Chapter 5
Chapter 6

4 Variables

All of the books in the world contain no more information than is broadcast as video in a single large American city in a single year. Not all bits have equal value.
—Carl Sagan

Believing oneself to be perfect is often the sign of a delusional mind.
—Lieutenant Commander Data

In this chapter:
- Variables: What are they?
- Declaring and initializing variables
- Common uses for variables
- Variables you get "for free" in Processing (a.k.a. *built-in* variables)
- Using random values for variables

4-1 What is a variable?

I admit it. When I teach programming, I launch into a diatribe of analogies in an attempt to explain the concept of a variable in an intuitive manner. On any given day, I might say, "A variable is like a bucket." You put something in the bucket, carry it around with you, and retrieve it whenever you feel inspired. "A variable is like a storage locker." Deposit some information in the locker where it can live safely, readily available at a moment's notice. "A variable is a lovely, yellow post-it note, on which is written the message: I am a variable. Write your information on me."

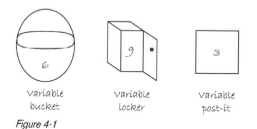

Figure 4-1

I could go on. But I won't. I think you get the idea. And I'm not entirely sure you really need an analogy since the concept itself is rather simple. Here's the deal.

The computer has memory. Why is it called memory? Because it's what the computer uses to *remember* stuff it needs.

Technically speaking, a *variable* is a named pointer to a location in the computer's memory ("memory address") where data is stored. Since computers only process information one instruction at a time, a variable allows a programmer to save information from one point in the program and refer back to it at a later time. For a Processing programmer, this is incredibly useful; variables can keep track of information related to shapes: color, size, location. Variables are exactly what you need to make a triangle change from blue to purple, a circle fly across the screen, and a rectangle shrink into oblivion.

Out of all the available analogies, I tend to prefer the *piece of paper* approach: *graph paper*.

Imagine that the computer's memory is a sheet of graph paper and each cell on the graph paper has an address. With pixels, I discussed how to refer to those cells by column and row numbers. Wouldn't it be nice if you could name those cells in memory? With variables, you can.

Let's name one "Jane's Score" (you'll see why I am calling it that in the next section) and give it the value 100. That way, whenever you want to use Jane's score in a program, you don't have to remember the value 100. It's there in memory and you can ask for it by name. See Figure 4-2.

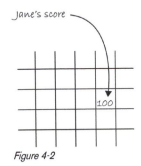

Figure 4-2

The power of a variable does not simply rest with the ability to remember a value. The whole point of a variable is that those values *vary*, and more interesting situations arise as you periodically alter that value.

Consider a game of Scrabble between Sasha and Malia. To keep track of the score, Sasha takes out paper and pencil, and scrawls down two column names: "Sasha's Score" and "Malia's Score." As the two play, a running tally is kept of each player's points below the headings. If you imagine this game to be virtual Scrabble programmed on a computer, you suddenly can see the concept emerge of a variable that *varies*. That piece of paper is the computer's memory and on that paper, information is written — "Sasha's Score" and "Malia's Score" are variables, locations in memory where each player's total points are stored and that change over time. See Figure 4-3.

Sasha's score	Malia's score
~~5~~	~~10~~
~~30~~	~~25~~
~~53~~	~~47~~
~~65~~	~~68~~
~~87~~	~~91~~
101	98

Figure 4-3

In the Scrabble example, the variable has two elements — a *name* (e.g., "Sasha's Score") and a *value* (e.g., 101). In Processing, variables can hold different kinds of values and you are required to explicitly define the *type* of value before you can use a given variable.

Exercise 4-1: Consider the game Pong. What variables would you need to program the game? (If you are not familiar with Pong, see http://en.wikipedia.org/wiki/Pong).

4-2 Variable declaration and initialization

Variables can hold *primitive* values or *references to objects and arrays*. For now, I'm just going to worry about primitives — I'll get to objects and arrays in a later chapter. Primitive values are the building blocks of data on the computer and typically involve a singular piece of information, like a number or character.

Variables are declared by first stating the type, followed by the name. Variable names must be one word (no spaces) and must start with a letter (they can include numbers, but cannot start with a number). They cannot include any punctuation or special characters, with the exception of the underscore: "_"

A *type* is the kind of data stored in that variable. This could be a whole number, a decimal number, or a character. Here are data types you will commonly use:

- **Whole numbers,** such as 0, 1, 2, 3, − 1, − 2, and so on are stored as *integers* and the type keyword for integer is `int`.

- **Decimal numbers,** such as 3.14159, 2.5, and −9.95 are typically stored as *floating point values* and the type keyword for floating point is `float`.

- **Characters,** such as the letters "a," "b," "c," and so on are stored in variables of type `char` and are declared as a letter enclosed in single quotes, that is, `'a'`. Characters are useful when determining what letter on the keyboard has been pressed, and for other uses involving *strings* of text (see Chapter 17).

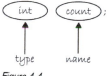
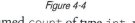

Figure 4-4

In Figure 4-4, I have a variable named `count` of type `int`, which stands for integer. Other possible data types are listed below.

Don't forget

- **Variables must have a type.** Why? This is how the computer knows exactly how much memory should be allocated to store that variable's data.

- **Variables must have a name.**

All primitive types

- `boolean`: true or false
- `char`: a character, "a," "b," "c," etc.
- `byte`: a small number, −128 to 127
- `short`: a larger number, −32,768 to 32,767
- `int`: a big number, −2,147,483,648 to 2,147,483,647
- `long`: a ridiculously huge number
- `float`: a decimal number, such as 3.14159
- `double`: a decimal number with a lot more decimal places (only necessary for advanced programs requiring mathematical precision).

Once a variable is declared, I can then assign it a value by setting it equal to something. In most cases, if you forget to initialize a variable, Processing will give it a default value, such as 0 for integers, 0.0 for floating points, and so on. However, it's good to get into the habit of always initializing variables in order to avoid confusion.

```
int count;
count = 50;
```
Declare and initialize a variable in two lines of code.

To be more concise, I can combine the above two statements into one.

```
int count = 50;
```
Declare and initialize a variable in one line of code.

What's in a name?

Tips for choosing good variable names

- Avoid using words that appear elsewhere in the Processing language. In other words, do not call your variable `mouseX`, since there already is one!

- Use names that mean something. This may seem obvious, but it's an important point. For example, if you are using a variable to keep track of score, call it "score" and not, say, "cat."

- Start your variable with a lowercase letter and join together words with capitals. Words that start with capitals are reserved for classes (Chapter 8). For example: "frogColor" is good, "Frogcolor" is not. this canTake some gettingUsedTo but it will comeNaturally soonEnough.

A variable can also be initialized by another variable (x equals y), or by evaluating a mathematical expression (x equals y plus z, etc.). Here are some examples:

Example 4-1. Variable declaration and initialization examples

```
int count = 0;          // Declare an int named count, assigned the value 0
char letter = 'a';      // Declare a char named letter, assigned the value 'a'
double d = 132.32;      // Declare a double named d, assigned the value 132.32
boolean happy = false;  // Declare a boolean named happy, assigned the value false
float x = 4.0;          // Declare a float named x, assigned the value 4.0
float y;                // Declare a float named y (no assignment)
y = x + 5.2;            // Assign the value of x plus 5.2 to the
                        // previously declared y
float z = x * y + 15.0; // Declare a variable named z, assign it the value which
                        // is x times y plus 15.0.
```

Exercise 4-2: Write out variable declaration and initialization for the game Pong.

4-3 Using a variable

Though it may initially seem more complicated to have words standing in for numbers, variables make our lives easier and more interesting.

Let's take a simple example of a program that draws a circle onscreen.

In a moment, I'll add variables at the top here.

```
void setup() {
  size(200, 200);
}

void draw() {
  background(255);
  stroke(0);
  fill(175);
  ellipse(100, 100, 50, 50);
}
```

In Chapter 3, you learned how to take this simple example one step further, changing the location of a shape to mouseX, mouseY in order to assign its location according to the mouse.

```
ellipse(mouseX, mouseY, 50, 50);
```

Can you see where this is going? mouseX and mouseY are named references to the horizontal and vertical location of the mouse. They are variables! However, because they are built into the Processing environment (note how they are colored red when you type them in your code), they can be used without being declared. Built-in variables (a.k.a. *system variables*) are discussed further in the next section.

What I want to do now is create my own variables by following the syntax for declaring and initializing outlined above, placing the variables at the top of my code. You can declare variables elsewhere in your code and I will get into this later. For now to avoid any confusion, all variables should be at the top.

Rule of thumb: when to use a variable

There are no hard and fast rules in terms of when to use a variable. However, if you find yourself hard-coding in a bunch of numbers as you program, take a few minutes, review your code, and change these values to variables.

Some programmers say that if a number appears three or more times, it should be a variable. Personally, I would say if a number appears once, use a variable. Always use variables!

Example 4-2. Using variables

```
int circleX = 100;
int circleY = 100;

void setup() {
  size(200, 200);
}

void draw() {
  background(255);
  stroke(0);
  fill(175);
  ellipse(circleX, circleY, 50, 50);
}
```

> Declare and initialize two integer variables at the top of the code.

> Use the variables to specify the location of an ellipse.

Running this code, you'll see the same result as in the first example: a circle appears in the middle of the screen. Nevertheless, you should open your heart and remind yourself that a variable is not simply a placeholder for one constant value. It's called a variable because it *varies*. To change its value, you write an *assignment operation*, which assigns a new value.

Up until now, every single line of code I wrote called a function: line(), ellipse(), stroke(), etc. Variables introduce assignment operations to the mix. Here is what one looks like (it's the same as how you initialize a variable, only the variable does not need to be declared).

```
// variable name = expression
x = 5;
x = a + b;              Examples of assigning a new value to a variable.
x = y - 10 * 20;
x = x * 5;
```

A common example is incrementation. In the above code, circleX starts with a value of 100. If you want to increment circleX by one, you say circleX equals itself plus 1. In code, this amounts to:

```
circleX = circleX + 1;
```

Let's try adding that to the sketch (and let's start circleX with the value of 0).

Example 4-3. Varying variables

```
int circleX = 0;
int circleY = 100;

void setup() {
  size(200, 200);
}

void draw() {
  background(255);
  stroke(0);
  fill(175);
  ellipse(circleX, circleY, 50, 50);

  circleX = circleX + 1;        An assignment operation that increments the value of circleX by
}                                1. Remember, this is not asking the question "does circleX
                                 equal circleX plus 1?" but rather is assigning circleX a new
                                 value: itself plus 1!
```

What happens? If you run Example 4-3 in Processing, you will notice that the circle moves from left to right. Remember, draw() loops over and over again, all the while retaining the value of circleX in memory. Let's pretend I am the computer for a moment. (This may seem overly simple and obvious, but it's key to your understanding of the principles of programming motion.)

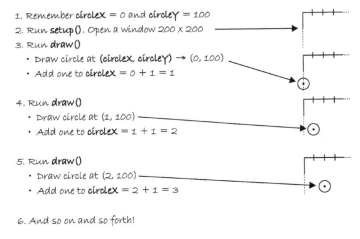

1. Remember *circleX* = 0 and *circleY* = 100
2. Run **setup**(). Open a window 200 x 200
3. Run **draw**()
   • Draw circle at (*circleX*, *circleY*) → (0, 100)
   • Add one to *circleX* = 0 + 1 = 1

4. Run **draw**()
   • Draw circle at (1, 100)
   • Add one to *circleX* = 1 + 1 = 2

5. Run **draw**()
   • Draw circle at (2, 100)
   • Add one to *circleX* = 2 + 1 = 3

6. And so on and so forth!

Figure 4-5

Practicing how to follow the code step-by-step will lead you to the questions you need to ask before writing your own sketches. *Be one with the computer.*

- What data I need to remember for the sketch?
- How do I use that data to draw shapes on the screen?
- How do I alter that data to make my sketch interactive and animated?

Exercise 4-3: Change Example 4-3 so that instead of the circle moving from left to right, the circle grows in size. What would you change to have the circle follow the mouse as it grows? How could you vary the speed at which the circle grows?

```
int circleSize = 0;
int circleX = 100;
int circleY = 100;

void setup() {
   size(200, 200);
}

void draw() {
   background(0);
   stroke(255);
   fill(175);

   _____

   _____
}
```

4-4 Many variables

Let's take the example one step further and use variables for every piece of information I can think of. I will also use floating point values to demonstrate greater precision in adjusting variable values.

Example 4-4. Many variables

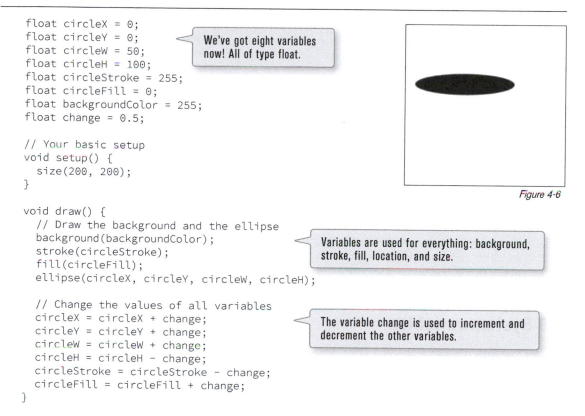

```
float circleX = 0;
float circleY = 0;
float circleW = 50;
float circleH = 100;
float circleStroke = 255;
float circleFill = 0;
float backgroundColor = 255;
float change = 0.5;

// Your basic setup
void setup() {
  size(200, 200);
}

void draw() {
  // Draw the background and the ellipse
  background(backgroundColor);
  stroke(circleStroke);
  fill(circleFill);
  ellipse(circleX, circleY, circleW, circleH);

  // Change the values of all variables
  circleX = circleX + change;
  circleY = circleY + change;
  circleW = circleW + change;
  circleH = circleH - change;
  circleStroke = circleStroke - change;
  circleFill = circleFill + change;
}
```

> We've got eight variables now! All of type float.

> Variables are used for everything: background, stroke, fill, location, and size.

> The variable change is used to increment and decrement the other variables.

Figure 4-6

Exercise 4-4: Recreate the images below.

- **Step 1:** Write code that draws the following screenshots with hard-coded values. (Feel free to use colors instead of grayscale.)
- **Step 2:** Replace all of the hard-coded numbers with variables.
- **Step 3:** Write assignment operations in draw() that change the value of the variables. For example variable1 = variable1 + 2;. Try different expressions and see what happens!

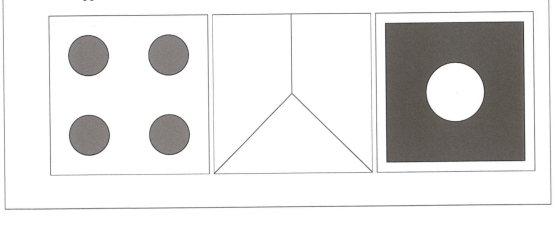

4-5 System variables

As you saw with mouseX and mouseY, Processing includes built-in variables for commonly needed pieces of data associated with all sketches (such as the *width* of the window, the *key* pressed on the keyboard, and more). When naming your own variables, it's best to avoid these built-in variable names, however, if you inadvertently use one, your variable will become primary and override the system one. Here is a list of commonly used built-in variables (there are more, which you can find in the Processing reference).

- **width** — Width (in pixels) of sketch window.
- **height** — Height (in pixels) of sketch window.
- **frameCount** — Number of frames processed.
- **frameRate** — Rate that frames are processed (per second).
- **displayWidth** — Width (in pixels) of entire screen.
- **displayHeight** — Height (in pixels) of entire screen.
- **key** — Most recent key pressed on the keyboard.
- **keyCode** — Numeric code for key pressed on keyboard.
- **keyPressed** — True or false? Is a key pressed?
- **mousePressed** — True or false? Is the mouse pressed?
- **mouseButton** — Which button is pressed? Left, right, or center?

Following is an example that makes use of several of the above variables; I'm not ready to use them all yet, as I'll need to cover some more concepts first.

Example 4-5. Using system variables

```
void setup() {
  size(200, 200);
}

void draw() {
  background(100);
  stroke(255);
  fill(frameCount/2);
  rectMode(CENTER);

  rect(width/2, height/2, mouseX + 10, mouseY + 10);
}

void keyPressed() {
  println("You pressed " + key);
}
```

> frameCount is used to color a rectangle.

> The rectangle will always be in the middle of the window if it's located at (width/2, height/2).

> The plus operator in this case is not for adding numbers. Rather it joins the string of characters "You pressed" with the variable key, which stores the key pressed. I'll cover more about how text is manipulated in Chapter 17.

Exercise 4-5: Using width *and* height, *recreate the following screenshot. Here's the catch: the shapes must resize themselves relative to the window size. (In other words, no matter what you specify for* size(), *the result should look identical.)*

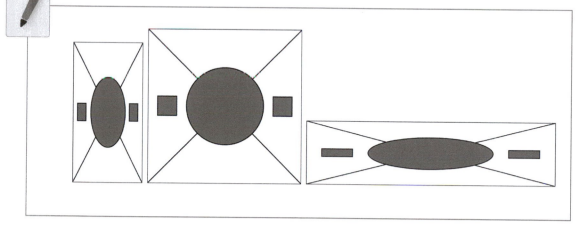

4-6 Random: variety is the spice of life

So, you may have noticed that the examples in this book so far are a bit, say, humdrum. A circle here. A square here. A grayish color. Another grayish color.

There is a method to the madness (or lack of madness in this case). It all goes back to the driving principle behind this book: *incremental development*. It's much easier to learn the fundamentals by looking at the individual pieces, programs that do one and only one thing. You can then begin to add functionality on top, step by step.

Nevertheless, you have waited patiently through four chapters and I have arrived at the time where you can begin to have a bit of fun. And this fun will be demonstrated via the use of the function random(). Consider, for a moment, Example 4-6, whose output is shown in Figure 4-7.

Example 4-6. Ellipse with variables

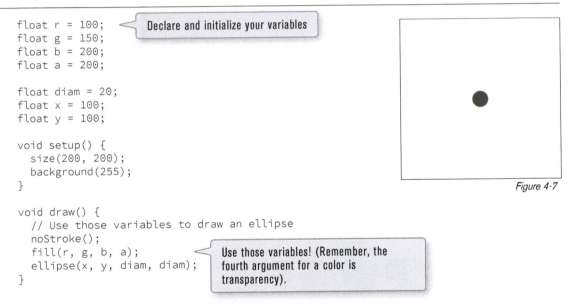

```
float r = 100;          Declare and initialize your variables
float g = 150;
float b = 200;
float a = 200;

float diam = 20;
float x = 100;
float y = 100;

void setup() {
  size(200, 200);
  background(255);
}
```

Figure 4-7

```
void draw() {
  // Use those variables to draw an ellipse
  noStroke();
  fill(r, g, b, a);          Use those variables! (Remember, the
  ellipse(x, y, diam, diam);  fourth argument for a color is
}                              transparency).
```

There it is, my dreary circle. Sure, I could adjust variable values and move the circle, grow its size, change its color, and so on. However, what if every time through draw(), I made a new circle, one with a random size, color, and position? The random() function allows me to do exactly that.

random() is a special kind of function; it's a function that *returns* a value. You have encountered this before. In Exercise 3-7 on page 41 I used the function abs() to calculate the absolute value of a number. The idea of a function that *calculates a value* and *returns it* will be explored fully in Chapter 7, but I am going to take some time to introduce the idea now and let it sink in a bit.

Unlike most of the functions you are comfortable with (e.g., line(), ellipse(), and rect()), random() does not draw or color a shape on the screen. Instead, random() answers a question; it returns that answer to you. Here is a bit of dialogue. Feel free to rehearse it with your friends.

Me: Hey random, what's going on? Hope you're well. Listen, I was wondering, could you give me a random number between 1 and 100?

Random: Like, no problem. How about the number 63?

Me: That's awesome, really great, thank you. OK, I'm off. Gotta draw a rectangle 63 pixels wide, OK?

Now, how would this sequence look in the slightly more formal, Processing environment? The code below the part of "me" is played by the variable w.

```
float w = random(1, 100);
rect(100, 100, w, 50);
```

A random float between 1 and 100.

The `random()` function requires two arguments and returns a random floating point number ranging from the first argument to the second. The second argument must be larger than the first for it to work properly. The function `random()` also works with one argument by assuming a range between zero and that argument.

In addition, `random()` only returns floating point numbers. This is why I declared w above as a `float`. However, if you want a random integer, you can convert the result of the random function to an `int`.

```
int w = int(random(1, 100));
rect(100, 100, w, 50);
```

A random integer between 1 and 100.

Notice the use of nested parentheses. This is a nice concept to get used to as it can sometimes be quite convenient to call functions inside of functions. The `random()` function returns a float, which is then passed to the `int()` function that converts it to an integer. If you wanted to go nuts nesting functions, you could even condense the above code into one line:

```
rect(100, 100, int(random(1, 100)), 50);
```

Incidentally, the process of converting one data type to another is referred to as *casting*. In Java (which Processing is based on) casting a `float` to an `int` can also be written this way:

```
int w = (int) random(1, 100);
```

The result of `random(1, 100)` is a floating point. It can be converted to an integer by "casting."

OK, I am now ready to experiment with `random()`. Example 4-7 shows what happens if you take every variable associated with drawing the ellipse (fill, location, size) and assign it to a random number each cycle through `draw()`. The output is shown in Figure 4-8.

Example 4-7. Filling variables with random values

```
float r;
float g;
float b;
float a;

float diam;
float x;
float y;

void setup() {
  size(200, 200);
  background(255);
}

void draw() {

  r = random(255);
  g = random(255);
  b = random(255);
  a = random(255);
  diam = random(20);
  x = random(width);
  y = random(height);

  // Use values to draw an ellipse
  noStroke();
  fill(r, g, b, a);
  ellipse(x, y, diam, diam);
}
```

> Each time through draw(), random values are picked for color, size, and position of a new ellipse.

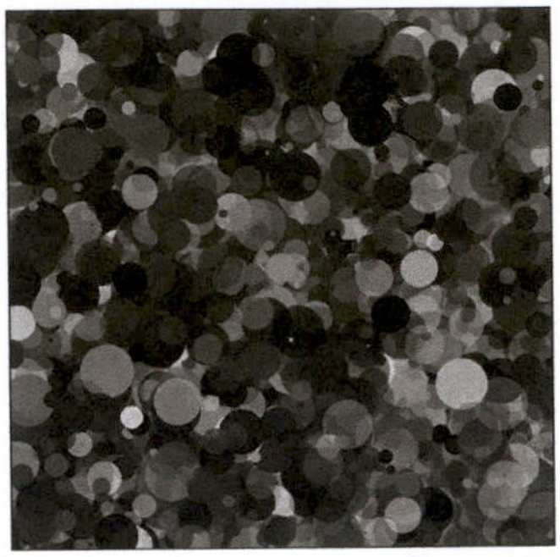

Figure 4-8

4-7 Variable Zoog

I am now ready to revisit Zoog, our alien friend, who was happily following the mouse around the screen when we last checked in. Here, I'll add two pieces of functionality to Zoog.

- **New feature #1** — Zoog will rise from below the screen and fly off into space (above the screen).
- **New feature #2** — Zoog's eyes will be colored randomly as Zoog moves.

Feature #1 is solved by simply taking the previous program that used mouseX and mouseY and substituting my variables in their place.

Feature #2 is implemented by creating three additional variables eyeRed, eyeGreen, and eyeBlue that will be used for the fill() function before displaying the eye ellipses.

Example 4-8. Variable Zoog

```
float zoogX;
float zoogY;

float eyeR;
float eyeG;
float eyeB;

void setup() {
  size(200, 200);
  zoogX = width/2; // Zoog always starts in the middle
  zoogY = height + 100; // Zoog starts below the screen
}

void draw() {
  background(255);

  // Set ellipses and rects to CENTER mode
  ellipseMode(CENTER);
  rectMode(CENTER);

  // Draw Zoog's body
  stroke(0);
  fill(150);
  rect(zoogX, zoogY, 20, 100);

  // Draw Zoog's head
  stroke(0);
  fill(255);
  ellipse(zoogX, zoogY-30, 60, 60);

  // Draw Zoog's eyes
  eyeR = random(255);
  eyeG = random(255);
  eyeB = random(255);
  fill(eyeR, eyeG, eyeB);
  ellipse(zoogX-19, zoogY-30, 16, 32);
  ellipse(zoogX+19, zoogY-30, 16, 32);

  // Draw Zoog's legs
  stroke(150);
  line(zoogX-10, zoogY+50, zoogX-10, height);
  line(zoogX+10, zoogY+50, zoogX+10, height);

  // Zoog moves up
  zoogY = zoogY - 1;
}
```

> Declaring variables. `zoogX` and `zoogY` are for feature #1. `eyeR`, `eyeG`, `eyeB` are for feature #2.

> Feature #1. `zoogX` and `zoogY` are initialized based on the size of the window. Note these variables must be initialized after `size()` is called since I am using the built-in variables `width` and `height`.

> Feature #1. `zoogX` and `zoogY` are used for the shape locations.

> Feature #2. `eyeR`, `eyeG`, and `eyeB` are given random values and used in the `fill()` function.

> Feature #1. `zoogY` is decreased by one so that Zoog moves upward on the screen.

Figure 4-9

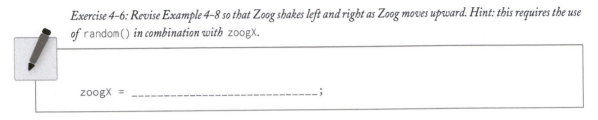

Exercise 4-6: Revise Example 4-8 so that Zoog shakes left and right as Zoog moves upward. Hint: this requires the use of `random()` *in combination with* `zoogX`.

```
zoogX = _____;
```

4-8 Translation

Examining Example 3-6 more closely, you might notice that all shapes are drawn relative to the point (zoogX, zoogY). Zoog's body is drawn directly at (zoogX, zoogY), Zoog's head is draw a bit higher up at (zoogX, zoogY-30), and the eyes a little bit to the right and left of Zoog's center. If zoogX and zoogY were equal to zero, where would Zoog appear? The top left of the window! You can see an example of this by removing zoogX and zoogY from the sketch and draw Zoog relative to (0,0). (Color functions like stroke() and fill() have been removed for simplicity.)

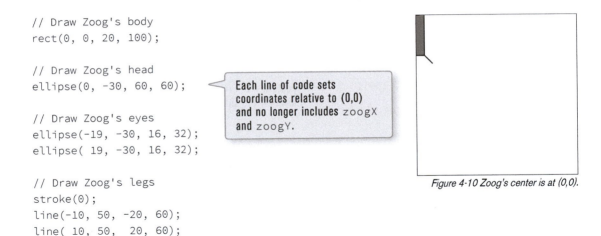

```
// Draw Zoog's body
rect(0, 0, 20, 100);

// Draw Zoog's head
ellipse(0, -30, 60, 60);

// Draw Zoog's eyes
ellipse(-19, -30, 16, 32);
ellipse( 19, -30, 16, 32);

// Draw Zoog's legs
stroke(0);
line(-10, 50, -20, 60);
line( 10, 50,  20, 60);
```

Each line of code sets coordinates relative to (0,0) and no longer includes zoogX and zoogY.

Figure 4-10 Zoog's center is at (0,0).

If you run the above code you'd see a partial Zoog in the top left as depicted in Figure 4-10. Another technique for moving Zoog (instead of adding zoogX and zoogY to each drawing function) is to use the Processing function translate(). translate() specifies a horizontal and vertical offset for shapes in the display window. In cases such as this, it can be more convenient to set an offset via translate() rather implement the math in each subsequent line of code. Here is an example implementation that moves Zoog relative to mouseX and mouseY.

Example 4-9. Translated Zoog

```
void setup() {
  size(200, 200);
}

void draw() {
  background(255);
  rectMode(CENTER);
  ellipseMode(CENTER);

  translate(mouseX, mouseY);

  // Draw Zoog's body
  stroke(0);
  fill(175);
  rect(0, 0, 20, 100);

  // Draw Zoog's head
  stroke(0);
  fill(255);
  ellipse(0, -30, 60, 60);
  // Draw Zoog's eyes
  stroke(0);
  fill(0);
  ellipse(-19, -30, 16, 32);
  ellipse( 19, -30, 16, 32);

  // Draw Zoog's legs
  stroke(0);
  line(-10, 50, -20, 60);
  line( 10, 50, 20, 60);
}
```

> All shapes drawn after `translate()` will be set relative to `mouseX` and `mouseY`.

Figure 4-11

There is a lot more to translation than what I've very briefly shown you here. So much so that an entire chapter later in this book (Chapter 14) is dedicated to `translate()` and other related functions known as *transformations*. Translation, for example, is required to rotate shapes in Processing as well as a key to unlocking how to draw in virtual three-dimensional space. However, I'm going to stop here since the first half of this book's focus is the fundamentals of programming. I'll leave more advanced topics in computer graphics for later. However, if you feel that exploring transformations now might add to your own work, it would not be so unreasonable to briefly skip to Chapter 14 and read up until Example 14-15 before returning to read Chapter 5. There the discussion starts to include topics I have not yet covered up until now.

Exercise 4-7: Using variables and the `random()` *function, revise your design from the Lesson One Project to move around the screen, change color, size, location, and so on. Consider using* `translate()` *to set Zoog's position in the window.*

5 Conditionals

That language is an instrument of human reason, and not merely a medium for the expression of thought, is a truth generally admitted.
—George Boole

The way I feel about music is that there is no right and wrong. Only true and false.
—Fiona Apple

In this chapter:
– Boolean expressions
– Conditional statements: How a program produces different results based on varying circumstances
– *If, else if, else*
– Relational and logical operators

5-1 Boolean expressions

What's your favorite kind of test? Essay format? Multiple choice? In the world of computer programming, one only takes one kind of test: a *boolean* test — true or false. A *boolean expression* (named for mathematician George Boole) is an expression that evaluates to either true or false. Let's look at some common language examples:

- My favorite color is pink. → true
- I am afraid of computer programming. → false
- This book is a hilarious read. → false

In the formal logic of computer science, relationships between numbers are tested.

- 15 is greater than 20 → false
- 5 equals 5 → true
- 32 is less than or equal to 33 → true

In this chapter, I will show how to use a variable in a boolean expression, allowing a sketch to take different paths depending on the current value stored in the variable.

- x > 20 → depends on current value of x
- y == 5 → depends on current value of y
- z <= 33 → depends on current value of z

The following operators can be used in a boolean expression.

Relational operators

```
>    greater than
<    less than
>=   greater than or equal to
<=   less than or equal to
==   equal to
!=   not equal to
```

5-2 Conditionals: if, else, else if

Boolean expressions (often referred to as "conditionals") operate within the sketch as questions. Is 15 greater than 20? If the answer is yes (i.e., true), you can choose to execute certain instructions (such as draw a rectangle); if the answer is no (i.e., false), those instructions are ignored. This introduces the idea of branching; depending on various conditions, the program can follow different paths.

In the physical world, this might amount to instructions like so:

If I am hungry then eat some food, otherwise if I am thirsty, drink some water, otherwise, take a nap.

In Processing, you might have something more like:

If the mouse is on the left side of the screen, draw a rectangle on the left side of the screen.

Or, more formally, with the output shown in Figure 5-1,

```
if (mouseX < width/2) {
  fill(255);
  rect(0, 0, width/2, height);
}
```

The boolean expression and resulting instructions in the above source code is contained within a block of code with the following syntax and structure:

```
if (boolean expression) {
  // code to execute if boolean expression is true
}
```

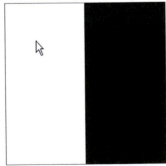

Figure 5-1

The structure can be expanded with the keyword *else* to include code that is executed if the boolean expression is false. This is the equivalent of "otherwise, do such and such."

```
if (boolean expression) {
  // code to execute if boolean expression is true
} else {
  // code to execute if boolean expression is false
}
```

For example, I could say the following, with the output shown in Figure 5-2.

If the mouse is on the left side of the screen, draw a white background, otherwise draw a black background.

```
if (mouseX < width/2) {
  background(255);
} else {
  background(0);
}
```

Finally, for testing multiple conditions, you can employ an `else if`. When an `else if` is used, the conditional statements are evaluated in the order presented. As soon as one boolean expression is found to be true, the corresponding code is executed and the remaining boolean expressions are ignored. See Figure 5-3.

Figure 5-2

```
if (boolean expression #1) {
  // code to execute if boolean expression #1 is
  true
} else if (boolean expression #2) {
  // code to execute if boolean expression #2 is
  true
} else if (boolean expression #n) {
  // code to execute if boolean expression #n is
  true
} else {
  // code to execute if none of the above
  // boolean expressions are true
}
```

Taking the simple mouse example a step further, I could say the following, with results shown in Figure 5-4.

If the mouse is on the left third of the window, draw a white background, if it's in the middle third, draw a gray background, otherwise, draw a black background.

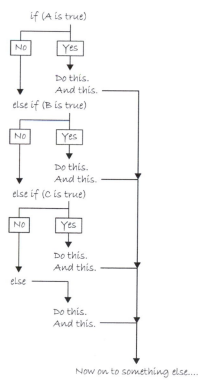

Figure 5-3

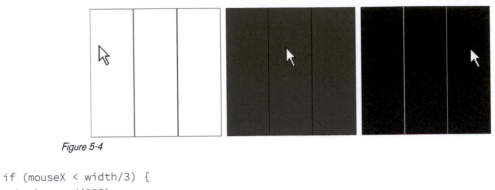

Figure 5-4

```
if (mouseX < width/3) {
  background(255);
} else if (mouseX < 2*width/3) {
  background(127);
} else {
  background(0);
}
```

Exercise 5-1: Consider a grading system where numbers are turned into letters. Fill in the blanks in the following code to complete the boolean expression.

```
float grade = random(0, 100);

if (_____) {
  println("Assign letter grade A.");

} else if (_____) {

  println(_____);

} else if (_____) {

  println(_____);

} else if (_____) {

  println(_____);

} else {

  println(_____);
}
```

> In one conditional statement, you can only ever have one `if` and one `else`. However, you can have as many `else` `if`s as you like!

Exercise 5-2: Examine the following code samples and determine what will appear in the message window. Write down your answer and then execute the code in Processing to compare.

Problem #1: Determine if a number is between 0 and 25, 26 and 50, or greater than 50.

```
int x = 75;

if (x > 50) {
  println(x + " > 50!");
} else if (x > 25) {
  println(x + " > 25!");
} else {
  println(x + " <= 25!");
}
```

```
int x = 75;

if(x > 25) {
  println(x + " > 25!");
} else if (x > 50) {
  println(x + " > 50!");
} else {
  println(x + " <= 25!");
}
```

OUTPUT:_____   **OUTPUT:**_____

Although the syntax is correct, what is problematic about the code in column two above?

Problem #2: If a number is 5, change it to 6. If a number is 6, change it to 5.

```
int x = 5;

println("x is now: " + x);
if (x == 5) {
  x = 6;
}
if (x == 6) {
  x = 5;
}
println("x is now: " + x);
```

```
int x = 5;

println("x is now: " + x);
if (x == 5) {
  x = 6;
} else if (x == 6) {
  x = 5;
}
println("x is now: " + x);
```

OUTPUT:_____   **OUTPUT:**_____

Although the syntax is correct, what is problematic about the code in column one above?

It's worth pointing out that in Exercise 5-2 on page 71 when I tested for equality I had to use *two* equal signs. This is because, when programming, asking if something is equal is different from assigning a value to a variable.

```
if (x == y) {
```
◁ "Is x equal to y?" Use double equals!

```
x = y;
```
◁ "Set x equal to y." Use single equals!

5-3 Conditionals in a sketch

Let's look at a very simple example of a program that performs different tasks based on the result of certain conditions. The pseudocode is below.

Step 1. Create variables to hold on to red, green, and blue color components. Call them *r*, *g*, and *b*.
Step 2. Continuously draw the background based on those colors.
Step 3. If the mouse is on the right-hand side of the screen, increment the value of *r*, if it's on the left-hand side decrement the value of *r*.
Step 4. Constrain the value *r* to be within 0 and 255.

This pseudocode is implemented in Processing in Example 5-1.

Example 5-1. Conditionals

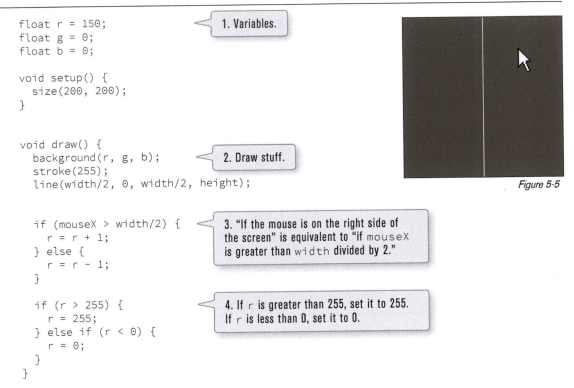

```
float r = 150;
float g = 0;
float b = 0;
```
← 1. Variables.

```
void setup() {
  size(200, 200);
}


void draw() {
  background(r, g, b);
  stroke(255);
  line(width/2, 0, width/2, height);
```
← 2. Draw stuff.

Figure 5-5

```
  if (mouseX > width/2) {
    r = r + 1;
  } else {
    r = r - 1;
  }
```
← 3. "If the mouse is on the right side of the screen" is equivalent to "if `mouseX` is greater than `width` divided by 2."

```
  if (r > 255) {
    r = 255;
  } else if (r < 0) {
    r = 0;
  }
}
```
← 4. If `r` is greater than 255, set it to 255. If `r` is less than 0, set it to 0.

Constraining the value of a variable, as in Step 4, is a common problem. Here, I do not want color values to increase to unreasonable extremes. In other examples, you might want to constrain the size or location of a shape so that it does not get too big or too small, or wander off the screen.

While using if statements is a perfectly valid solution to the constrain problem, Processing does offer a function entitled constrain() that will get you the same result in one line of code.

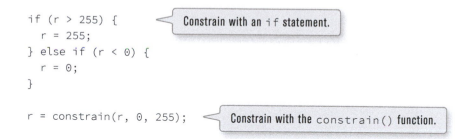

```
if (r > 255) {                    Constrain with an if statement.
   r = 255;
} else if (r < 0) {
   r = 0;
}


r = constrain(r, 0, 255);         Constrain with the constrain() function.
```

constrain() takes three arguments: the value you intend to constrain, the minimum limit, and the maximum limit. The function *returns* the "constrained" value and is assigned back to the variable r. (Remember what it means for a function to *return* a value? See the discussion of random().)

Getting into the habit of *constraining* values is a great way to avoid errors; no matter how sure you are that your variables will stay within a given range, there are no guarantees other than constrain() itself. And someday, as you work on larger software projects with multiple programmers, functions such as constrain() can ensure that sections of code work well together. Handling errors before they happen in code is emblematic of good style.

Let's make my first example a bit more advanced and change all three color components according to the mouse location and click state. Note the use of constrain() for all three variables. The system variable mousePressed is true or false depending on whether the user is holding down the mouse button.

Example 5-2. More conditionals

```
float r = 0;
float b = 0;
float g = 0;
```
Three variables for the background color.

```
void setup() {
   size(200, 200);
}

void draw() {
 background(r, g, b);
 stroke(0);
```
Color the background and draw lines to divide the window into quadrants.

Figure 5-6

```
 line(width/2, 0, width/2, height);
 line(0, height/2, width, height/2);


 if(mouseX > width/2) {
   r = r + 1;
 } else {
   r = r - 1;
 }
```
If the mouse is on the right-hand side of the window, increase red. Otherwise, it is on the left-hand side and decrease red.

```
 if (mouseY > height/2) {
   b = b + 1;
 } else {
   b = b - 1;
 }
```
If the mouse is on the bottom of the window, increase blue. Otherwise, it is on the top and decrease blue.

```
 if (mousePressed) {
   g = g + 1;
 } else {
   g = g - 1;
 }
```
If the mouse is pressed (using the system variable `mousePressed`) increase green.

```
 r = constrain(r, 0, 255);
 g = constrain(g, 0, 255);
 b = constrain(b, 0, 255);
}
```
Constrain all color values to between 0 and 255.

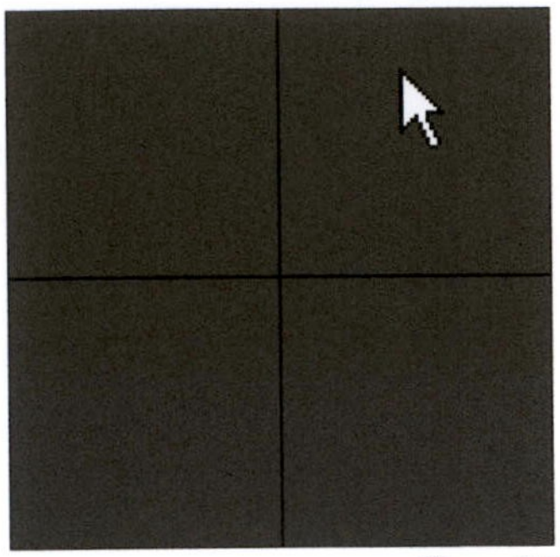

Exercise 5-3: Move a rectangle across a window by incrementing a variable. Start the shape at x coordinate 0 and use an if statement to have it stop at coordinate 100. Rewrite the sketch to use constrain() *instead of the* if *statement. Fill in the missing code.*

```
// Rectangle starts at location x
float x = 0;

void setup() {
  size(200, 200);
}

void draw() {
  background(255);
  // Display object
  fill(0);
  rect(x, 100, 20, 20);

  // Increment x
  x = x + 1;

  _____

  _____

  _____
}
```

5-4 Logical operators

You have conquered the simple if statement:

>*If my temperature is greater than 98.6, then take me to the doctor.*

Sometimes, however, simply performing a task based on one condition is not enough. For example:

>*If my temperature is greater than 98.6 **OR** I have a rash on my arm, take me to the doctor.*

>*If I am stung by a bee **AND** I am allergic to bees, take me to the doctor.*

The same idea applies in programming.

>*If the mouse is on the right side of the screen **AND** the mouse is on the bottom of the screen, draw a rectangle in the bottom right corner.*

Your first instinct might be to write the above code using a nested if statement, like so:

```
if (mouseX > width/2) {
  if (mouseY > height/2) {
    fill(255);
    rect(width/2,height/2,width/2,height/2);
  }
}
```

In other words, you would have to get a true answer for *two* if statements before the code is executed. This works, yes, but can be accomplished in a simpler way using what is called a "logical and," written as two ampersands ("&&"). A single ampersand ("&") means something else[1] in Processing so make sure you include two!

|| (logical OR)
&& (logical AND)
! (logical NOT)

A "logical or" is two vertical bars (a.k.a. two "pipes") "||". If you can't find the pipe, it's typically on the keyboard as shift-backslash.

```
if (mouseX > width/2 && mouseY > height/2) {
  fill(255);
  rect(width/2, height/2, width/2, height/2);
}
```

If the mouse is on the right side and on the bottom.

In addition to && and ||, you also have access to the logical operator "not," written as an exclamation point: !

*If my temperature is **NOT** greater than 98.6, I won't call in sick to work.*

*If I am stung by a bee **AND** I am **NOT** allergic to bees, I'll be fine!*

A Processing example is:

*If the mouse is **NOT** pressed, draw a circle, otherwise draw a square.*

```
if (!mousePressed) {
  ellipse(width/2, height/2, 100, 100);
} else {
  rect(width/2, height/2, 100, 100);
}
```

! means not. mousePressed is a boolean variable that acts as its own boolean expression. Its value is either true or false (depending on whether or not the mouse is currently pressed). Boolean variables will be explored in greater detail in Section 5-6 on page 79.

---

[1] "&" or "|" are reserved for *bitwise* operations in Processing. A bitwise operation compares each bit (0 or 1) of the binary representations of two numbers. It's used in rare circumstances where you require low-level access to bits.

Notice this example could also be written omitting the *not*, saying:

If the mouse is pressed, draw a square, otherwise draw a circle.

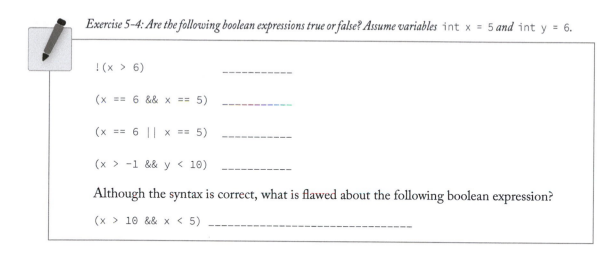

Exercise 5-4: Are the following boolean expressions true or false? Assume variables int x = 5 and int y = 6.

```
!(x > 6)                    _____

(x == 6 && x == 5)    _____

(x == 6 || x == 5)    _____

(x > -1 && y < 10)    _____
```

Although the syntax is correct, what is flawed about the following boolean expression?

```
(x > 10 && x < 5) _____
```

Exercise 5-5: Write a program that implements a simple rollover. In other words, if the mouse is over a rectangle, the rectangle changes color. Here is some code to get you started. (How might you do this for a circle?)

```
int x = 50;
int y = 50;
int w = 100;
int h = 75;

void setup() {
  size(200, 200);
}
void draw() {
  background(255);

  stroke(0);

  if (_____ && _____ && _____ && _____) {

    _____

  } _____ {

    _____

  }

  rect(x, y, w, h);
}
```

5-5 Multiple rollovers

Let's solve a simple problem together, a slightly more advanced version of Exercise 5-5 on page 77. Consider the four screenshots shown in Figure 5-7 from one single sketch. A black square is displayed in one of four quadrants, according to the mouse location.

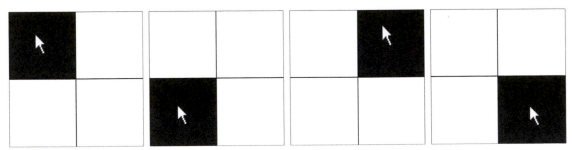

Figure 5-7

Let's first write the logic of the program in pseudocode (i.e., English).

Setup:

1. Set up a window of 200 × 200 pixels.

Draw:

1. Draw a white background.
2. Draw horizontal and vertical lines to divide the window in four quadrants.
3. If the mouse is in the top left corner, draw a black rectangle in the top left corner.
4. If the mouse is in the top right corner, draw a black rectangle in the top right corner.
5. If the mouse is in the bottom left corner, draw a black rectangle in the bottom left corner.
6. If the mouse is in the bottom right corner, draw a black rectangle in the bottom right corner.

For instructions 3-6, I'll ask the question: "How do you know if the mouse is in a given corner?" To accomplish this, you need to develop a more specific if statement. For example, you might say: "If the mouseX location is greater than 100 pixels and the mouseY location is greater than 100 pixels, draw a black rectangle in the bottom right corner. As an exercise, you may want to try writing this program yourself based on the above pseudocode. The answer, for your reference, is given in Example 5-3.

Example 5-3. Rollovers

```
void setup() {
  size(200, 200);
}

void draw() {
  background(255);
  stroke(0);
  line(100, 0, 100, 200);
  line(0, 100, 200, 100);

  noStroke();
  fill(0);
  if (mouseX < 100 && mouseY < 100) {
    rect(0, 0, 100, 100);
  } else if (mouseX > 100 && mouseY < 100) {
    rect(100, 0, 100, 100);
  } else if (mouseX < 100 && mouseY > 100) {
    rect(0, 100, 100, 100);
  } else if (mouseX > 100 && mouseY > 100) {
    rect(100, 100, 100, 100);
  }
}
```

Depending on the mouse location, a different rectangle is displayed.

 Exercise 5-6: *Rewrite Example 5-3 so that the squares fade from white to black when the mouse leaves their area. Hint: you need four variables, one for each rectangle's color.*

5-6 Boolean variables

The natural next step up from programming a rollover is a button. After all, a button is just a rollover that responds when clicked. Now, it may feel ever so slightly disappointing to be programming rollovers and buttons. Perhaps you're thinking: "Can't I just select 'Add Button' from the menu or something?" For us, right now, the answer is no. Yes, I will eventually cover how to use code from a library (and you might use a library to make buttons in your sketches more easily), but there is value in learning how to program GUI (graphical user interface) elements from scratch.

For one, practicing programming buttons, rollovers, and sliders is an excellent way to learn the basics of variables and conditionals. And two, using the same old buttons and rollovers that every program has is not terribly exciting. If you care about and are interested in developing new interfaces, understanding how to build an interface from scratch is a skill you will need.

OK, with that out of the way, I am going to look at how to use a *boolean variable* to program a button. A boolean variable (or a variable of type boolean) is a variable that can only be true or false. Think of it as a switch. It is either on or off. Press the button, turn the switch on. Press the button again, turn it off. I just used a boolean variable in Example 5-2: the built-in variable `mousePressed`. `mousePressed` is true when the mouse is pressed and false when the mouse is not.

And so my button example will include one boolean variable with a starting value of false (the assumption being that the button starts in the off state).

```
boolean button = false;
```
> A boolean variables is either true of false.

In the case of a rollover, any time the mouse hovered over the rectangle, it turned white. The sketch will turn the background white when the button is pressed and black when it is not.

```
if (button) {
  background(255);
} else {
  background(0);
}
```
> If the value of button is true, the background is white. If it is false, black.

I can then check to see if the mouse location is inside the rectangle and if the mouse is pressed, setting the value of button to true or false accordingly. Here is the full example:

Example 5-4. Hold down the button

```
boolean button = false;

int x = 50;
int y = 50;
int w = 100;
int h = 75;

void setup() {
  size(200, 200);
}

void draw() {

  if (mouseX > x && mouseX < x+w && mouseY > y && mouseY < y+h && mousePressed) {
    button = true;
  } else {
    button = false;
  }

  if (button) {
    background(255);
    stroke(0);
  } else {
    background(0);
    stroke(255);
  }

  fill(175);
  rect(x, y, w, h);

}
```
> The button is pressed if (mouseX, mouseY) is inside the rectangle and mousePressed is true.

This example simulates a button connected to a light that is only on when the button is pressed. As soon as you let go, the light goes off. While this might be a perfectly appropriate form of interaction for some instances, it's not what I am really going for in this section. What I want is a button that operates like a switch; when you flip the switch (press the button), if the light is off, it turns on. If it's on, it turns off.

For this to work properly, I must check to see if the mouse is located inside the rectangle inside mousePressed() rather than as above in draw(). By definition, when the user clicks the mouse, the code inside mousePressed() is executed once and only once (see Section 3-4 on page 42). When the mouse is clicked, I want the switch to turn on or off (once and only once).

I now need to write some code that "toggles" the switch, changes its state from on to off, or off to on. This code will go inside mousePressed().

If the variable button equals true, it should be set to false. If it is false, it should be set to true.

```
if (button) {
  button = false;
} else {
  button = true;
}
```

The explicit way to toggle a boolean variable. If the value of button is true, set it equal to false. Otherwise, it must be false, so set it equal to true.

There is a simpler way to go which is the following:

```
button = !button;
```

Not true is false. Not false is true!

Here, the value of button is set to *not* itself. In other words, if the button is true then I set it to *not true* (false). If it is false then I set it to *not false* (true). Armed with this odd but effective line of code, you are ready to look at the button in action in Example 5-5.

Example 5-5. Button as switch

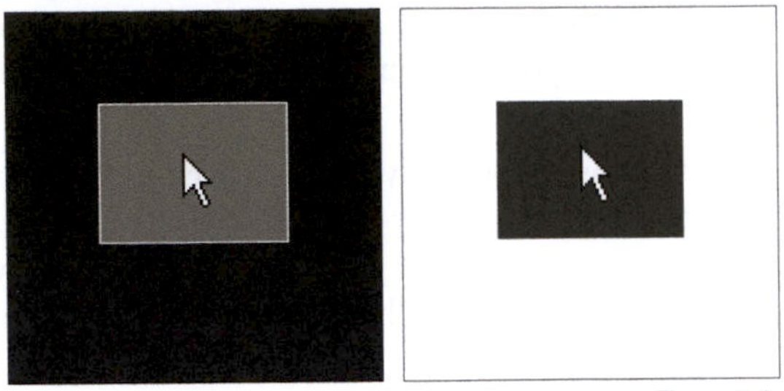

```
boolean button = false;

int x = 50;
int y = 50;
int w = 100;
int h = 75;

void setup() {
  size(200, 200);
}

void draw() {
  if (button) {
    background(255);
    stroke(0);
  } else {
    background(0);
    stroke(255);
  }

  fill(175);
  rect(x, y, w, h);
}

void mousePressed() {
  if (mouseX > x & & mouseX < x + w & & mouseY > y & & mouseY < y + h) {
    button = !button;
  }
}
```

Figure 5-8

> When the mouse is pressed, the state of the button is toggled. Try moving this code to `draw()` like in the rollover example. (See Exercise 5-7 below.)

Exercise 5-7: Why doesn't the following code work properly when it's moved to draw()?

```
if (mouseX > x && mouseX < x+w &&
    mouseY > y && mouseY < y+h && mousePressed) {
    button = !button;
}
```

Exercise 5-8: Example 4-3 in the previous chapter moved a circle across the window. Change the sketch so that the circle only starts moving once the mouse has been pressed. Use a boolean variable.

```
boolean _____ = _____;

int circleX = 0;
int circleY = 100;

void setup() {
  size(200, 200);
}

void draw() {
  background(100);
  stroke(255);
  fill(0);
  ellipse(circleX, circleY, 50, 50);

  _____

  _____

  _____

}

void mousePressed() {

  _____

}
```

5-7 A bouncing ball

It's time again to return to my friend Zoog. Let's review what you have done so far. First, you learned to draw Zoog with shape functions available from the Processing reference. Afterward, you realized you could use variables instead of hard-coded values. Having these variables allowed you to move Zoog. If Zoog's location is x, draw it at x, then at x + 1, then at x + 2, and so on.

It was an exciting, yet sad moment. The pleasure you experienced from discovering the motion was quickly replaced by the lonely feeling of watching Zoog leave the screen. Fortunately, conditional statements are here to save the day, allowing me to ask the question: *Has Zoog reached the edge of the screen? If so, turn Zoog around!*

To simplify things, let's start with a simple circle instead of Zoog's entire pattern.

> Write a program where Zoog (a simple circle) moves across the screen horizontally from left to right. When it reaches the right edge it reverses direction.

From the previous chapter on variables, you know you need global variables to keep track of Zoog's location.

```
int x = 0;
```

Is this enough? No. In the previous example Zoog always moved one pixel.

```
x = x + 1;
```

This tells Zoog to move to the right. But what if I want it to move to the left? Easy, right?

```
x = x - 1;
```

In other words, sometimes Zoog moves with a speed of "+1" and sometimes "−1." The speed of Zoog *varies.* Yes, bells are ringing. In order to switch the direction of Zoog's speed, I need another *variable*: speed.

```
int x = 0;
int speed = 1;
```
A variable for Zoog's speed. When speed is positive Zoog moves to the right, when speed is negative Zoog moves to the left.

Now that I have variables, I can move on to the rest of the code. Assuming `setup()` sets the size of the window, I can go directly to examining the steps required inside of `draw()`. I can also refer to Zoog as a ball in this instance since I am just going to draw a circle.

```
background(255);
stroke(0);
fill(100);
ellipse(x, 100, 32, 32);
```
For simplicity, Zoog is just a circle.

Elementary stuff. Now, in order for the ball to move, the value of its x location should change each cycle through `draw()`.

```
x = x + speed;
```

If you ran the program now, the circle would start on the left side of the window, move toward the right, and continue off the edge of the screen — this is the result I achieved in Chapter 4. In order for it to turn around, I need a conditional statement.

> *If the ball goes off the edge, turn the ball around.*

Or more formally...

> *If x is greater than width, reverse speed.*

```
if (x > width) {
    speed = speed * -1;
}
```

> Multiplying by -1 reverses the speed.

Reversing the polarity of a number

When I want to reverse the polarity of a number, I mean that I want a positive number to become negative and a negative number to become positive. This is achieved by multiplying by -1. Remind yourself of the following:

- -5 * -1 = 5
- 5 * -1 = -5
- 1 * -1 = -1
- -1 * -1 = 1

Running the sketch, I now have a circle that turns around when it reaches the right-most edge, but runs off the left-most edge of the screen. I'll need to revise the conditional slightly.

If the ball goes off either the right or left edge, turn the ball around.

Or more formally...

If x is greater than width or if x is less than zero, reverse speed.

```
if ((x > width) || (x < 0)) {
    speed = speed * -1;
}
```

> Remember, || means "or."

Example 5-6 puts it all together.

Example 5-6. Bouncing ball

```
int x = 0;
int speed = 1;

void setup() {
  size(200, 200);
}

void draw() {
  background(255);

  x = x + speed;                        Add the current speed to x.

  if ((x > width) || (x < 0)) {         If the object reaches either edge,
    speed = speed * -1;                 multiply speed by -1 to turn it around.
  }

  // Display circle at x location
  stroke(0);
  fill(175);
  ellipse(x, 100, 32, 32);
}
```

Exercise 5-9: Rewrite Example 5-6 so that the ball not only moves horizontally, but vertically as well. Can you implement additional features, such as changing the size or color of the ball based on certain conditions? Can you make the ball speed up or slow down in addition to changing direction?

The "bouncing ball" logic of incrementing and decrementing a variable can be applied in many ways beyond the motion of shapes onscreen. For example, just as a square moves from left to right, a color can go from less red to more red. Example 5-7 takes the same bouncing ball algorithm and applies it to changing color.

Example 5-7. "Bouncing" color

```
float c1 = 0;
float c2 = 255;

float c1Change = 1;
float c2Change = -1;

void setup() {
  size(200, 200);
}

void draw() {
  noStroke();

  // Draw rectangle on left
  fill(c1, 0, c2);
  rect(0, 0, 100, 200);

  // Draw rectangle on right
  fill(c2, 0, c1);
  rect(100, 0, 100, 200);

  // Adjust color values
  c1 = c1 + c1Change;
  c2 = c2 + c2dc2Changeir;

  // Reverse direction of color change
  if (c1 < 0 || c1 > 255) {
    c1Change *= -1;
  }

  if (c2 < 0 || c2 > 255) {
    c2Change *= -1;
  }
}
```

> Two variables for color.

> Start by incrementing c1.
> Start by decrementing c2.

> Instead of reaching the edge of a window, these variables reach the "edge" of color: 0 for no color and 255 for full color. When this happens, just like with the bouncing ball, the direction is reversed.

Figure 5-9

Having the conditional statement in your collection of programming tools allows for more complex motion. For example, consider a rectangle that follows the edges of a window.

One way to solve this problem is to think of the rectangle's motion as having four possible states, numbered 0 through 3. See Figure 5-10.

- State #0: left to right.
- State #1: top to bottom.
- State #2: right to left.
- State #3: bottom to top.

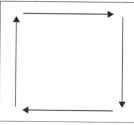

Figure 5-10

I can use a variable to keep track of the state number and adjust the (x,y) coordinate of the rectangle according to that state. For example: "If the state equals 2, set x equal to itself minus 1."

Once the rectangle reaches the endpoint for that state, I can change the state variable. "If the state equals 2: (a) set x equal to itself minus 1, (b) if x is less than zero, set state equal to 3."

The following example implements this logic.

Example 5-8. Square following edge, uses a "state" variable

```
int x = 0;      // x location of square
int y = 0;      // y location of square
int speed = 5; // speed of square

int state = 0;

void setup() {
  size(200, 200);
}

void draw() {
  background(255);

  // Display the square
  noStroke();
  fill(0);
  rect(x, y, 10, 10);

  if (state == 0) {
    x = x + speed;
    if (x > width - 10) {
      x = width - 10;
      state = 1;
    }
  } else if (state == 1) {
    y = y + speed;
    if (y > height - 10) {
      y = height - 10;
      state = 2;
    }
  } else if (state == 2) {
    x = x - speed;
    if (x < 0) {
      x = 0;
      state = 3;
    }
  } else if (state == 3) {
    y = y - speed;
    if (y < 0) {
      y = 0;
      state = 0;
    }
  }
}
```

A variable to keep track of the square's "state." Depending on the value of its state, it will either move right, down, left, or up.

If the state is 0, move to the right.

If, while the state is 0, it reaches the right side of the window, change the state to 1. Repeat this same logic for all states!

Figure 5-11

5-8 Physics 101

For me, one of the happiest moments of my programming life was the moment I realized I could code gravity. And in fact, armed with variables and conditionals, you are now ready for this moment.

The bouncing ball sketch demonstrated that an object moves by altering its location according to speed.

location = location + speed

Gravity is a force of attraction between all masses. When you drop a pen, the force of gravity from the earth (which is overwhelmingly larger than the pen) causes the pen to accelerate toward the ground. What I must add to the bouncing ball is the concept of "acceleration" (which is caused by gravity, but could be caused by any number of forces). Acceleration increases (or decreases) speed. In other words, acceleration is the rate of change of speed. And speed is the rate of change of location. So I just need another line of code:

speed = speed + acceleration

And now I have a simple gravity simulation.

Example 5-9. Simple gravity

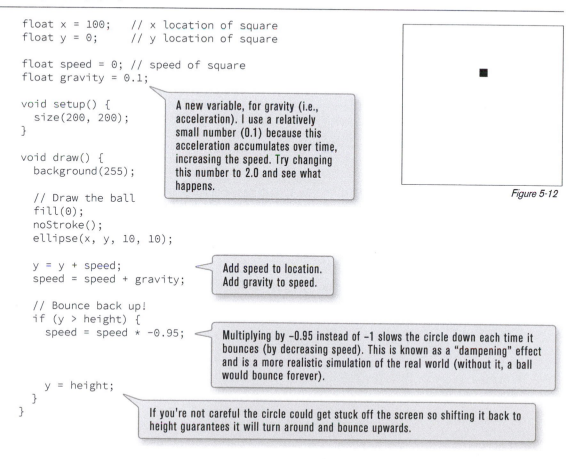

```
float x = 100;    // x location of square
float y = 0;      // y location of square

float speed = 0; // speed of square
float gravity = 0.1;

void setup() {
  size(200, 200);
}

void draw() {
  background(255);

  // Draw the ball
  fill(0);
  noStroke();
  ellipse(x, y, 10, 10);

  y = y + speed;
  speed = speed + gravity;

  // Bounce back up!
  if (y > height) {
    speed = speed * -0.95;



    y = height;
  }
}
```

A new variable, for gravity (i.e., acceleration). I use a relatively small number (0.1) because this acceleration accumulates over time, increasing the speed. Try changing this number to 2.0 and see what happens.

Figure 5-12

Add speed to location.
Add gravity to speed.

Multiplying by –0.95 instead of –1 slows the circle down each time it bounces (by decreasing speed). This is known as a "dampening" effect and is a more realistic simulation of the real world (without it, a ball would bounce forever).

If you're not careful the circle could get stuck off the screen so shifting it back to height guarantees it will turn around and bounce upwards.

Exercise 5-10: Continue with your design and add some of the functionality demonstrated in this chapter. Some options:

- Make parts of your design rollovers that change color when the mouse is over certain areas.

- Move it around the screen. Can you make it bounce off all edges of the window?

- Fade colors in and out.

Here is a simple version with Zoog.

Example 5-10. Zoog and conditionals

```
float x = 100;
float y = 100;
float w = 60;
float h = 60;
float eyeSize = 16;

float xspeed = 3;          Zoog has variables for speed in the
float yspeed = 1;          horizontal and vertical direction.

void setup() {
  size(200, 200);
}


void draw() {
  // Change the location of Zoog by speed
  x = x + xspeed;
  y = y + yspeed;

  if ((x > width) || (x < 0)) {     An if statement with a logical or determines if Zoog has
    xspeed = xspeed * -1;           reached either the right or left edges of the screen. When this
  }                                 is true, multiply the speed by -1, reversing Zoog's direction!

  if ((y > height) || (y < 0)) {
    yspeed = yspeed * -1;
  }                              Identical logic is applied to the y direction as well.

  background(255);
  ellipseMode(CENTER);
  rectMode(CENTER);

  // Draw Zoog's body
  stroke(0);
  fill(150);
  rect(x, y, w/6, h*2);

  // Draw Zoog's head
  fill(255);
```

```
  ellipse(x, y-h/2, w, h);

  // Draw Zoog's eyes
  fill(0);
  ellipse(x-w/3, y-h/2, eyeSize, eyeSize*2);
  ellipse(x+w/3, y-h/2, eyeSize, eyeSize*2);

  // Draw Zoog's legs
  stroke(0);
  line(x-w/12, y+h, x-w/4, y+h+10);
  line(x+w/12, y+h, x+w/4, y+h+10);
}
```

6 Loops

Repetition is the reality and the seriousness of life.
—Soren Kierkegaard

What's the key to comedy? Repetition. What's the key to comedy? Repetition.
—Anonymous

In this chapter:
- The concept of iteration
- Two types of loops: `while` and `for`. When do you use them?
- Variable scope: *local* vs. *global*
- Iteration in the context of computer graphics

6-1 What is iteration? I mean, what is iteration? Seriously, what is iteration?

Iteration is the generative process of repeating a set of rules or steps over and over again. It's a fundamental concept in computer programming and you will soon come to discover that it makes your life as a coder quite delightful. Let's begin.

For the moment, think about legs. Lots and lots of legs on little Zoog. If you had only read Chapter 1 of this book, you would probably write some code as in Example 6-1.

Example 6-1. Many lines

```
size(200, 200);
background(255);

// Legs
stroke(0);
line(50, 60, 50, 80);
line(60, 60, 60, 80);
line(70, 60, 70, 80);
line(80, 60, 80, 80);
line(90, 60, 90, 80);
line(100, 60, 100, 80);
line(110, 60, 110, 80);
line(120, 60, 120, 80);
line(130, 60, 130, 80);
line(140, 60, 140, 80);
line(150, 60, 150, 80);
```

Figure 6-1

In the above example, legs are drawn from x position 50 all the way to x position 150, with one leg every 10 pixels. Although the code accomplishes this, I can make some substantial improvements and eliminate the hard-coded values by using the variables I discussed in Chapter 4.

First, I'll set up variables for each parameter of the system: the legs' (x,y) positions, length, and the spacing between the legs. Note that for each leg drawn, only the x value changes. All other variables stay the same (but they could change if you wanted them to!).

Example 6-2. Many lines with variables

```
size(200, 200);
background(255);

// Legs
stroke(0);

int y = 80;        // Vertical location of each line
int x = 50;        // Initial horizontal location for first line
int spacing = 10;  // How far apart is each line
int len = 20;      // Length of each line

line(x, y, x, y+len);
```
—< Draw the first leg.

```
x = x + spacing;
line(x, y, x, y+len);
```
—< Add spacing so the next leg appears 10 pixels to the right.

```
x = x + spacing;
line(x, y, x, y+len);
```
—< Continue this process for each leg, repeating it over and over.

```
x = x + spacing;
line(x, y, x, y+len);

x = x + spacing;
line(x, y, x, y+len);

x = x + spacing;
line(x, y, x, y+len);

x = x + spacing;
line(x, y, x, y+len);

x = x + spacing;
line(x, y, x, y+len);

x = x + spacing;
line(x, y, x, y+len);

x = x + spacing;
line(x, y, x, y+len);

x = x + spacing;
line(x, y, x, y+len);
```

Not too bad, I suppose. Strangely enough, although this is technically more efficient (I could adjust the spacing variable, for example, by changing only one line of code), I have taken a step backward, having produced twice as much code! And what if I wanted to draw 100 legs? For every leg, I need two lines of code. That's 200 lines of code for 100 legs! To avoid this dire, carpal-tunnel inducing problem, I want to be able to say something like:

Draw one line one hundred times.

Aha, only one line of code!

Obviously, you are not the first programmer to reach this dilemma and it's easily solved with the very commonly used *control structure* — the *loop*. A loop structure is similar in syntax to a conditional (see Chapter 5). However, instead of asking a yes or no question to determine whether a block of code should be executed one time, the code will ask a yes or no question to determine *how many times* the block of code should be *repeated*. This is known as iteration.

6-2 The `while` loop, the only loop you really need

There are three types of loops: the `while` loop, the `do-while` loop, and the `for` loop. To get started, I yam going to focus on the `while` loop for a little while (sorry, couldn't resist). For one thing, the only loop you really need is `while`. The `for` loop, as you will see, is simply a convenient alternative, a great shorthand for the majority of counting operations. `do-while`, however, is rarely used (not one example in this book requires it) and so I will ignore it.

Just as with conditional (`if/else`) structures, a `while` loop employs a boolean test condition. If the test evaluates to true, the instructions enclosed in curly brackets are executed; if it is false, the sketch continues on to the next line of code. The difference here is that the instructions inside the `while` block continue to be executed over and over again until the test condition becomes false. See Figure 6-2.

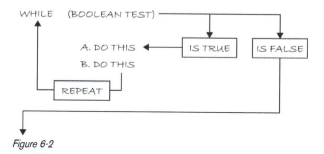

Figure 6-2

Let's take the code from the legs problem. Assuming the following variables...

```
int y = 80;           // Vertical location of each line
int x = 50;           // Initial horizontal location for first line
int spacing = 10;     // How far apart is each line
int len = 20;         // Length of each line
```

... I had to manually repeat the following code:

```
stroke(255);
line(x, y, x, y+len); // Draw the first leg

x = x + spacing;       // Add "spacing" to x
line(x, y, x, y+len); // The next leg is 10 pixels to the right

x = x + spacing;       // Add "spacing" to x
line(x, y, x, y+len); // The next leg is 10 pixels to the right

x = x + spacing;       // Add "spacing" to x
line(x, y, x, y+len); // The next leg is 10 pixels to the right

// etc. etc. repeating with new legs
```

Now, with the knowledge of the existence of while loops, I can rewrite the code as in Example 6-3, adding a variable that specifies when to stop looping, that is, at what pixel the legs stop.

Example 6-3. While loop

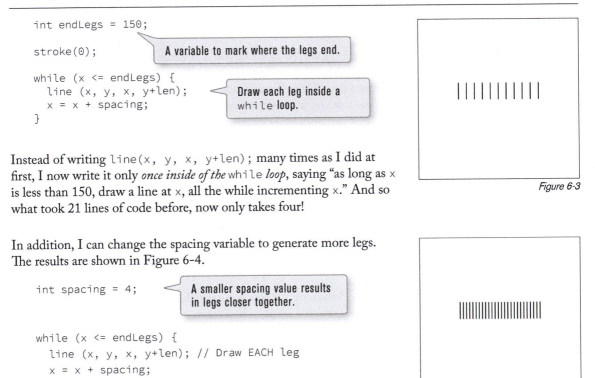

```
int endLegs = 150;

stroke(0);          A variable to mark where the legs end.

while (x <= endLegs) {
    line (x, y, x, y+len);      Draw each leg inside a
    x = x + spacing;            while loop.
}
```

Figure 6-3

Instead of writing line(x, y, x, y+len); many times as I did at first, I now write it only *once inside of the* while *loop*, saying "as long as x is less than 150, draw a line at x, all the while incrementing x." And so what took 21 lines of code before, now only takes four!

In addition, I can change the spacing variable to generate more legs. The results are shown in Figure 6-4.

```
int spacing = 4;        A smaller spacing value results
                        in legs closer together.


while (x <= endLegs) {
    line (x, y, x, y+len); // Draw EACH leg
    x = x + spacing;
}
```

Figure 6-4

Let's look at one more example, this time using rectangles instead of
lines, as shown in Figure 6-5, and ask three key questions.

1. What is the initial condition for your loop? Here, since the first
   rectangle is at y location 10, you want to start your loop with `y` =
   `10`.

   ```
   int y = 10;
   ```

2. When should your loop stop? Since you want to display rectangles
   all the way to the bottom of the window, the loop should stop when
   y is greater than height. In other words, you want the loop to keep
   going *as long as y is less than height.*

   ```
   while (y < height) {
       // Loop!
   }
   ```

Figure 6-5

3. What is your loop operation? In this case, each time through the loop, you want to draw a new
   rectangle below the previous one. You can accomplish this by calling the `rect()` function and
   incrementing y by 20.

   ```
   rect(100, y, 100, 10);
   y = y + 20;
   ```

Putting it all together:

```
int y = 10;
```
Initial condition.

```
while (y < height) {
    rect(100, y, 100, 10);
```
The loop continues while the boolean expression is true. Therefore, the loop
stops when the boolean expression is false.

```
    y = y + 20;
}
```
y increments by 20 each time through the loop, drawing rectangle after
rectangle until y is no longer less than height.

Exercise 6-1: Fill in the blanks in the code to recreate the following screenshots.

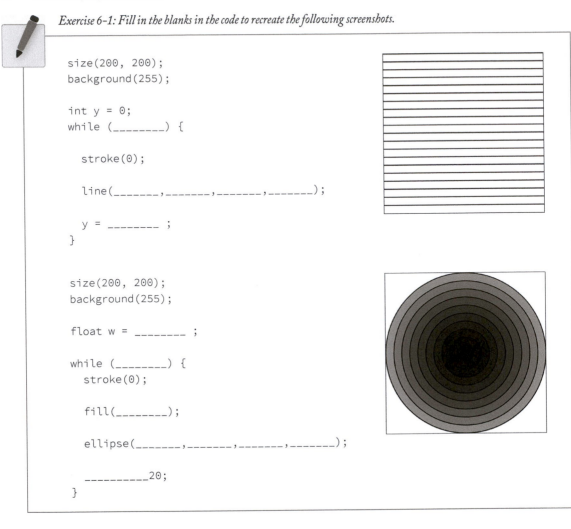

```
size(200, 200);
background(255);

int y = 0;
while (_____) {

  stroke(0);

  line(_____,_____,_____,_____);

  y = _____ ;
}


size(200, 200);
background(255);

float w = _____ ;

while (_____) {
  stroke(0);

  fill(_____);

  ellipse(_____,_____,_____,_____);

  _____20;
}
```

6-3 "Exit" conditions

Loops, as you're probably starting to realize, are quite handy. Nevertheless, there is a dark, seedy underbelly in the world of loops, where nasty things known as *infinite loops* live. See Figure 6-6.

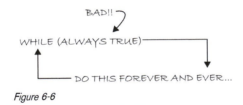

Figure 6-6

Examining the legs in Example 6-3, you can see that as soon as x is greater than 150, the loop stops. And this always happens because x increments by spacing, which is always a positive number. This is not an accident; whenever you embark on programming with a loop structure, you must make sure that the exit condition for the loop will eventually be met!

Processing will not give you an error should your exit condition never occur. The result is Sisyphean, as your loop rolls the boulder up the hill over and over and over again to infinity.

Example 6-4. Infinite loop. Don't do this!

```
int x = 0;
while (x < 10) {
  println(x);
  x = x - 1;
}
```

> Decrementing x results in an infinite loop here because the value of x will never be 10 or greater. Be careful!

For kicks, try running the above code (make sure you have saved all your work and are not running some other mission-critical software on your computer). You will quickly see that Processing hangs. The only way out of this predicament is probably to force-quit Processing. Infinite loops are not often as obvious as in Example 6-4. Here is another flawed program that will *sometimes* result in an infinite loop crash.

Example 6-5. Another infinite loop. Don't do this!

```
int y = 80;          // Vertical location of each line
int x = 0;           // Horizontal location of first line
int spacing = 10;    // How far apart is each line
int len = 20;        // Length of each line
int endLegs = 150;   // Where should the lines stop?

void setup() {
  size(200, 200);
}

void draw() {
  spacing = mouseX / 2;

  background(0);
  stroke(255);

  x = 0;
  while (x <= endLegs) {

    line(x, y, x, y+len);

    x = x + spacing;
  }
}
```

> The spacing variable, which sets the distance in between each line, is assigned a value equal to mouseX divided by two.

> Exit condition – when x is greater than endlegs.

> Incrementation of x. x always increases by the value of spacing. What is the range of possible value for spacing?

Will an infinite loop occur? You know you will be stuck looping forever if x never is greater than 150. And since x increments by spacing, if spacing is zero (or a negative number) x will always remain the same value (or go down in value.)

Recalling the `constrain()` function described in Chapter 4, you can guarantee no infinite loop by constraining the value of spacing to a positive range of numbers:

```
int spacing = constrain(mouseX/2, 1, 100);
```

> Using `constrain()` to ensure the exit condition is met.

Since spacing is directly linked with the necessary exit condition, I can enforce a specific range of values to make sure no infinite loop is ever reached. In other words, in pseudocode I would say: *"Draw a series of lines spaced out by* n *pixels where* n *can never be less than one!"*

This is also a useful example because it reveals an interesting fact about `mouseX`. You might be tempted to try putting `mouseX` directly in the incrementation expression as follows:

```
while (x <= endLegs) {
  line(x, y, x, y+len);
  x = x + mouseX/2;
}
```

> Placing `mouseX` inside the loop is not a solution to the infinite loop problem.

Wouldn't this solve the problem, since even if the loop gets stuck as soon as the user moves the mouse to a horizontal location greater than zero, the exit condition would be met? It's a nice thought, but one that is sadly quite flawed. `mouseX` and `mouseY` are updated with new values at the beginning of each cycle through `draw()`. So even if the user moves the mouse to x location 50 from location 0, `mouseX` will never know this new value because it will be stuck in its infinite loop and not able to get to the next cycle through `draw()`.

6-4 The `for` loop

A certain style of `while` loop where one value is incremented repeatedly (demonstrated in Section 6-2 on page 95) is particularly common. This will become even more evident once you look at arrays in Chapter 9. The `for` loop is a nifty shortcut for commonly occurring `while` loops. Before I get into the details, let's talk through some common loops you might write in Processing and how they are written as a `for` loop.

Start at 0 and count up to 9.	`for (int i = 0; i < 10; i = i + 1)`
Start at 0 and count up to 100 by 10.	`for (int i = 0; i < 101; i = i + 10)`
Start at 100 and count down to 0 by 5.	`for (int i = 100; i >= 0; i = i - 5)`

Looking at the above examples, you can see that a `for` loop consists of three parts:

- **Initialization** — Here, a variable is declared and initialized for use within the body of the loop. This variable is most often used inside the loop as a counter.
- **Boolean Test** — This is exactly the same as the boolean tests found in conditional statements and `while` loops. It can be any expression that evaluates to true or false.

• **Iteration Expression** — The last element is an instruction that you want to happen with each loop cycle. Note that the instruction is executed at the end of each cycle through the loop. (You can have multiple iteration expressions, as well as variable initializations, but for the sake of simplicity let's not worry about this now.)

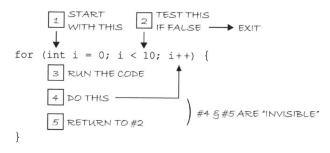

Figure 6-7

In English, the above code means: repeat this code 10 times. Or to put it even more simply: count from zero to nine!

To the machine, it means the following:

• Declare a variable `i`, and set its initial value to 0.

• While `i` is less than 10, repeat this code.

• At the end of each iteration, add one to `i`.

> A `for` loop can have its own variable just for the purpose of counting. A variable not declared at the top of the code is called a `local variable`. I will explain and define it shortly.

Increment and decrement operators

The shortcut for adding or subtracting one from a variable is as follows:

• `x++;` is equivalent to: `x = x + 1;` (meaning: "increment x by 1" or "add 1 to the current value of x")

• `x--;` is equivalent to: `x = x - 1;`

There is also:

• `x += 2;` same as `x = x + 2;`

• `x *= 3;` same as `x = x * 3;`

and so on.

The same exact loop can be programmed with the `while` format:

```
int i = 0;
while (i < 10) {
  // Lines of code to execute here
  i++;
}
```

> This is the translation of the `for` loop, using a `while` loop.

Rewriting the leg drawing code to use a `for` statement looks like this:

Example 6-6. Legs with a `for` loop

```
int y = 80;          // Vertical location of each line
int spacing = 10;    // How far apart is each line
int len = 20;        // Length of each line

for (int x = 50; x <= 150; x += spacing) {
  line(x, y, x, y + len);
}
```

> Translation of the legs `while` loop to a `for` loop.

Exercise 6-2: Rewrite Exercise 6-1 on page 98 using a for *loop.*

```
size(200, 200);
background(255);

for (int y =_____;_____;_____) {
    stroke(0);

    line(_____,_____,_____,_____);
}
```

```
size(200, 200);
background(255);

for (_____;_____;_____-= 20) {
    stroke(0);

    fill(_____);

    ellipse(_____,_____,_____,_____);
}
```

Exercise 6-3: Following are some additional examples of loops. Match the appropriate screenshot with the loop structure. Each example assumes the same four lines of initial code.

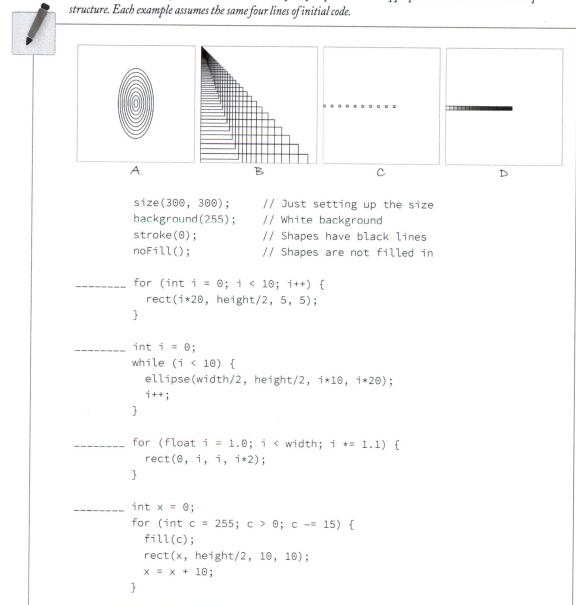

A   B   C   D

```
size(300, 300);      // Just setting up the size
background(255);      // White background
stroke(0);           // Shapes have black lines
noFill();            // Shapes are not filled in
```

```
_____  for (int i = 0; i < 10; i++) {
            rect(i*20, height/2, 5, 5);
          }
```

```
_____  int i = 0;
          while (i < 10) {
            ellipse(width/2, height/2, i*10, i*20);
            i++;
          }
```

```
_____  for (float i = 1.0; i < width; i *= 1.1) {
            rect(0, i, i, i*2);
          }
```

```
_____  int x = 0;
          for (int c = 255; c > 0; c -= 15) {
            fill(c);
            rect(x, height/2, 10, 10);
            x = x + 10;
          }
```

6-5 Local vs. global variables (a.k.a. "variable scope")

Up until this moment, any time that I used a variable, I declared it at the top of the sketch above `setup()`.

```
int x = 0;

void setup() {
  size(200, 200);
}
```

> I have always declared variables at the top of the code.

This was a nice simplification and allowed me to focus on the fundamentals of declaring, initializing, and using variables. Variables, however, can be declared anywhere within a program, and I will now look at what it means to declare a variable somewhere other than the top and how you might go about choosing the right location for declaring a variable.

Imagine, for a moment, that a computer program is running your life. And in this life, variables are pieces of data written on post-its that you need to remember. One post-it might have the address of a restaurant for lunch. You write it down in the morning and throw it away after enjoying a nice kale burger. But another post-it might contain crucial information (such as a bank account number), and you save it in a safe place for years on end. This is the concept of *scope*. Some variables exist (i.e., are accessible) throughout the entire course of a program's life — *global variables* — and some live temporarily, only for the brief moment when their value is required for an instruction or calculation — *local variables*.

In Processing, global variables are declared at the top of the program, outside of both `setup()` and `draw()`. These variables can be used in any line of code anywhere in the program. This is the easiest way to use a variable since you do not have to remember when you can and cannot use that variable. You can *always* use that variable (and this is why I started with global variables only).

Local variables are variables declared within a block of code. So far, you have seen many different examples of blocks of code: `setup()`, `draw()`, `mousePressed()`, and `keyPressed()`, `if` statements, and `while` and `for` loops.

A local variable declared within a block of code is only available for use inside that specific block of code where it was declared. If you try to access a local variable outside of the block where it was declared, you will get this error:

   The variable "variableName" doesn't exist.

This is the same exact error you would get if you did not bother to declare the variable `variableName` at all. Processing does not know what it is because no variable with that name exists within the block of code you happen to be in.

Here is an example where a local variable is used inside of draw() for the purpose of executing a while loop.

Example 6-7. Local variable

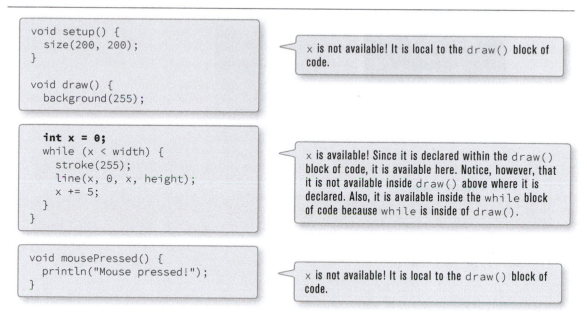

```
void setup() {
  size(200, 200);
}

void draw() {
  background(255);
```

> x is not available! It is local to the draw() block of code.

```
  int x = 0;
  while (x < width) {
    stroke(255);
    line(x, 0, x, height);
    x += 5;
  }
}
```

> x is available! Since it is declared within the draw() block of code, it is available here. Notice, however, that it is not available inside draw() above where it is declared. Also, it is available inside the while block of code because while is inside of draw().

```
void mousePressed() {
  println("Mouse pressed!");
}
```

> x is not available! It is local to the draw() block of code.

Why bother? Couldn't I just have declared x as a global variable? While this is true, since I am only using x within the draw() function, it's wasteful to have it as a global variable. It's more efficient and ultimately less confusing when programming to declare variables only within the scope of where they are necessary. Certainly, many variables *need* to be global, but this is not the case here.

A for loop offers up a spot for a local variable within the "initialization" part:

```
for (int i = 0; i < 100; i += 10) {
  stroke(255);
  fill(i);
  rect(i, 0, 10, height);
}
```

> i is only available inside the for loop.

It's not required to use a local variable in the for loop, however, it's usually convenient to do so.

It's theoretically possible to declare a local variable with the same name as a global variable. In this case, the program will use the local variable within the current scope and the global variable outside of that scope.

Exercise 6-4: Predict the result of the following two sketches. After 100 frames, what will the screen look like? Test your theory by running them.

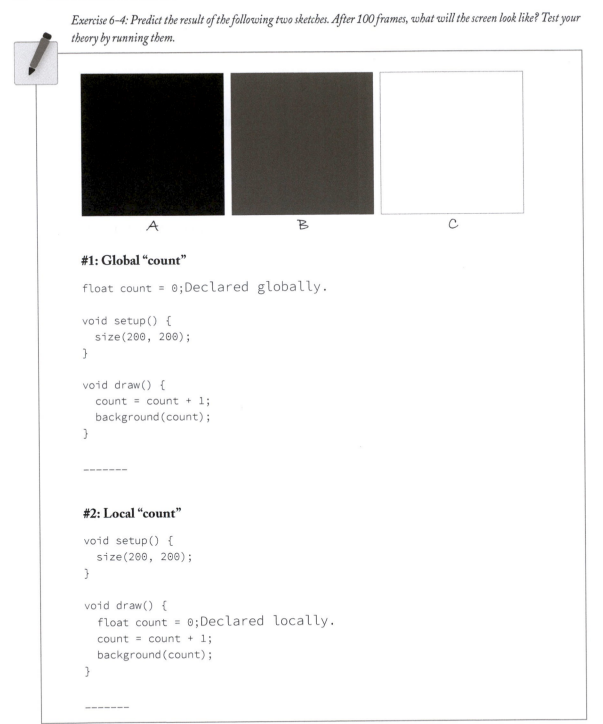

#1: Global "count"

```
float count = 0;Declared globally.

void setup() {
  size(200, 200);
}

void draw() {
  count = count + 1;
  background(count);
}
```

#2: Local "count"

```
void setup() {
  size(200, 200);
}

void draw() {
  float count = 0;Declared locally.
  count = count + 1;
  background(count);
}
```

6-6 Loop inside the `draw()` loop

The distinction between local and global variables moves you one step further toward successfully integrating a loop structure into Zoog. Before you finish this chapter, I want to take a look at one of the most common points of confusion that comes with writing your first loop in the context of a "dynamic" Processing sketch.

Consider the following loop (which happens to be the answer to Exercise 6-2 on page 102). The outcome of the loop is shown in Figure 6-8.

```
for (int y = 0; y < height; y += 10) {
  stroke(0);
  line(0, y, width, y);
}
```

Let's say you want to take the above loop and display each line one at a time so that you see the lines appear animated from top to bottom. Your first thought might be to take the above loop and bring it into a dynamic Processing sketch with `setup()` and `draw()`.

```
void setup() {
  size(200, 200);
}
void draw() {
  background(255);
  for (int y = 0; y < height; y += 10) {
    stroke(0);
    line(0, y, width, y);
  }
}
```

Figure 6-8

If you read the code, it seems to make sense that you would see each line appear one at a time. "Set up a window of size 200 by 200 pixels. Draw a black background. Draw a line at y position 0. Draw a line at y position 10. Draw a line at y position 20."

Referring back to Chapter 2, however, you may recall that Processing does not actually update the display window until the end of `draw()` is reached. This is crucial to remember when using `while` and `for` loops.

These loops serve the purpose of repeating something in the context of *one cycle* through `draw()`. They are a loop inside of the sketch's main loop, `draw()`.

Displaying the lines one at a time is something you can do with a global variable in combination with the very looping nature of `draw()` itself.

Example 6-8. Lines one at a time

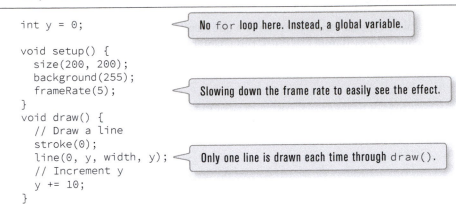

```
int y = 0;
```
> No `for` loop here. Instead, a global variable.

```
void setup() {
  size(200, 200);
  background(255);
  frameRate(5);
}
```
> Slowing down the frame rate to easily see the effect.

```
void draw() {
  // Draw a line
  stroke(0);
  line(0, y, width, y);
  // Increment y
  y += 10;
}
```
> Only one line is drawn each time through `draw()`.

The logic of this sketch is identical to Example 4-3, this book's first motion sketch with variables. Instead of moving a circle across the window horizontally, I am moving a line vertically (but not clearing the background for each frame).

Exercise 6-5: It's possible to achieve the effect of rendering one line at a time using a `for` loop. See if you can figure out how this is done. Part of the code is below.

```
int endY;

void setup() {
  size(200, 200);
  frameRate(5);

  endY = _____;
}

void draw() {
  background(0);

  for (int y = _____; _____; _____) {
    stroke(255);
    line(0, y, width, y);
  }

  _____;
}
```

Using a loop inside draw() also opens up the possibility of interactivity. Example 6-9 displays a series of rectangles (from left to right), each one colored with a brightness according to its distance from the mouse.

Example 6-9. Simple while loop with interactivity

```
void setup() {
  size(255, 255);
  background(0);
}

void draw() {
  background(0);
  // Start with i as 0
  int i = 0;
  // While i is less than the width of the window
  while (i < width) {
    noStroke();
    float distance = abs(mouseX - i);
    fill(distance);
    rect(i, 0, 10, height);

    // Increase i by 10
    i += 10;
  }
}
```

> The distance between the current rectangle and the mouse is equal to the absolute value of the difference between i and mouseX. That distance is used to fill the color of a rectangle at horizontal location i.

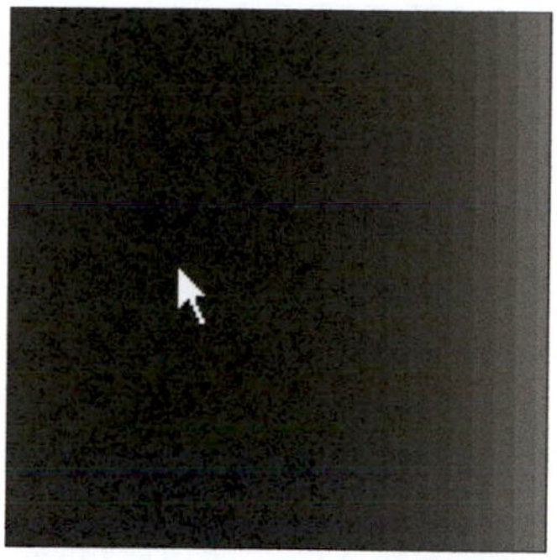

Figure 6-9

Exercise 6-6: Rewrite Example 6-9 using a for *loop.*

6-7 Zoog grows arms

I last left Zoog bouncing back and forth in the Processing window. This new version of Zoog comes with one small change. Example 6-10 uses a for loop to add a series of lines to Zoog's body, resembling arms.

Example 6-10. Zoog with arms

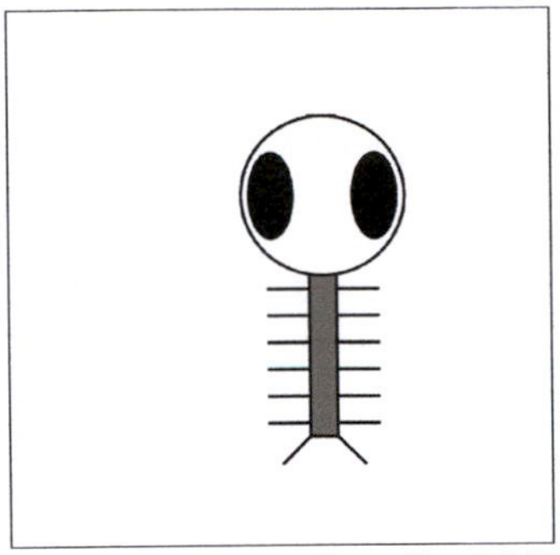

```
int x = 100;
int y = 100;
int w = 60;
int h = 60;
int eyeSize = 16;
int speed = 1;

void setup() {
  size(200, 200);
}

void draw() {
  // Change the x location of Zoog by speed
  x = x + speed;

  // If Zoog has reached an edge, reverse speed (i.e., multiply it by -1)
  //(Note if speed is a + number, square moves to the right,- to the left)
  if ((x > width)|(x < 0)) {
    speed = speed * -1;
  }

  background(255); // Draw a white background

  // Set ellipses and rects to CENTER mode
  ellipseMode(CENTER);
  rectMode(CENTER);

  // Draw Zoog's arms with a for loop
  for (int i = y + 5; i < y + h; i += 10) {
    stroke(0);
    line(x-w/3, i, x+w/3, i);
  }

  // Draw Zoog's body
  stroke(0);
  fill(175);
  rect(x, y, w/6, h*2);

  // Draw Zoog's head
  fill(255);
  ellipse(x, y-h/2, w, h);

  // Draw Zoog's eyes
  fill(0);
  ellipse(x-w/3, y-h/2, eyeSize, eyeSize*2);
  ellipse(x+w/3, y-h/2, eyeSize, eyeSize*2);

  // Draw Zoog's legs
  stroke(0);
  line(x-w/12, y+h, x-w/4, y+h+10);
  line(x+w/12, y+h, x+w/4, y+h+10);
}
```

Arms are incorporated into Zoog's design with a `for` loop drawing a series if lines.

Figure 6-10

I can also use a loop to draw multiple instances of Zoog by placing the code for Zoog's body inside of a for loop. See Example 6-11.

Example 6-11. Multiple Zoogs

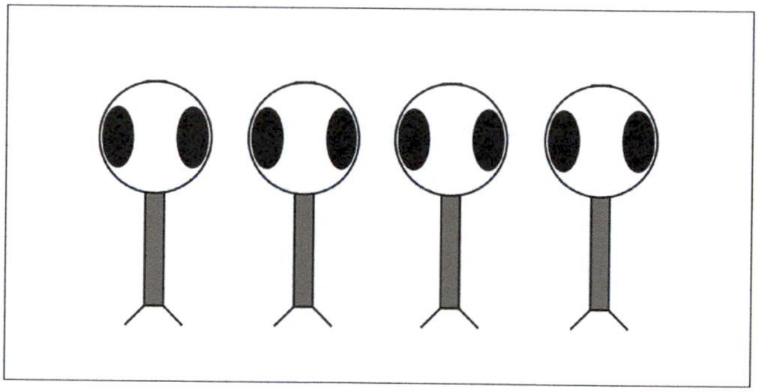

```
int w = 60;
int h = 60;
int eyeSize = 16;

void setup() {
  size(400, 200);
}

void draw() {
  background(255);
  ellipseMode(CENTER);
  rectMode(CENTER);

  int y = height/2;

  // Multiple versions of Zoog
  for (int x = 80; x < width; x + = 80) {

    // Draw Zoog's body
    stroke(0);
    fill(175);
    rect(x, y, w/6, h*2);

    // Draw Zoog's head
    fill(255);
    ellipse(x, y-h/2, w, h);

    // Draw Zoog's eyes
    fill(0);
    ellipse(x-w/3, y-h/2, eyeSize, eyeSize*2);
    ellipse(x+w/3, y-h/2, eyeSize, eyeSize*2);

    // Draw Zoog's legs
    stroke(0);
    line(x-w/12, y+h, x-w/4, y+h+10);
    line(x+w/12, y+h, x+w/4, y+h+10);
  }
}
```

Figure 6-11

> The variable x is now included in a for loop, in order to iterate and display multiple Zoogs!

Exercise 6-7: Add something to your design using a `for` *or* `while` *loop. Is there anything you already have that could be made more efficient with a loop?*

Exercise 6-8: Create a grid of squares (each colored randomly) using a `for` *loop. (Hint: You will need two* `for` *loops!) Recode the same pattern using a* `while` *loop instead of* `for`.

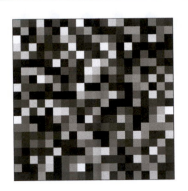

Lesson Two Project

1. Take your Lesson One design and rewrite it with variables instead of hard-coded values. Consider using a `for` loop in the creation of your design.

2. Write a series of assignment operations that alter the values of those variables and make the design dynamic. You might also use system variables, such as `width`, `height`, `mouseX`, and `mouseY`.

3. Using conditional statements, alter the behavior of your design based on certain conditions. What happens if it touches the edge of the screen, or if it grows to a certain size? What happens if you move the mouse over elements in your design?

If your original design was extraordinarily complex with lots of code, you might consider changing it to something very simple, possibly even just starting over from scratch with a single circle or rectangle, to be able to more easily focus on animation behaviors that use variables, conditionals, and loops.

Use the space provided below to sketch designs, notes, and pseudocode for your project.

Lesson Three

Organization

Chapter 7
Chapter 8

7 Functions

When it's all mixed up, better break it down.
—Tears for Fears

In this chapter:
– Modularity
– Declaring and defining a function
– Calling a function
– Arguments and parameters
– Returning a value
– Reusability

7-1 Break it down

The examples provided in Chapter 1 through Chapter 6 are short. I probably have not shown a sketch with more than 100 lines of code. These programs are the equivalent of writing the opening paragraph of this chapter, as opposed to the whole chapter itself.

Processing is great because you can make interesting visual sketches with small amounts of code. But as you move forward to looking at more complex projects, such as network applications or image processing programs, you will start to have hundreds of lines of code. You will be writing essays, not paragraphs. And these large amounts of code can prove to be unwieldy inside of your two main blocks — setup() and draw().

Functions are a means of taking the parts of a program and separating them out into modular pieces, making code easier to read, as well as to revise. Let's consider the video game Space Invaders. The steps for draw() might look something like:

- Erase background.
- Draw spaceship.
- Draw enemies.
- Move spaceship according to user keyboard interaction.
- Move enemies.

What's in a name?

Functions are often called other things, such as "procedures" or "methods" or "subroutines." In some programming languages, there is a distinction between a procedure (performs a task) and a function (calculates a value). In this chapter, I am choosing to use the term function for simplicity's sake. Nevertheless, the technical term in the Java programming language is *method* (related to Java's object-oriented design) and once I get into objects in Chapter 8, I will use the term "method" to describe functions inside of objects.

Before this chapter on functions, I would have translated the above pseudocode into actual code, and placed it inside draw(). Functions, however, will let you approach the problem as follows:

```
void draw() {
   background(0);
   drawSpaceShip();        I am calling functions I made up inside of draw()!
   drawEnemies();
   moveShip();
   moveEnemies();
}
```

The above demonstrates how functions make life easier with clear and easy to manage code. Nevertheless, I am missing an important piece: the function *definitions*. Calling a function is old hat. You do this all the time when you write line(), rect(), fill(), and so on. Defining a new "made-up" function is going to require some more work on your part.

Before I launch into the details, let's reflect on why writing your own functions is so important:

- **Modularity** — Functions break down a larger program into smaller parts, making code more manageable and readable. Once I have figured out how to draw a spaceship, for example, I can take that chunk of spaceship drawing code, store it away in a function, and call upon that function whenever necessary (without having to worry about the details of the operation itself).
- **Reusability** — Functions allow you to reuse code without having to retype it. What if I want to make a two player Space Invaders game with two spaceships? I can *reuse* the drawSpaceShip() function by calling it multiple times without having to repeat code over and over.

In this chapter, I will look at some of my previous sketches, written without functions, and demonstrate the power of modularity and reusability by incorporating functions. In addition, I will further emphasize the distinctions between local and global variables, as functions are independent blocks of code that will require the use of local variables. Finally, I will continue to follow Zoog's story with functions.

Exercise 7-1: Write your answers below.

What functions might you write for your Lesson Two Project?	What functions might you write in order to program the game Pong?

7-2 "User-defined" functions

In Processing, you have been using functions all along. When you say line(0, 0, 200, 200); you are calling the function line(), a built-in function of the Processing environment. The ability to draw a line by calling the function line() does not magically exist. Someone, somewhere, defined (i.e., wrote the underlying code for) how Processing should display a line. One of Processing's strengths is its library of available functions, which you have started to explore throughout the first six chapters of this book. Now it's time to move beyond the built-in functions of Processing and write your own *user-defined* (a.k.a. "made-up") functions.

7-3 Defining a function

A function definition (sometimes referred to as a "declaration") has three parts:

- Return type.
- Function name.
- Arguments.

It looks like this:

```
returnType functionName(parameters) {
  // Code body of function
}
```

Déjà vu?

Remember when in Chapter 3 I introduced the functions setup() and draw()? Notice that they follow the same format you are learning now.

setup() and draw() are functions you define and are called automatically by Processing in order to run the sketch. All other functions you write have to be called by you.

For now, let's focus solely on the *function name* and *code body*, ignoring *return type* and *parameters*.

Here is a simple example:

Example 7-1. Defining a function

```
void drawBlackCircle() {
  fill(0);
  ellipse(50, 50, 20, 20);
}
```

This is a simple function that performs one basic task: drawing an ellipse colored black at coordinate (50,50). Its name — drawBlackCircle() — is arbitrary (I made it up) and its code body consists of two instructions (you can have as much or as little code as you choose). It's also important to remind ourselves that this is only the definition of the function. The code will never happen unless the function is actually called from a part of the program that is being executed. This is accomplished by referencing the function name, that is, calling a function, as shown in Example 7-2.

Example 7-2. Calling a function

```
void draw() {
  background(255);
  drawBlackCircle();
}
```

Exercise 7-2: Write a function that displays Zoog (or your own design). Call that function from within `draw()`.

```
void setup() {
  size(200, 200);
}

void draw() {
  background(0);


  _____
}

_____  _____  _____  {


  _____


  _____


  _____


  _____


  _____
```

7-4 Simple modularity

Let's examine the bouncing ball example from Chapter 5 and rewrite it using functions, illustrating one technique for breaking a program down into modular parts. Example 5-6 is reprinted here for your convenience.

Example 7-3. Bouncing ball

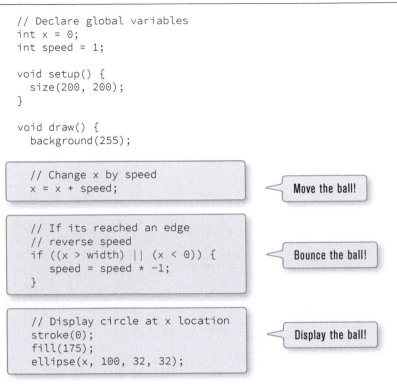

```
// Declare global variables
int x = 0;
int speed = 1;

void setup() {
  size(200, 200);
}

void draw() {
  background(255);
```

```
// Change x by speed
x = x + speed;
```
Move the ball!

```
// If its reached an edge
// reverse speed
if ((x > width) || (x < 0)) {
    speed = speed * -1;
}
```
Bounce the ball!

```
// Display circle at x location
stroke(0);
fill(175);
ellipse(x, 100, 32, 32);
```
Display the ball!

```
}
```

Once I have determined how I want to divide the code up into functions, I can take the pieces out of draw() and insert them into function definitions, calling those functions inside draw(). Functions typically are written below draw().

Example 7-4. Bouncing ball with functions

```
// Declare all global variables (stays the same)
int x = 0;
int speed = 1;

// Setup does not change
void setup() {
  size(200, 200);
}

void draw() {
  background(255);
  move();
  bounce();
  display();
}
```

> Instead of writing out all the code about the ball in draw(), I simply call three functions. How do I know the names of these functions? I made them up!

```
// A function to move the ball
void move() {
  // Change the x location by speed
  x = x + speed;
}
```

> Where should functions be placed? You can define your functions anywhere in the code outside of setup() and draw(). However, the convention is to place your function definitions below draw().

```
// A function to bounce the ball
void bounce() {
  // If its reached an edge, reverse speed
  if ((x > width) || (x < 0)) {
    speed = speed * -1;
  }
}

// A function to display the ball
void display() {
  stroke(0);
  fill(175);
  ellipse(x, 100, 32, 32);
}
```

Note how simple draw() has become. The code is reduced to function *calls*; the detail for how variables change and shapes are displayed is left for the function *definitions*. One of the main benefits here is the programmer's sanity. If you wrote this program right before leaving on a two-week vacation in the Caribbean, upon returning with a nice tan, you would be greeted by well-organized, readable code. To change how the ball is rendered, you only need to make edits to the display() function, without having to search through long passages of code or worrying about the rest of the program. For example, try replacing display() with the following:

```
void display() {
  background(255);
  rectMode(CENTER);
  noFill();
  stroke(0);
  rect(x, y, 32, 32);
  fill(255);
```

> If you want to change the appearance of the shape, the display() function can be rewritten leaving all the other features of the sketch intact.

```
    rect(x-4, y-4, 4, 4);
    rect(x+4, y-4, 4, 4);
    line(x-4, y+4, x+4, y+4);
}
```

Another benefit of using functions is greater ease in debugging. Suppose, for a moment, that the bouncing ball function was not behaving appropriately. In order to find the problem, I now have the option of turning on and off parts of the program. For example, I might simply run the program with `display()` only, by commenting out `move()` and `bounce()`:

```
void draw() {
    background(0);
    // move();
    // bounce();
    display();
}
```

Functions can be commented out to determine if they are causing a bug or not.

The function definitions for `move()` and `bounce()` still exist, only now the functions are not being called. By adding function calls one by one and executing the sketch each time, I can more easily find the location of the problematic code.

Exercise 7-3: Take any Processing program you have written and modularize it using functions, as above. Use the following space to make a list of functions you need to write.

7-5 Arguments

Just a few pages ago I said "Let's ignore **ReturnType** and **Arguments**." I did this in order to ease into functions by sticking with the basics. However, functions possess greater powers than simply breaking a program into parts. One of the keys to unlocking these powers are the concepts of *arguments* and *parameters*.

Arguments are values that are "passed" into a function. You can think of them as inputs that a function needs to do its job. A function that causes a creature to move a certain number of steps needs to know how many steps you want the creature to move. Instead of merely saying "move," you might say, "move ten steps," where "ten" is the argument.

When you define such a "move" function, you are required to give each argument a name. That way, the function can refer to the arguments it receives by the particular name that you specify. To illustrate, let's rewrite drawBlackCircle() to include a parameter:

```
void drawBlackCircle(int diameter) {
    fill(0);
    ellipse(50, 50, diameter, diameter);
}
```

> diameter **is a parameter to the function** drawBlackCircle().

A parameter is simply a variable declaration inside the parentheses in the function definition. This variable is a *local variable* (remember the discussion in Section 6-5 on page 104?) to be used in that function (and only in that function). The black circle will be sized according to the value of diameter, which will automatically be assigned the value that you pass the function when you call it. For example, when you say drawBlackCircle(100), the value 100 is the argument. That 100 gets assigned to the diameter parameter, and the function itself uses diameter to draw the circle. When you call drawBlackCircle(80), the argument 80 is assigned to parameter diameter, and the function body then uses diameter to draw the circle.

```
drawBlackCircle(16);   // Draw the circle with a diameter of 16
drawBlackCircle(32);   // Draw the circle with a diameter of 32
```

You could also pass another variable or the result of a mathematical expression (such as mouseX divided by 10) into the function. For example:

```
drawBlackCircle(mouseX / 10);
```

This, by the way, is exactly what you did in Chapter 1 when you first started drawing in Processing. To draw a line, for example, you couldn't just say draw a line. Rather, you had to say draw a line from some (x,y) to some other (x,y). You needed *four arguments*.

```
line(10, 25, 100, 75);   // Draw a line from (10,25) to (100,75).
```

The key difference here is that you didn't write the line() function! The creators of Processing did, and if you delve into the Processing source itself, you'll find a function definition with *four parameters*.

```
void line(float x1, float y1, float x2, float y2) {
    // This functions requires four parameters
    // which define the end points (x1,y1) and (x2,y2)
    // of a line!
}
```

Parameters pave the way for more flexible, and therefore reusable, functions. To demonstrate this, let's look at code for drawing a collection of shapes and examine how functions allow you to draw multiple versions of the pattern without retyping the same code over and over.

Leaving Zoog until a bit later, consider the following pattern resembling a car (viewed from above as shown in Figure 7-1):

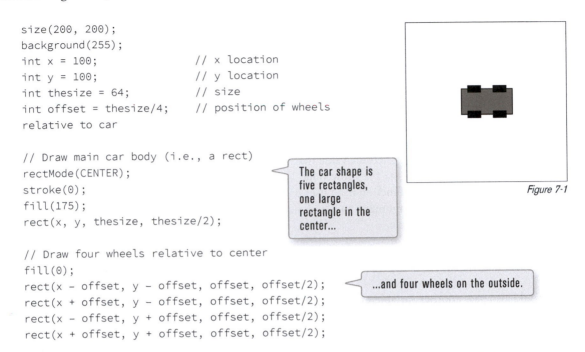

```
size(200, 200);
background(255);
int x = 100;              // x location
int y = 100;              // y location
int thesize = 64;         // size
int offset = thesize/4;   // position of wheels
relative to car

// Draw main car body (i.e., a rect)
rectMode(CENTER);
stroke(0);
fill(175);
rect(x, y, thesize, thesize/2);
```

> The car shape is five rectangles, one large rectangle in the center...

```
// Draw four wheels relative to center
fill(0);
rect(x - offset, y - offset, offset, offset/2);
rect(x + offset, y - offset, offset, offset/2);
rect(x - offset, y + offset, offset, offset/2);
rect(x + offset, y + offset, offset, offset/2);
```

> ...and four wheels on the outside.

Figure 7-1

To draw a second car, I'll repeat the above code with different values, as shown in Figure 7-2.

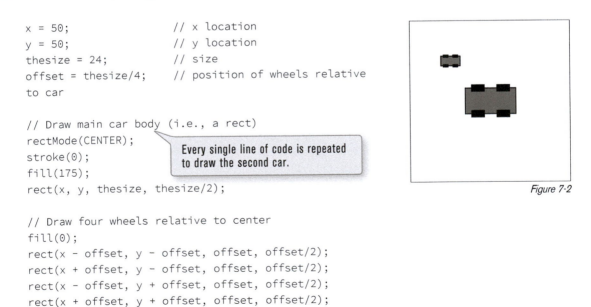

```
x = 50;                   // x location
y = 50;                   // y location
thesize = 24;             // size
offset = thesize/4;       // position of wheels relative
to car

// Draw main car body (i.e., a rect)
rectMode(CENTER);
stroke(0);
fill(175);
rect(x, y, thesize, thesize/2);
```

> Every single line of code is repeated to draw the second car.

Figure 7-2

```
// Draw four wheels relative to center
fill(0);
rect(x - offset, y - offset, offset, offset/2);
rect(x + offset, y - offset, offset, offset/2);
rect(x - offset, y + offset, offset, offset/2);
rect(x + offset, y + offset, offset, offset/2);
```

It should be fairly apparent where this is going. After all, I am doing the same thing twice — why bother repeating all that code? To escape this repetition, I can move the code into a function that displays the car according to several parameters (position, size, and color).

```
void drawCar(int x, int y, int theSize, color c) {
    // Using a local variable "offset "
    int offset = theSize/4;
    // Draw main car body
    rectMode(CENTER);
    stroke(200);
    fill(c);
    // Draw four wheels relative to center
    fill(200);
    rect(x - offset, y - offset, offset, offset/2);
    rect(x + offset, y - offset, offset, offset/2);
    rect(x - offset, y + offset, offset, offset/2);
    rect(x + offset, y + offset, offset, offset/2);
}
```

> Local variables can be declared and used in a function!

> This code is the **function definition**. The function drawCar() draws a car shape based on four arguments: horizontal location, vertical location, size, and color.

In the draw() function, I then call the drawCar() function three times, passing four *arguments* each time. See the output in Figure 7-3.

```
void setup() {
    size(200, 200);
}

void draw() {
    background(255);
    drawCar(100, 100, 64, color(200, 200, 0));
    drawCar(50, 75, 32, color(0, 200, 100));
    drawCar(80, 175, 40, color(200, 0, 0));
}
```

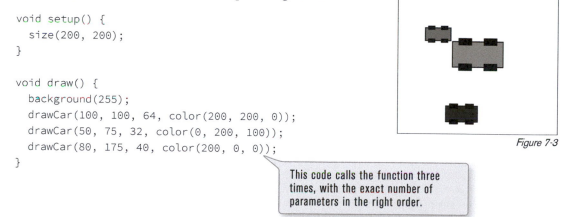

Figure 7-3

> This code calls the function three times, with the exact number of parameters in the right order.

Technically speaking, *parameters* are the variables that live inside the parentheses in the function definition, that is, void drawCar(int x, int y, int thesize, color c). *Arguments* are the values passed into the function when it is called, that is, drawCar(80, 175, 40, color(100, 0, 100)). The semantic difference between arguments and parameters is somewhat trivial and you should not be terribly concerned if you confuse the use of the two words from time to time.

The concept to focus on is this ability to *pass* arguments. You will not be able to advance your programming knowledge unless you are comfortable with this technique.

Let's go with the word *pass*. Imagine a lovely, sunny day and you're playing catch with a friend in the park. You have the ball. You (the main program) call the function (your friend) and pass the ball (the argument). Your friend (the function) now has the ball (the argument) and can use it however he or she pleases (the code itself inside the function). See Figure 7-4.

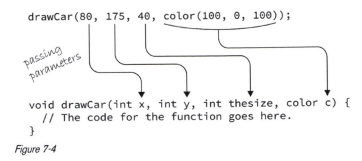

```
void drawCar(int x, int y, int thesize, color c) {
    // The code for the function goes here.
}
```

Figure 7-4

Important things to remember about passing arguments

- You must pass the same number of arguments as defined in the function's parameters.

- When an argument is passed, it must be of the same *type* as declared within the parameters in the function definition. An integer must be passed into an integer, a floating point into a floating point, and so on.

- The value you pass to a function can be a literal value (20, 5, 4.3, etc.), a variable (x, y, etc.), or the result of an expression (8 + 3, 4 * x/2, random(0, 10), etc.)

- Parameters act as local variables to a function and are only accessible within that function.

Exercise 7-4: The following function takes three numbers, adds them together, and prints the sum to the message window.

```
void sum(int a, int b, int c) {
    int total = a + b + c;
    println(total);
}
```

Looking at the function definition above, write the code that calls the function.

_____

Exercise 7-5: OK, here is the opposite problem. Here is a line of code that assumes a function that takes two numbers, multiplies them together, and prints the result to a message window. Write the function definition that goes with this function call.

```
multiply(5.2, 9.0);
```

Exercise 7-6: Create a design for a flower. Can you write a function with parameters that vary the flower's appearance (height, color, number of petals, etc.)? If you call that function multiple times with different arguments, can you create a garden with a variety of flowers?

7-6 Passing a copy

There is a slight problem with the "playing catch" analogy. What I really should have said is the following. Before tossing the ball (the argument), you make a copy of it (a second ball), and pass it to the receiver (the function).

Whenever you pass a primitive value (int, float, char, etc.) to a function, you do not actually pass the value itself, but a copy of that variable. This may seem like a trivial distinction when passing a hard-coded number, but it's not so trivial when passing a variable.

The following code has a function entitled randomizer() that receives one parameter (a floating point number) and adds a random number between -2 and 2 to it. Here is the pseudocode.

- **num** is the number 10.
- **num** is displayed: **10**
- **A copy of num** is passed into the parameter **newnum** in the function randomizer().
- In the function randomizer():
  - — a random number is added to **newnum**.
  - — **newnum** is displayed: **10.34232**
- **num** is displayed again: **Still 10! A copy was sent into newnum, so num has not changed.**

And here is the code:

```
void setup() {
  float num = 10;
  println("The number is: " + num);
  randomizer(num);
  println("The number is: " + num);
}

void randomizer(float newnum) {
  newnum = newnum + random(-2, 2);
  println("The new number is: " + newnum);
}
```

Even though the variable **num** was passed into the variable **newnum**, which then quickly changed values, the original value of the variable **num** was not affected because a copy was made.

I like to refer to this process as "pass by copy," however, it's more commonly referred to as "pass by value." This holds true for all primitive data types (the only kinds I've covered so far: integer, float, etc.), but is not quite the same with *objects*, which you will learn about in the next chapter.

This example also provides a nice opportunity to review the *flow* of a program when using a function. Notice how the code is executed in the order that the lines are written, but when a function is called, the code leaves its current line, executes the lines inside of the function, and then comes back to where it left off. Here is a description of the preceding example's flow:

1. Set num equal to 10.

2. Print the value of num.

3. Call the function randomizer.

   a. Set newnum equal to newnum plus a random number.

   b. Print the value of newnum.

4. Print the value of num.

Exercise 7-7: Predict the output of this program by writing out what would appear in the message window.

```
void setup() {
  println("a");
  function1();
  println("b");
}

void draw() {
  println("c");
  function2();
  println("d");
  function1();
  noLoop();
}

void function1() {
  println("e");
  println("f");
}

void function2() {
  println("g");
  function1();
  println("h");
}
```

> New! `noLoop()` is a built-in function in Processing that stops `draw()` from looping. In this case, I can use it to ensure that `draw()` only executes one time. I could restart it at some other point in the code by calling the function `loop()`.

> It's perfectly reasonable to call a function from within a function. In fact, you do this all the time whenever you call any function from inside of `setup()` or `draw()`.

Output:

1: _____   7: _____

2: _____   8: _____

3: _____   9: _____

4: _____   10: _____

5: _____   11: _____

6: _____   12: _____

7-7 Return type

So far you have seen how functions can separate a sketch into smaller parts, as well as incorporate arguments to make it reusable. However, there is one piece still missing from this discussion, and it is the answer to the question you have been wondering all along: "What does *void* mean?"

As a reminder, let's examine the structure of a function definition again:

```
returnType functionName(parameters) {
  // Code body of function
}
```

OK, now let's look at one of the functions:

```
void drawCar(int x, int y, int theSize, color c) {
  int offset = theSize/4;
  // Draw main car body
  rectMode(CENTER);
  stroke(200);
  fill(c);
  // Draw four wheels relative to center
  fill(200);
  rect(x - offset, y - offset, offset, offset/2);
  rect(x + offset, y - offset, offset, offset/2);
  rect(x - offset, y + offset, offset, offset/2);
  rect(x + offset, y + offset, offset, offset/2);
}
```

drawCar is the *function name*, x is a *parameter* to the function, and void is the *return type*. All the functions I have defined so far did not have a return type; this is precisely what void means: no return type. But what is a return type and when might you need one?

Let's recall for a moment the random() function examined in Chapter 4. I asked the function for a random number between 0 and some value, and random() graciously heeded my request and gave back a random value within the appropriate range. The random() function *returned* a value. What type of a value? A floating point number. In the case of random(), therefore, its *return type* is a *float*.

The *return type* is the data type that the function returns. In the case of random(), I did not specify the return type, however, the creators of Processing did, and it's documented on the reference page for random().

> Each time the random() *function is called, it returns an unexpected value within the specified range. If one argument is passed to the function it will return a float between zero and the value of the argument. The function call* random(5) *returns values between 0 and 5. If two arguments are passed, it will return a float with a value between the arguments. The function call* random(-5, 10.2) *returns values between −5 and 10.2.*
>
> —*From http://www.processing.org/reference/random.html*

If you want to write your own function that returns a value, you have to specify the type in the function definition. Let's create a trivially simple example:

```
int sum(int a, int b, int c) {

    int total = a + b + c;
    return total;
}
```

> This function, which adds three numbers together, has a return type: int.

> A return statement is required! A function with a return type must always return a value of that type.

Instead of writing void as the return type as I have in previous examples, I now write int. This specifies that the function must return a value of type integer. In order for a function to return a value, a *return statement* is required. A return statement looks like this:

return valueToReturn;

If you do not include a return statement, Processing will give you an error:

- *This function must return a result of type int.*

As soon as the return statement is executed, the program exits the function and sends the returned value back to the location in the code where the function was called. That value can be used in an assignment operation (to give another variable a value) or in any appropriate expression. See the illustration in Figure 7-5. Here are some examples:

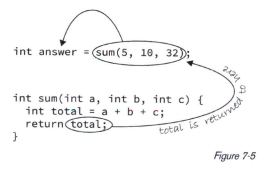

Figure 7-5

```
int x = sum(5, 6, 8);
int y = sum(8, 9, 10) * 2;
int z = sum(x, y, 40);
line(100, 100, 110, sum(x, y, z));
```

I hate to bring up playing catch in the park again, but you can think of it as follows. You (*the main program*) throw a copy of a ball to your friend (*a function*). After your friend catches that ball, he or she thinks for a moment, puts a number inside the ball (*the return value*) and passes it back to you.

Functions that return values are traditionally used to perform complex calculations that may need to be performed multiple times throughout the course of the program. One example is calculating the distance between two points: (x1,y1) and (x2,y2). The distance between pixels is a very useful piece of information in interactive applications. Processing, in fact, has a built-in distance function that you can use. It's called dist().

```
float d = dist(100, 100, mouseX, mouseY);
```

> Calculating the distance between (100,100) and (mouseX,mouseY).

This line of code calculates the distance between the mouse location and the point (100, 100). For the moment, let's pretend Processing did not include this function in its library. Without it, you would have to calculate the distance manually, using the Pythagorean Theorem, as shown in Figure 7-6.

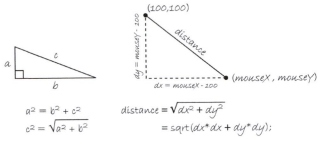

Figure 7-6

```
float dx = mouseX - 100;
float dy = mouseY - 100;
float d = sqrt(dx*dx + dy*dy);
```

If you wanted to perform this calculation many times over the course of a program with many different pairs of coordinates, it would be easier to move it into a function that returns the value *d*.

```
float distance(float x1, float y1, float x2, float y2) {
  float dx = x1 - x2;
  float dy = y1 - y2;
  float d = sqrt(dx*dx + dy*dy);
  return d;
}
```

> Our version of Processing's `dist()` function.

Note the use of the return type `float`. Again, I do not have to write this function because Processing supplies it for me. But since I did, I can now show an example that makes use of this function.

Example 7-5. Using a function that returns a value, distance

```
void setup() {
  size(200, 200);
}


void draw() {
  background(255);
  stroke(0);

  float d = distance(width/2, height/2, mouseX, mouseY);

  fill(d*3, d*2, d);
  ellipseMode(CENTER);
  ellipse(width/2, height/2, 100, 100);
}

float distance(float x1, float y1, float x2, float y2) {
  float dx = x1 - x2;
  float dy = y1 - y2;
  float d = sqrt(dx*dx + dy*dy);
  return d;
}
```

> The result of the `distance()` function is used to color a circle. I could have used the built-in function `dist()` instead, but I am demonstrating how how to define a function that returns a value.

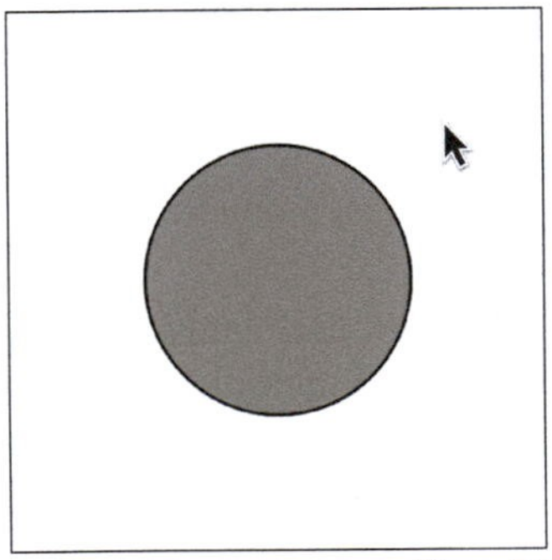

Figure 7-7

Exercise 7-8: Write a function that takes one argument — F for Fahrenheit — and computes the result of the following equation (converting the temperature to Celsius). Hint: in Processing if you divide an integer by an integer you will get an integer, same with floating point! In other words, 1/2 evaluates to 0 while 1.0/2.0 evaluates to 0.5.

```
// Formula: C = (F - 32) * (5/9)

_____ convertToCelsius(float _____) {

    _____ _____ = _____

    _____
}
```

7-8 Zoog reorganization

Zoog is now ready for a fairly major overhaul.

- Reorganize Zoog with two functions: `drawZoog()` and `jiggleZoog()`. Just for variety, I am going to have Zoog jiggle (move randomly in both the x and y directions) instead of bouncing back and forth.

- Incorporate parameters so that Zoog's jiggliness is determined by the `mouseX` position and Zoog's eye color is determined by Zoog's distance to the mouse.

Example 7-6. Zoog with functions

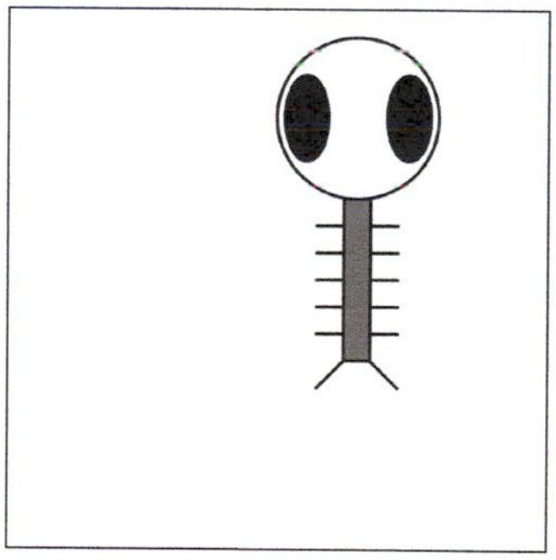

```
float x = 100;
float y = 100;
float w = 60;
float h = 60;
float eyeSize = 16;

void setup() {
  size(200, 200);
}

void draw() {
  background(255); // Draw a white background

  // A color based on distance from the mouse
  float d = dist(x, y, mouseX, mouseY);
  color c = color(d);

  // mouseX position determines speed factor for moveZoog function
  float factor = constrain(mouseX/10, 0, 5);

  jiggleZoog(factor);
  drawZoog(c);
```

Figure 7-8

> The code for changing the variables associated with Zoog and displaying Zoog is moved outside of `draw()` and into functions called here. The functions are given arguments, such as "jiggle Zoog by the following factor" and "draw Zoog with the following eye color."

```
}

void jiggleZoog(float speed) {
  // Change the x and y location of Zoog randomly
  x = x + random(-1, 1) * speed;
  y = y + random(-1, 1) * speed;

  // Constrain Zoog to window
  x = constrain(x, 0, width);
  y = constrain(y, 0, height);
}

void drawZoog(color eyeColor) {
  // Set ellipses and rects to CENTER mode
  ellipseMode(CENTER);
  rectMode(CENTER);

  // Draw Zoog's arms with a for loop
  for (float i = y - h/3; i < y + h/2; i += 10) {
    stroke(0);
    line(x - w/4, i, x + w/4, i);
  }

  // Draw Zoog's body
  stroke(0);
  fill(175);
  rect(x, y, w/6, h);

  // Draw Zoog's head
  stroke(0);
  fill(255);
  ellipse(x, y - h, w, h);

  // Draw Zoog's eyes
  fill(eyeColor);
  ellipse(x - w/3, y - h, eyeSize, eyeSize*2);
  ellipse(x + w/3, y - h, eyeSize, eyeSize*2);

  // Draw Zoog's legs
  stroke(0);
  line(x - w/12, y + h/2, x - w/4, y + h/2 + 10);
  line(x + w/12, y + h/2, x + w/4, y + h/2 + 10);
}
```

Exercise 7-9: Write a function that draws Zoog based on a set of parameters. Some ideas are: Zoog's x and y coordinates, its width and height, eye color.

Exercise 7-10: Another idea (if you're feeling tired of Zoog) is to create a design for a spaceship and draw several to the screen with slight variations based on arguments you pass to a function. Here's a screenshot and the beginnings of some example code.

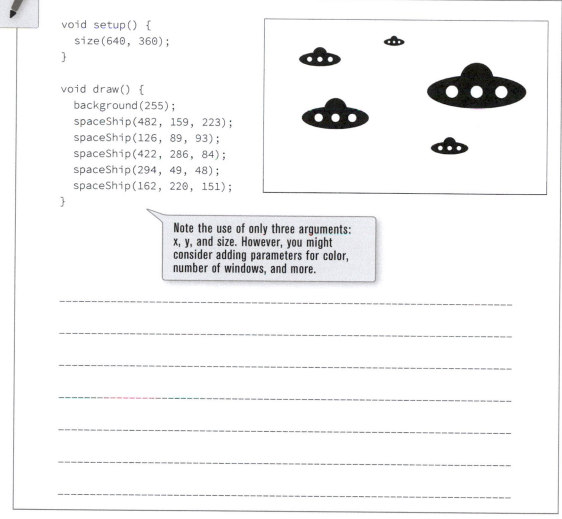

```
void setup() {
  size(640, 360);
}

void draw() {
  background(255);
  spaceShip(482, 159, 223);
  spaceShip(126, 89, 93);
  spaceShip(422, 286, 84);
  spaceShip(294, 49, 48);
  spaceShip(162, 220, 151);
}
```

Note the use of only three arguments: x, y, and size. However, you might consider adding parameters for color, number of windows, and more.

Exercise 7-11: Rewrite your Lesson Two Project using functions.

8 Objects

No object is so beautiful that, under certain conditions, it will not look ugly.
—Oscar Wilde

In this chapter:
- Data and functionality, together at last
- What is an object?
- What is a class?
- Writing your own classes
- Creating your own objects
- Processing tabs

8-1 I'm down with OOP

Before I begin discussing the details of how object-oriented programming (OOP) works in Processing, let's embark on a short conceptual discussion of "objects" themselves. It's important to understand that I am not introducing any new programming fundamentals. Objects use everything you have already learned: variables, conditional statements, loops, functions, and so on. What is entirely new, however, is a way of thinking, a way of structuring and organizing everything you have already learned.

Imagine you were not programming in Processing, but were instead writing out a program for your day, a list of instructions, if you will. It might start out something like:

- Wake up.
- Drink coffee (or tea).
- Eat breakfast: cereal, blueberries, and soy milk.
- Ride the subway.

What is involved here? Specifically, what *things* are involved? First, although it may not be immediately apparent from how I wrote the above instructions, the main thing is *you*, a human being, a person. You exhibit certain properties. You look a certain way; perhaps you have brown hair, wear glasses, and appear slightly nerdy. You also have the ability to do stuff, such as wake up (presumably you can also sleep), eat, or ride the subway. An object is just like you, a thing that has properties and can do stuff.

So how does this relate to programming? The properties of an object are variables; and the stuff an object can do are functions. Object-oriented programming is the marriage of everything I covered in Chapter 1 through Chapter 7; data and functionality, all rolled into one *thing*.

Let's map out the data and functions for a very simple human object:

Human data

- Height.
- Weight.
- Gender.
- Eye color.
- Hair color.

Human functions

- Sleep.
- Wake up.
- Eat.
- Ride some form of transportation.

Now, before I get too much further, I need to embark on a brief metaphysical digression. The above structure is not a human being itself; it simply describes the idea, or the concept, behind a human being. It describes what it is to be human. To be human is to have height, hair, to sleep, to eat, and so on. This is a crucial distinction for programming objects. This human being template is known as a *class*. A *class* is different from an *object*. You are an object. I am an object. That guy on the subway is an object. Albert Einstein is an object. We are all people, real world *instances* of the idea of a human being.

Think of a cookie cutter. A cookie cutter makes cookies, but it is not a cookie itself. The cookie cutter is the *class*, the cookies are the *objects*.

Exercise 8-1: Consider a car as an object. What data would a car have? What functions would it have?

Car data   Car functions

-      -

-      -

-      -

-      -

-      -

8-2 Using an object

Before I look at the actual writing of a *class* itself, let's briefly look at how using objects in the main program (i.e., setup() and draw()) makes the world a better place.

Returning to the car example from Chapter 7, you may recall that the pseudocode for the sketch looked something like this:

Data (Global Variables):

- Car color.
- Car x location.
- Car y location.
- Car x speed.

Setup:

- Initialize car color.
- Initialize car location to starting point.
- Initialize car speed.

Draw:

- Fill background.
- Display car at location with color.
- Increment car's location by speed.

In Chapter 7, I defined global variables at the top of the program, initialized them in setup(), and called *functions* to move and display the car in draw().

Object-oriented programming allows me to take all of the variables and functions out of the main program and store them inside a car object. A car object will know about its data — *color*, *location*, *speed*. That is part one. Part two of the car object is the stuff it can do, the methods (functions inside an object). The car can *move* and it can be *displayed*.

Using object-oriented design, the pseudocode improves to look something like this:

Data (Global Variables):

- Car object.

Setup:

- Initialize car object.

Draw:

- Fill background.
- Display car object.
- Move car object.

Notice I removed all of the global variables from the first example. Instead of having separate variables for car color, car location, and car speed, I now have only one variable, a Car variable! And instead of initializing those three variables, I initialize one thing, the Car object. Where did those variables go? They still exist, only now they live inside of the Car object (and will be defined in the Car class, which I will get to in a moment).

Moving beyond pseudocode, the actual body of the sketch might look like:

```
Car myCar;        <──  An object in Processing.

void setup() {
   myCar = new Car();
}

void draw() {
   background(255);
   myCar.move();
```

```
    myCar.display();
  }
```

I am going to get into the details regarding the previous code in a moment, but before I do so, let's take a look at how the Car *class* itself is written.

8-3 Writing the cookie cutter

The simple car example above demonstrates how the use of object in Processing makes for clean, readable code. The hard work goes into writing the object template, that is the *class* itself. When you're first learning about object-oriented programming, it's often a useful exercise to take a program written without objects and, not changing the functionality at all, rewrite it using objects. I will do exactly this with the car example from Chapter 7, recreating exactly the same look and behavior in an object-oriented manner. And at the end of the chapter, I will remake Zoog as an object.

All classes must include four elements: *name*, *data*, *constructor*, and *methods*. (Technically, the only actual required element is the class name, but the point of doing object-oriented programming is to include all of these.)

Figure 8-1 shows how you can take the elements from a simple non-object-oriented sketch and place them into a Car class, from which you will then be able to make Car objects.

- **The Class Name** — The name is specified by "class WhateverNameYouChoose". You then enclose all of the code for the class inside curly brackets after the name declaration. Class names are traditionally capitalized (to distinguish them from variable names, which traditionally are lowercase).
- **Data** — The data for a class is a collection of variables. These variables are often referred to as *instance* variables since each *instance* of an object contains this set of variables.
- **A Constructor** — The constructor is a special function inside of a class that creates the instance of the object itself. It's where you give the instructions on how to set up the object. It's just like Processing's setup() function, only here it's used to create an individual object within the sketch, whenever a new object is created from this *class*. It always has the same name as the class and is called by invoking the new operator: "Car myCar = new Car();".
- **Functionality** — We can add functionality to an object by writing methods. These are done in the same way as described in Chapter 7, with a return type, name, arguments, and a body of code.

This code for a *class* exists as its own block and can be placed anywhere outside of setup() and draw().

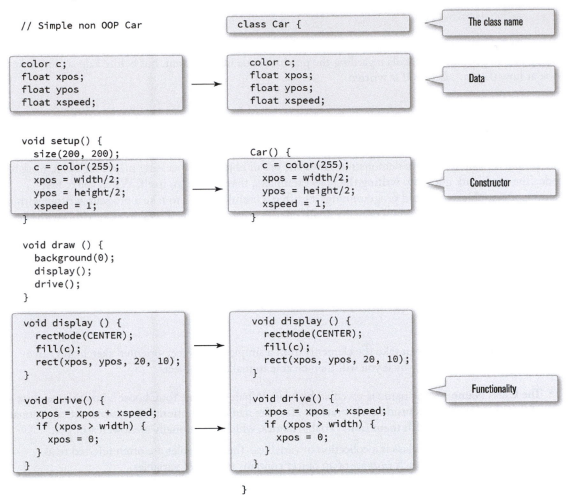

```
// Simple non OOP Car
```

```
class Car {
```
The class name

```
color c;
float xpos;
float ypos
float xspeed;
```

```
color c;
float xpos;
float ypos;
float xspeed;
```
Data

```
void setup() {
  size(200, 200);
  c = color(255);
  xpos = width/2;
  ypos = height/2;
  xspeed = 1;
}
```

```
Car() {
  c = color(255);
  xpos = width/2;
  ypos = height/2;
  xspeed = 1;
}
```
Constructor

```
void draw () {
  background(0);
  display();
  drive();
}
```

```
void display () {
  rectMode(CENTER);
  fill(c);
  rect(xpos, ypos, 20, 10);
}

void drive() {
  xpos = xpos + xspeed;
  if (xpos > width) {
    xpos = 0;
  }
}
```

```
void display () {
  rectMode(CENTER);
  fill(c);
  rect(xpos, ypos, 20, 10);
}

void drive() {
  xpos = xpos + xspeed;
  if (xpos > width) {
    xpos = 0;
  }
}
```
Functionality

```
}
```

Figure 8-1

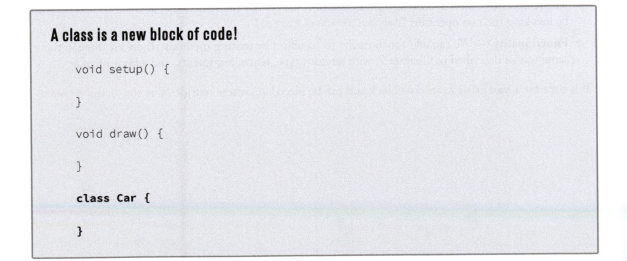

A class is a new block of code!

```
void setup() {

}

void draw() {

}

class Car {

}
```

Exercise 8-2: Fill in the blanks in the following Human class definition. Include a function called sleep() *or make up your own function. Follow the syntax of the Car example. (There are no right or wrong answers in terms of the actual code itself; it's the structure that is important.)*

```
_____ _____ {
    color hairColor;
    float height;


    _____ {


        _____


        _____
    }


    _____ {


        _____


        _____
    }
}
```

8-4 Using an object: the details

In Section 8-2 on page 141, I took a quick peek at how an object can greatly simplify the main parts of a Processing sketch (setup() and draw()).

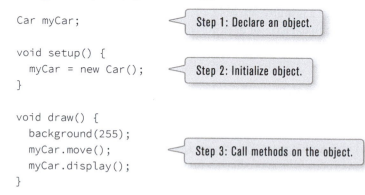

```
Car myCar;                    Step 1: Declare an object.

void setup() {
    myCar = new Car();        Step 2: Initialize object.
}

void draw() {
    background(255);
    myCar.move();             Step 3: Call methods on the object.
    myCar.display();
}
```

Let's look at the details behind the above three steps outlining how to use an object in your sketch.

Step 1. Declaring an object variable.

If you flip back to Chapter 4, you may recall that a variable is declared by specifying a *type* and a *name*.

```
// Variable declaration
// type name
int var;
```

The above is an example of a variable that holds onto *a primitive*, in this case an integer. As you learned in Chapter 4, primitive data types are singular pieces of information: an integer, a floating point number, a character. Declaring a variable that holds onto an object is quite similar. The difference is that here the type is the class name, something I will make up, in this case Car. Objects, incidentally, are not primitives and are considered *complex* data types. (This is because they store multiple pieces of information: data and functionality. Primitives only store data.)

Step 2. Initializing an object.

Again, you may recall from Chapter 4 that in order to initialize a variable (i.e., give it a starting value), I use an assignment operation — *variable* equals *something*.

```
// Variable Initialization
// var equals 10
var = 10;
```

Initializing an object is a bit more complex. Instead of simply assigning it a primitive value, like an integer or floating point number, you have to construct the object. An object is made with the new operator.

```
// Object Initialization
myCar = new Car();
```

> The new operator is used to make a new object.

In the above example, myCar is the object variable name and "=" indicates you are setting it equal to something, that something being a new instance of a Car object. What I am really doing here is initializing a Car object. When you initialize a primitive variable, such as an integer, you just set it equal to a number. But an object may contain multiple pieces of data. Recalling the Car class from the previous section, you can see that this line of code calls the *constructor*, a special function named Car() that initializes all of the object's variables and makes sure the Car object is ready to go.

One other thing; with the primitive integer var, if you had forgotten to initialize it (set it equal to 10), Processing would have assigned it a default value, zero. An object variable (such as myCar), however, has no default value. If you forget to initialize an object, Processing will give it the value null. null means *nothing*. Not zero. Not negative one. Utter nothingness. Emptiness. If you encounter an error in the message window that says NullPointerException (and this is a pretty common error), that error is most likely caused by having forgotten to initialize an object. (See the Appendix for more details.)

Step 3. Using an object

Once you have successfully declared and initialized an object variable, you can use it. Using an object involves calling functions that are built into that object. A human object can eat, a car can drive, a dog can bark. Functions that are inside of an object are technically referred to as "methods" in Java so I can begin to use this nomenclature (see Section 7-1 on page 117). Calling a method inside of an object is accomplished via dot syntax:

variableName.objectMethod(method arguments);

In the case of the car, none of the available functions has an argument so it looks like:

```
myCar.draw();
myCar.display();
```
> Functions are called with the "dot syntax."

Exercise 8-3: Assume the existence of a Human class. You want to write the code to declare a Human object as well as call the function `sleep()` *on that human object. Write out the code below:*

Declare and initialize the Human *object:* _____

Call the `sleep()` *function:* _____

8-5 Putting it together with a tab

Now that I have covered how to define a class and use an object born from that class, I can take the code from Section 8-2 on page 141 and Section 8-3 on page 143 and put them together in one sketch.

Example 8-1. A Car class and a Car object

```
Car myCar;                              Declare car object as a global variable.

void setup() {
  size(200, 200);

  // Initialize Car object
  myCar = new Car();                    Initialize car object in setup() by calling constructor.
}

void draw() {
  background(255);
  // Operate Car object.
  myCar.move();                         Operate the car object in draw() by calling object methods
  myCar.display();                      using the dots syntax.
}

class Car {                             Define a class below the rest of the program.

  color c;
  float xpos;                           Variables.
  float ypos;
  float xspeed;

  Car() {                               A constructor.
    c = color(255);
    xpos = width/2;
    ypos = height/2;
    xspeed = 1;
  }

  void display() {                      Function.
    // The car is just a square
    rectMode(CENTER);
    fill(c);
    rect(xpos, ypos, 20, 10);
  }

  void move() {                         Function.
    xpos = xpos + xspeed;
    if (xpos > width) {
      xpos = 0;
    }
  }
}
```

You will notice that the code block that contains the Car class is placed below the main body of the program (under draw()). This spot is identical to where I placed user-defined functions in Chapter 7. Technically speaking, the order does not matter, as long as the blocks of code (contained within curly brackets) remain intact. The Car class could go above setup() or it could even go between setup() and draw(). Though any placement is technically correct, when programming, it's nice to place things where they make the most logical sense to our human brains, the bottom of the code being a good starting point. Nevertheless, Processing offers a useful means for separating blocks of code from each other through the use of tabs.

In your Processing window, look for the upside-down triangle next to the name of your sketch. If you click that triangle, you will see that it offers the "New Tab" option shown in Figure 8-2.

Figure 8-2

Upon selecting "New Tab," you will be prompted to type in a name for the new tab, as shown in Figure 8-3.

Figure 8-3

Although you can pick any name you like, it's probably a good idea to name the tab after the class you intend to put there. You can then put your main code (`setup()` and `draw()`) on the original tab (named "ObjectExample" in Figure 8-4) and type the code for your class in the new one (named "Car").

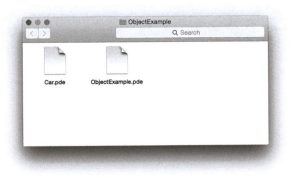

Figure 8-4

Toggling between the tabs is simple, just click on the tab name itself. Also, it should be noted that when a new tab is created, a new .pde file is created inside the sketch folder, as shown in Figure 8-5. The program has both an ObjectExample.pde file and Car.pde file.

Figure 8-5

Exercise 8-4: Create a sketch with multiple tabs. Try to get the Car example to run without any errors.

8-6 Constructor arguments

In the previous examples, the car object was initialized using the *new* operator followed by the *constructor* for the class.

```
Car myCar = new Car();
```

This was a useful simplification while you learned the basics of OOP. Nonetheless, there is a rather serious problem with the above code. What if I wanted to write a program with two car objects?

```
Car myCar1 = new Car();     Creating two Car objects.
Car myCar2 = new Car();
```

This accomplishes my goal; the code will produce two car objects, one stored in the variable myCar1 and one in myCar2. However, if you study the Car class, you will notice that these two cars will be identical: each one will be colored white, start in the middle of the screen, and have a speed of 1. In English, the above reads:

Make a new car.

I want to instead say:

Make a new red car, at location (0,10) with a speed of 1.

So that I could also say:

Make a new blue car, at location (0,100) with a speed of 2.

I can do this by placing arguments inside of the constructor.

```
Car myCar = new Car(color(255, 0, 0), 0, 100, 2);
```

The constructor must be rewritten to incorporate these arguments:

```
Car(color tempC, float tempXpos, float tempYpos, float tempXspeed) {
  c = tempC;
  xpos = tempXpos;
  ypos = tempYpos;
  xspeed = tempXspeed;
}
```

In my experience, the use of constructor arguments to initialize object variables can be somewhat bewildering. Please don't blame yourself. The code is strange-looking and can seem awfully redundant: "For every single variable I want to initialize in the constructor, I have to duplicate it with a temporary argument to that constructor?"

Nevertheless, this is quite an important skill to learn, and, ultimately, is one of the things that makes object-oriented programming powerful. But for now, it may feel painful. Let's briefly revisit parameter passing again to understand how it works in this context. See Figure 8-6.

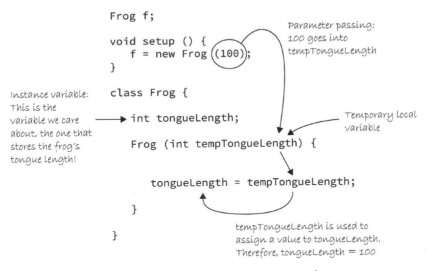

Translation: Make a new frog with a tongue length of 100.

Figure 8-6

Arguments are local variables used inside the body of a function that get filled with values when the function is called. In the examples, they have *one purpose only*, to initialize the variables inside of an object. These are the variables that count, the car's actual color, the car's actual x location, and so on. The constructor's arguments are just *temporary*, and exist solely to pass a value from where the object is made into the object itself.

This allows you to make a variety of objects using the same constructor. You might also just write the word *temp* in your argument names to remind you of what is going on (x vs. tempX). You will also see programmers use an underscore (x vs. x_) in many examples. I'll probably do it this way in some examples towards the end of this book. You can name these whatever you want, of course. However, it's advisable to choose a name that makes sense to you, and also to stay consistent.

I can now write the same program with multiple object instances, each with unique properties.

Example 8-2. Two Car objects

```
Car myCar1;          Two objects!
Car myCar2;

void setup() {
  size(200, 200);

  myCar1 = new Car(color(255, 0, 0), 0, 100, 2);
  myCar2 = new Car(color(0, 0, 255), 0, 10, 1);
}
```

> Arguments go inside the
> parentheses when the
> object is constructed.

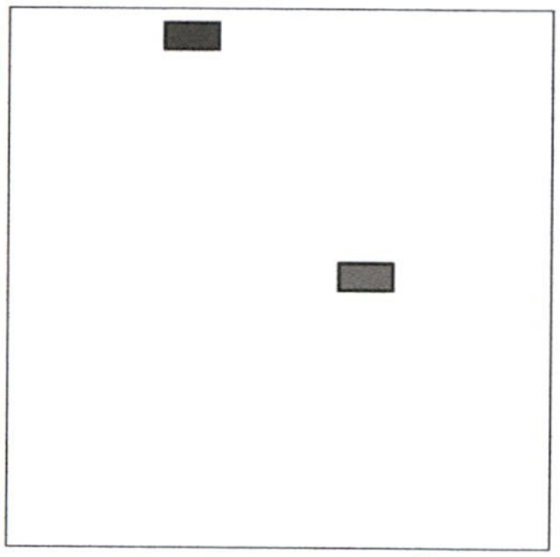

```
void draw() {
  background(255);
  myCar1.move();
  myCar1.display();
  myCar2.move();
  myCar2.display();
}
```

> Even though there are multiple objects,
> you still only need one class. No matter
> how many cookies you make, only one
> cookie cutter is needed. Isn't object-
> oriented programming swell?

```
class Car {

  color c;
  float xpos;
  float ypos;
  float xspeed;

  Car(color tempC, float tempXpos, float tempYpos, float tempXspeed) {
    c = tempC;
    xpos = tempXpos;          The constructor is defined with
    ypos = tempYpos;          parameters.
    xspeed = tempXspeed;
  }

  void display() {
  stroke(0);
    fill(c);
    rectMode(CENTER);
    rect(xpos, ypos, 20, 10);
  }

  void move() {
    xpos = xpos + xspeed;
    if (xpos > width) {
      xpos = 0;
    }
  }

}
```

Figure 8-7

Exercise 8-5: Rewrite the gravity example from Chapter 5 using objects with a `Ball` *class. The original example is included here for your reference with a framework to help you get started. Once you get one object working, make two without changing the class! Can you add variables for color or size in your class?*

```
_____ _____;
float gravity = 0.1;

void setup() {
  size(200, 200);

  ball = new _____(50, 0);
}

void draw() {
  background(255);
  ball.display();


  _____
}


_____ {
  float x;


  _____
  float speed;


  _____(_____,_____,_____) {


    x = _____;


    _____

    speed = 0;
  }

  void _____() {


    _____


    _____


    _____
  }
```

```
// Simple gravity example

// (x,y) location
float x = 100;
float y = 0;

// Starting speed
float speed = 0;
// Gravity
float gravity = 0.1;

void setup() {
  size(200, 200);
}

void draw() {
  background(255);

  // Display the circle
  fill(175);
  stroke(0);
  ellipse(x, y, 10, 10);

  // Add speed to y location
  y = y + speed;
  // Add gravity to speed
  speed = speed + gravity;

  // If square reaches the bottom
  // Reverse speed
  if (y > height) {
    speed = speed * -0.95;
    y = height;
  }
}
```

```
              -------------------------------

              -------------------------------

              -------------------------------

              -------------------------------

              --------------------------------

              -------------------------------

              -------------------------------
  }
```

8-7 Objects are data types too!

This is your first experience with object-oriented programming, so I want to take it easy. The examples in this chapter all use just one class and make, at most, two or three objects from that class. Nevertheless, there are no actual limitations. A Processing sketch can include as many classes as you feel like writing. If you were programming the Space Invaders game, for example, you might create a `Spaceship` class, an `Enemy` class, and a `Bullet` class, using an object for each entity in your game.

In addition, although not *primitive*, classes are data types just like integers and floats. And since classes are made up of data, an object can therefore contain other objects! For example, let's assume you had just finished programming a `Fork` and `Spoon` class. Moving on to a `PlaceSetting` class, you would likely include variables for both a `Fork` object and a `Spoon` object inside that class itself. This is perfectly reasonable and quite common in object-oriented programming.

```
class PlaceSetting {

  Fork fork;            A class can include other objects among its variables.
  Spoon spoon;

  PlaceSetting() {
    fork = new Fork();
    spoon = new Spoon();
  }
}
```

Objects, just like any data type, can also be passed in as arguments to a function. In the Space Invaders game example, if the spaceship shoots the bullet at the enemy, you would probably want to write a function inside the `Enemy` class to determine if the enemy had been hit by the bullet.

```
void hit(Bullet b) {
  // Code to determine if
  // the bullet struck the enemy
}
```

> A function can have an object as its argument.

In Chapter 7, I showed how when a primitive value (int, float, etc.) is passed into a function, a copy of the variable is made and the original variable remains the same no matter what happens in the function. This is known as *pass by value*. With objects, things work a bit differently. If changes are made to an object after it is passed into a function, those changes will affect the original object. Instead of copying the object and passing it into the function, a copy of a *reference* to the object is passed. You can think of a reference as the address in memory where the object's data is stored. So while there are in fact two distinct variables holding on their own value, that value is simply an address pointing to only one object. Any changes to those object variables affect the same object.

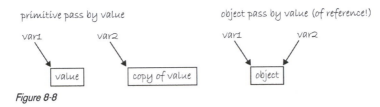

Figure 8-8

As you move forward through this book and the examples become more advanced, you will see examples that use multiple objects, pass objects into functions, and more. The next chapter, in fact, focuses on how to make lists of objects. And Chapter 10 walks through the development of a project that includes multiple classes. For now, as I close out the chapter with Zoog, I will stick with just one class.

8-8 Object-oriented Zoog

Invariably, the question comes up: "When should I use object-oriented programming?" For me, the answer is *always*. Objects allow you to organize the concepts inside of a software application into modular, reusable packages. You will see this again and again throughout the course of this book. However, it's not always convenient or necessary to start out every project using object-orientation, especially while you're learning. Processing makes it easy to quickly "sketch" out visual ideas with non object-oriented code.

For any Processing project you want to make, my advice is to take a step-by-step approach. You do not need to start out writing classes for everything you want to try to do. Sketch out your idea first by writing code in setup() and draw(). Nail down the logic of what you want to do as well as how you want it to look. As your project begins to grow, take the time to reorganize your code, perhaps first with functions, then with objects. It's perfectly acceptable to dedicate a significant chunk of your time to this reorganization process (often referred to as *refactoring*) without making any changes to the end result, that is, what your sketch looks like and does on screen.

This is exactly what I have been doing with cosmonaut Zoog from Chapter 1 until now. I sketched out Zoog's look and experimented with some motion behaviors. Now that I have something, I can take the time to *refactor* by making Zoog into an object. This process will give you a leg up in programming Zoog's future life in more complex sketches.

And so it is time to take the plunge and make a Zoog class. Our little Zoog is almost all grown up. The following example is virtually identical to Example 7-6 (Zoog with functions) with one major difference. All of the variables and all of the functions are now incorporated into the Zoog class with setup() and draw() containing barely any code.

Example 8-3. Zoog object

```
Zoog zoog;               [Zoog is an object!]

void setup() {
  size(200, 200);
  zoog = new Zoog(100, 125, 60, 60, 16);   [Zoog is given initial properties via
}                                            the constructor.]

void draw() {
  background(255);
  // mouseX position determines speed factor
  float factor = constrain(mouseX/10, 0, 5);
  zoog.jiggle(factor);
  zoog.display();
}                    [Zoog can do stuff with functions!]


class Zoog {              [Everything about Zoog is contained in this one
                          class. Zoog has properties (location, width, height,
  // Zoog's variables     eye size) and Zoog has abilities (jiggle, display).]
  float x, y, w, h, eyeSize;

  // Zoog constructor
  Zoog(float tempX, float tempY, float tempW, float tempH, float tempEyeSize) {
    x = tempX;
    y = tempY;
    w = tempW;
    h = tempH;
    eyeSize = tempEyeSize;
  }

  // Move Zoog
  void jiggle(float speed) {
    // Change the location of Zoog randomly
    x = x + random(-1, 1)*speed;
    y = y + random(-1, 1)*speed;

    // Constrain Zoog to window
    x = constrain(x, 0, width);
    y = constrain(y, 0, height);
  }

  // Display Zoog
  void display() {
    // Set ellipses and rects to CENTER mode
    ellipseMode(CENTER);
    rectMode(CENTER);

    // Draw Zoog's arms with a for loop
```

```
    for (float i = y - h/3; i < y + h/2; i += 10) {
      stroke(0);
      line(x - w/4, i, x + w/4, i);
    }

    // Draw Zoog's body
    stroke(0);
    fill(175);
    rect(x, y, w/6, h);

    // Draw Zoog's head
    stroke(0);
    fill(255);
    ellipse(x, y - h, w, h);

    // Draw Zoog's eyes
    fill(0);
    ellipse(x - w/3, y - h, eyeSize, eyeSize*2);
    ellipse(x + w/3, y - h, eyeSize, eyeSize*2);

    // Draw Zoog's legs
    stroke(0);
    line(x - w/12, y + h/2, x - w/4, y + h/2 + 10);
    line(x + w/12, y + h/2, x + w/4, y + h/2 + 10);
  }
}
```

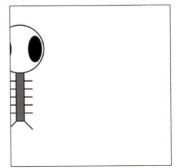

Figure 8-9

Exercise 8-6: Rewrite Example 8-3 to include two Zoogs. Can you vary their appearance? Behavior? Consider adding color as a Zoog variable.

Lesson Three Project

1. Take your Lesson Two Project and reorganize the code using functions.

2. Reorganize the code one step further using a class and an object variable.

3. Add arguments to the Constructor of your class and try making two or three objects with different variables.

Use the space provided below to sketch designs, notes, and pseudocode for your project.

Lesson Four

More of the Same

Chapter 9

9 Arrays

I might repeat to myself slowly and soothingly, a list of quotations beautiful from minds profound—if I can remember any of the damn things.
—Dorothy Parker

In this chapter:
– What is an array?
– Declaring an array
– Initializing an array
– Array operations – using a `for` loop with an array
– Arrays of objects

9-1 Arrays, why do you care?

Let's take a moment to revisit the car example from the previous chapter on object-oriented programming. You may remember I spent a great deal of effort on developing a program that contained multiple instances of a class, that is, two objects.

```
Car myCar1;
Car myCar2;
```

This was indeed an exciting moment in the development of your life as a computer programmer. It's likely, however, that you're contemplating a somewhat obvious question. How could you take this further and write a program with 100 `Car` objects? With some clever copying and pasting, you might write a program with the following beginning:

```
Car myCar1
Car myCar2
Car myCar3
Car myCar4
Car myCar5
Car myCar6
Car myCar7
Car myCar8
Car myCar9
Car myCar10
Car myCar11
Car myCar12
Car myCar13
Car myCar14
Car myCar15
Car myCar16
Car myCar17
Car myCar18
Car myCar19
```

```
Car myCar20
Car myCar21
Car myCar22
Car myCar23
Car myCar24
Car myCar25
Car myCar26
Car myCar27
Car myCar28
Car myCar29
Car myCar30
Car myCar31
Car myCar32
Car myCar33
Car myCar34
Car myCar35
Car myCar36
Car myCar37
Car myCar38
Car myCar39
Car myCar40
Car myCar41
Car myCar42
Car myCar43
Car myCar44
Car myCar45
Car myCar46
Car myCar47
Car myCar48
Car myCar49
Car myCar50
Car myCar51
Car myCar52
Car myCar53
Car myCar54
Car myCar55
Car myCar56
Car myCar57
Car myCar58
Car myCar59
Car myCar60
Car myCar61
Car myCar62
Car myCar63
Car myCar64
Car myCar65
Car myCar66
Car myCar67
```

```
Car myCar68
Car myCar69
Car myCar70
Car myCar71
Car myCar72
Car myCar73
Car myCar74
Car myCar75
Car myCar76
Car myCar77
Car myCar78
Car myCar79
Car myCar80
Car myCar81
Car myCar82
Car myCar83
Car myCar84
Car myCar85
Car myCar86
Car myCar87
Car myCar88
Car myCar89
Car myCar90
Car myCar91
Car myCar92
Car myCar93
Car myCar94
Car myCar95
Car myCar96
Car myCar97
Car myCar98
Car myCar99
Car myCar100
```

If you really want to give yourself a headache, try completing the rest of the program modeled after the above start. It will not be a pleasant endeavor. I am certainly not about to leave you any workbook space in this book to practice.

An array will allow you to take these 100 lines of code and put them into one line. Instead of having 100 variables, an array is *one* thing that contains a *list* of variables.

Any time a program requires multiple instances of similar data, it might be time to use an array. For example, an array can be used to store the scores of four players in a game, a selection of 10 colors in a design program, or a list of fish objects in an aquarium simulation.

Exercise 9-1: Looking at all of the sketches you have created so far, do any merit the use of an array? Why?

9-2 What is an array?

From Chapter 4, you may recall that a variable is a named pointer to a location in memory where data is stored. In other words, variables allow programs to keep track of information over a period of time. An array is exactly the same, only instead of pointing to one singular piece of information, an array points to multiple pieces. See Figure 9-1.

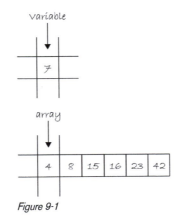

Figure 9-1

You can think of an array as a list of variables. A list, it should be noted, is useful for two important reasons. Number one, the list keeps track of the elements in the list themselves. Number two, the list keeps track of *the order* of those elements (which element is the first in the list, the second, the third, etc.). This is a crucial point since in many programs, the order of information is just as important as the information itself.

In an array, each element of the list has a unique *index,* an integer value that designates its position in the list (element #1, element #2, etc.). In all cases, the name of the array refers to the list as a whole, while each element is accessed via its position.

Notice how in Figure 9-2, the indices range from 0 to 9. The array has a total of 10 elements, but the first element number is 0 and the last element is 9. You might be tempted to stomp your feet and complain: "Hey, why aren't the elements numbered from 1 to 10? Wouldn't that be easier?"

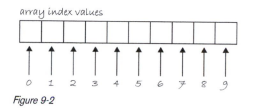

Figure 9-2

While at first, it might intuitively seem like I should start counting at 1 (and some programming languages do), I start at 0 because technically the first element of the array is located at the start of the array, a distance of zero from the beginning. Numbering the elements starting at 0 also makes many *array operations* (the process of executing a line of code for every element of the list) a great deal more convenient. As I continue through several examples, you will begin to believe in the power of counting from zero.

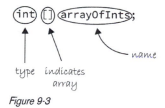

Exercise 9-2: If you have an array with 1,000 elements, what is the range of index values for that array?

Answer: _____ through _____

9-3 Declaring and creating an array

In Chapter 4, you learned that all variables must have a name and a data type. Arrays are no different. The declaration statement, however, does look different. You denote the use of an array by placing empty square brackets ([]) after the type declaration. Let's start with an array of primitive values, for example, integers. (You can have arrays of any data type, and I will soon show how you can make an array of objects.) See Figure 9-3.

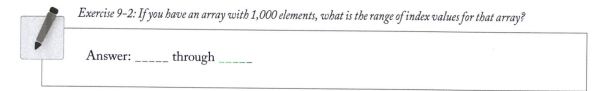

Figure 9-3

The declaration in Figure 9-3 indicates that `arrayOfInts` will store a list of integers. The array name `arrayOfInts` can be absolutely anything you want it to be (I only include the word "array" here to illustrate what you are learning).

One fundamental property of arrays, however, is that they are of fixed size. Once I define the size for an array, it can never change. A list of 10 integers can never *go to 11*. But where in the above code is the size of the array defined? It is not. The code simply declares the array; I must also make sure I *create* the actual instance of the array with a specified size.

To do this, I use the new operator, in a similar manner as I did in calling the constructor of an object. In the object's case, I am saying "Make a *new* Car" or "Make a *new* Zoog." With an array, I am saying "Make a *new* array of integers," or "Make a *new* array of Car objects," and so on. See array declaration in Figure 9-4.

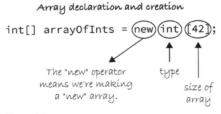

Array declaration and creation

```
int[] arrayOfInts = new int [42];
```

The "new" operator   type
means we're making   size of
a "new" array.   array

Figure 9-4

The array declaration in Figure 9-4 allows me to specify the array size: how many elements I want the array to hold (or, technically, how much memory in the computer I am asking for to store my beloved data). I write this statement as follows: the new operator, followed by the data type, followed by the size of the array enclosed in brackets. This size must be an integer. It can be a hard-coded number, a variable (of type integer), or an expression that evaluates to an integer (like 2 + 2).

Example 9-1. Additional array declaration and creation examples

```
float[] scores = new float[4];                   // A list of 4 floating point numbers
Human[] people = new Human[100];                 // A list of 100 Human objects
int num = 50;
Car[] cars = new Car[num];                        // Using a variable to specify size
Spaceship[] ships = new Shapeship[num*2 + 3];    // Using an expression to
                                                 //    specify size
```

Exercise 9-3: Write the declaration statements for the following arrays:

30 integers: _____

100 floating point numbers: _____

56 Zoog objects: _____

Exercise 9-4: Which of the following array declarations are valid and which are invalid (and why)?

```
int[] numbers = new int[10];          _____

float[] numbers = new float[5 + 6];   _____

int num = 5;
float[] numbers = new int[num];       _____

float num = 5.2;
Car[] cars = new Car[num];            _____

int num = (5 * 6)/2;
float[] numbers = new float[num = 5]; _____

int num = 5;
Zoog[] zoogs = new Zoog[num * 10];    _____
```

Things are looking up. Not only did I successfully declare the existence of an array, but I have given it a size and allocated physical memory for the stored data. A major piece is missing, however: the data stored in the array itself!

9-4 Initializing an array

One way to fill an array is to hard-code the values stored in each spot of the array.

Example 9-2. Initializing the elements of an array one at a time

```
int[] stuff = new int[3];

stuff[0] = 8; // The first element of the array equals 8
stuff[1] = 3; // The second element of the array equals 3
stuff[2] = 1; // The third element of the array equals 1
```

As you can see, each element of the array is referred to individually by specifying an index, starting at 0. The syntax for this is the name of the array, followed by the index value enclosed in brackets.

```
arrayName[INDEX]
```

A second option for initializing an array is to manually type out a list of values enclosed in curly braces and separated by commas.

Example 9-3. Initializing the elements of an array all at once

```
int[] arrayOfInts = { 1, 5, 8, 9, 4, 5 } ;
float[] floatArray = { 1.2, 3.5, 2.0, 3.4123, 9.9 } ;
```

Exercise 9-5: Declare an array of three Zoog *objects. Initialize each spot in the array with a* Zoog *object via its index.*

```
Zoog__ zoogs = new _____[___];

_____[_____] = _____ _____(100, 100, 50, 60, 16);

_____[_____] = _____ _____(_____);

_____[_____] = _____ _____(_____);
```

Both of these approaches are not commonly used and you will not see them in most of the examples throughout the book. In fact, neither initialization method has really solved the problem posed at the beginning of the chapter. Imagine initializing each element individually with a list of 100 or (gasp) 1,000 or (gasp gasp!) 1,000,000 elements.

The solution to all of your woes involves a means for *iterating* through the elements of the array. Ding ding ding. Hopefully a loud bell is ringing in your head. Loops! (If you're lost, revisit Chapter 6.)

9-5 Array operations

Consider, for a moment, the following problem:

1. Create an array of 1,000 floating point numbers.
2. Initialize every element of that array with a random number between 0 and 10.

Part 1 you already know how to do.

```
float[] values = new float[1000];
```

What I want to avoid is having to do this for Part 2:

```
values[0] = random(0, 10);
values[1] = random(0, 10);
values[2] = random(0, 10);
values[3] = random(0, 10);
values[4] = random(0, 10);
values[5] = random(0, 10);
// etc. etc.
```

Let's describe in English what I want to program.

For every number *n* from 0 to 999, initialize the *nth* element stored in array as a random value between 0 and 10. Translating into code, I have:

```
int n = 0;
values[n] = random(0, 10);
values[n + 1] = random(0, 10);
values[n + 2] = random(0, 10);
values[n + 3] = random(0, 10);
values[n + 4] = random(0, 10);
values[n + 5] = random(0, 10);
```

Unfortunately, the situation has not improved. I have, nonetheless, taken a big leap forward. By using a variable (n) to describe an index in the array, I can now employ a while loop to initialize every n element.

Example 9-4. Using a while loop to initialize all elements of an array

```
int n = 0;
while (n < 1000) {
  values[n] = random(0, 10);
  n = n + 1;
}
```

A for loop allows you to be even more concise, as Example 9-5 shows.

Example 9-5. Using a for loop to initialize all elements of an array

```
for (int n = 0; n < 1000; n++) {
  values[n] = random(0, 10);
}
```

What was once 1,000 lines of code is now three!

I can exploit the same technique for any type of array operation I might like to do beyond simply initializing the elements. For example, I could take the array and double the value of each element. (I will use i from now on instead of n as it is more commonly used by programmers.)

Example 9-6. An array operation

```
for (int i = 0; i < 1000; i++) {
  values[i] = values[i] * 2;
}
```

There is one problem with Example 9-6: the use of the hard-coded value 1,000. Striving to be better programmers, you should always question the existence of a hard-coded number. In this case, what if you wanted to change the array to have 2,000 elements? If your program was very long with many array operations, you would have to make this change everywhere throughout your code. Fortunately, Processing offers a nice means for accessing the size of an array dynamically, using the dot syntax you learned for objects in Chapter 8. length is a property of every array and you can access it by saying:

arrayName dot length

Let's use length while clearing an array. This will involve resetting every value to 0.

Example 9-7. An array operation using dot length

```
for (int i = 0; i < values.length; i++) {
  values[i] = 0;
}
```

Exercise 9-6: Assuming an array of 10 integers, that is,

```
int[] nums = { 5, 4, 2, 7, 6, 8, 5, 2, 8, 14 };
```

Write code to perform the following array operations (Note that the number of clues vary, just because a [____] is not explicitly written in does not mean there should not be brackets).

Square each number (i.e., multiply each by itself)	`for (int i _____; i < _____; i++) {`
	
	`  _____[i] = _____*_____;`
	
	`}`

Add a random number between zero and 10 to each number.	`_____`
	
	`  _____ += int(_____);`
	
	`---`

Add to each number the number that follows in the array. Skip the last value in the array.	`for (int i = 0; i < _____; i++) {`
	
	`  _____ += _____[_____];`
	
	`}`

Calculate the sum of all the numbers.	`_____ _____ = _____;`
	`for (int i = 0; i < nums.length; i++) {`
	
	`  _____ += _____;`
	
	`}`

9-6 Simple array example: the snake

A seemingly trivial task, programming a trail following the mouse, is not as easy as it might initially appear. The solution requires an array, which will serve to store the history of mouse locations. I will use two arrays, one to store horizontal mouse locations, and one for vertical. Let's say, arbitrarily, that I want to store the last 50 mouse locations.

First, I declare the two arrays.

```
int[] xpos = new int[50];
int[] ypos = new int[50];
```

Second, in setup(), I must initialize the arrays. Since at the start of the program there has not been any mouse movement, I will just fill the arrays with 0's.

```
for (int i = 0; i < xpos.length; i++) {
  xpos[i] = 0;
  ypos[i] = 0;
}
```

Each time through the main draw() loop, I want to update the array with the current mouse location. Let's choose to put the current mouse location in the last spot of the array. The length of the array is 50, meaning index values range from 0–49. The last spot is index 49, or the length of the array minus one.

```
xpos[xpos.length - 1] = mouseX;      The last spot in an array is length minus one.
ypos[ypos.length - 1] = mouseY;
```

Now comes the hard part. I want to keep only the last 50 mouse locations. By storing the current mouse location at the end of the array, I am overwriting what was previously stored there. If the mouse is at (10,10) during one frame and (15,15) during another, I want to put (10,10) in the second to last spot and (15,15) in the last spot. A solution is to shift all of the elements of the array down one spot before updating the current location. This is shown in Figure 9-5.

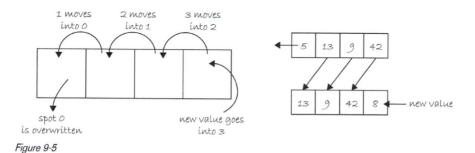

Figure 9-5

Element index 49 moves into spot 48, 48 moves into spot 47, 47 into 46, and so on. I can do this by looping through the array and setting each element index i to the value of element i+1. Note I must stop at the second to last value since for element 49 there is no element 50 (49 plus 1). In other words, instead of having an exit condition

```
i < xpos.length;
```

I must instead say:

```
i < xpos.length - 1;
```

The full code for performing this array shift is as follows:

```
for (int i = 0; i < xpos.length - 1; i++) {
  xpos[i] = xpos[i + 1];
  ypos[i] = ypos[i + 1];
}
```

Finally, I can use the history of mouse locations to draw a series of circles. For each element of the xpos array and ypos array, draw an ellipse at the corresponding values stored in the array.

```
for (int i = 0; i < xpos.length; i++) {
  stroke(0);
  fill(175);
  ellipse(xpos[i], ypos[i], 32, 32);
}
```

Making this a bit fancier, you might choose to link the brightness of the circle as well as the size of the circle to the location in the array, that is, the earlier (and therefore older) values will be bright and small and the later (newer) values will be darker and bigger. This is accomplished by using the counting variable i to evaluate color and size.

```
for (int i = 0; i < xpos.length; i++) {
  noStroke();
  fill(255 - i * 5);
  ellipse(xpos[i], ypos[i], i, i);
}
```

Putting all of the code together, I have the following example, with the output shown in Figure 9-6.

Example 9-8. A snake following the mouse

```
// x and y positions
int[] xpos = new int[50];        Declare two arrays with
int[] ypos = new int[50];        50 elements.

void setup() {
  size(200, 200);

  // Initialize
  for (int i = 0; i < xpos.length; i++) {
    xpos[i] = 0;
    ypos[i] = 0;
  }                            Initialize all elements of each
}                              array to zero.

void draw() {
  background(255);

  // Shift array values
  for (int i = 0; i < xpos.length - 1; i++) {
    xpos[i] = xpos[i + 1];
    ypos[i] = ypos[i + 1];
  }                            Shift all elements down one spot.
                               xpos[0] = xpos[1], xpos[1] = xpos
                               = [2], and so on. Stop at the
                               second to last element.

  // New location
  xpos[xpos.length - 1] = mouseX;
  ypos[ypos.length - 1] = mouseY;    Update the last spot in the array
                                     with the mouse location.

  // Draw everything
  for (int i = 0; i < xpos.length; i++) {
    noStroke();
    fill(255 - i*5);
    ellipse(xpos[i], ypos[i], i, i);    Draw an ellipse for each element in
  }                                     the arrays. Color and size are tied to
}                                       the loop's counter: i.
```

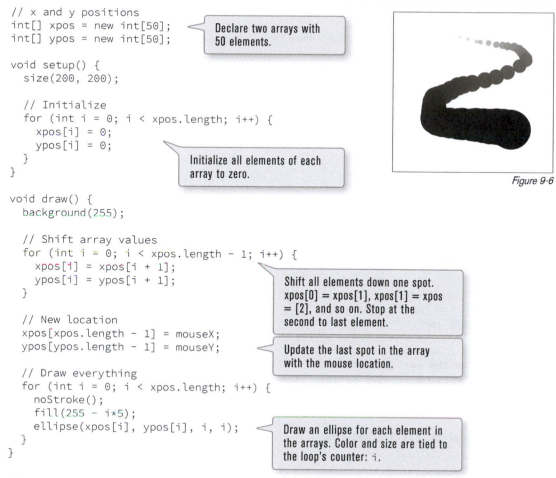

Figure 9-6

Exercise 9-7: Rewrite the snake example in an object-oriented fashion with a Snake *class. Can you make snakes with slightly different looks (different shapes, colors, sizes)? (For an advanced problem, create a* Point *class that stores an x and y coordinate as part of the sketch. Each snake object will have an array of Point objects, instead of two separate arrays of x and y values. This involves arrays of objects, covered in the next section.)*

9-7 Arrays of objects

I know, I know. I still have not fully answered the question. How can you write a program with 100 car objects?

One of the nicest features of combining object-oriented programming with arrays is the simplicity of transitioning a program from one object to 10 objects to 10,000 objects. In fact, if I have been careful, I will not have to change the Car class whatsoever. A class does not care how many objects are made from it. So, assuming I keep the identical `Car` class code, let's look at how to expand the main program to use an array of objects instead of just one.

Let's revisit the main program for one `Car` object.

```
Car myCar;

void setup() {
  myCar = new Car(color(255, 0, 0), 0, 100, 2);
}

void draw() {
  background(255);
  myCar.move();
  myCar.display();
}
```

There are three steps in the above code and each one needs to be changed to account for an array.

Before	After
`// Declare the car` `Car myCar;`	`// Declare the car array` `Car[] cars = new Car[100];`

`// Initialize the car`
`myCar = new Car(color(255), 0, 100, 2);`
	`// Initialize each element of the array`
	`for (int i = 0; i < cars.length; i++) {`
	`   cars[i] = new Car(color(i*2), 0, i*2, i);`
	`}`

`// Run the car by calling methods`
`myCar.move();`
`myCar.display();`
	`// Run each element of the array`
	`for (int i = 0; i < cars.length; i++) {`
	`   cars[i].move();`
	`   cars[i].display();`
	`}`

This leaves you with Example 9-9. Note how changing the number of cars present in the program requires only altering the array definition. Nothing else anywhere has to change!

Example 9-9. An array of Car objects

```
Car[] cars = new Car[100];
```
An array of 100 Car objects!

```
void setup() {
  size(200, 200);

  for (int i = 0; i < cars.length; i++) {
    cars[i] = new Car(color(i*2), 0, i*2, i/20.0);
  }
}
```
Initialize each car using a for loop.

```
void draw() {

  background(255);

  for (int i = 0; i < cars.length; i++) {
    cars[i].move();
    cars[i].display();
  }
}
```
Run each car using a for loop.

```
class Car {
```
The Car class does not change whether you are making one car, 100 cars or 1,000 cars!

```
  color c;
  float xpos;
  float ypos;
  float xspeed;

  Car(color c_, float xpos_, float ypos_, float xspeed_) {
    c = c_;
    xpos = xpos_;
    ypos = ypos_;
    xspeed = xspeed_;
  }

  void display() {
    rectMode(CENTER);
    stroke(0);
    fill(c);
    rect(xpos, ypos, 20, 10);
  }

  void move() {
    xpos = xpos + xspeed;
    if (xpos > width) {
      xpos = 0;
    }
  }

}
```

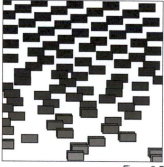

Figure 9-7

9-8 Interactive objects

When you first learned about variables (Chapter 4) and conditionals (Chapter 5), you programmed a simple rollover effect. A rectangle appears in the window and is one color when the mouse is on top and another color when the mouse is not. The following is an example that takes this simple idea and puts it into a Stripe class. Even though there are 10 stripes, each one individually responds to the mouse by having its own rollover() function.

```
void rollover(int mx, int my) {
  if (mx > x & & mx < x + w) {
    mouse = true;
  } else {
    mouse = false;
  }
}
```

This function checks to see if a point (mx,my) is contained within the vertical stripe. Is it greater than the left edge and less than the right edge? If so, a boolean variable mouse is set to true. When designing your classes, it's often convenient to use a boolean variable to keep track of properties of an object that resemble a switch. For example, a Car object could be running or not running. Zoog could be happy or not happy.

This boolean variable is used in a conditional statement inside of the Stripe object's display() function to determine the stripe's color.

```
void display() {
  if (mouse) {
    fill(255);
  } else {
    fill(255, 100);
  }
  noStroke();
  rect(x, 0, w, height);
}
```

When I call the rollover() function on that object, I can then pass in mouseX and mouseY as arguments.

```
stripes[i].rollover(mouseX, mouseY);
```

Even though I could have accessed mouseX and mouseY directly inside of the rollover() function, it's better to use arguments. This allows for greater flexibility. The Stripe object can check and determine if any (x,y) coordinate is contained within its rectangle. Perhaps later, I will want the stripe to turn white when another object, rather than the mouse, is over it.

Here is the full "interactive stripes" example.

Example 9-10. Interactive stripes

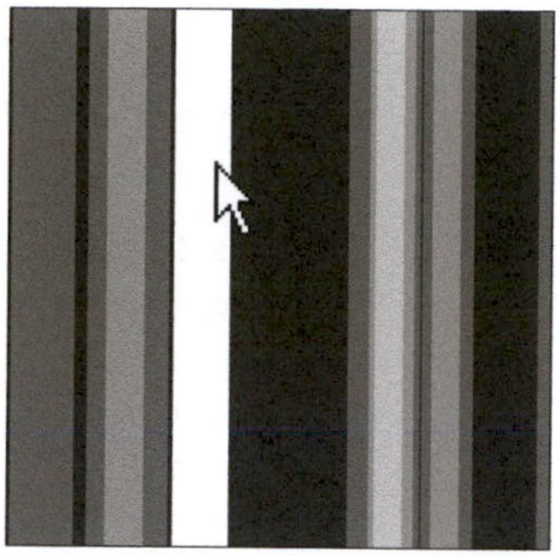

```
Stripe[] stripes = new Stripe[10];

void setup() {
  size(200, 200);
  for (int i = 0; i < stripes.length; i++) {
    stripes[i] = new Stripe();
  }
}
```

> array of `Stripe` objects

Figure 9-8

```
void draw() {
  background(100);
  // Move and display all stripes
  for (int i = 0; i < stripes.length; i++) {
    stripes[i].rollover(mouseX, mouseY);
    stripes[i].move();
    stripes[i].display();
  }
}
```

> Check in the mouse is over a stripe by passing the the mouse coordinates into the `Stripe` class `rollover()` function.

```
class Stripe {
  float x;        // horizontal location of stripe
  float speed;    // speed of stripe
  float w;        // width of stripe
  boolean mouse;  // Is the mouse over the stripe?
```

> A boolean variable keeps track of the object's state.

```
  Stripe() {
    x = 0;                   // All stripes start at 0
    speed = random(1);       // All stripes have a random positive speed
    w = random(10, 30);
    mouse = false;
  }

  void display() {
    if (mouse) {
      fill(255);
    } else {
      fill(255, 100);
    }
    noStroke();
    rect(x, 0, w, height);
  }
```

> That boolean variable determines stripe color.

```
  void move() {
    x += speed;
    if (x > width + 20) x = -20;
  }

  void rollover(int mx, int my) { {
    // Left edge is x, right edge is x + w
    if (mx > x & & mx < x + w)
      mouse = true;
    } else {
      mouse = false;
    }
  }
}
```

> This function checks to see if the point (mx,my) is inside the stripe (returning `true`) or outside (returning `false`).

Exercise 9-8: Write a Button *class (see Example 5-5 for a non–object-oriented button). The* Button *class should register when a mouse is pressed over the button and change color. Create buttons of different sizes and locations using an array. Before writing the main program, sketch out the* Button *class. Assume the button is off when it first appears. Here is a code framework:*

```
class Button {
  float x;
  float y;
  float w;
  float h;
  boolean on;

  Button(float tempX, float tempY, float tempW, float tempH) {
    x = tempX;
    y = tempY;
    w = tempW;
    h = tempH;

    on = _____;
  }
```



```
}
```

9-9 Processing's array functions

OK, so I have a confession to make. I lied. Well, sort of. See, earlier in this chapter, I made a very big point of emphasizing that once you set the size of an array, you can never change that size. Once you have made 10 Button objects, you can't make an 11th.

And I stand by those statements. Technically speaking, when you allocate 10 spots in an array, you have told Processing exactly how much space in memory you intend to use. You can't expect that block of memory to happen to have more space next to it so that you can expand the size of your array.

However, there is no reason why you couldn't just make a new array (one that has 11 spots in it), copy the first 10 from your original array, and pop a new Button object in the last spot. Processing, in fact, offers a set of array functions that manipulate the size of an array by managing this process for you. They are: shorten(), concat(), subset(), append(), splice(), and expand(). In addition, there are functions for changing the order in an array, such as sort() and reverse().

Details about all of these functions can be found in the reference. Let's look at one example that uses append() to expand the size of an array. This example (which includes an answer to Exercise 8-5 on page 154) starts with an array of one object. Each time the mouse is pressed, a new object is created and appended to the end of the original array.

Example 9-11. Resizing an array using append()

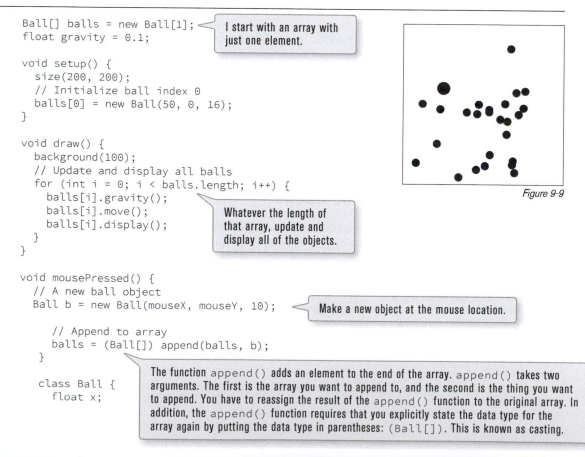

```
Ball[] balls = new Ball[1];      ◁  I start with an array with
float gravity = 0.1;                just one element.

void setup() {
  size(200, 200);
  // Initialize ball index 0
  balls[0] = new Ball(50, 0, 16);
}

void draw() {
  background(100);
  // Update and display all balls
  for (int i = 0; i < balls.length; i++) {
    balls[i].gravity();
    balls[i].move();            Whatever the length of
    balls[i].display();         that array, update and
  }                             display all of the objects.
}

void mousePressed() {
  // A new ball object
  Ball b = new Ball(mouseX, mouseY, 10);   ◁  Make a new object at the mouse location.

  // Append to array
  balls = (Ball[]) append(balls, b);
}

class Ball {
  float x;
```

Figure 9-9

The function append() adds an element to the end of the array. append() takes two arguments. The first is the array you want to append to, and the second is the thing you want to append. You have to reassign the result of the append() function to the original array. In addition, the append() function requires that you explicitly state the data type for the array again by putting the data type in parentheses: (Ball[]). This is known as casting.

```
    float y;
    float speed;
    float w;

    Ball(float tempX, float tempY, float tempW) {
      x = tempX;
      y = tempY;
      w = tempW;
      speed = 0;
    }

    void gravity() {
      // Add gravity to speed
      speed = speed + gravity;
    }

    void move() {
      // Add speed to y location
      y = y + speed;
      // If square reaches the bottom
      // Reverse speed
      if (y > height) {
        speed = speed * -0.95;
        y = height;
      }
    }

    void display() {
    // Display the circle
    fill(255);
    noStroke();
    ellipse(x, y, w, w);
  }
}
```

Another means of having a resizable array is through the use of a special object known as an `ArrayList`, which will be covered in Chapter 23.

9-10 One thousand and one Zoogs

It's time to complete Zoog's journey and look at how to move from one Zoog to many. In the same way that I generated the `Car` array or `Stripe` array example, I can simply copy the exact `Zoog` class created in Example 8-3 and implement an array.

Example 9-12. 200 Zoog objects in an array

```
Zoog[] zoogies = new Zoog[200];

void setup() {
  size(400, 400);
  for (int i = 0; i < zoogies.length; i++) {
    zoogies[i] = new Zoog(random(width), random(height), 30, 30, 8);
  }
```

> The only difference between this example and the previous chapter is the use of an array for multiple `Zoog` objects.

```
}

void draw() {
  background(255);
  for (int i = 0; i < zoogies.length; i++) {
    zoogies[i].display();
    zoogies[i].jiggle();
  }
}

class Zoog {

  // Zoog's variables
  float x;
  float y;
  float w;
  float h;
  float eyeSize;

  // Zoog constructor
  Zoog(float tempX, float tempY, float tempW, float tempH, float tempEyeSize) {
    x = tempX;
    y = tempY;
    w = tempW;
    h = tempH;
    eyeSize = tempEyeSize;
  }

  void jiggle() {
    // Change the location
    x = x + random(-1, 1);
    y = y + random(-1, 1);

    // Constrain Zoog to window
    x = constrain(x, 0, width);
    y = constrain(y, 0, height);
  }

  // Display Zoog
  void display() {


    // Draw Zoog's arms with a for loop
    for (float i = y - h/3; i < y + h/2; i += 10) {
      stroke(0);
      line(x - w/4, i, x + w/4, i);
    }

    // Set ellipses and rects to CENTER mode
    ellipseMode(CENTER);
    rectMode(CENTER);

    // Draw Zoog's body
    stroke(0);
    fill(175);
    rect(x, y, w/6, h);

    // Draw Zoog's head
```

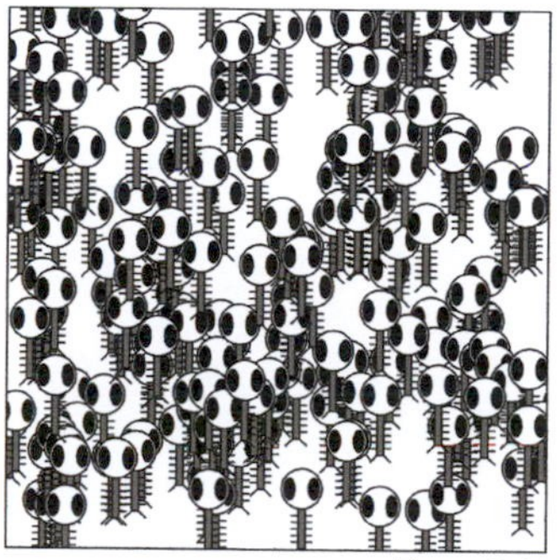

> For simplicity I have also removed the `speed` parameter from the `jiggle()` function. Try adding it back in as an exercise.

Figure 9-10

```
        stroke(0);
        fill(255);
        ellipse(x, y - h, w, h);

        // Draw Zoog's eyes
        fill(0);
        ellipse(x - w/3, y - h, eyeSize, eyeSize*2);
        ellipse(x + w/3, y - h, eyeSize, eyeSize*2);

        // Draw Zoog's legs
        stroke(0);
        line(x - w/12, y + h/2, x - w/4, y + h/2 + 10);
        line(x + w/12, y + h/2, x + w/4, y + h/2 + 10);
    }
}
```

Lesson Four Project

1. Take the Class you made in Lesson Three and make an array of objects from that class.

2. Can you make the objects react to the mouse? Try using the dist() function to determine the object's proximity to the mouse. For example, could you make each object jiggle more the closer it is to the mouse?

How many objects can you make before the sketch runs too slow?

Use the space provided below to sketch designs, notes, and pseudocode for your project.

Lesson Five

Putting It All Together

Chapter 10

Chapter 11

Chapter 12

10 Algorithms

Lather. Rinse. Repeat.
—Unknown

10-1 Where have we been? Where are we going?

Our friend Zoog had a nice run. Zoog taught you the basics of the shape drawing libraries in *Processing*. From there, Zoog advanced to interacting with the mouse, to moving autonomously via variables, changing direction with conditionals, expanding its body with a loop, organizing its code with functions, encapsulating its data and functionality into an object, and finally duplicating itself with an array. It's a good story, and one that treated us well. Nonetheless, it's highly unlikely that all of the programming projects you intend to do after reading this book will involve a collection of alien creatures jiggling around the screen (if they do, you are one lucky programmer!). What I'd like to do now is pause for a moment and consider what you have learned and how it can apply to what *you want to do*. What is your idea and how can variables, conditionals, loops, functions, objects, and arrays help you?

In earlier chapters I focused on straightforward "one feature" programming examples. Zoog would jiggle and only jiggle. Zoog didn't suddenly start hopping. And Zoog was usually all alone, never interacting with other alien creatures along the way. Certainly, I could have taken these early examples further, but it was important at the time to stick with basic functionality so that you could really learn the fundamentals.

In the real world, software projects usually involve many moving parts. This chapter aims to demonstrate how a larger project is created out of many smaller "one feature" programs like the ones you are starting to feel comfortable making. You, the programmer, will start with an overall vision, but must learn how to break it down into individual parts to successfully execute that vision.

I will start with an idea. Ideally, I would pick a sample "idea" that could set the basis for any project you want to create after reading this book. Sadly, there is no such thing. Programming your own software is terrifically exciting because of the immeasurable array of possibilities for creation. Ultimately, you will have to make your own way. However, just as I picked a simple creature for learning the fundamentals, knowing you will not really be programming creatures all of your life, I can attempt to make a generic choice, one that will hopefully serve for learning about the process of developing larger projects.

My choice will be a simple game with interactivity, multiple objects, and a goal. The focus will not be on good game design, but rather on good *software design*. How do you go from thought to code? How do you implement your own algorithm to realize your ideas? I will show how this larger project can be divided into four mini-projects and attack them one by one, ultimately bringing all parts together to execute the original idea.

I will continue to emphasize object-oriented programming, and each one of these parts will be developed using a class. The payoff will be seeing how easy it then is to create the final program by bringing the self-contained, fully functional classes together. Before I get to the idea and its parts, let's review the concept of an *algorithm* which you'll need for steps 2a and 2b.

Process

1. **Idea** — Start with an idea.
2. **Parts** — Break the idea down into smaller parts.

    a. **Algorithm Pseudocode** — For each part, work out the algorithm for that part in pseudocode.

    b. **Algorithm Code** — Implement that algorithm with code.

    c. **Objects** — Take the data and functionality associated with that algorithm and build it into a class.

3. **Integration** — Take all the classes from Step 2 and integrate them into one larger algorithm.

10-2 Algorithms: Dance to the beat of your own drum

An algorithm is a procedure or formula for solving a problem. In computer programming, an algorithm is the sequence of steps required to perform a task. Every single example I have created so far in this book involved an algorithm.

An algorithm is not too far off from a recipe.

1. Preheat the oven to 400°F.
2. Whisk together balsamic vineger, olive oil, and mustard.
3. Bake four portabello mushrooms for 12-15 minutes.
4. Arrange mushrooms on a serving platter and top with dressing.

The above is a nice algorithm for cooking portabello mushrooms. Clearly I am not going to write a Processing program to cook mushrooms. Nevertheless, if I did, the above pseudocode might turn into the following code.

```
preheatOven(400);
placeMushrooms(4, "baking dish");
bake(400, 15);
whisk("balsamic", "olive oil", "mustard");
combine("mushrooms", dressing");
```

An example that uses an algorithm to solve a math problem is more relevant to your pursuits. Let's describe an algorithm to evaluate the sum of a sequence of numbers 1 through N.

$SUM(N) = 1 + 2 + 3 + ... + N$

where N is any given whole number greater than zero.

1. Set SUM = 0 and a counter $i = 1$

2. Repeat the following steps while i is less than or equal to N.

    a. Calculate SUM + i and save the result in SUM.

    b. Increase the value of i by 1.

3. The solution is now the number saved in SUM.

Translating the preceding algorithm into code, I have:

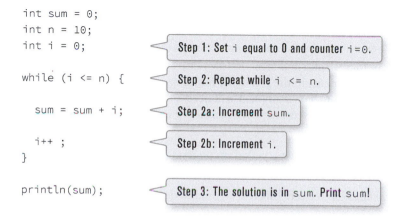

```
int sum = 0;
int n = 10;
int i = 0;              Step 1: Set i equal to 0 and counter i=0.

while (i <= n) {        Step 2: Repeat while i <= n.

    sum = sum + i;      Step 2a: Increment sum.

    i++ ;               Step 2b: Increment i.
}

println(sum);           Step 3: The solution is in sum. Print sum!
```

Traditionally, programming is thought of as the process of (1) developing an idea, (2) working out an algorithm to implement that idea, and (3) writing out the code to implement that algorithm. This is what I have accomplished in both the mushroom and summation examples. Some ideas, however, are too large to be finished in one fell swoop. And so I am going to revise these three steps and say that programming is the process of (1) developing an idea, (2) breaking that idea into smaller manageable parts, (3) working out the algorithm for each part, (4) writing the code for each part, (5) working out the algorithm for all the parts together, and (6) integrating the code for all of the parts together.

This does not mean to say you shouldn't experiment along the way, even altering the original idea completely. And certainly, once the code is finished, there will almost always remain work to do in terms of cleaning up code, bug fixes, and additional features. It is this thinking process, however, that should guide you from idea to code. If you practice developing your projects with this strategy, creating code that implements your ideas will hopefully feel less daunting.

10-3 From idea to parts

To practice this development strategy, I will begin with the idea, a very simple game. Before I can get anywhere, I should describe the game in paragraph form.

Rain game

The object of this game is to catch raindrops before they hit the ground. Every so often (depending on the level of difficulty), a new drop falls from the top of the screen at a random horizontal location with a random vertical speed. The player must catch the raindrops with the mouse with the goal of not letting any raindrops reach the bottom of the screen.

Exercise 10-1: Write out an idea for a project you want to create. Keep it simple, just not too simple. A few elements, a few behaviors will do.

Now let's see if I can take the "Rain Game" idea and break it down into smaller parts. How do I do this? For one, I can start by thinking of the elements in the game: the raindrops and the catcher. Secondly, I should think about these elements' behaviors. For example, I will need a timing mechanism so that the drops fall "every so often". I will also need to determine when a raindrop is "caught." Let's organize these parts more formally.

1. Develop a program with a circle controlled by the mouse. This circle will be the user-controlled "rain catcher."

2. Write a program to test if two circles intersect. This will be used to determine if the rain catcher has caught a raindrop.

3. Write a timer program that executes a function every N seconds.

4. Write a program with circles falling from the top of the screen to the bottom. These will be the raindrops.

Parts 1 through 3 are simple and each can be completed in one fell swoop. However, with Part 4, even though it represents one piece of the larger project, it's complex enough that I will need to complete this exact exercise by breaking it down into smaller steps and building it back up.

Exercise 10-2: Take your idea from Exercise 10-1 on page 192 and write out the individual parts. Try to make the parts as simple as possible (almost to the point that it seems absurd). If the parts are too complex, break them down even further.

Section 10-4 on page 193 to Section 10-7 on page 204 will follow the process of Steps 2a, 2b, and 2c (see "Process" on page 190) for each individual part. For each part, I will first work out the algorithm in pseudocode, then in actual code, and finish with an object-oriented version. If I do my job correctly, all of the functionality needed will be built into a class which can then be easily copied into the final project itself when I get to Step 3 (integration of all parts).

10-4 Part 1: The catcher

This is the simplest part to construct and requires little beyond what I covered in Chapter 3. Having pseudocode that is only two lines long is a good sign, indicating that this step is small enough to handle and does not need to be made into even smaller parts.

Pseudocode:

- Erase background.
- Draw an ellipse at the mouse location.

Translating it into code is easy:

```
void setup() {
  size(400, 400);
}

void draw() {
  background(255);      ◁ Erase background.
  stroke(0);
  fill(175);
  ellipse(mouseX, mouseY, 64, 64);      ◁ Draw an ellipse at the
}                                            mouse location.
```

This is a good step, but I'm not done. As stated, my goal is to develop the rain catcher program in an object-oriented manner. When I take this code and incorporate it into the final program, I will want to have it separated out into a class so that I can make a `Catcher` object. My pseudocode is therefore revised to look like the following.

Setup:

- Initialize catcher object.

Draw:

- Erase background.
- Set catcher location to mouse location.
- Display catcher.

Example 10-1 shows the code rewritten assuming a `Catcher` object.

Example 10-1. Catcher

```
Catcher catcher;

void setup() {
  size(400, 400);
  catcher = new Catcher(32);
}

void draw() {
  background(255);          Erase background.

  catcher.setLocation(mouseX, mouseY);

                            Set catcher location to mouse location.
  catcher.display();
}
                            Display catcher.
```

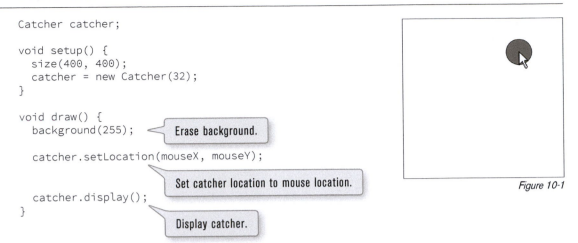

Figure 10-1

The Catcher class itself is rather simple, with variables for location and size, and two functions, one to set the location and one to display.

```
class Catcher {
  float r;    // radius
  float x;    // location
  float y;

  Catcher(float tempR) {
    r = tempR;
    x = 0;
    y = 0;
  }

  void setLocation(float tempX, float tempY) {
    x = tempX;
    y = tempY;
  }

  void display() {
    stroke(0);
    fill(175);
    ellipse(x, y, r*2, r*2);
  }
}
```

10-5 Part 2: Intersection

Part 2 of the list requires me to determine when the catcher and a raindrop intersect. Intersection *functionality* is what I want to focus on developing in this step. I will start with a simple bouncing ball class (which you saw in Example 5-6) and work out how to determine when two bouncing circles intersect. During the "integration" process, this `intersect()` function will be incorporated into the `Catcher` class to catch raindrops.

Here is an algorithm for this intersection part.

Setup:

- Create two ball objects.

Draw:

- Move balls.
- If ball #1 intersects ball #2, change color of both balls to white. Otherwise, leave color gray.
- Display balls.

Certainly the hard work here is the intersection test, which I will get to in a moment. First, here is what I need for a simple bouncing `Ball` class without an intersection test.

Data:

- x and y location.
- Radius.
- Speed in x and y directions.

Functions:

- Constructor.
  - Set radius based on argument.
  - Pick random location.
  - Pick random speed.
- Move.
  - Increment x by speed in x direction.
  - Increment y by speed in y direction.
  - If ball hits any edge, reverse direction.
- Display.
  - Draw a circle at x and y location.

I am now ready to translate this into code.

Example 10-2. Bouncing ball class

```
class Ball {
    float r;                // radius
    float x, y;             // location
    float xspeed, yspeed;   // speed

    Ball(float tempR) {

        r = tempR;                          Set radius based on argument.


        x = random(width);         Pick random location.
        y = random(height);

        xspeed = random(-5, 5);    Pick random speed.
        yspeed = random(-5, 5);
    }

    void move() {

        x += xspeed;           Increment x and y speed.
        y += yspeed;

        // Check horizontal edges
        if (x > width || x < 0) {
            xspeed *= -1;
        }                              If ball hits any edge, reverse direction.

        // Check vertical edges
        if (y > height || y < 0) {
            yspeed *= -1;
        }
    }

    // Draw the ball
    void display() {
        stroke(0);
        fill(0, 50);
        ellipse(x, y, r*2, r*2);       Draw a circle at location.
    }
}
```

From here, it's pretty easy to create a sketch with two ball objects. Ultimately, in the final sketch, I'll need an array for many raindrops, but for now, two ball variables will be simpler.

Example 10-3. Two ball objects

```
// Two Ball variables
Ball ball1;
Ball ball2;

void setup() {
  size(400, 400);
  // Initialize Ball objects
  ball1 = new Ball(64);
  ball2 = new Ball(32);
}

void draw() {
  background(255);
  // Move and display Ball objects
  ball1.move();
  ball2.move();
  ball1.display();
  ball2.display();
}
```

Figure 10-2

Now that I have set up a system for having two circles moving around the screen, I need to develop an algorithm for determining if the circles intersect. In Processing, the `dist()` function calculates the distance between two points (see Section 7-7 on page 132). I also have access to the radius of each circle (the variable `r` inside each object). The diagram in Figure 10-3 shows how I can compare the distance between the circles and the sum of the radii to determine if the circles overlap.

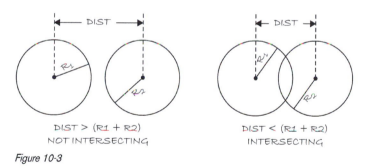

Figure 10-3

OK, so assuming the following:

- x_1,y_1: coordinates of circle one

- x_2,y_2: coordinates of circle two

- r_1: radius of circle one

- r_2: radius of circle two

I have the statement:

If the distance between (x_1,y_1) and (x_2,y_2) is less than the sum of r_1 and r_2, circle one intersects circle two.

My job now is to write a function that returns true or false based on the above statement.

```
// A function that returns true or false based on whether two circles intersect
boolean intersect(float x1, float y1, float x2, float y2, float r1, float r2) {
  // Calculate distance
  float distance = dist(x1, y2, x2, y2);
  if (distance < r1 + r2) {
    return true;
  } else {
    return false;
  }
}
```

> If distance is less than the sum of radii, the circles touch.

Now that the function is complete, I can test it with data from `ball1` and `ball2`.

```
boolean intersecting = intersect(ball1.x,ball1.y,ball2.x,ball2.y,ball1.r,ball2.r);
if (intersecting) {
  println("The circles are intersecting!");
}
```

The above code is awkward due to the number of arguments to `intersect()` and it is useful to go one step further, incorporating the intersection test into the `Ball` class itself. Let's first look at the entire main program as it stands.

```
// Two ball variables
Ball ball1;
Ball ball2;

void setup() {
  size(400, 400);
  // Initialize Ball objects
  ball1 = new Ball(64);
  ball2 = new Ball(32);
}

void draw() {
  background(255);
  // Move and display Ball objects
  ball1.move();
  ball2.move();
  ball1.display();
  ball2.display();
  boolean intersecting = intersect(ball1.x,ball1.y,ball2.x,ball2.y,ball1.r,ball2.r);
  if (intersecting) {
    println("The circles are intersecting!");
  }
}

// A function that returns true or false based on whether two circles intersect
```

```
// If distance is less than the sum of radii the circles touch
boolean intersect(float x1, float y1, float x2, float y2, float r1, float r2) {
  float distance = dist(x1, y2, x2, y2);    // Calculate distance
  if (distance < r1 + r2) {                  // Compare distance to r1 + r2
    return true;
  } else {
    return false;
  }
}
```

Since I have programmed the balls in an object-oriented fashion, it's not terribly logical to suddenly have an `intersect()` function that lives outside of the ball class. A ball object should know how to test if it is intersecting another ball object. The code can be improved by incorporating the intersect logic into the class itself, saying `ball1.intersect(ball2)`; or, "Does ball one intersect ball two?"

```
void draw() {
  background(255);
  // Move and display Ball objects
  ball1.move();
  ball2.move();
  ball1.display();
  ball2.display();
  boolean intersecting = ball1.intersect(ball2);    ← Assumes a function
  if (intersecting) {                                  intersect() inside the
    println("The circles are intersecting!");          Ball class that returns true
  }                                                     or false.
}
```

Following this model and the algorithm for testing intersection, here is a function for inside the ball class itself. Notice how the function makes use of both its own location (x and y) as well as the other ball's location (b.x and b.y).

```
// A function that returns true or false based on whether two Ball objects intersect
boolean intersect(Ball b) {
  float distance = dist(x, y, b.x, b.y);    ← The function is testing this object's
  if (distance < r + b.r) {                   position and radius vs the position and
    return true;                              radius for Ball b.
  } else {
    return false;
  }
}
```

Putting it all together, I have the code in Example 10-4.

Example 10-4. Bouncing ball with intersection

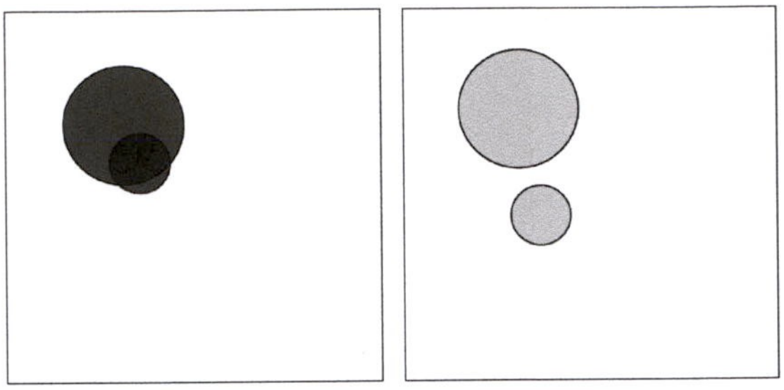

```
// Two ball variables
Ball ball1;
Ball ball2;

void setup() {
  size(400, 400);
  // Initialize Ball objects
  ball1 = new Ball(64);
  ball2 = new Ball(32);
}

void draw() {
  background(255);
  // Move and display Ball objects
  ball1.move();
  ball2.move();
  if (ball1.intersect(ball2)) {
    ball1.highlight();
    ball2.highlight();
  }
  ball1.display();
  ball2.display();
}

class Ball {
  float r; // radius
  float x, y;
  float xspeed, yspeed;
  color c = color(100, 50);

  // Constructor
  Ball(float tempR) {
    r = tempR;
    x = random(width);
    y = random(height);
    xspeed = random(-5, 5);
    yspeed = random(-5, 5);
  }

  void move() {
    x += xspeed;    // Increment x
    y += yspeed;    // Increment y

    // Check horizontal edges
    if (x > width || x < 0) {
      xspeed *= -1;
    }
    // Check vertical edges
    if (y > height || y < 0) {
      yspeed *= -1;
    }
  }

  void highlight() {
    c = color(0, 150);
  }
```

Figure 10-4

> New! An object can have a function that takes another object as an argument. This is one way to have objects communicate. In this case they are checking to see if they intersect.

> Whenever the circles are touching, this highlight() function is called and the color is darkened.

```
// Draw the ball
void display() {
  stroke(0);
  fill(c);
  ellipse(x ,y, r*2, r*2);
  c = color(100, 50);
}
```

> After the ball is displayed, the color is reset back to a darker gray.

```
// A function that returns true or false based on whether two circles intersect
// If distance is less than the sum of radii the circles touch
boolean intersect(Ball b) {
  float distance = dist(x, y, b.x, b.y); // Calculate distance
  if (distance < r + b.r) {              // Compare distance
    return true;                         // to sum of radii
  } else {
    return false;
  }
}
```

> Objects can be passed into functions as arguments too!

10-6 Part 3: The timer

Our next task is to develop a timer that executes a function every *N* seconds. Again, we will do this in two steps, first just using the main body of a program and second, taking the logic and putting it into a `Timer` class. Processing has the functions `hour()`, `second()`, `minute()`, `month()`, `day()`, and `year()` to deal with time. I could conceivably use the `second()` function to determine how much time has passed. However, this is not terribly convenient, since `second()` rolls over from 60 to 0 at the end of every minute.

For creating a timer, the function `millis()` is best. First of all, `millis()`, which returns the number of milliseconds since a sketch started, allows for a great deal more precision. One millisecond is one one-thousandth of a second (1,000 ms = 1 s). Secondly, `millis()` never rolls back to zero, so asking for the milliseconds at one moment and subtracting it from the milliseconds at a later moment will always result in the amount of time passed.

Let's say I want a sketch to change the background color to red five seconds after it started. Five seconds is 5,000 ms, so it's as easy as checking if the result of the `millis()` function is greater than 5,000.

```
if (millis() > 5000) {
  background(255, 0, 0);
}
```

Making the problem a bit more complicated, I can expand the program to change the background to a new random color every 5 seconds.

Setup:

- Save the time at startup (note this should always be zero, but it's useful to save it in a variable anyway). Call this savedTime.

Draw:

- Calculate the time passed as the current time (i.e., millis()) minus savedTime. Save this as passedTime.
- If passedTime is greater than 5,000, fill a new random background and *reset* savedTime *to the current time*. This step will restart the timer.

Example 10-5 translates this into code.

Example 10-5. Implementing a timer

```
int savedTime;
int totalTime = 5000;

void setup() {
  size(200, 200);
  background(0);
  savedTime = millis();          Save the time.
}

void draw() {
  int passedTime = millis() - savedTime;      Calculate how much time has passed.


  if (passedTime > totalTime) {    Has five seconds passed?

    println("5 seconds have passed!");
    background(random(255)); // Color a new background
    savedTime = millis();    // Save the current time to restart the timer!
  }
}
```

With the above logic worked out, I can now move the timer into a class. Let's think about what data is involved in the timer. A timer must know the time at which it started (savedTime) and how long it needs to run (totalTime).

Data:

- savedTime
- totalTime

The timer must also be able to *start* as well as check and see if it *is finished*.

Functions:

- start()

- isFinished()—returns true or false

Taking the code from the non-object-oriented example and building it out with the above structure, I have the code shown in Example 10-6.

Example 10-6. Object-oriented timer

```
Timer timer;

void setup() {
  size(200, 200);
  background(0);
  timer = new Timer(5000);
  timer.start();
}

void draw() {
  if (timer.isFinished()) {
    background(random(255));
    timer.start();
  }
}

class Timer {
  int savedTime;   // When Timer started
  int totalTime;   // How long Timer should last

  Timer(int tempTotalTime) {
    totalTime = tempTotalTime;
  }

  // Starting the timer
  void start() {
    savedTime = millis();
  }

  boolean isFinished() {
    // Check how much time has passed
    int passedTime = millis() - savedTime;
    if (passedTime > totalTime) {
      return true;
    } else {
      return false;
    }
  }
}
```

> When the timer starts it stores the current time in milliseconds.

> The function isFinished() returns true if 5,000 ms have passed. The work of the timer is farmed out to this method.

10-7 Part 4: Raindrops

I'm almost there. I have created a `Catcher` class, I know how to test for intersection, and I have completed the `Timer` class. The final piece of the puzzle is the raindrops themselves. Ultimately, I want an array of `Drop` objects falling from the top of the window to the bottom. Since this step involves creating an array of objects that move, it's useful to approach this fourth part as a series of even smaller steps, subparts of Part 4, thinking again of the individual elements and behaviors I will need.

Part 4 Subparts:

> **Part 4.1:** A single moving raindrop.

> **Part 4.2:** An array of raindrop objects.

> **Part 4.3:** Flexible number of raindrops (appearing one at a time).

> **Part 4.4:** Fancier raindrop appearance.

Part 4.1, creating the motion of a raindrop (a simple circle for now) is easy — Chapter 3 easy.

- Increment raindrop's y position.
- Display raindrop.

Translating into code, I have *Part 4.1 — A single moving raindrop*, shown in Example 10-7.

Example 10-7. Simple raindrop behavior

```
float x, y; // Variables for drop location

void setup() {
  size(400, 400);
  x = width/2;
  y = 0;
}

void draw() {
  background(255);
  // Display the drop
  fill(50, 100, 150);
  noStroke();
  ellipse(x, y, 16, 16);
  // Move the drop
  y++;
}
```

Again, however, I need to go a step further and make a `Drop` class — after all I will ultimately want an array of drops. In making the class, I can add a few more variables, such as speed and size, as well as a function to test if the raindrop reaches the bottom of the screen, which will be useful later for scoring the game.

```
class Drop {

    float x, y;      // Variables for location of raindrop
    float speed;     // Speed of raindrop
    color c;
    float r;         // Radius of raindrop
```

> A raindrop object has a location, speed, color, and size.

```
    Drop() {
        r = 8;                    // All raindrops are the same size
        x = random(width);        // Start with a random x location
        y = -r*4;                 // Start a little above the window
        speed = random(1, 5);     // Pick a random speed
        c = color(50, 100, 150);  // Color
    }

    // Move the raindrop down
    void move() {
        y += speed;
    }
```

> Incrementing y is now in the move() function.

```
    // Check if it hits the bottom
    boolean reachedBottom() {
        if (y > height + r*4) {
            return true;
        } else {
            return false;
        }
    }
```

> In addition, I have a function that determines if the drop leaves the window.

```
    // Display the raindrop
    void display() {
        fill(50, 100, 150);
        noStroke();
        ellipse(x, y, r*2, r*2);
    }
}
```

Before I move on to Part 4.3, the array of drops, I should make sure that a singular Drop object functions properly. As an exercise, complete the code in Exercise 10-3 on page 206 that would test a single drop object.

Exercise 10-3: Fill in the blanks below completing the "test drop" sketch.

```
Drop drop;

void setup() {
  size(200, 200);


  _____

}

void draw() {
  background(255);

  drop._____


  _____

}
```

Now that this is complete, the next step is to go from one drop to an array of drops — *Part 4.2*. This is exactly the technique you perfected in Chapter 9.

```
// An array of drops
Drop[] drops = new Drop[50];        Instead of one Drop object, an array of 50.

void setup() {
  size(400, 400);
  // Initialize all drops
  for (int i = 0; i < drops.length; i++) {    Using a loop to initialize all drops.
    drops[i] = new Drop();
  }
}

void draw() {
  background(255);
  // Move and display all drops
  for (int i = 0; i < drops.length; i++) {    Move and display all drops.
    drops[i].move();
    drops[i].display();
  }
}
```

The problem with the above code is that the raindrops appear all at once. According to the specifications I made for the game, the raindrops should appear one at a time, every *N* seconds — I am now at *Part 4.3* — *Flexible number of raindrops (appearing one at a time)*. I can skip worrying about the timer for now and just have one new raindrop appear every frame. I should also make the array much larger, allowing for many more raindrops.

To make this work, I need a new variable to keep track of the total number of drops — `totalDrops`. Most array examples involve walking through the entire array in order to deal with the entire list. Now, I want to access a portion of the list, the number stored in `totalDrops`. Let's write some pseudocode to describe this process:

Setup:

- Create an array of drops with 1,000 spaces in it.
- Set `totalDrops` equal to 0.

Draw:

- Create a new drop in the array (at the index `totalDrops`). Since `totalDrops` starts at 0, I will first create a new raindrop in the first spot of the array.
- Increment `totalDrops` (so that the next time, a drop is created in the next spot in the array).
- If `totalDrops` exceeds the array size, reset it to zero and start over.
- Move and display all available drops (i.e., `totalDrops`).

Example 10-8 translates the above pseudocode into code.

Example 10-8. Drops one at a time

```
// An array of drops
Drop[] drops = new Drop[1000];

int totalDrops = 0;        New variable to keep track of
                           total number of drops!

void setup() {
  size(400, 400);
}

void draw() {
  background(255);

  // Initialize one drop
  drops[totalDrops] = new Drop();
  // Increment totalDrops
  totalDrops++ ;
  // If totalDrops hits the end of the array
  if (totalDrops >= drops.length) {
    totalDrops = 0; //Start over
  }

  // Move and display drops
  for (int i = 0; i < totalDrops; i++) {
    drops[i].move();
    drops[i].display();      New! All drops are no longer displayed, rather
  }                          only the totalDrops that are currently
}                            present in the game are shown.
```

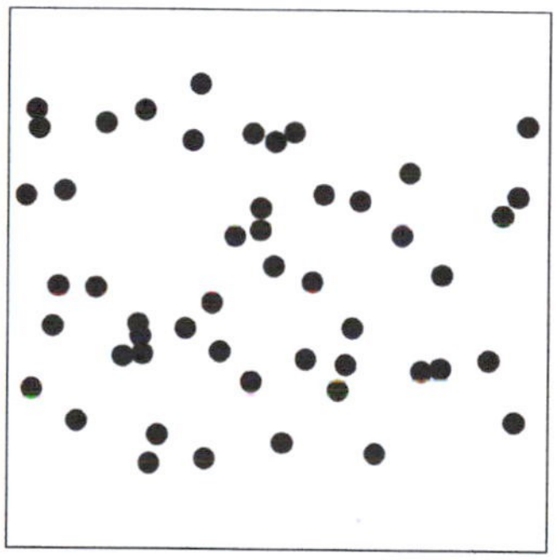

Figure 10-5

I have taken the time to figure out how the raindrop moves, created a class that exhibits that behavior, and made an array of objects from that class. All along, however, I have just been using a circle to display the drop. The advantage to this is that I was able to delay worrying about the code required for visual design and focus on the motion behaviors and organization of data and functions. Now I can focus on how the drops look — *Part 4.4 — Finalize raindrop appearance.*

One way to create a more "drop-like" look is to draw a sequence of circles in the vertical direction, starting small, and getting larger as they move down.

Example 10-9. Fancier looking raindrop

```
background(255);
for (int i = 2; i < 8; i++) {
  noStroke();
  fill(0);
  ellipse(width/2, height/2 + i*4, i*2, i*2);
}
```

I can incorporate this algorithm in the Drop class from Example 10-8, using x and y for the start of the ellipse locations, and the raindrop radius as the maximum value for i in the for loop. The output is shown in Figure 10-7.

Figure 10-6

```
void display() {
  noStroke();
  fill(c);
  for (int i = 2; i < r; i++) {
    ellipse(x, y + i*4, i*2, i*2);
  }
}
```

Figure 10-7

10-8 Integration: Puttin' on the ritz

It is time. Now that I have developed the individual pieces and confirmed that each one works properly, I can assemble them together in one program. The first step is to create a new Processing sketch that has four tabs, one for each of the three classes and one main program, as shown in Figure 10-8.

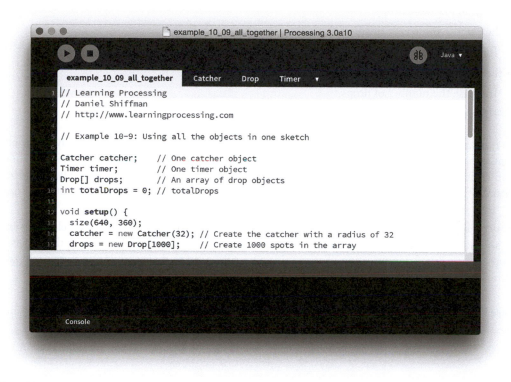

```
// Learning Processing
// Daniel Shiffman
// http://www.learningprocessing.com

// Example 10-9: Using all the objects in one sketch

Catcher catcher;      // One catcher object
Timer timer;          // One timer object
Drop[] drops;         // An array of drop objects
int totalDrops = 0;   // totalDrops

void setup() {
  size(640, 360);
  catcher = new Catcher(32);  // Create the catcher with a radius of 32
  drops = new Drop[1000];     // Create 1000 spots in the array
```

Figure 10-8

The first step is to copy and paste the code for each class into each tab. Individually, they will not need to change, so there is no need to revisit the code. What I do need to revisit is the main program — what goes in setup() and draw(). Referring back to the original game description and knowing how the pieces were assembled, I can write the pseudocode algorithm for the entire game.

Setup:

- Create Catcher object.
- Create array of Drop objects.
- Set totalDrops equal to 0.
- Create Timer object.
- Start timer.

Draw:

- Set catcher location to mouse location.
- Display catcher.
- Move all available drops.
- Display all available drops.
- If the catcher intersects any drop.
  — Remove drop from screen.
- If the timer is finished:
  — Increase the number of drops.
  — Restart timer.

Notice how every single step in the above program has already been worked out previously in the chapter with one exception: "Remove drop from screen." This is rather common. Even with breaking the idea down into parts and working them out one at a time, little bits can be missed. Fortunately, this piece of functionality is simple enough and with some ingenuity, you will see how I can slip it in during assembly.

One way to approach assembling the above algorithm is to start by combining all of the elements into one sketch and not worrying about how they interact. In other words, everything but having the timer trigger the drops and testing for intersection. To get this going, all I need to do is copy/paste from each part's global variables, `setup()` and `draw()`!

Here are the global variables: a `Catcher` object, an array of `Drop` objects, a `Timer` object, and an integer to store the total number of drops.

```
Catcher catcher;      // One catcher object
Timer timer;          // One timer object
Drop[] drops;         // An array of drop objects

int totalDrops = 0;   // totalDrops
```

In `setup()`, the variables are initialized. Note, however, I can skip initializing the individual drops in the array since they will be created one at a time. I will also need to call the timer's `start()` function.

```
void setup() {
  size(400, 400);

  catcher = new Catcher(32);     // Create the catcher with a radius of 32
  drops = new Drop[1000];        // Create 1000 spots in the array
  timer = new Timer(2000);       // Create a timer that goes off every 2 seconds
  timer.start();                 // Starting the timer
}
```

In `draw()`, the objects call their methods. Again, I am just taking the code from each part I did separately earlier in this chapter and pasting in sequence.

Example 10-10. Using all the objects in one sketch

```
Catcher catcher;      // One catcher object
Timer timer;          // One timer object
Drop[] drops;         // An array of drop objects

int totalDrops = 0;   // totalDrops

void setup() {
  size(400, 400);

  catcher = new Catcher(32);   // Create the catcher with a radius of 32
  drops = new Drop[1000];      // Create 1000 spots in the array
  timer = new Timer(2000);     // Create a timer that goes off every 2 seconds

  timer.start();               // Starting the timer
}

void draw() {
  background(255);
```

```
  // Set catcher location
  catcher.setLocation(mouseX, mouseY);
  // Display the catcher
  catcher.display();
```
From Part 1. The Catcher!

```
  // Check the timer
  if (timer.isFinished()) {
    println("2 seconds have passed!");
    timer.start();
  }
```
From Part 3. The Timer!

```
  // Initialize one drop
  drops[totalDrops] = new Drop();
  // Increment totalDrops
  totalDrops++;
  // If totalDrops hit the end of the array
  if (totalDrops >= drops.length) {
    totalDrops = 0; // Start over
  }

  // Move and display all drops
  for (int i = 0; i < totalDrops; i++) {
    drops[i].move();
    drops[i].display();
  }
```
From Part 4. The Raindrops!

```
}
```

The next step is to take these concepts I have developed and have them work together. For example, a new raindrop should only be created when two seconds have passed (as indicated by the timer's isFinished() function).

```
// Check the timer
if (timer.isFinished()) {

  // Initialize one drop
  drops[totalDrops] = new Drop();
  // Increment totalDrops
  totalDrops++;
  // If totalDrops hit the end of the array
  if (totalDrops >= drops.length) {
    totalDrops = 0; // Start over
  }
  timer.start();
}
```

> Concepts working together! Here when the timer "is finished," a Drop object is added (by incrementing totalDrops).

I also need to find out when the Catcher object intersects a drop. In Section 10-5 on page 195, I tested for intersection by calling the intersect() function inside the Ball class.

```
boolean intersecting = ball1.intersect(ball2);
if (intersecting) {
  println("The circles are intersecting!");
}
```

I can do the same thing here, calling an intersect() function in the Catcher class and passing through every raindrop in the system. Instead of printing out a message, I want to affect the raindrop itself, telling it to disappear, perhaps. This code assumes that the caught() function will do the job.

```
// Move and display all drops
for (int i = 0; i < totalDrops; i++) {
  drops[i].move();
  drops[i].display();
  if (catcher.intersect(drops[i])) {
    drops[i].caught();
  }
}
```

> Concepts working together! Here, the Catcher object checks to see if it intersects any Drop object in the drops array.

Our Catcher class did not originally contain the function intersect(), nor did the Drop class include caught(). So these are new functions I will need to write as part of the integration process.

intersect() is easy to incorporate; that problem was solved already in Section 10-5 on page 195 and can be copied into the Catcher class (changing the parameter from a Ball object to a Drop object).

```
// A function that returns true or false based if the catcher intersects a raindrop
boolean intersect(Drop d) {
  // Calculate distance
  float distance = dist(x, y, d.x, d.y);
  // Compare distance to sum of radii
```

```
    if (distance < r + d.r) {
        return true;
    } else {
        return false;
    }
}
```

> In addition to calling functions, variables inside of an object can be accessed using the dot syntax.

When the drop is caught, I can set its location to somewhere offscreen (so that it can't be seen, the equivalent of "disappearing") and stop it from moving by setting its speed equal to 0. Although I did not work out this functionality in advance of the integration process, it's simple enough to throw in right now.

```
// If the drop is caught
void caught() {
    speed = 0;      // Stop it from moving by setting speed equal to zero
    y = -1000;      // Set the location to somewhere way off-screen
}
```

And it's finished! For reference, Example 10-11 is the entire sketch. The timer is altered to execute every 300 ms, making the game ever so slightly more difficult.

Example 10-11. The raindrop catching game

```
Catcher catcher;        // One catcher object
Timer timer;            // One timer object
Drop[] drops;           // An array of drop objects

int totalDrops = 0;     // totalDrops
void setup() {
    size(400, 400);

    // Create the catcher with a radius of 32
    catcher = new Catcher(32);
    // Create 1000 spots in the array
    drops = new Drop[1000];
    // Create and start a timer that goes off every 300
milliseconds
    timer = new Timer(300);
    timer.start();
}

void draw() {
    background(255);
    catcher.setLocation(mouseX, mouseY);    // Set catcher location
    catcher.display();                      // Display the catcher

    // Check the timer
    if (timer.isFinished()) {
        // Initialize one drop
        drops[totalDrops] = new Drop();
        // Increment totalDrops
        totalDrops++ ;
        // If totalDrops hit the end of the array
        if (totalDrops >= drops.length) {
            totalDrops = 0; // Start over
```

Figure 10-9

```
    }
    timer.start();
  }

  // Move and display all drops
  for (int i = 0; i < totalDrops; i++) {
    drops[i].move();
    drops[i].display();
    if (catcher.intersect(drops[i])) {
      drops[i].caught();
    }
  }
}

class Catcher {
  float r;      // radius
  color col;    // color
  float x, y;   // location

  Catcher(float tempR) {
    r = tempR;
    col = color(50, 10, 10, 150);
    x = 0;
    y = 0;
  }

  void setLocation(float tempX, float tempY) {
    x = tempX;
    y = tempY;
  }

  void display() {
    stroke(0);
    fill(col);
    ellipse(x, y, r*2, r*2);
  }

  // Returns true if the catcher intersects a raindrop, otherwise false
  boolean intersect(Drop d) {
    float distance = dist(x, y, d.x, d.y);    // Calculate distance
    if (distance < r + d.r) {                 // Compare distance to sum of radii
      return true;
    } else {
      return false;
    }
  }

}

class Drop {

  float x, y;      // Variables for location of raindrop
  float speed;     // Speed of raindrop
  color c;
  float r;         // Radius of raindrop

  Drop() {
    r = 8;                          // All raindrops are the same size
```

```
    x = random(width);        // Start with a random x location
    y = -r*4;                 // Start a little above the window
    speed = random(1, 5);     // Pick a random speed
    c = color(50, 100, 150);  // Color
  }

  // Move the raindrop down
  void move() {
    y += speed; // Increment by speed
  }

  // Display the raindrop
  void display() {
    // Display the drop
    fill(c);
    noStroke();
    for (int i = 2; i < r; i++) {
     ellipse(x, y+i*4, i*2, i*2);
    }
  }

  // If the drop is caught
  void caught() {
    speed = 0; // Stop it from moving by setting speed equal to zero
    y = -1000; // Set the location to somewhere way off-screen
  }
}

class Timer {

  int savedTime; // When Timer started
  int totalTime; // How long Timer should last

  Timer(int tempTotalTime) {
    totalTime = tempTotalTime;
  }

  // Starting the timer
  void start() {
    savedTime = millis();
  }

  boolean isFinished() {
    // Check out much time has passed
    int passedTime = millis()- savedTime;
    if (passedTime > totalTime) {
      return true;
    } else {
      return false;
    }
  }

}
```

Exercise 10-4: Implement a scoring system for the game. Start the player off with 10 points. For every raindrop that reaches the bottom, decrease the score by 1. If all 1,000 raindrops fall without the score getting to zero, a new level begins and the raindrops appear faster. If 10 raindrops reach the bottom during any level, the player loses. Show the score onscreen as a rectangle that decreases in size. Do not try to implement all of these features at once. Do them one step at a time! Following is a clue to get you started, a function for the Drop *class to determine if the* Drop *object has reached the bottom of the window.*

```
boolean reachedBottom() {
  // If the drop goes a little beyond the bottom
  if (y > height + r*4) {
    return true;
  } else {
    return false;
  }
}
```

10-9 Getting ready for Act II

The point of this chapter is not to learn how to program a game of catching falling raindrops, rather it's to develop an approach to problem solving — taking an idea, breaking it down into parts, developing pseudocode for those parts, and implementing them one very small step at a time.

It's important to remember that getting used to this process takes time and it takes practice. Everyone struggles through it when first learning to program.

Before you embark on the rest of this book, let's take a moment to consider what you have learned and where you are headed. In these 10 chapters, I have focused entirely on the fundamentals of programming:

- **Data** — in the form of variables and arrays.
- **Control Flow** — in the form of conditional statements and loops.
- **Organization** — in the form of functions and objects.

These concepts are not unique to Processing and will carry you through to any and all programming languages and environments, such as C++, Python, JavaScript, and more. The syntax may change, but the fundamental concepts will not.

Starting with Chapter 13, the book will focus on some advanced concepts available in Processing, such as three-dimensional translation and rotation, image processing and video capture, networking, and sound. Although these concepts are certainly not unique to Processing, the details of their implementation will be more specific to this particular environment.

Before I move on to these advanced topics I will take a quick look at basic strategies for fixing errors in your code (Chapter 11: Debugging) as well as how to use Processing libraries (Chapter 12). Many of these advanced topics require importing libraries that come with Processing as well as libraries made by third parties. One of the strengths of Processing is its ability to be easily extended with libraries. You will read some hints of how to create your own libraries in the final chapter of this book.

Onward, ho!

Lesson Five Project

1. Develop an idea for a project that can be created with Processing using simple shape drawing and the fundamentals of programming. If you feel stuck, try making a game such as Pong or Tic-Tac-Toe.

2. Follow the strategy outlined in this chapter and break the idea down into smaller parts, implementing the algorithm for each one individually. Make sure to use object-oriented programming for each part.

3. Bring the smaller parts together in one program. Did you forget any elements or features?

Use the space provided below to sketch designs, notes, and pseudocode for your project.

11 Debugging

The difference between the right word and the almost-right word is the difference between lightning and a lightning bug.
—Mark Twain

"L'appétit vient en mangeant."
—The French

Bugs happen.

Five minutes ago, your code was working perfectly and you swear, all you did was change the color of some object! But now, when the spaceship hits the asteroid, it doesn't spin any more. But it was totally spinning five minutes ago! And your friend agrees: "Yeah, I saw it spin. That was cool." The `rotate()` function is there. What happened? It should work. This makes no sense at all! The computer is probably broken. Yeah. *Yeah.* It is definitely the computer's fault.

No matter how much time you spend studying computer science, reading programming books, or playing audio recordings of code while you sleep hoping it will soak in that way, there is just no way to avoid getting stuck on a bug.

It can be really frustrating.

A bug is any defect in a program. Sometimes it's obvious that you have a bug; your sketch will quit (or not run at all) and display an error in the message console. These types of bugs can be caused by simple typos, variables that were never initialized, looking for an element in an array that doesn't exist, and so on. For some additional clues on "error" bugs, take a look at the Appendix on errors at the end of this book.

Bugs can also be more sinister and mysterious. If your Processing sketch does not function the way you intended it to, you have a bug. In this case, your sketch might run without producing any errors in the message console. Finding this type of bug is more difficult since it will not necessarily be as obvious where to start looking in the code.

In this chapter, I will discuss a few basic strategies for fixing bugs ("debugging") with Processing.

11-1 Tip #1: Take a break

Seriously. Go away from your computer. Sleep. Go jogging. Eat an orange. Play scrabble. Do something other than working on your code. I can't tell you how many times I have stared at my code for hours unable to fix it, only to wake up the next morning and solve the problem in five minutes.

11-2 Tip #2: Get another human being involved

Talk through the problem with a friend. The process of showing your code to another programmer (or non-programmer, even) and walking through the logic out loud will often reveal the bug. In many cases, it's something obvious that you did not see because you know your code so well. The process of explaining it to someone else, however, forces you to go through the code more slowly. If you do not have a friend nearby, you can also do this out loud to yourself. Yes, you will look silly, but it helps.

11-3 Tip #3: Simplify

Simplify. Simplify! SIMPLIFY!

In Chapter 10, I focused on the process of incremental development. The more you develop your projects step-by-step, in small, easy-to-manage pieces, the fewer errors and bugs you will end up having. Of course, there is no way to avoid problems completely, so when they do occur, the philosophy of incremental development can also be applied to debugging. Instead of building the code up piece by piece, debugging involves taking the code apart piece by piece.

One way to accomplish this is to comment out large chunks of code in order to isolate a particular section. Following is the main tab of an example sketch. The sketch has an array of Snake objects, a Button object, and an Apple object. (The code for the classes is not included.) Let's assume that everything about the sketch is working properly, except that the Apple is invisible. To debug the problem, everything is commented out except for the few lines of code that deal directly with initializing and displaying the Apple object.

```
// Snake[] snakes = new Snake[100];
// Button button;
Apple apple;

void setup() {
  size(200, 200);
  apple = new Apple();
  /*for (int i = 0; i < snakes.length; i ++) {
    snakes[i] = new Snake();
  }
  button = new Button(10, 10, 100, 50);*/
}

void draw() {
```

> Only the code that makes the Apple object is left in. This way, you can be sure that none of the other code is the cause of the issue.

```
    background(0);
    apple.display();
    // apple.move();
}
```

Once again, only the code that displays the `Apple` object is left uncommented.

```
/*
    for (int i = 0; i < snakes.length; i++) {
        snakes[i].display();
        snakes[i].slither();
        snakes[i].eat(apple);
    }

    if (button.pressed()) {
        apple.restart();
    }
*/


}
```

Large blocks of code can be commented out between /* and */

```
/*All of this is
commented out */
```

```
/*
void mousePressed() {
    button.click(mouseX, mouseY);
}*/
```

Once all the code is commented out, there are two possible outcomes. Either the apple still does not appear or it does. In the former, the issue is most definitely caused by the apple itself, and the next step would be to investigate the insides of the `display()` function and look for a mistake.

If the apple does appear, then the problem is caused by one of the other lines of code. Perhaps the `move()` function sends the apple offscreen so that you do not see it. Or maybe the snakes cover it up by accident. To figure this out, I would recommend putting back lines of code, one at a time. Each time you add back in a line of code, run the sketch and see if the apple disappears. As soon as it does, you have found the culprit and can root out the cause. Having an object-oriented sketch as above (with many classes) can really help the debugging process. Another tactic you can try is to create a new sketch and just use one of the classes, testing its basic features. In other words, do not worry about fixing your entire program just yet. First, create a new sketch that only does one thing with the relevant class (or classes) and reproduce the error. Let's say that, instead of the apple, the snakes are not behaving properly. To simplify and find the bug, you could create a sketch that just uses one snake (instead of an array) without the apple or the button. Without the bells and whistles, the code will be much easier to deal with.

```
Snake snake;

void setup() {
  size(200, 200);
  snake = new Snake();
}

void draw() {
  background(0);
  snakes.display();
  snakes.slither();
  // snakes.eat(apple);
}
```

> Since this version does not include an `Apple` object, I cannot use this line of code. As part of the debugging process, however, I might incrementally add back in the apple and uncomment this line.

Although I have not yet looked at examples that involve external devices (I will in many of the chapters that follow), simplifying your sketch can also involve turning off connections to these devices, such as a camera, microphone, or network connection and replacing them with "dummy" information. For example, it's much easier to find an image analysis problem if you just load a JPG, rather than use a live video source. Or load a local text file instead of connecting to a URL XML feed. If the problem goes away, you can then say definitively: "Aha, the web server is probably down" or "My camera must be broken." If it does not, then you can dive into your code knowing the problem is there. If you're worried about worsening the problem by taking out sections of code, just make a copy of your sketch first before you begin removing features.

11-4 Tip #4: `println()` is your friend

Using the message window to display the values of variables can be really helpful. If an object is completely missing on the screen and you want to know why, you can print out the values of its location variables. It might look something like this:

```
println(x, y);
```

Let's say the result is:

```
9000000 -900000
9000116 -901843
9000184 -902235
9000299 -903720
9000682 -904903
```

It's pretty obvious that these values are not reasonable pixel coordinates. So something would be off in the way the object is calculating its (x,y) location. However, if the values were perfectly reasonable, then you would move on. Maybe the color is the problem?

```
println("brightness: " + brightness(thing.col) + " alpha: " + alpha(thing.col));
```

Resulting in:

```
brightness: 150.0 alpha: 0.0
```

Well, if the alpha value of the object's color is zero, that would explain why you can't see it! Let's take a moment here to remember Tip #3: Simplify. This process of printing variable values will be much more effective if you are doing it in a sketch that only deals with the Thing object. This way, you can be sure that it is not another class which is, say, drawing over the top of the thing by accident.

You may have also noticed that the above print statements are written two different ways. The first one includes two variables separated by a comma. println() can receive any number of variables and will automatically display them separated by a space. You can also concatenate actual text with the variables or the results of function calls, as seen with brightness() and alpha(). The specifics of how this works will be explained in Chapter 17. It's generally a good idea to do this. For example, take the following line of code that only prints the value of x, with no explanation.

```
println(x);
```

This can be confusing to follow in the message window, especially if you're printing different values in different parts of the code. How do you know what is x and what is y ? If you include your own notes in println(), there can't be any confusion:

```
println("The x value of the thing I'm looking for is: " + x);
```

In addition, println() can be used to indicate whether or not a certain part of the code has been reached. For example, what if in the "bouncing ball" example, the ball never bounces off of the right-hand side of the window? The problem could be (a) you are not properly determining when it hits the edge, or (b) you are doing the wrong thing when it hits the edge. To know if your code correctly detects when it hits the edge, you could write:

```
if (x > width) {
  println("x is greater than width. This code is happening now!");
  xspeed *= -1;
}
```

If you run the sketch and never see the message printed, then something is probably flawed with your boolean expression.

Finally, for examining the contents of an array in the console, printArray() should be used. The printArray() function will format the array contents nicely as well as show the index values.

```
float[] values = new float[10];
for (int i = 0; i < values.length; i++) {
  values[i] = random(10);
}
printArray(values);
```

Admittedly, println() and printArray() are not perfect debugging tools. It can be hard to track multiple pieces of information with the message window. It can also slow your sketch down rather significantly (depending on how much printing you are doing). The newest version of Processing (3) also includes a debugging tool (which you can enable via the "Debug" menu option or by clicking the debugger icon as pictured below).

The debugger allows you to pause the program (by specifying a *breakpoint*) and advance line by line in the code (known as *stepping*). Figure 11-1 shows a sketched paused at a specific breakpoint. You can see the state of current variables in the debugger window. You then have the option of either continuing which will run the code again until the next breakpoint or stepping line by line.

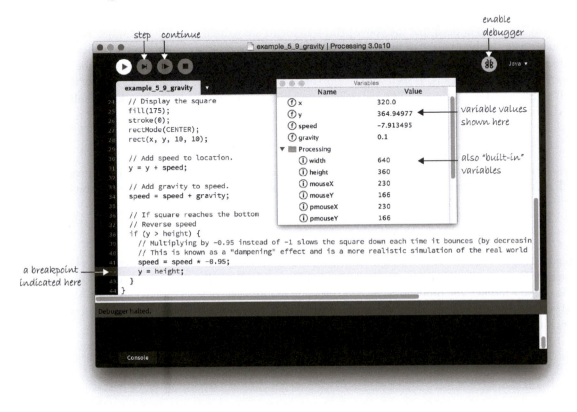

Figure 11-1

While the debugger tool is very useful, sometimes some sleep, a friend to talk to, and a little common sense is all you need.

12 Libraries

If truth is beauty, how come no one has their hair done in the library?
—Lily Tomlin

Many of the chapters that follow require the use of Processing libraries. This chapter will cover how to download, install, and use these libraries. I recommend that you read the chapter for a basic sense of libraries now and, if necessary, refer back to it when you suddenly find yourself downloading one (which first occurs in Chapter 15: Video).

12-1 Libraries

Whenever you call a Processing function, such as line(), background(), stroke(), and so on, you are calling a function that you learned about from the Processing reference page (or perhaps even from this book!). That reference page is a list of all the available functions in the Processing's *core library*. In computer science, a library refers to a collection of "helper" code. A library might consist of functions, variables, and objects. The bulk of things you do are made possible by the core Processing library.

In most programming languages, you are required to specify which libraries you intend to use at the top of your code. This tells the compiler (see Chapter 2) where to look things up in order to translate your source code into machine code. If you were to investigate the files inside of the Processing application itself, you would find a file named *core.jar*. That file contains the compiled code for just about everything you do in Processing. Since it's used in every program, Processing just assumes that it should be imported and does not require that you explicitly write an import statement. However, if this were not the case, you would have the following line of code at the top of every single sketch:

```
import processing.core.*;
```

import indicates you are going to make use of a library, and the library you using is "processing.core" The ".*" is a wildcard, meaning you would like access to everything in the library. The naming of the library using the dot syntax (processing dot core) has to do with how collections of classes are organized into "packages" in the Java programming language. As you get more comfortable with Processing and programming, this is likely a topic you will want to investigate further. For now, all you need to know is that "processing.core" is the name of the library.

While the *core* library covers all the basics, for other more advanced functionality, you will have to import specific libraries that are not *assumed*. Your first encounter with this will come in Chapter 16, where in order pull images from a camera, the Processing video library will be required:

```
import processing.video.*;
```

Many of the chapters that follow will require the explicit use of Processing libraries, such as video, networking, serial, and so on. Documentation for these libraries can be found on the Processing website libraries page (*http://www.processing.org/reference/libraries/*). There, you will find a list of libraries that come with Processing, as well as links to third party libraries available for download on the web.

12-2 Built-in libraries

Some built-in libraries require no installation process. These libraries come with your Processing application. The list of built-in libraries (full list available at above URL) is not terribly long and the following libraries are covered in this book. The last two (video and sound) require a separate installation process as described in the next section.

- **Serial** — For sending data between Processing and an external device via serial communication. Covered in Chapter 19.
- **Network** — For creating client and server sketches that can communicate across the internet. Covered in Chapter 19.
- **PDF** — For creating high resolution PDFs of graphics generated in Processing. Covered in Chapter 21.
- **Video** — For capturing images from a camera and playing movie files. Covered in Chapter 16.
- **Sound** — For sound analysis, synthesis, and playback. Covered in Chapter 20.

Examples specifically tailored toward using the above libraries are found in the chapters listed. The Processing website also has superb documentation for these libraries (found on the "libraries" page). The only generic knowledge you need regarding Processing built-in libraries is that you must include the appropriate import statement at the top of your program. This statement will automatically be added to the sketch if you select Sketch → Import Library. Or, you can simply type the code in manually (using the import library menu option does not do anything other than just add the text for the import statement).

```
import processing.video.*;
import processing.serial.*;
import processing.net.*;
import processing.pdf.*;
import processing.sound.*;
```

12-3 Contributed libraries

The world of third party (also known as "contributed") libraries for Processing resembles the wild west. As of the writing of this book, there are 113 contributed libraries officially listed on the Processing site, with capabilities ranging from physics simulation to packet sniffing to computer vision to generative text to GUI controls. Online searches will reveal probably another hundred more not listed (and possibly not compatible with current versions of Processing). I'll discuss the code for several contributed libraries during the course of the remainder of this book. For now, let's focus on installing libraries themselves.

The process for installing a contributed library is the same as for installing the Processing Foundation libraries video and sound. I'll use video as an example below. The first step is to open the Processing contributions manager. This can be accessed by the menu option Sketch → Import Library → Add Library.

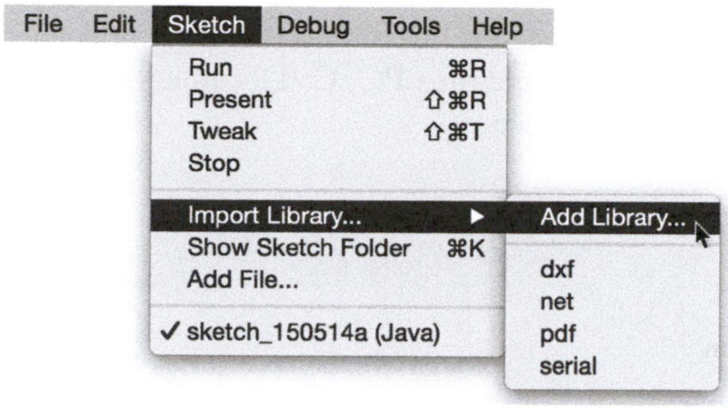

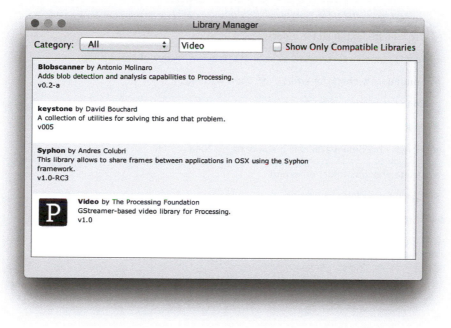

Figure 12-1

This will reveal the Library Manager. There, you can search through the list of libraries to find the one you're looking for. You can filter the list by category or by typing into the search box. For example, I can quickly find the Processing Foundation video library by typing "video".

Figure 12-2

To install a library, simply press the "install" button and wait for the library to download. That's all! While it's not required, if you run into issues, try re-starting Processing after installing. You can also update libraries through the manager if and when an update is released. You can check which libraries have updates available with the Library Manager.

12-4 Manually installing libraries

I hesitate to even include this section given that the recommended way to install a library is through the manager. And all libraries listed in the manager have been tested by the Processing Foundation. However, there are some useful libraries that you might find online that are not listed. These have to be installed through a manual process. To do so, the first thing you need to do is find your sketch folder. On a Mac, this is typically /Documents/Processing/ and on a PC, C:/Documents/Processing. If you're not sure you can always check via the Processing preferences.

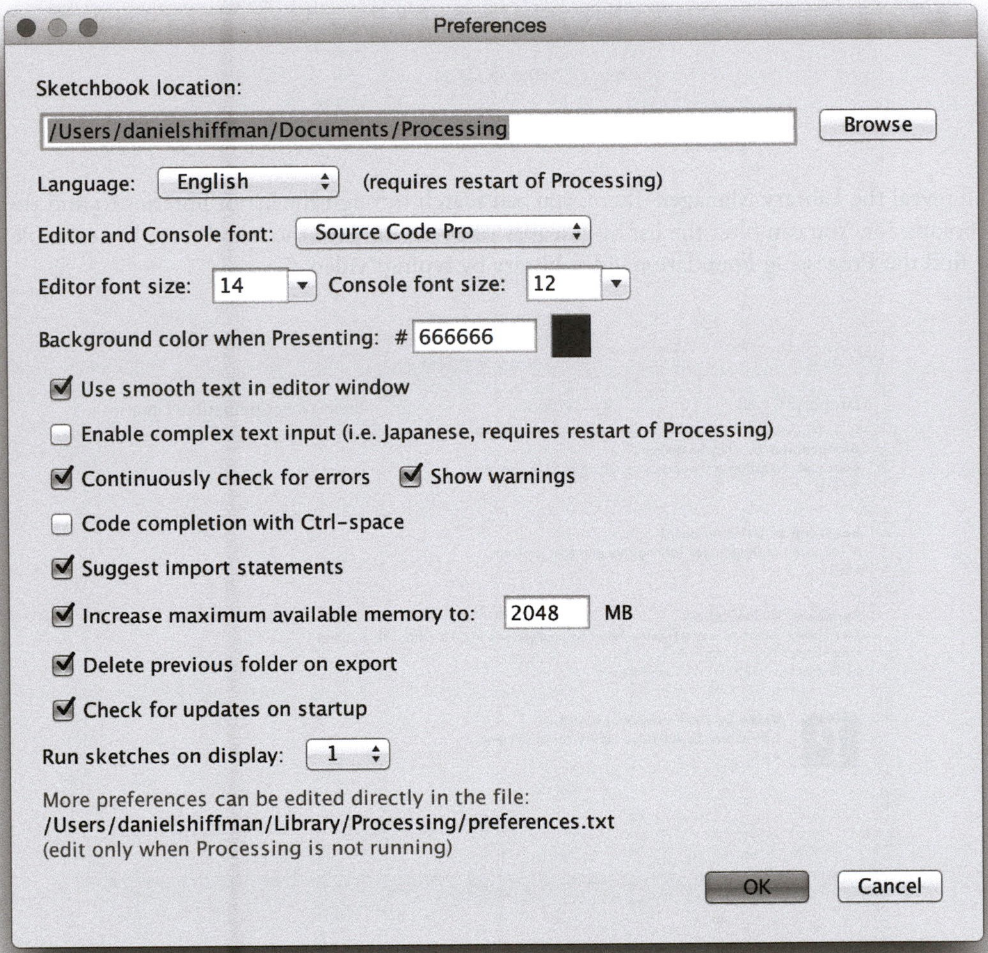

Figure 12-3

Once you have determined the sketch folder location, find the subfolder named "libraries".

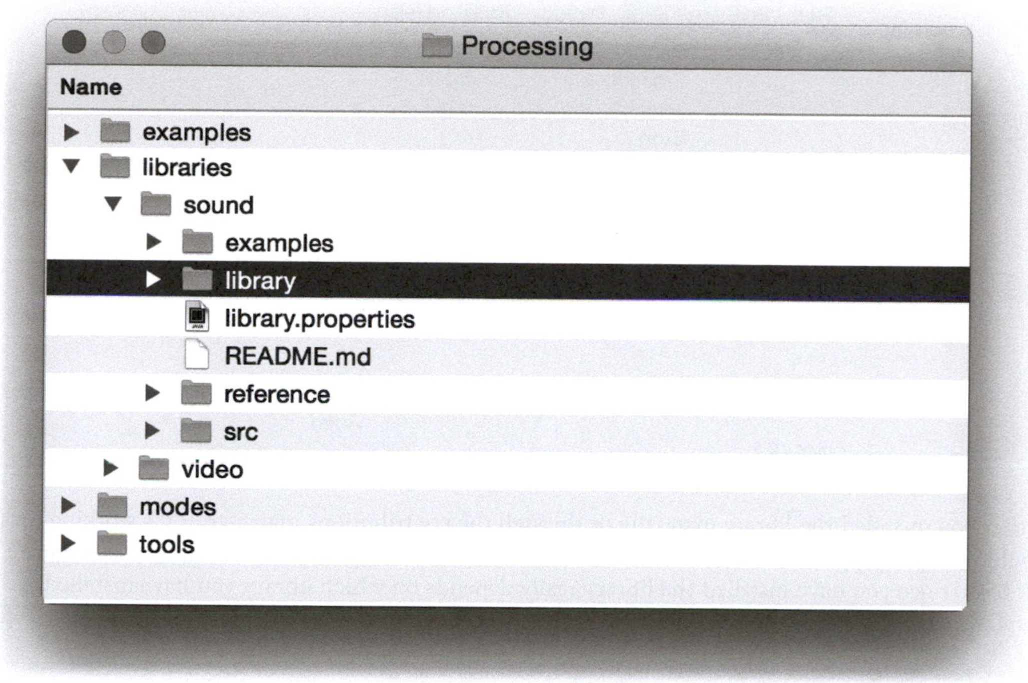

Figure 12-4

The libraries directory is where you can manually install contributed libraries. A library is just a directory of files and assuming you've found one you'd like to download, it will most likely arrive as a zip file. Once you've got the file, follow the instructions below, referencing Figure 12-4.

1. Extract the ZIP file. This can usually be accomplished by double-clicking the file or with any decompression application, such as Winzip on a PC.

2. Copy the extracted files to the libraries folder. Most libraries you download will automatically unpack with the right directory structure. The full directory structure should look like this: *libraries/libraryName/library/libraryName.jar*

   Most libraries include additional files such as source code and examples. If the library does not automatically unpack itself with the above directory structure, you can manually create these folders (using the finder or explorer) and place the libraryName.jar file in the appropriate location yourself.

3. Restart Processing. If Processing was running while you performed Step 2, you will need to quit Processing and restart it in order for the library to be recognized.

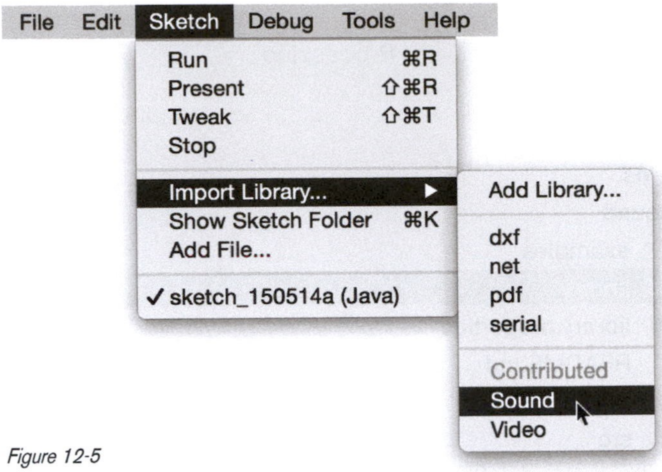

Figure 12-5

Whether you installed the library manually or through the contributions manager, if it's working properly it should now now appear in the list under the "Sketch → Import Library" option shown in Figure 12-5. What to do once you have installed the library really depends on which library you have installed. Examples that make use of code in a library can be found in Chapter 16, Chapter 18, and Chapter 20.

Although it's a topic beyond the scope of the book, you can also create your own Processing libraries. Instructions and information for how to do so can be found in the Processing github repository (*https://github.com/processing/processing/wiki/Library-Overview*). Finally, in addition to libraries, the Processing development environment ("PDE") itself can be extended with tools and modes. Tools provide smaller features to the PDE and modes offer radical large changes (like writing your code in an entirely different programming language!). These can be installed with the contributions manager as well and live in the "tools" and "modes" subdirectories of your sketchbook.

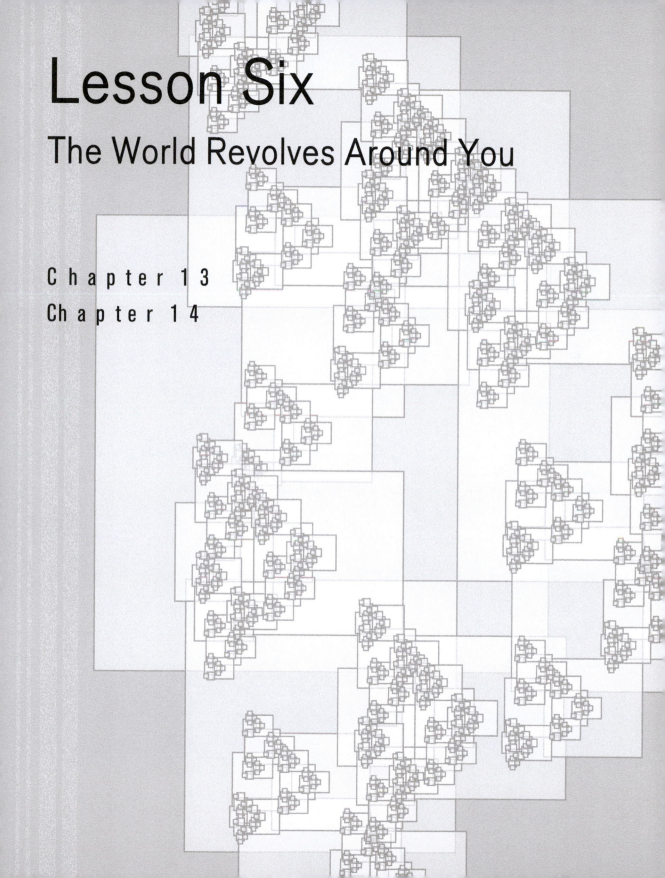

Lesson Six

The World Revolves Around You

Chapter 13
Chapter 14

13 Mathematics

If people do not believe that mathematics is simple, it is only because they do not realize how complicated life is.
—John von Neumann

If you were cosine squared, I'd be sine squared, because together we'd be one.
—Anonymous

In this chapter:
– Modulus
– Probability
– Perlin noise
– The `map()` function
– Trigonometry
– Recursion
– Two-dimensional arrays

Here we are. The fundamentals are finished, and I am going to start looking at some more sophisticated topics in Processing. You may find there is less of a story to follow from chapter to chapter. Nonetheless, although the concepts do not necessarily build on each other as fluidly as they did previously, the chapters are ordered with a step-by-step learning approach in mind.

Everything I do from here on out will still employ the same flow structure of `setup()` and `draw()`. I will continue to use functions from the Processing library and algorithms made of conditional statements and loops, and organize sketches with an object-oriented approach in mind. At this point, however, the descriptions will assume a knowledge of these essential topics, and I encourage you to return to earlier chapters to review as needed.

13-1 Mathematics and programming

Did you ever start to feel the sweat beading on your forehead the moment your teacher called you up to the board to write out the solution to the latest algebra assignment? Does the mere mention of the word "calculus" cause a trembling sensation in your extremities?

Relax; there is no need to be afraid. There is nothing to fear but the fear of mathematics itself. Perhaps at the beginning of reading this book, you feared computer programming. I certainly hope that, by now, any terrified sensations associated with code have been replaced with feelings of serenity, if not outright joy. This chapter aims to take a relaxed and friendly approach to a few useful topics from mathematics that will help you along the journey of developing Processing sketches.

You know, you have been using math all along.

For example, you have likely had an algebraic expression on almost every single page since learning variables.

```
float x = width/2;
```

And most recently, in Chapter 10, you tested intersection using the Pythagorean Theorem.

```
float d = dist(x1, x2, y1, y2);
```

These are just a few examples you have seen so far, and as you get more and more advanced, you may even find yourself online, late at night, googling "Sinusoidal Spiral Inverse Curve." For now, I will start with a selection of useful mathematical topics.

13-2 Modulus

Let's begin with a discussion of the *modulo operator*, written as a percent sign, in Processing. *Modulus* is a very simple concept (one that you learned without referring to it by name when you first studied division) that is incredibly useful for keeping a number within a certain boundary (a shape on the screen, an index value within the range of an array, etc.) The modulo operator calculates the remainder when one number is divided by another. It works with both integers and floats.

20 divided by 6 equals 3 remainder 2. (In other words 6 times 3 plus 2 equals 20.)

therefore:

20 modulo 6 equals 2 or 20 % 6 = 2

Here are a few more, with some blanks for you to fill in.

17 divided by 4 equals 4 remainder 1	`17 % 4 = 1`
3 divided by 5 equals 0 remainder 3	`3 % 5 = 3`
10 divided by 3.75 equals 2 remainder 2.5	`10 % 3.75 = 2.5`
100 divided by 50 equals _____ remainder _____	`100 % 40 = _____`
9.25 divided by 0.5 equals _____ remainder _____	`9.25 % 0.5 = _____`

You will notice that if A = B % C, A can never be larger than C. The remainder can never be greater than or equal to the divisor.

0 % 3 = 0
1 % 3 = 1
2 % 3 = 2
3 % 3 = 0
4 % 3 = 1
etc.

Therefore, modulo can be used whenever you need to cycle a counter variable back to zero. The following lines of code:

```
x = x + 1;
if (x >= limit) {
  x = 0;
}
```

can be replaced by:

```
x = (x + 1) % limit;
```

This is very useful if you want to count through the elements of an array one at a time, always returning to zero when you get to the length of the array.

Example 13-1. Modulo

```
// 4 random numbers
float[] randoms = new float[4];
int index = 0; // Which number from the array

void setup() {
  size(200, 200);
  // Fill array with random values
  for (int i = 0; i < randoms.length; i++) {
    randoms[i] = random(0, 256);
  }
  frameRate(1);
}

void draw() {
  // Every frame access one element of the array
  background(randoms[index]);
  // And then go on to the next one
  index = (index + 1) % randoms.length;
}
```

> Using the modulo operator to cycle a counter back to 0.

13-3 Random numbers

In Chapter 4, you were introduced to the `random()` function, which allowed you to randomly fill variables. Processing's random number generator produces what is known as a "uniform" distribution of numbers. For example, I ask for a random number between 0 and 9, 0 will come up 10 percent of the time, 1 will come up 10 percent of the time, 2 will come up 10 percent of the time, and so on. I could write a simple sketch using an array to prove this fact. See Example 13-2.

Pseudo-random numbers

The random numbers you get from the `random()` function are not truly random and are known as "pseudo-random." They are the result of a mathematical function that simulates randomness. This function would yield a pattern over time, but that time period is so long that for us, it's just as good as pure randomness!

Example 13-2. Random number distribution

```
// An array to keep track of how often random numbers
are picked.
float[] randomCounts;

void setup() {
  size(200, 200);
  randomCounts = new float[20];
}

void draw() {
  background(255);

  // Pick a random number and increase the count
  int index = int(random(randomCounts.length));
  randomCounts[index]++ ;

  // Draw a rectangle to graph results
  stroke(0);
  fill(175);
  for (int x = 0; x < randomCounts.length; x++) {
    rect(x * 10, 0, 9, randomCounts[x]);
  }
}
```

Figure 13-1

With a few tricks, you can change the way you use `random()` to produce a nonuniform distribution of random numbers and generate *probabilities* for certain events to occur. For example, what if you wanted to create a sketch where the background color had a 10 percent chance of being green and a 90 percent chance of being blue?

13-4 Probability review

Let's review the basic principles of probability, first looking at single event probability, that is, the likelihood of something to occur.

Given a system with a certain number of possible outcomes, the probability of any given event occurring is the number of outcomes which qualify as that event divided by total number of possible outcomes. The simplest example is a coin toss. There are a total of two possible outcomes (heads or tails). There is only one way to flip heads, therefore the probability of heads is one divided by two, that is, 1/2 or 50 percent.

Consider a deck of 52 cards. The probability of drawing an ace from that deck is:

number of aces/number of cards = 4/52 = 0.077 = ~8%

The probability of drawing a diamond is:

(number of diamonds) / (total cards) = 13/52 = 0.25 = 25%

You can also calculate the probability of multiple events occurring in sequence as the product of the individual probabilities of each event.

The probability of a coin flipping up heads three times in a row is:

*(1/2) * (1/2) * (1/2) = 1/8 (or 0.125).*

In other words, a coin will land heads three times in a row one out of eight times (with each "time" being three tosses).

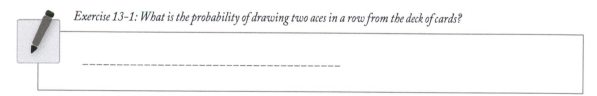

Exercise 13-1: What is the probability of drawing two aces in a row from the deck of cards?

13-5 Event probability in code

There are few different techniques for using the `random()` function with probability in code. For example, if I fill an array with a selection of numbers (some repeated), I can randomly pick from that array and generate events based on what I select.

```
int[] stuff = new int[5];
stuff[0] = 1;
stuff[1] = 1;
stuff[2] = 2;
```

```
stuff[3] = 3;
stuff[4] = 3;
int index = int(random(stuff.length));        Picking a random element from an array.
if (stuff[index] == 1) {
  // Do something
}
```

If you run this code, there will be a 40 percent chance of selecting the value 1, a 20 percent chance of selecting the value 2, and a 40 percent chance of selecting the value 3.

Another strategy is to ask for a random number (for simplicity, let's consider random floating point values between 0 and 1) and only allow the event to happen if the random number picked is within a certain range. For example:

```
float prob = 0.10;      // A probability of 10%
float r = random(1);    // A random floating point value between 0 and 1
if (r < prob) {         // If the random number is less than 0.1

  // Instigate the event here!        This code will only be executed 10 percent of the time.
}
```

This same technique can also be applied to multiple outcomes.

Outcome A — 60 percent | Outcome B — 10 percent | Outcome C — 30 percent

To implement this in code, I'll pick one random float and check where it falls.

- *Between 0.00 and 0.60 (60%)* → *outcome A*
- *Between 0.60 and 0.70 (10%)* → *outcome B*
- *Between 0.70 and 1.00 (30%)* → *outcome C*

Example 13-3 draws a circle with a three different colors, each with the above probability (red: 60 percent, green: 10 percent, blue: 30 percent). This example is displayed in Figure 13-2.

Example 13-3. Probabilities

```
void setup() {
  size(200, 200);
  background(255);
  noStroke();
}



void draw() {

  float red_prob = 0.60;
  float green_prob = 0.10;
  float blue_prob = 0.30;
```

Figure 13-2

> Here, the probabilities for three different possibilities are defined: 60 percent chance of red (0.6), 10 percent chance of green (0.1), and 30 chance change of blue (0.3). These need to add up to 100 percent (1.0)!

```
  float num = random(1);
```

> Pick a random number between 0 and 1

```
  if (num < red_prob) {
```

> If the number is less than 0.6

```
    fill(255, 53, 2, 150);

  } else if (num < green_prob + red_prob) {
```

> If it's between 0.6. and 0.7

```
    fill(156, 255, 28, 150);

  } else {
```

> And in all other cases (between 0.7. and 1)

```
    fill(10, 52, 178, 150);
  }

  // Now draw that circle!
  ellipse(random(width), random(height), 64, 64);
}
```

Exercise 13-2: Fill in the blanks in the following code so that the circle has a 10 percent chance of moving up, a 20% chance of moving down, and a 70 percent chance of doing nothing.

```
float y = 100;

void setup() {
  size(200, 200);
}

void draw() {
  background(0);
  float r = random(1);

  _____

  _____

  _____

  _____

  _____

  _____

  ellipse(width/2, y, 16, 16);
}
```

13-6 Perlin noise

One of the qualities of a good random number generator is that the numbers produced appear to have no relationship. If they exhibit no discernible pattern, they are considered *random*.

In programming behaviors that have an organic, almost lifelike quality, a little bit of randomness is a good thing. However, you might not want too much randomness. This is the approach taken by Ken Perlin, who developed a function in the early 1980s entitled "Perlin noise" that produces a naturally ordered (i.e., "smooth") sequence of pseudo-random numbers. It was originally designed to create procedural textures, for which Ken Perlin won an Academy Award for Technical Achievement. Perlin noise can be used to generate a variety of interesting effects including clouds, landscapes, marble textures, and so on.

Figure 13-3 shows two graphs, a graph of Perlin noise over time (the x-axis represents time; note how the curve is smooth) compared to a graph of pure random numbers over time. (Visit this book's website for the code that generated these graphs.)

Perlin noise

random

Figure 13-3

Noise detail

If you visit the processing.org noise reference, you will find that noise is calculated over several "octaves." You can change the number of octaves and their relative importance by calling the `noiseDetail()` function. This, in turn, can change how the noise function behaves. See *http://processing.org/reference/noiseDetail_.html.*

You can read more about how noise works from Ken Perlin himself (*http://www.noisemachine.com/talk1/*).

Processing has a built-in implementation of the Perlin noise algorithm with the function `noise()`. The `noise()` function takes one, two, or three arguments (referring to the "space" in which noise is computed: one, two, or three dimensions). This chapter will look at one-dimensional noise only. Visit the Processing website for further information about two-dimensional and three-dimensional noise.

One-dimensional Perlin noise produces as a linear sequence of values over time. For example:

0.364, 0.363, 0.363, 0.364, 0.365

Note how the numbers move up or down randomly, but stay close to the value of their predecessor. Now, in order to get these numbers out of Processing, you have to do two things: (1) call the function `noise()`, and (2) pass in as an argument the current "time." You would typically start at time $t = 0$ and therefore call the function like so: `noise(t);`

```
float t = 0.0;
float noisevalue = noise(t); // Noise at time 0
```

You can also take the above code and run it looping in `draw()`.

```
float t = 0.0;
void draw() {
   float noisevalue = noise(t);
   println(noisevalue);
}
```

```
Output:
0.28515625
0.28515625
0.28515625
0.28515625
0.28515625
```

The above code results in the same value printed over and over. This is because I am asking for the result of the noise() function at the same point in *time* — 0.0 — over and over. If I increment the time variable t, however, I'll get a different result.

```
float t = 0.0;
void draw() {
    float noisevalue = noise(t);
    println(noisevalue);

    t += 0.01;
}
```

Time moves forward!

```
Output:
0.12609221
0.12697512
0.12972163
0.13423012
0.1403218
```

How quickly you increment t also affects the smoothness of the noise. Try running the code several times, incrementing t by 0.01, 0.02, 0.05, 0.1, 0.0001, and so on.

By now, you may have noticed that noise() always returns a floating point value between 0 and 1. This detail cannot be overlooked, as it affects how you use Perlin noise in a Processing sketch. Example 13-4 assigns the result of the noise() function to the size of a circle. The noise value is scaled by multiplying by the width of the window. If the width is 200, and the range of noise() is between 0.0 and 1.0, the range of noise() multiplied by the width is 0.0 to 200.0. This is illustrated by the table below and by Example 13-4.

Noise Value	Multiplied by	Equals
0	200	0
0.12	200	24
0.57	200	114
0.89	200	178
1	200	200

Example 13-4. Perlin noise

```
float time = 0.0;
float increment = 0.01;

void setup() {
  size(200, 200);
}


void draw() {
  background(255);

  float n = noise(time) * width;
```

> Get a noise value at `time` and scale it according to the window's width.

```
  fill(0);
  ellipse(width/2, height/2, n, n);
```

> The circle's diameter is set to the noise value `n`.

```
  time += increment;
}
```

> With each cycle, increment the "time"

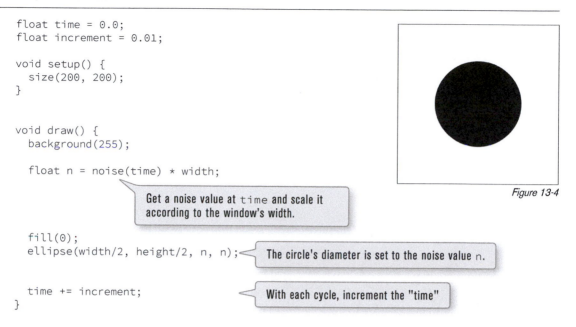

Figure 13-4

Exercise 13-3: Complete the following code that uses Perlin noise to set the location of a circle. Run the code. Does the circle appear to be moving "naturally"?

```
// Noise "time" variables
float xtime = 0.0;
float ytime = 100.0;

float increment = 0.01;

void setup() {
  size(200, 200);
}

void draw() {
  background(0);

  float x = _____;

  float y = _____;

  _____;

  _____;

  // Draw the ellipse with location determined by Perlin noise
  fill(200);

  ellipse(_____,_____,_____,_____);
}
```

> In this sketch, I want to use noise for two different values. So that the output of the noise function is not identical, I start at two different points in time.

13-7 The map() function

Using Perlin noise values for setting a color or x-position was easy. If, say, the x-position for an ellipse ranges between 0 and width all I need to do is multiply the result of the noise function (which outputs a range between 0 and 1) by width.

```
float x = width * noise(t);
ellipse(x, 100, 20, 20);
```

This range conversion is known as *mapping*. I *mapped* a Perlin noise value between 0 and 1 to an x-position between 0 and width. This sort of conversion comes up all the time in programming. Perhaps you want to map the mouse x-position (ranging between 0 and width) to a color value (ranging between 0 and 255). The math is a bit more complex but manageable.

```
float r = 255.0 * mouseX / width;
fill(r, 0, 0);
```

> Dividing `mouseX` by `width` results in a value between 0 and 1 which is then multiplied by 255. You must include ".0" in order to guarantee that floating point math is used.

Now let's consider a more complex scenario. Let's say you are reading values from a sensor that range between 65 and 324. And you want to map those values to a color range between 0 and 255. Now things are getting trickier. Fortunately, Processing includes a map() function that handles the math for converting values from one range to another. map() expects four arguments as listed below:

1. **value**: this is the value you want to map.
2. **current min**: the minimum of the value's range.
3. **current max**: the maximum of the value's range.
4. **new min**: the minimum of the new value's range.
5. **new max**: the maximum of the new value's range.

In the scenario I just described, the value is the sensor reading. The current min and max is the sensor's range: 65 and 324. The new min and max is the range fill() expects: 0 and 255.

```
float r = map(sensor, 65, 324, 0, 255);
fill(r, 0, 0);
```

Using "min" and "max" to describe the new range isn't exactly accurate. map() will happily invert the relationship as well. If you wanted the shape to appear red when the sensor value is low and black when it is high, you can simply swap the placement of 0 and 255.

```
float r = map(sensor, 65, 324, 255, 0);
fill(r, 0, 0);
```

Following is an example that demonstrates the map() function. Here the red and blue values of the background are tied to the mouse's x and y positions.

Example 13-5. Using map()

```
void setup() {
  size(640, 360);
}

void draw() {
  float r = map(mouseX, 0, width, 0, 255);
  float b = map(mouseY, 0, height, 255, 0);
  background(r, 0, b);
}
```

> Note how the mapping is inverted. The background is most blue when the mouse is at the top.

Exercise 13–4: Rewrite your answer to Exercise 13-3 on page 244 using the map() function.

13-8 Angles

Some of the examples in this book will require a basic understanding of how angles are defined in *Processing*. In Chapter 14, for example, you will need to know about angles in order to feel comfortable using the rotate() function to rotate and spin objects.

In order to get ready for these upcoming examples, you need to learn about *radians* and *degrees*. It's likely you're familiar with the concept of an angle in degrees. A full rotation goes from zero to 360°. An angle of 90° (a right angle) is one-fourth of 360°, shown in Figure 13-5 as two perpendicular lines.

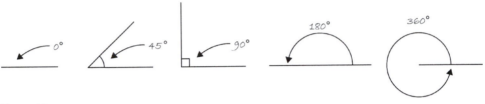

Figure 13-5

It's fairly intuitive to think angles in terms of degrees. For example, the rectangle in Figure 13-6 is rotated 45° around its center.

Processing, however, requires angles to be specified in *radians*. A radian is a unit of measurement for angles defined by the ratio of the length of the arc of a circle to the radius of that circle. One radian is the angle at which that ratio equals one (see Figure 13-7). An angle of 180° = π radians (π is the symbol for pi, more on this below.) An angle of 360° = 2π radians, and 90° = π/2 radians, and so on.

Figure 13-6

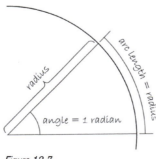

Figure 13-7

The formula to convert from degrees to radians is:

radians = 2π × (*degrees* ÷ 360)

Fortunately for us, if you prefer to think in degrees but code with radians, Processing makes this easy. The `radians()` function will automatically convert values from degrees to radians. In addition, the constants `PI` and `TWO_PI` are available for convenient access to these commonly used numbers (equivalent to 180° and 360°, respectively). The following code, for example, will rotate shapes by 60° (rotation will be fully explored in the next chapter).

```
float angle = radians(60);
rotate(angle);
```

Pi, what is it?

The mathematical constant pi (or π) is a real number defined as the ratio of a circle's circumference (the distance around the perimeter) to its diameter (a straight line that passes through the circle center). It is equal to approximately 3.14159.

Exercise 13-5: A dancer spins around two full rotations. How many degrees did the dancer rotate? How many radians?

Degrees: _____ Radians: _____

13-9 Trigonometry

Sohcahtoa. Strangely enough, this seemingly nonsense word, *sohcahtoa*, is the foundation for a lot of computer graphics work. Any time you need to calculate an angle, determine the distance between points, deal with circles, arcs, lines, and so on, you will find that a basic understanding of trigonometry is essential.

Trigonometry is the study of the relationships between the sides and angles of triangles and *sohcahtoa* is a mnemonic device for remembering the definitions of the trigonometric functions, sine, cosine, and tangent. See Figure 13-8.

- **soh**: sine = opposite/hypotenuse
- **cah**: cosine = adjacent/hypotenuse
- **toa**: tangent = opposite/adjacent

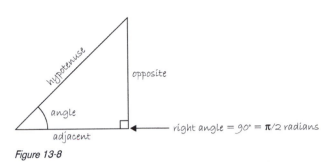

Figure 13-8

Any time you display a shape in Processing, you have to specify a pixel location, given as (x,y) coordinates. These coordinates are known as Cartesian coordinates, named for the French mathematician René Descartes, who developed the ideas behind Cartesian space.

Another useful coordinate system, known as *polar coordinates*, describes a point in space as an angle of rotation around the origin and a radius from the origin. You can't use polar coordinates as arguments to a function in Processing. However, the trigonometric formulas allow you convert those coordinates to Cartesian, which can then be used to draw a shape. See Figure 13-9.

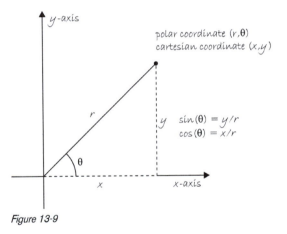

Figure 13-9

$$sine(theta) = y/r \rightarrow y = sine(theta) \times r$$

$$cosine(theta) = y/r \rightarrow y = cosine(theta) \times r$$

For example, assuming a radius r and an angle theta, I can calculate x and y using the above formula. The functions for sine and cosine in Processing are `sin()` and `cos()`, respectively. They each take one argument, a floating point angle measured in radians.

```
float r = 75;
float theta = PI / 4;      // You could also say: float theta = radians(45);
float x = r * cos(theta);
float y = r * sin(theta);
```

This type of conversion can be useful in certain applications. For example, how would you move a shape along a circular path using Cartesian coordinates? It would be tough. Using polar coordinates, however, this task is easy. Simply increment the angle!

Here is how it's done with global variables r and theta.

Example 13-6. Polar to Cartesian

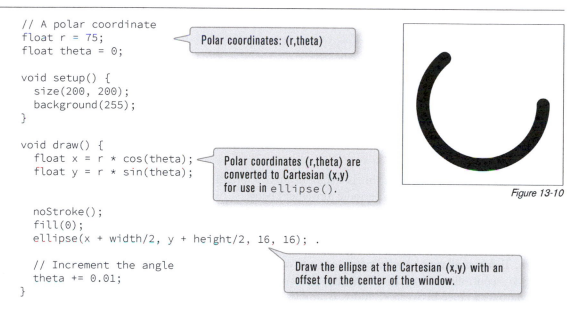

```
// A polar coordinate
float r = 75;                    Polar coordinates: (r,theta)
float theta = 0;

void setup() {
  size(200, 200);
  background(255);
}

void draw() {
  float x = r * cos(theta);      Polar coordinates (r,theta) are
  float y = r * sin(theta);      converted to Cartesian (x,y)
                                 for use in ellipse().

  noStroke();
  fill(0);
  ellipse(x + width/2, y + height/2, 16, 16); .

  // Increment the angle        Draw the ellipse at the Cartesian (x,y) with an
  theta += 0.01;                offset for the center of the window.
}
```

Figure 13-10

Exercise 13-6: Using Example 13-6, draw a spiral path. Start in the center and move outward. Note that this can be done by changing only one line of code and adding one line of code!

13-10 Oscillation

Trigonometric functions can be used for more than geometric calculations associated with right triangles. Let's take a look at Figure 13-11, a graph of the sine function where $y = sine(x)$.

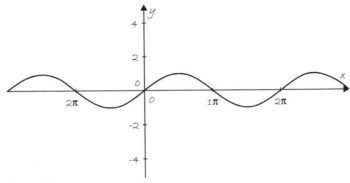

Figure 13-11

You will notice that the output of sine is a smooth curve alternating between –1 and 1. This type of behavior is known as *oscillation*, a periodic movement between two points. A swinging pendulum, for example, oscillates.

I can simulate oscillation in a Processing sketch by assigning the output of the sine function to an object's location. This is similar to how I used `noise()` to control the size of a circle (see Example 13-4), only with `sin()` controlling a location. Note that while `noise()` produces a number between 0 and 1.0, `sin()` outputs a range between –1 and 1. Example 13-7 shows the code for an oscillating pendulum.

Example 13-7. Oscillation

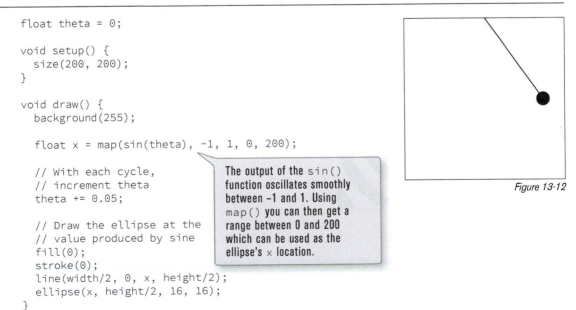

```
float theta = 0;

void setup() {
  size(200, 200);
}

void draw() {
  background(255);

  float x = map(sin(theta), -1, 1, 0, 200);

  // With each cycle,
  // increment theta
  theta += 0.05;

  // Draw the ellipse at the
  // value produced by sine
  fill(0);
  stroke(0);
  line(width/2, 0, x, height/2);
  ellipse(x, height/2, 16, 16);
}
```

> The output of the `sin()` function oscillates smoothly between –1 and 1. Using `map()` you can then get a range between 0 and 200 which can be used as the ellipse's x location.

Figure 13-12

Exercise 13-7: Encapsulate the above functionality into an Oscillator object. Create an array of Oscillators, each moving at different rates along the x and y axes. Here is some code for the Oscillator class to help you get started.

```
class Oscillator {
    float xtheta;
    float ytheta;

    _____

    Oscillator() {
        xtheta = 0;
        ytheta = 0;

    _____

    }

    void oscillate() {

    _____

    _____

    }

    void display() {

        float x = _____

        float y = _____
        ellipse(x, y, 16, 16);
    }
}
```

Exercise 13-8: Use the sine function to create a "breathing" shape, that is, one whose size oscillates.

I can also produce some interesting results by drawing a sequence of shapes along the path of the sine function. See Example 13-8.

Example 13-8. Wave

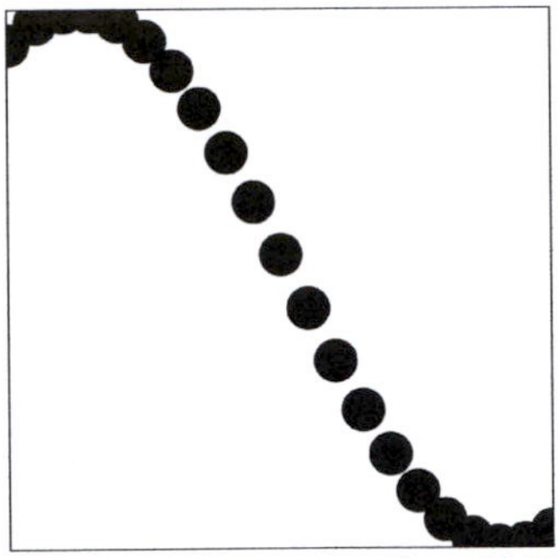

```
// Starting angle
float theta = 0.0;

void setup() {
  size(200, 200);
}

void draw() {
  background(255);

  // Increment theta (try different values for "angular
velocity" here)
  theta += 0.02;

  noStroke();
  fill(0);

  float x = theta;
  // A simple way to draw the wave with an ellipse at each location
  for (int i = 0; i <= 20; i++) {
    // Calculate y value based off of sine function using map()
    float y = map(sin(angle), -1, 1, 0, height);
    // Draw an ellipse
    ellipse(i * 10, y, 16, 16);
    // Move along x-axis
    x += 0.2;
  }
}
```

> A for loop is used to draw all the points along a sine wave (scaled to the pixel dimension of the window).

Figure 13-13

 Exercise 13-9: Rewrite the above example to use the noise() *function instead of* sin().

13-11 Recursion

Figure 13-14 The Mandelbrot set: http://processing.org/learning/topics/mandelbrot.html

In 1975, Benoit Mandelbrot coined the term *fractal* to describe self-similar shapes found in nature. Much of the stuff you encounter in the physical world can be described by idealized geometrical forms — a postcard has a rectangular shape, a ping-pong ball is spherical, and so on. However, many naturally occurring structures cannot be described by such simple means. Some examples are snowflakes, trees, coastlines, and mountains. Fractals provide a geometry for describing and simulating these types of self-similar shapes (by "self-similar," I mean no matter how "zoomed out" or "zoomed in," the shape ultimately appears the same). One process for generating these shapes is known as recursion.

You know that a function can call another function. You do this whenever you call any function inside of the draw() function. But can a function call itself? Can draw() call draw()? In fact, it can (although calling draw() from within draw() is a terrible example, since it would result in an infinite loop).

Functions that call themselves are *recursive* and are appropriate for solving different types of problems. This occurs in mathematical calculations; the most common example of this is "factorial."

The factorial of any number *n*, usually written as *n*!, is defined as:

$$n! = (n - 1) \times (n - 2) \times (n - 3) \ldots \times 1$$

In other words, factorial is the product of all whole numbers from 1 to *n*. For example.

$$5! = 5 \times 4 \times 3 \times 2 \times 1$$

I could write a function to calculate factorial using a `for` loop in Processing:

```
int factorial(int n) {
  int f = 1;
  for (int i = 0; i < n; i++) {
    f = f * (i + 1);
  }
  return f;
}
```

If you look closely at how factorial works, however, you will notice something interesting. Let's examine 4! and 3!

$$4! = 4 \times 3 \times 2 \times 1$$

$$3! = 3 \times 2 \times 1$$

therefore... $4! = 4 \times 3!$

Let's describe this in more general terms. For any positive integer n :

$$n! = n \times (n - 1)!$$

$$1! = 1$$

Written in English:

The *factorial of n* is defined as n times the *factorial of (n − 1)*.

The definition of factorial includes factorial?! It's kind of like saying "tired" is defined as "the feeling you get when you're tired." This concept of self-reference in functions is known as *recursion*. And you can use recursion to write a function for factorial that calls itself.

```
int factorial(int n) {
  if (n == 1) {
    return 1;
  } else {
    return n * factorial(n-1);
  }
}
```

Crazy, I know. But it works. Figure 13-15 walks through the steps that happen when `factorial(4)` is called.

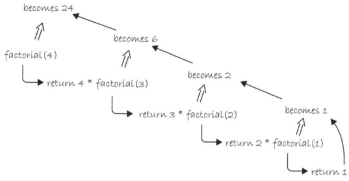

Figure 13-15

The same principle can be applied to graphics with interesting results. Take a look at the following recursive function. The results are shown in Figure 13-16.

```
void drawCircle(int x, int y, float radius) {
  ellipse(x, y, radius, radius);
  if (radius > 2) {
    radius * = 0.75;
    drawCircle(x, y, radius);
  }
}
```

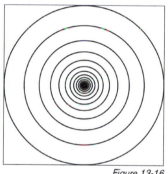

Figure 13-16

What does drawCircle() do? It draws an ellipse based on a set of parameters received as arguments, and then calls itself with the same parameters (adjusting them slightly). The result is a series of circles each drawn inside the previous circle.

Notice that the above function only recursively calls itself if the radius is greater than two. This is a crucial point. *All recursive functions must have an exit condition!* This is identical to iteration. In Chapter 6, you learned that all for and while loops must include a boolean test that eventually evaluates to false, thus exiting the loop. Without one, the program would crash, caught inside an infinite loop. The same can be said about recursion. If a recursive function calls itself forever and ever, you will most likely be treated to a nice frozen screen.

The preceding circles example is rather trivial, since it could easily be achieved through simple iteration. However, in more complex scenarios where a method calls itself more than once, recursion becomes wonderfully elegant.

Let's revise drawCircle() to be a bit more complex. For every circle displayed, draw a circle half its size to the left and right of that circle. See Example 13-9.

Example 13-9. Recursion

```
void setup() {
  size(200, 200);
}

void draw() {
  background(255);
  stroke(0);
  noFill();
  drawCircle(width/2, height/2, 100);
}

void drawCircle(float x, float y, float radius) {
  ellipse(x, y, radius, radius);
  if (radius > 2) {
    drawCircle(x + radius/2, y, radius/2);
    drawCircle(x - radius/2, y, radius/2);
  }
}
```

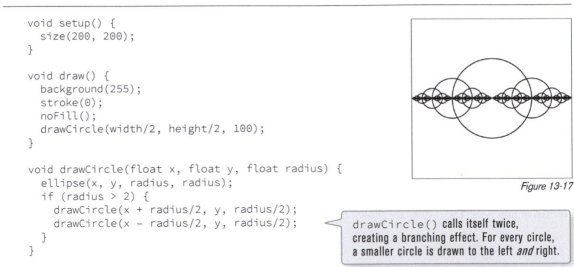

Figure 13-17

> drawCircle() calls itself twice, creating a branching effect. For every circle, a smaller circle is drawn to the left *and* right.

With a teeny bit more code, I can add a circle above and below. This result is shown in Figure 13-18.

```
void drawCircle(float x, float y, float radius) {
  ellipse(x, y, radius, radius);
  if (radius > 8) {
    drawCircle(x + radius/2, y, radius/2);
    drawCircle(x - radius/2, y, radius/2);
    drawCircle(x, y + radius/2, radius/2);
    drawCircle(x, y - radius/2, radius/2);
  }
}
```

Figure 13-18

Just try recreating this sketch with iteration instead of recursion! I dare you!

Exercise 13-10: Complete the code which generates the following pattern (Note: the solution uses lines, although it would also be possible to create the image using rotated rectangles, which you will learn how to do in Chapter 14).

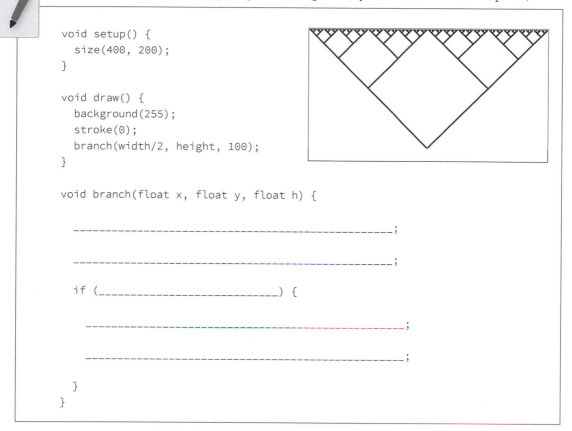

```
void setup() {
  size(400, 200);
}

void draw() {
  background(255);
  stroke(0);
  branch(width/2, height, 100);
}

void branch(float x, float y, float h) {

  _____;

  _____;

  if (_____) {

    _____;

    _____;

  }
}
```

13-12 Two-dimensional arrays

In Chapter 9, you learned that an array keeps track of multiple pieces of information in linear order, a one-dimensional list. However, the data associated with certain systems (a digital image, a board game, etc.) lives in two dimensions. To visualize this data, you need a multi-dimensional data structure, that is, a multi-dimensional array.

A two-dimensional array is really nothing more than an array of arrays (a three-dimensional array is an array of arrays of arrays). Think of your dinner. You could have a one-dimensional list of everything you eat:

(lettuce, tomatoes, salad dressing, steak, mashed potatoes, string beans, cake, ice cream, coffee)

Or you could have a two-dimensional list of three courses, each containing three things you eat:

(lettuce, tomatoes, salad dressing) and (steak, mashed potatoes, string beans) and (cake, ice cream, coffee)

In the case of an array, an old-fashioned one-dimensional array looks like this:

```
int[] myArray = {0, 1, 2, 3};
```

And a two-dimensional array looks like this:

```
int[][] myArray = { {0, 1, 2, 3}, {3, 2, 1, 0}, {3, 5, 6, 1}, {3, 8, 3, 4} } ;
```

For me, it's easier to think of the two-dimensional array as a matrix. A matrix can be thought of as a grid of numbers, arranged in rows and columns, kind of like a bingo board. I'll write the two-dimensional array out as follows to illustrate this point:

```
int[][] myArray = { {0, 1, 2, 3} ,
                    {3, 2, 1, 0} ,
                    {3, 5, 6, 1} ,
                    {3, 8, 3, 4} };
```

To access an individual element of a two-dimensional array, you need two indices. The first specifies which array is the array of arrays and the second specifies which element of that array. Thus `myArray[2][1]` is 5 (bolded above to illustrate this point).

Let's use this type of data structure to encode information about an image. For example, the grayscale image in Figure 13-19 could be represented by the following array:

```
int[][] myArray = { {236, 189, 189,   0} ,
                    {236,  80, 189, 189} ,
                    {236,   0, 189,  80} ,
                    {236, 189, 189,  80} };
```

Figure 13-19

To walk through every element of a one-dimensional array, I'll use a `for` loop, that is:

```
int[] myArray = new int[10];
for (int i = 0; i < myArray.length; i++) {
  myArray[i] = 0;
}
```

For a two-dimensional array, in order to reference every element, I must use two nested loops. This provides a counter variable for every column and every row in the matrix. See Figure 13-20.

```
int cols = 10;
int rows = 10;
int[][] myArray = new int[cols][rows];
```

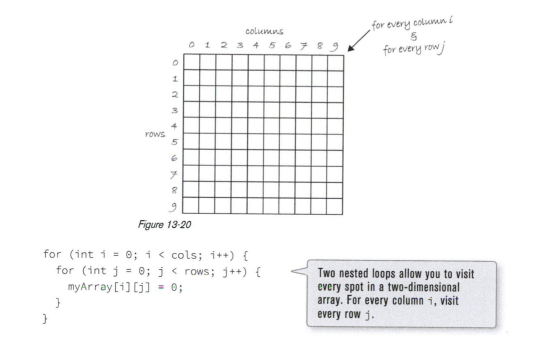

Figure 13-20

```
for (int i = 0; i < cols; i++) {
  for (int j = 0; j < rows; j++) {
    myArray[i][j] = 0;
  }
}
```

Two nested loops allow you to visit every spot in a two-dimensional array. For every column i, visit every row j.

For example, you might write a program using a two-dimensional array to draw a grayscale image as in Example 13-10.

Example 13-10. Two-dimensional array

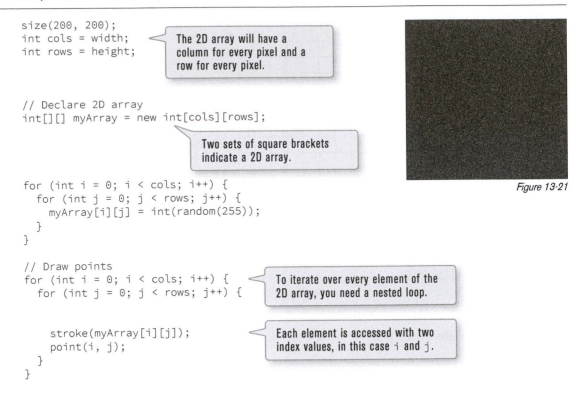

```
size(200, 200);
int cols = width;
int rows = height;
```
> The 2D array will have a column for every pixel and a row for every pixel.

```
// Declare 2D array
int[][] myArray = new int[cols][rows];
```
> Two sets of square brackets indicate a 2D array.

```
for (int i = 0; i < cols; i++) {
  for (int j = 0; j < rows; j++) {
    myArray[i][j] = int(random(255));
  }
}
```

Figure 13-21

```
// Draw points
for (int i = 0; i < cols; i++) {
  for (int j = 0; j < rows; j++) {
```
> To iterate over every element of the 2D array, you need a nested loop.

```
    stroke(myArray[i][j]);
    point(i, j);
  }
}
```
> Each element is accessed with two index values, in this case i and j.

A two-dimensional array can also be used to store objects, which is especially convenient for programming sketches that involve some sort of "grid" or "board." Example 13-11 displays a grid of Cell objects stored in a two-dimensional array. Each cell is a rectangle whose brightness oscillates from 0–255 with a sine function.

Example 13-11. Two-dimensional array of objects

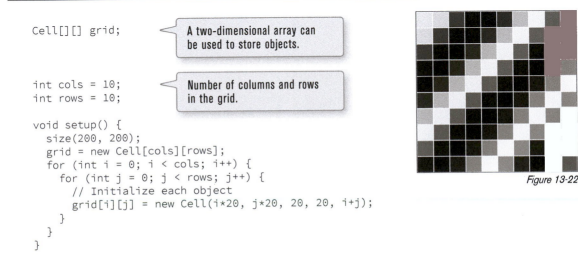

```
Cell[][] grid;
```
> A two-dimensional array can be used to store objects.

```
int cols = 10;
int rows = 10;
```
> Number of columns and rows in the grid.

```
void setup() {
  size(200, 200);
  grid = new Cell[cols][rows];
  for (int i = 0; i < cols; i++) {
    for (int j = 0; j < rows; j++) {
      // Initialize each object
      grid[i][j] = new Cell(i*20, j*20, 20, 20, i+j);
    }
  }
}
```

Figure 13-22

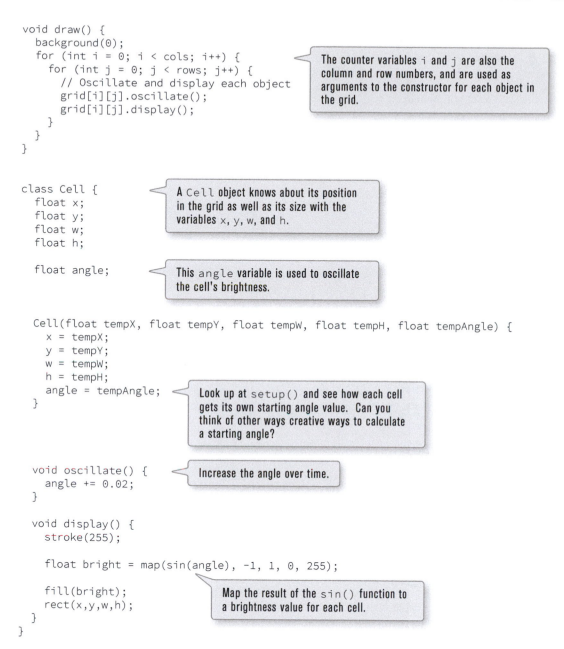

```
void draw() {
  background(0);
  for (int i = 0; i < cols; i++) {
    for (int j = 0; j < rows; j++) {
      // Oscillate and display each object
      grid[i][j].oscillate();
      grid[i][j].display();
    }
  }
}
```

The counter variables i and j are also the column and row numbers, and are used as arguments to the constructor for each object in the grid.

```
class Cell {
  float x;
  float y;
  float w;
  float h;

  float angle;
```

A Cell object knows about its position in the grid as well as its size with the variables x, y, w, and h.

This angle variable is used to oscillate the cell's brightness.

```
  Cell(float tempX, float tempY, float tempW, float tempH, float tempAngle) {
    x = tempX;
    y = tempY;
    w = tempW;
    h = tempH;
    angle = tempAngle;
  }
```

Look up at setup() and see how each cell gets its own starting angle value. Can you think of other ways creative ways to calculate a starting angle?

```
  void oscillate() {
    angle += 0.02;
  }
```

Increase the angle over time.

```
  void display() {
    stroke(255);

    float bright = map(sin(angle), -1, 1, 0, 255);

    fill(bright);
    rect(x,y,w,h);
  }
}
```

Map the result of the sin() function to a brightness value for each cell.

Exercise 13-11: Develop the beginnings of a Tic-Tac-Toe game. Create a Cell *object that can exist in one of two states: O or nothing. When you click on the cell, its state changes from nothing to "O". Here is a framework to get you started.*

```
Cell[][] board;

int cols = 3;
int rows = 3;

void setup() {
  // What goes here?
}

void draw() {
  background(0);
  for (int i = 0; i < cols; i++) {
    for (int j = 0; j < rows; j + +) {
      board[i][j].display();
    }
  }
}

void mousePressed() {
  // What goes here?
}

// A Cell object
class Cell {
  float x, y;
  float w, h;
  int state;

  // Cell Constructor
  Cell(float tempX, float tempY, float tempW, float tempH) {
    // What goes here?
  }

  void click(int mx, int my) {
    // What goes here?
  }

  void display() {
    // What goes here?
  }
}
```

Exercise 13-12: If you are feeling saucy, go ahead and complete the Tic-Tac-Toe game adding X and alternating player turns with mouse clicks.

14 Translation and Rotation (in 3D!)

What is the Matrix?
—Neo

In this chapter:
- 2D and 3D translation
- Using P3D and P2D renderers
- Vertex shapes
- 2D and 3D rotation
- Saving and restoring the transformation state: `pushMatrix()` and `popMatrix()`

14-1 The z-axis

As you have seen throughout this book, pixels in a two-dimensional window are described using Cartesian coordinates: an x (horizontal) and a y (vertical) position. This concept dates all the way back to Chapter 1, when I discussed thinking of the screen as a digital piece of graph paper.

In three-dimensional space (such as the actual, real-world space where you're reading this book), a third axis (commonly referred to as the z-axis) refers to the depth of any given point. In a Processing sketch's window, a coordinate along this z-axis indicates how far in front or behind the window a pixel lives. Scratching your head is a perfectly reasonable response here. After all, a computer window is only two dimensional. There are no pixels floating in the air in front of or behind your LCD monitor! In this chapter, I will examine how using the theoretical z-axis will create the *illusion* of three-dimensional space in your Processing window.

I can, in fact, create a three-dimensional illusion with what you have learned so far. For example, if I were to draw a rectangle in the middle of the window and slowly increase its width and height, it might appear as if it's moving toward the viewer. See Example 14-1.

Example 14-1. A growing rectangle, or a rectangle moving toward you?

```
float r = 8;

void setup() {
  size(200, 200);
}

void draw() {
  background(255);

  // Display a rectangle in the middle of the screen
  stroke(0);
  fill(175);
  rectMode(CENTER);
  rect(width/2, height/2, r, r);

  // Increase the rectangle size
  r++;
}
```

Figure 14-1

Is this rectangle flying off of the computer screen about to bump into your nose? Technically, this is, of course, not the case. It's simply a rectangle growing in size. But I have created the *illusion* of the rectangle moving toward you.

Fortunately, if you choose to use 3D coordinates, Processing will create the illusion for you. While the idea of a third dimension on a flat computer monitor may seem imaginary, it is quite real for Processing. Processing knows about perspective, and selects the appropriate two-dimensional pixels in order to create the three-dimensional effect. You should recognize, however, that as soon as you enter the world of 3D pixel coordinates, a certain amount of control must be relinquished to the Processing renderer. You can no longer control exact pixel locations as you might with 2D shapes, because (x,y) locations will be adjusted to account for 3D perspective.

In order to specify points in three dimensions, the coordinates are specified in the order you would expect: (x,y,z). Cartesian 3D systems can be described as *left-handed* or *right-handed*. If you use your right hand to point your index finger in the positive y-direction (up) and your thumb in the positive x direction (to the right), the rest of your fingers will point toward the positive z direction. It's left-handed if you use your left hand and do the same. In Processing, the system is left-handed, as shown in Figure 14-2.

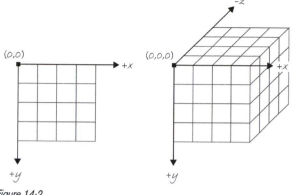

Figure 14-2

My first goal is to rewrite Example 14-1 using the 3D capabilities of Processing. Assume the following variables:

```
int x = width/2;
int y = height/2;
int z = 0;
int r = 10;
```

In order to specify the location for a rectangle, the `rect()` function takes four arguments: x location, y location, width, and height.

```
rect(x, y, w, h);
```

Your first instinct might be to add another argument to the `rect()` function.

```
rect(x, y, z, w, h);
```

> Incorrect! You cannot use an (x,y,z) coordinate in Processing's shape functions such as `rect()`, `ellipse()`, `line()`, and so on. Other functions in Processing can take three arguments for (x,y,z) and you will see this later in the chapter.

The Processing reference page for `rect()`, however, does not allow for this possibility. In order to specify 3D coordinates for shapes in the Processing world, you must learn to use a new function, called `translate()`.

The `translate()` function is not exclusive to 3D sketches, so let's return to two dimensions to see how it works.

The function `translate()` moves the origin point — (0,0) — relative to its previous state. When a sketch first starts, the origin point lives on the top left of the window. If you were to call the function `translate()` with the arguments (50,50), the result would be as shown in Figure 14-3.

Where is the origin?

The "origin" in a Processing sketch is the point (0,0) in two dimensions or (0,0,0) in three dimensions. It's always at the top left corner of the window unless you move it using `translate()`.

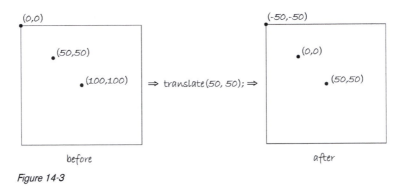

Figure 14-3

You can think of it as moving a pen around the screen, where the pen indicates the origin point.

In addition, the origin always resets itself back to the top left corner at the beginning of `draw()`. Any calls to `translate()` only apply to the current cycle through the `draw()` loop. See Example 14-2.

Example 14-2. Multiple translations

```
void setup() {
  size(200, 200);
}

void draw() {
  background(255);
  stroke(0);
  fill(175);

  // Grab mouse coordinates, constrained to window
  int mx = constrain(mouseX, 0, width);
  int my = constrain(mouseY, 0, height);
```

Figure 14-4

```
  translate(mx, my);
  ellipse(0, 0, 8, 8);
```
> Translate to the mouse location.

```
  translate(100, 0);
  ellipse(0, 0, 8, 8);
```
> Translate 100 pixels to the right.

```
  translate(0, 100);
  ellipse(0, 0, 8, 8);
```
> Translate 100 pixels down.

```
  translate(-100, 0);
  ellipse(0, 0, 8, 8);
}
```
> Translate 100 pixels left.

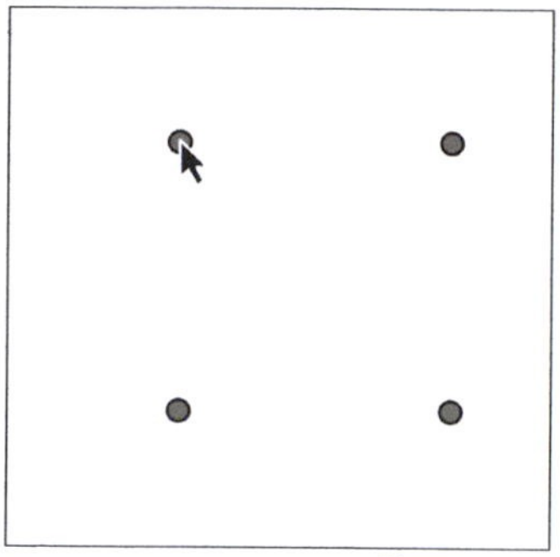

Now that I've discussed how translate() works, I can return to the original problem of specifying 3D coordinates. translate(), unlike rect(), ellipse(), and other shape functions, can accept a third argument for a z position.

```
translate(0, 0, 50);
rectMode(CENTER);
rect(100, 100, 8, 8);
```
> Translation along the z-axis!

The above code translates 50 units along the z-axis, and then draws a rectangle at (100,100). While the above is technically correct, when using translate(), it's a good habit to specify the (x,y) location as part of the translation, that is:

```
translate(100, 100, 50);
rectMode(CENTER);
rect(0, 0, 8, 8);
```
> When using translate(), the rectangle's location is (0,0) since translate() moved the location for the rectangle.

Finally, I can use a variable for the z position and animate the shape moving toward the viewer, as seen in Example 14-3.

Example 14-3. A rectangle moving along the z-axis

```
float z = 0; // A variable for the z (depth) coordinate

void setup() {
  size(200, 200, P3D);
}

void draw() {
  background(0);
  stroke(255);
  fill(100);

  // Translate to an (x,y,z) coordinate
  translate(width/2, height/2, z);
  rectMode(CENTER);
  rect(0, 0, 8, 8);

  z++;
}
```

> When using (x,y,z) coordinates, you must alert Processing that you want a 3D sketch. This is accomplished by adding a third argument P3D to size(). See Section 14-2 on page 271 for more details.

> Increment z (i.e., move the shape toward the viewer)

Although the result does not *look* different from Example 14-1, it's quite different conceptually as I have opened the door to creating a variety of three-dimensional effects on the screen with Processing's 3D engine.

Exercise 14-1: Fill in the appropriate translate() *functions to create this pattern. Once you're finished, try adding a third argument to* translate() *to move the pattern into three dimensions.*

```
size(200, 200);
background(0);
stroke(255);
fill(255, 100);

translate(_____, _____);
rect(0, 0, 100, 100);

translate(_____, _____);
rect(0, 0, 100, 100);

translate(_____, _____);
line(0, 0, -50, 50);
```

The translate() function is particularly useful when you're drawing a collection of shapes relative to a given centerpoint. Harking back to Zoog from the first 10 chapters of this book, you saw code like this:

```
void display() {
  // Draw Zoog's body
  fill(150);
  rect(x, y, w/6, h*2);

  // Draw Zoog's head
  fill(255);
  ellipse(x, y-h/2, w, h);
}
```

The display() function above draws all of Zoog's parts (body and head, etc.) relative to Zoog's (x,y) location. It requires that x and y be used in both rect() and ellipse(). translate() allows me to simply set Processing's origin (0,0) at Zoog's (x,y) location and therefore draw the shapes relative to (0,0).

```
void display() {
  // Move origin (0,0) to (x,y)
  translate(x, y);

  // Draw Zoog's body
  fill(150);
  rect(0, 0, w/6, h*2);

  // Draw Zoog's head
  fill(255);
  ellipse(0, -h/2, w, h);
}
```

> translate() can be used to draw a collection of shapes relative to a given point.

14-2 What is P3D exactly?

If you look closely at Example 14-3, you will notice that I have added a third argument to the size() function. Traditionally, size() has served one purpose: to specify the width and height of a Processing window. The size() function, however, also accepts a third parameter indicating a drawing mode or "renderer". The renderer tells Processing what to do behind the scenes when rendering the display window. The default renderer (when none is specified) employs existing Java 2D libraries to draw shapes, set colors, and so on. You do not have to worry about how this works. The creators of Processing took care of the details.

If you want to employ 3D translation (or rotation as you will see later in this chapter), the default renderer will no longer suffice. Running the example results in the following error:

"translate(), or this particular variation of it, is not available with this renderer."

Instead of switching back translate(x, y), you'll want to select a different renderer: P3D. P3D is a 3D renderer that employs hardware acceleration. If you have an OpenGL compatible graphics card installed on your computer (which is pretty much every computer), you can use this renderer. P3D also often has an added advantage: speed. If you are planning to display large numbers of shapes onscreen in a high-resolution window, this mode will likely have the best performance. There is also a P2D renderer for the case where you would like the features of OpenGL but are drawing 2D graphics.

To specify the rendering mode, add a third argument in all caps to the `size()` function.

```
size(200, 200);        // using the default renderer
size(200, 200, P3D);   // using P3D
size(200, 200, P2D);   // using P2D
```

Finally, in the case of high "pixel density" displays (for example, an Apple "Retina" display), Processing can also render at "2X" with `pixelDensity()`. Pixel density is different than pixel resolution which is defined as the actual width and height of an image in pixels. A high density display is measured in DPI ("dots per inch"). Density here refers to how many pixels (i.e., dots) fit into each physical inch of your display. For high density displays, Processing offers renderers that double the number of pixels to make shapes appear finer to the human eye. This all happens behind the scenes and you don't need to change the values in your code — the `width` and `height` of your sketch remain the same. However, some complications are introduced when working with direct access to pixels which I'll briefly discuss in the next chapter.

```
size(200, 200);
pixelDensity(2);
```

> This specifies that Processing should render at "2X" for a high density display. This can only be called once during a sketch and only in `setup()` after `size()`.

    Exercise 14-2: Run any Processing sketch in the default renderer, then switch to P2D and P3D. Notice any difference?

14-3 Vertex shapes

Up until now, your ability to draw to the screen has been limited to a small list of primitive two-dimensional shapes: rectangles, ellipses, triangles, lines, and points. For some projects, however, creating your own custom shapes is desirable. This can be done through the use of the functions `beginShape()`, `endShape()`, and `vertex()`.

Consider a rectangle. A rectangle in Processing is defined as a reference point, as well as a width and height.

```
rect(50, 50, 100, 100);
```

But you could also consider a rectangle to be a polygon (a closed shape bounded by line segments) made up of four points. The points of a polygon are called vertices (plural) or vertex (singular). The following code draws exactly the same shape as the `rect()` function by setting the vertices of the rectangle individually. See Figure 14-5.

```
beginShape();
vertex(50, 50);
vertex(150, 50);
vertex(150, 150);
vertex(50, 150);
endShape(CLOSE);
```

Figure 14-5

beginShape() indicates that you are going to create a custom shape made up of some number of vertex points: a single *polygon*. vertex() specifies the points for each vertex in the polygon and endShape() indicates that you are finished adding vertices. The argument CLOSE inside of endShape(CLOSE) declares that the shape should be closed, that is, that the last vertex point should connect to the first.

The nice thing about using a custom shape over a simple rectangle is flexibility. For example, the sides are not required to be perpendicular. See Figure 14-6.

```
stroke(0);
fill(175);
beginShape();
vertex(50, 50);
vertex(150, 25);
vertex(150, 175);
vertex(25, 150);
endShape(CLOSE);
```

Figure 14-6

You also have the option of creating more than one shape, for example, in a loop, as shown in Figure 14-7.

```
stroke(0);
for (int i = 0; i < 10; i++) {
  beginShape();
  fill(175);
  vertex(i*20, 10 - i);
  vertex(i*20 + 15, 10 + i);
  vertex(i*20 + 15, 180 + i);
  vertex(i*20, 180-i);
  endShape(CLOSE);
}
```

Figure 14-7

You can also add an argument to beginShape() specifying exactly what type of shape you want to make. This is particularly useful if you want to make more than one polygon. For example, if you create six vertex points, there is no way for Processing to know that you really want to draw two triangles (as opposed to one hexagon) unless you say beginShape(TRIANGLES). If you do not want to make a polygon at all, but want to draw points or lines, you can by saying beginShape(POINTS) or beginShape(LINES). See Figure 14-8.

```
stroke(0);
beginShape(LINES);
for (int i = 10; i < width; i += 20) {
  vertex(i, 10);
  vertex(i, height-10);
}
endShape();
```

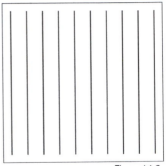

Figure 14-8

Note that LINES is meant for drawing a series of individual lines, not a continous loop. For a continuous loop, do not use any argument. Instead, simply specify all the vertex points you need and include noFill(). See Figure 14-9.

```
noFill();
stroke(0);
beginShape();
for (int i = 10; i < width; i += 20) {
  vertex(i, 10);
  vertex(i, height - 10);
}
endShape();
```

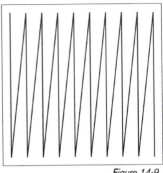

Figure 14-9

The full list of possible arguments for beginShape() is available in the Processing reference (*http://processing.org/reference/beginShape_.html*): POINTS, LINES, TRIANGLES, TRIANGLE_FAN, TRIANGLE_STRIP, QUADS, and QUAD_STRIP.

In addition, vertex() can be replaced with curveVertex() to join the points with curves instead of straight lines. With curveVertex(), note how the first and last points are not displayed. This is because they are required to define the curvature of the line as it begins at the second point and ends at the second to last point. See Figure 14-10.

```
noFill();
stroke(0);
beginShape();
for (int i = 10; i < width; i +=20) {
  curveVertex(i, 10);
  curveVertex(i, height - 10);
}
endShape();
```

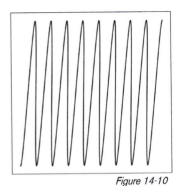

Figure 14-10

Exercise 14-3: Complete the vertices for the shape pictured.

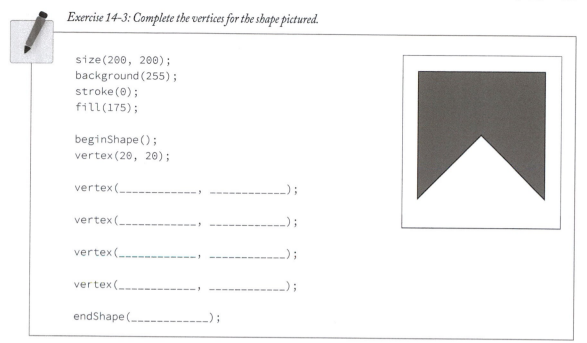

```
size(200, 200);
background(255);
stroke(0);
fill(175);

beginShape();
vertex(20, 20);

vertex(_____, _____);

vertex(_____, _____);

vertex(_____, _____);

vertex(_____, _____);

endShape(_____);
```

14-4 Custom 3D shapes

Three-dimensional shapes can be created using `beginShape()`, `endShape()`, and `vertex()` by placing multiple polygons side by side in the proper configuration. Let's say you want to draw a four-sided pyramid made up of four triangles, all connected to one point (the apex) and a flat plane (the base). If the shape is simple enough, you might be able to get by with just writing out the code. In most cases, however, it's best to start sketching it out with pencil and paper to determine the location of all the vertices. One example for a pyramid is shown in Figure 14-11.

Example 14-4 takes the vertices from Figure 14-11 and puts them in a function that allows the pyramid to be drawn at any size. (As an exercise, try making the pyramid into an object.)

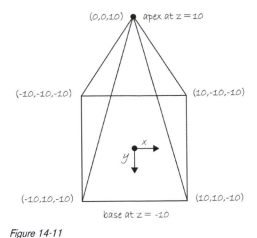

Figure 14-11

Example 14-4. Pyramid using beginShape(TRIANGLES)

```
void setup() {
  size(200, 200, P3D);
}

void draw() {
  background(255);
  translate(100, 100, 0);
  drawPyramid(150);
}


void drawPyramid(int t) {
  stroke(0);

  beginShape(TRIANGLES);
  fill(255, 150);
  vertex(-t, -t, -t);
  vertex( t, -t, -t);
  vertex( 0,  0,  t);

  fill(150, 150);
  vertex(t, -t, -t);
  vertex(t,  t, -t);
  vertex(0,  0,  t);

  fill(255, 150);
  vertex( t,  t, -t);
  vertex(-t,  t, -t);
  vertex( 0,  0,  t);

  fill(150, 150);
  vertex(-t,  t, -t);
  vertex(-t, -t, -t);
  vertex( 0,  0,  t);
  endShape();
}
```

> Since the pyramid's vertices are drawn relative to a centerpoint, you must call `translate()` to place the pyramid properly in the window.

> The function sets the vertices for the pyramid around the centerpoint at a flexible distance, depending on the number passed in as an argument.

> This pyramid has 4 sides, each drawn as a separate triangle. each side has three vertices, making up a triangle shape. The parameter `t` determines the size of the pyramid.

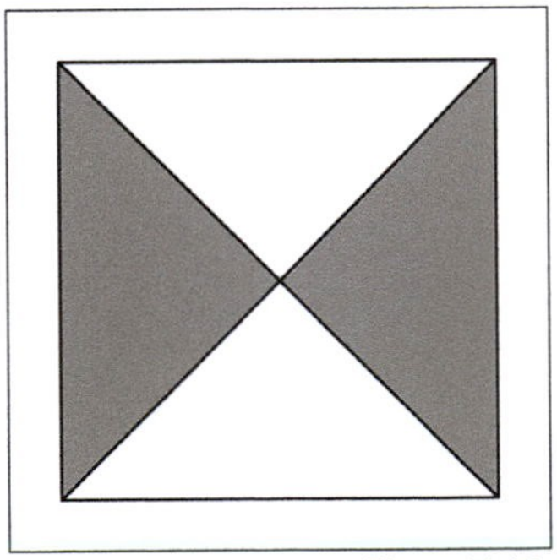

Figure 14-12

Exercise 14-4: Create a pyramid with only three sides. Include the base (for a total of four triangles). Use the space below to sketch out the vertex locations as in Figure 14-11.

Exercise 14-5: Create a three-dimensional cube using eight quads — `beginShape(QUADS)`. *(Note that a simpler way to make a cube in Processing is with the* `box()` *function.)*

14-5 Simple rotation

There is nothing particularly three-dimensional about the visual result of the pyramid example. The image looks more like a flat rectangle with two lines connected diagonally from end to end. Again, you have to remind yourself that I am only creating a three-dimensional *illusion*, and it's not a particularly effective one without animating the pyramid structure within the virtual space. One way for me to demonstrate the difference would be to rotate the pyramid. So let's learn about rotation.

For most people, in the physical world, rotation is a pretty simple and intuitive concept. Grab a baton, twirl it, and you have a sense of what it means to rotate an object.

Programming rotation, unfortunately, is not so simple. All sorts of questions come up. Around what axis should you rotate? At what angle? Around what origin point? Processing offers several functions related to rotation, which I will explore slowly, step by step. My goal will be to program a solar system simulation with multiple planets rotating around a star at different rates (as well as to rotate the pyramid in order to better experience its three dimensionality).

But first, let's try something simple and attempt to rotate one rectangle around its center. I should be able to get rotation going with the following three principles:

1. Shapes are rotated in Processing with the `rotate()` function.
2. The `rotate()` function takes one argument, an angle measured in radians.
3. `rotate()` will rotate the shape in the *clockwise* direction (to the right).

OK, armed with this knowledge, I should be able to just call the `rotate()` function and pass in an angle. Say, 45° (or PI/4 radians) in Processing. Here is a first (albeit flawed) attempt, with the output shown in Figure 14-13.

```
rotate(radians(45));
rectMode(CENTER);
rect(width/2, height/2, 100, 100);
```

Shoot. What went wrong? The rectangle looks rotated, but it's in the wrong place!

The single most important fact to remember about rotation in Processing is that *shapes always rotate around the point of origin.* Where is the point of origin in this example? The top left corner! The origin has not been translated. The rectangle therefore will not spin around its own center. Instead, it rotates around the top left corner. See Figure 14-14.

Figure 14-13

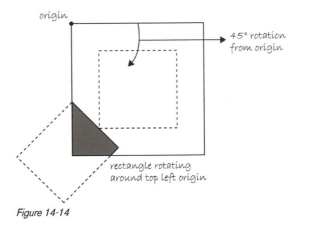

Figure 14-14

Sure, there may come a day when all you want to do is rotate shapes around the top left corner, but until that day comes, you will always need to first move the origin to the proper location before rotating, and then display the rectangle. translate() to the rescue!

```
translate(width/2, height/2);
rotate(radians(45));
rectMode(CENTER);
rect(0, 0, 100, 100);
```

> Because I translated in order to rotate, the rectangle now lives at the point (0,0).

I can expand the above code using the mouseX location to calculate an angle of rotation and thus animate the rectangle, allowing it to spin. See Example 14-5.

Example 14-5. Rectangle rotating around center

```
void setup() {
  size(200, 200);
}

void draw() {
  background(255);
  stroke(0);
  fill(175);

  // Translate origin to center
  translate(width/2, height/2);

  // theta is a common name of a variable to store an
angle

  float theta = map(mouseX, 0, width, 0, TWO_PI);

  // Rotate by the angle theta
  rotate(theta);

  // Display rectangle with CENTER mode
  rectMode(CENTER);
  rect(0, 0, 100, 100);
}
```

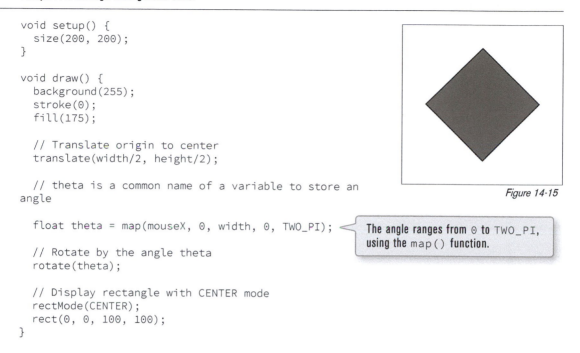

Figure 14-15

> The angle ranges from 0 to TWO_PI, using the map() function.

Exercise 14-6: Create a line that spins around its center (like twirling a baton). Draw a circle at both endpoints.

14-6 Rotation around different axes

Now that I have basic rotation out of the way, you can ask the next important rotation question:

Around which axis do I want to rotate?

In the previous section, the square rotated around the z-axis. This is the default axis for two-dimensional rotation. See Figure 14-16.

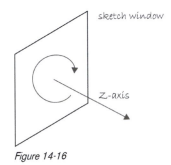

Figure 14-16

Processing also allows for rotation around the x or y-axis with the functions `rotateX()` and `rotateY()`, which each require the P3D renderer. The function `rotateZ()` also exists and is the equivalent of `rotate()`. See Example 14-6, Example 14-7 and Example 14-8.

Example 14-6. rotateZ

```
float theta = 0.0;

void setup() {
  size(200, 200, P3D);
}

void draw() {
  background(255);
  stroke(0);
  fill(175);

  translate(100, 100);
  rotateZ(theta);
  rectMode(CENTER);
  rect(0, 0, 100, 100);

  theta += 0.02;
}
```

Figure 14-17

Example 14-7. rotateX

```
float theta = 0.0;

void setup() {
  size(200, 200, P3D);
}

void draw() {
  background(255);
  stroke(0);
  fill(175);

  translate(100, 100);
  rotateX(theta);
  rectMode(CENTER);
  rect(0, 0, 100, 100);

  theta += 0.02;
}
```

Figure 14-18

Example 14-8. rotateY

```
float theta = 0.0;

  void setup() {
  size(200, 200, P3D);
}

void draw() {
  background(255);
  stroke(0);
  fill(175);

  translate(100, 100);
  rotateY(theta);
  rectMode(CENTER);
  rect(0, 0, 100, 100);

  theta += 0.02;
}
```

Figure 14-19

The rotate functions can also be used in combination. The results of Example 14-9 are shown in Figure 14-20.

Example 14-9. Rotate around more than one axis

```
void setup() {
  size(200, 200, P3D);
}

void draw() {
  background(255);
  stroke(0);
  fill(175);

  translate(width/2, height/2);
  rotateX(map(mouseY, 0, height, 0, TWO_PI));
  rotateY(map(mouseX, 0, width, 0, TWO_PI));
  rectMode(CENTER);
  rect(0, 0, 100, 100);
}
```

Figure 14-20

Returning to the pyramid example, you will see how rotating makes the three-dimensional quality of the shape more apparent. The example is also expanded to include a second pyramid that is offset from the first pyramid using translate. Note, however, that it rotates around the same origin point as the first pyramid (since rotateX() and rotateY() are called before the second translate()).

Example 14-10. Pyramid

```
float theta = 0.0;

void setup() {
  size(200, 200, P3D);
}

void draw() {
  background(255);
  theta += 0.01;

  translate(100, 100, 0);
  rotateX(theta);
  rotateY(theta);
  drawPyramid(50);

  translate(50, 50, 20);
  drawPyramid(10);
}


void drawPyramid(int t) {
  stroke(0);

  fill(150, 0, 0, 127);
  beginShape(TRIANGLES);
  vertex(-t, -t, -t);
  vertex( t, -t, -t);
  vertex( 0,  0,   t);

  fill(0, 150, 0, 127);
  vertex( t, -t, -t);
  vertex( t,  t, -t);
  vertex( 0,  0,   t);

  fill(0, 0, 150, 127);
  vertex( t,  t, -t);
  vertex(-t,  t, -t);
  vertex( 0,  0,   t);

  fill(150, 0, 150, 127);
  vertex(-t,  t, -t);
  vertex(-t, -t, -t);
  vertex( 0,  0,   t);
  endShape();
}
```

> Translate for the first pyramid.

> Now translate again for a second, smaller one. Its location is offset from the first translation and will rotate around it according to the rotateX() and rotateY calls.

> This function hasn't changed. Again, the pyramid has 4 sides, each drawn as a separate triangle sized according to the parameter t.

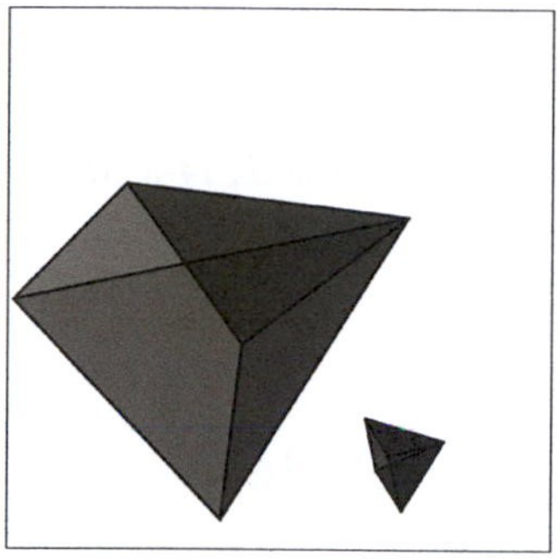

Figure 14-21

Exercise 14-7: Rotate the 3D cube you made in Exercise 14-5 on page 277. Can you rotate it around the corner or center? You can also use the Processing function box() *to make the cube.*

Exercise 14-8: Make a Pyramid class.

14-7 Scale

In addition to translate() and rotate(), there is one more function, scale(), that affects the way shapes are oriented and drawn onscreen. scale() increases or decreases the size of objects onscreen. Just as with rotate(), the scaling effect is performed relative to the origin's location.

scale() takes a floating point value, a percentage at which to scale: 1.0 is 100%. For example, scale(0.5) draws an object at 50% of its size and scale(3.0) increases the object's size to 300%.

Following is a re-creation of Example 14-1 (the growing square) using scale() .

Example 14-11. A growing rectangle, using *scale()*

```
float r = 0.0;

void setup() {
  size(200, 200);
}

void draw() {
  background(0);

  // Translate to center of window
  translate(width/2, height/2);

  scale(r);

  stroke(255);
  fill(100);
  rectMode(CENTER);
  rect(0, 0, 10, 10);

  r += 0.02;
}
```

> scale() increases the dimensions of an object relative to the origin by a percentage (1 equals 100 percent). Notice how in this example the scaling effect causes the outline of the shape to become thicker.

Figure 14-22

scale() can also take two arguments (for scaling along the x and y axes with different values) or three arguments (for the x, y, and z axes).

14-8 The matrix: pushing and popping

What is the matrix?

In order to keep track of rotations and translations and how to display the shapes according to different transformations, Processing (and just about any computer graphics software) uses a matrix.

How matrix transformations work is beyond the scope of this book; however, it's useful to simply know that the information related to the coordinate system is stored in what is known as a *transformation matrix*. When a translation or rotation is applied, the transformation matrix changes. From time to time, it's useful to save the current state of the matrix to be restored later. This will ultimately allow you to move and rotate individual shapes without them affecting others.

What is the matrix?

A matrix is a table of numbers with rows and columns. In Processing, a *transformation* matrix is used to describe the window *orientation* — is it translated or rotated? You can view the current matrix at any time by calling the function `printMatrix()`. This is what the matrix looks like in its "normal" state, with no calls to `translate()` or `rotate()`.

```
1.0000 0.0000 0.0000
0.0000 1.0000 0.0000
```

This concept is best illustrated with an example. Let's give ourselves an assignment: Create a Processing sketch where two rectangles rotate at different speeds in different directions around their respective center points.

As I start developing this example, you will see where the problems arise and how I'll need to utilize the functions `pushMatrix()` and `popMatrix()`.

Starting with essentially the same code from Section 14-4 on page 275, I can rotate a square around the z-axis in the top left corner of the window. See Example 14-12.

Example 14-12. Rotating one square

```
float theta1 = 0;

void setup() {
  size(200, 200, P3D);
}

void draw() {
  background (255);
  stroke(0);
  fill(175);
  rectMode(CENTER);

  translate(50, 50);
  rotateZ(theta1);
  rect(0, 0, 60, 60);
  theta1 += 0.02;
}
```

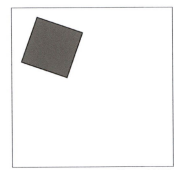

Figure 14-23

Making some minor adjustments, let's now implement a rotating square in the bottom right-hand corner.

Example 14-13. Rotating another square

```
float theta2 = 0;

void setup() {
  size(200, 200, P3D);
}

void draw() {
  background(255);
  stroke(0);
  fill(175);
  rectMode(CENTER);

  translate(150, 150);
  rotateY(theta2);
  rect(0, 0, 60, 60);

  theta2 += 0.02;
}
```

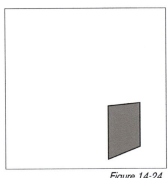

Figure 14-24

Without careful consideration, I might think to simply combine the two programs. The setup() function should stay the same, I should incorporate two global variables, theta1 and theta2, and call the appropriate translation and rotation for each rectangle. I should also adjust translation for the second square from translate(150, 150); to translate(100, 100);, since I've already translated to (50,50) with the first square. This should work, right?

```
float theta1 = 0;
float theta2 = 0;

void setup() {
  size(200, 200, P3D);
}

void draw() {
  background(255);
  stroke(0);
  fill(175);
  rectMode(CENTER);

  translate(50, 50);
  rotateZ(theta1);
  rect(0, 0, 60, 60);

  theta1 += 0.02;

  translate(100, 100);
  rotateY(theta2);
  rect(0, 0, 60, 60);

  theta2 += 0.02;
}
```

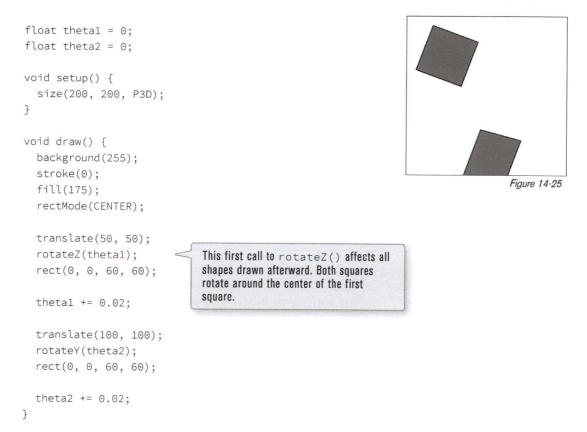

Figure 14-25

This first call to `rotateZ()` affects all shapes drawn afterward. Both squares rotate around the center of the first square.

Running this example quickly reveals a problem. The first (top left) square rotates around its center. However, while the second square does rotate around its center, it also rotates around the first square! Remember, all calls to translate and rotate are relative to the coordinate system's previous state. I need a way to restore the matrix to its original state so that individual shapes can act independently.

Saving and restoring the rotation/translation state is accomplished with the functions `pushMatrix()` and `popMatrix()`. To get started, let's think of them as *saveMatrix()* and *restoreMatrix()*. (Note there are no such functions.) Push = save. Pop = restore.

For each square to rotate on its own, I can write the following algorithm (with the new parts bolded).

1. **Save the current transformation matrix.** This is where I started, with (0,0) in the top left corner of the window and no rotation.
2. Translate and rotate the first rectangle.
3. Display the first rectangle.
4. **Restore matrix from Step 1 so that the second rectangle isn't affected by Steps 2 and 3!**
5. Translate and rotate the second rectangle.
6. Display the second rectangle.

Rewriting the code in Example 14-14 gives the correct result as shown in Figure 14-26.

Example 14-14. Rotating both squares

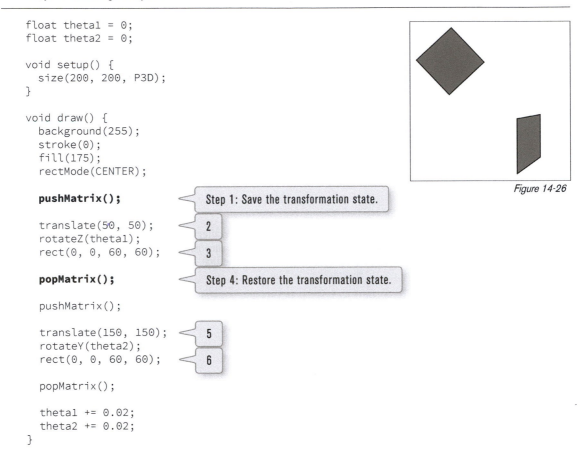

```
float theta1 = 0;
float theta2 = 0;

void setup() {
  size(200, 200, P3D);
}

void draw() {
  background(255);
  stroke(0);
  fill(175);
  rectMode(CENTER);

  pushMatrix();              Step 1: Save the transformation state.

  translate(50, 50);         2
  rotateZ(theta1);
  rect(0, 0, 60, 60);        3

  popMatrix();               Step 4: Restore the transformation state.

  pushMatrix();

  translate(150, 150);       5
  rotateY(theta2);
  rect(0, 0, 60, 60);        6

  popMatrix();

  theta1 += 0.02;
  theta2 += 0.02;
}
```

Figure 14-26

Although technically not required, it's a good habit to place pushMatrix() and popMatrix() around the second rectangle as well (in case I was to add more to this code). A nice rule of thumb when starting is to use pushMatrix() and popMatrix() before and after translation and rotation for all shapes so that they can be treated as individual entities. In fact, this example should really be object oriented, with every object making its own calls to pushMatrix(), translate(), rotate() , and popMatrix(). See Example 14-15.

Example 14-15. Rotating many things using objects

```
// An array of Rotater objects
Rotater[] rotaters;

void setup() {
  size(200, 200);
  rotaters = new Rotater[20];

  // Rotaters are made randomly
  for (int i = 0; i < rotaters.length; i++) {
    rotaters[i] = new Rotater(random(width),
      random(height), random(-0.1, 0.1), random(48));
  }
}
```

Figure 14-27

```
void draw() {
  background(255);
  // All Rotaters spin and are displayed
  for (int i = 0; i < rotaters.length; i++) {
    rotaters[i].spin();
    rotaters[i].display();
  }
}

// A Rotater class
class Rotater {
  float x, y;    // x,y location
  float theta;   // angle of rotation
  float speed;   // speed of rotation
  float w;       // size of rectangle

  Rotater(float tempX, float tempY, float tempSpeed, float tempW) {
    x = tempX;
    y = tempY;
    theta = 0;        // Angle is always initialized to 0
    speed = tempSpeed;
    w = tempW;
  }

  // Increment angle
  void spin() {
    theta += speed;
  }

  // Display rectangle
  void display() {
    rectMode(CENTER);
    stroke(0);
    fill(0, 100);
    pushMatrix();
    translate(x, y);
    rotate(theta);
    rect(0, 0, w, w);
    popMatrix();
  }
}
```

> pushMatrix() is called inside the class's display() method...

> ...and popMatrix() is here too. This way, every Rotater object is rendered with its own independent translation and rotation!

Interesting results can also be produced from *nesting* multiple calls to pushMatrix() and popMatrix(). There must always be an equal number of calls to both pushMatrix() and popMatrix(), but they do not always have to come one right after the other.

To understand how this works, let's take a closer look at the meaning of "push" and "pop." "Push" and "pop" refer to a concept in computer science known as a *stack*. Knowledge of how a stack works will help you use pushMatrix() and popMatrix() properly.

A stack is exactly that: a stack. Consider an English teacher getting settled in for a night of grading papers stored in a pile on a desk, a stack of papers. The teacher piles them up one by one and reads them in reverse order of the pile. The first paper placed on the stack is the last one read. The last paper added is the first one read. Note this is the exact opposite of a queue. If you're waiting in line to buy tickets to a movie, the first person in line is the first person to get to buy tickets, the last person is the last. See Figure 14-28.

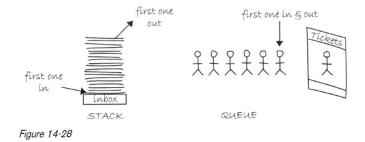

Figure 14-28

Pushing refers to the process of putting something in the stack, *popping* to taking something out. This is why you must always have an equal number of pushMatrix() and popMatrix() calls. You can't pop something if it does not exist! If your numbers are off, an error will appear in the console. For example, with too many calls to popMatrix(), Processing will report: "Missing a pushMatrix() to go along with that popMatrix()."

Using the rotating squares program as a foundation, you can hopefully see how nesting pushMatrix() and popMatrix() is useful. The following sketch has one circle in the center (let's call it the sun) with another circle rotating it (let's call it earth) and another two rotating around it (let's call them moon #1 and moon #2).

Example 14-16. Simple solar system

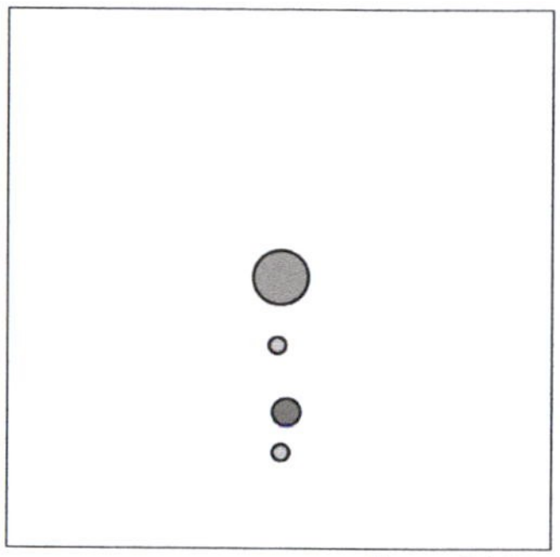

```
// Angle of rotation around sun and planets
float theta = 0;

void setup() {
  size(200, 200);
}

void draw() {

  background(255);
  stroke(0);

  // Translate to center of window to draw the sun.
  translate(width/2, height/2);
  fill(255, 200, 50);
  ellipse(0, 0, 20, 20);

  // The earth rotates around the sun
  pushMatrix();
  rotate(theta);
  translate(50, 0);
  fill(50, 200, 255);
  ellipse(0, 0, 10, 10);

  // Moon #1 rotates around the earth

  pushMatrix();
  rotate(-theta*4);
  translate(15, 0);
  fill(50, 255, 200);
  ellipse(0, 0, 6, 6);
  popMatrix();

  // Moon #2 also rotates around the earth
  pushMatrix();
  rotate(theta*2);
  translate(25, 0);
  fill(50, 255, 200);
  ellipse(0, 0, 6, 6);
  popMatrix();

  popMatrix();

  theta += 0.01;
}
```

Figure 14-29

> pushMatrix() is called to save the transformation state before drawing moon #1. This way I can pop and return to earth before drawing moon #2. Both moons rotate around the earth (which itself is rotating around the sun).

pushMatrix() and popMatrix() can also be nested inside for or while loops with rather unique and interesting results. The following example is a bit of a brainteaser, but I encourage you to play around with it.

Example 14-17. Nested push and pop

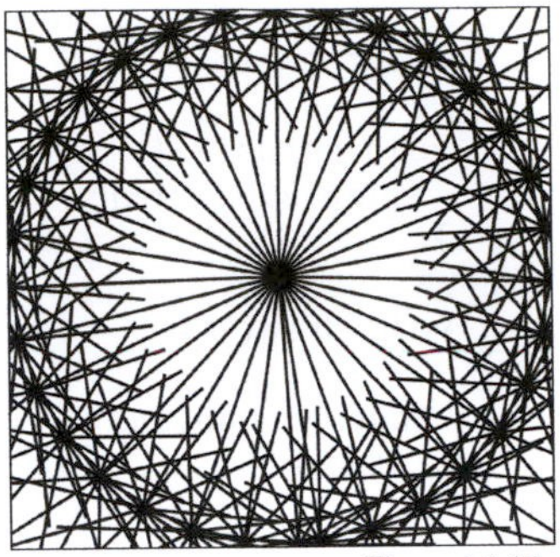

```
// Global angle for rotation
float theta = 0;

void setup() {
  size(200, 200);
}

void draw() {
  background(100);
  stroke(255);

  // Translate to center of window
  translate(width/2, height/2);

  // Loop from 0 to 360 degrees (2*PI radians)
  for(float i = 0; i < TWO_PI; i += 0.2) {
    // Push, rotate and draw a line!
    pushMatrix();
    rotate(theta + i);
    line(0, 0, 100, 0);
    // From 0 to 360 degrees (2*PI radians)
    for(float j = 0; j < TWO_PI; j + = 0.5) {

      // Push, translate, rotate!
      pushMatrix();
      translate(100, 0);
      rotate(-theta - j);
      line(0, 0, 50, 0);
      // Done with the inside loop, pop!
      popMatrix();
    }
    // Done with the outside loop, pop!
    popMatrix();
  }
  endShape();

  // Increment theta
  theta += 0.01;
}
```

Figure 14-30

> The transformation state is saved at the beginning of each cycle through the for loop and restored at the end. Try commenting out these lines to see the difference!

> Another `pushMatrix()`.

> Another `popMatrix()`.

> Final `popMatrix()`.

 Exercise 14-9: Take either your pyramid or your cube shape and make it into a class. Have each object make its own call to `pushMatrix()` *and* `popMatrix()`. *Can you make an array of objects all rotating independently in 3D?*

14-9 A Processing solar system

Using all the translation, rotation, pushing, and popping techniques in this chapter, you are ready to build a Processing solar system. This example is an updated version of Example 14-16 in the previous section (without any moons), with two major changes:

- Every planet is an object, a member of a `Planet` class.
- An array of planets orbits the sun.

Example 14-18. Object-oriented solar system

```
// An array of 8 planet objects
Planet[] planets = new Planet[8];

void setup() {
  size(200, 200);

  // The planet objects are initialized using the
counter variable
  for (int i = 0; i < planets.length; i++) {
    planets[i] = new Planet(20 + i*10, i + 8);
  }
}

void draw() {

  background(255);

  // Drawing the Sun
  pushMatrix();
  translate(width/2, height/2);
  stroke(0);
  fill(255);
  ellipse(0, 0, 20, 20);

  // Drawing all Planets
  for (int i = 0; i < planets.length; i++) {
    planets[i].update();
    planets[i].display();
  }

  popMatrix();
}

class Planet {

  float theta;      // Rotation around sun
  float diameter;   // Size of planet
  float distance;   // Distance from sun
  float orbitspeed; // Orbit speed

  Planet(float distance_, float diameter_) {
    distance = distance_;
    diameter = diameter_;
    theta = 0;
    orbitspeed = random(0.01, 0.03);
  }

  void update() {
    // Increment the angle to rotate
    theta += orbitspeed;
  }
```

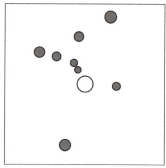

Figure 14-31

> Each planet object keeps track of its own angle of rotation.

```
void display() {

    pushMatrix();
    // Rotate orbit
    rotate(theta);
    // Translate out distance
    translate(distance, 0);
    stroke(0);
    fill(175);
    ellipse(0, 0, diameter, diameter);
    popMatrix();
  }
}
```

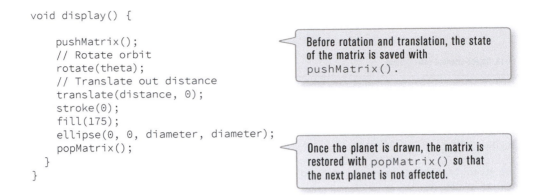

Before rotation and translation, the state of the matrix is saved with `pushMatrix()`.

Once the planet is drawn, the matrix is restored with `popMatrix()` so that the next planet is not affected.

Exercise 14-10: How would you add moons to the planets? Hint: Write a Moon *class that is virtually identical to the* Planet *one. Then, incorporate a* Moon *variable into the* Planet *class. (In Chapter 22, I will show how this could be made more efficient with advanced OOP techniques.)*

Exercise 14-11: Extend the solar system example into three dimensions. Try using sphere() *or* box() *instead of* ellipse(). *Note* sphere() *takes one argument, the sphere's radius.* box() *can take one argument (size, in the case of a cube) or three arguments (width, height, and depth.)*

14-10 PShape

At the very beginning of this book, the first thing you learned is how to draw "primitive" shapes to the screen: rectangles, ellipses, lines, triangles, and more. You've now seen in this chapter a more advanced drawing option using beginShape() and endShape() to specify the vertices of a custom polygon in both two and three dimensions.

This is all well and good and will get you pretty far. There's very little you can't draw just knowing the above. However, there is another step. A step that can, in some cases, improve the speed of your rendering as well as offer a more advanced organizational model for your code — PShape().

By now, you are hopefully quite comfortable with the idea of data types. You specify them often — a float variable called speed, an int named x, perhaps even a char entitled letterGrade. These are all *primitive* data types, bits sitting in the computer's memory ready for your use. Though perhaps a bit trickier, you are also beginning to feel at ease with objects, *complex* data types that store multiple pieces of data (along with functionality) — the Zoog class, for example, included floating point variables for location, size, and speed as well as methods to move, display itself, and so on. Zoog, of course, is a user-defined class; I brought Zoog into this programming world, defined what it means to be a Zoog, and defined the data and functions associated with a Zoog object.

In addition to user-defined objects, Processing has a bunch of built-in classes for you to use. The next chapter will be entirely dedicated to one of these built-in Processing objects: PImage, a class for loading and displaying images.

Before I move onto the next chapter, let's wade into the waters by examining PShape, a datatype for storing shapes. A PShape can store custom geometry you build via an algorithm as well as shapes that you load from an external file, such as a scalable vector graphics files (SVG), a standard file format for storing shape data.

A PShape object can be created with either the createShape function or loadShape(), in the case of loading from a file. Let's take a look at a quick example, a more thorough discussion of PShape, beyond the scope of this book, is included at the Processing tutorials page (*https://processing.org/tutorials/pshape/*).

Example 14-19. PShape

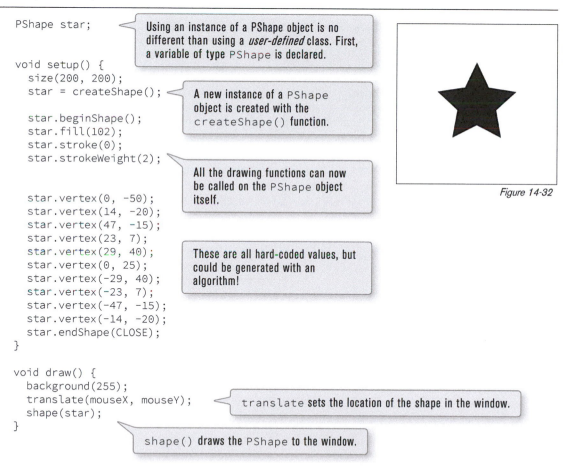

```
PShape star;
```
Using an instance of a PShape object is no different than using a *user-defined* class. First, a variable of type PShape is declared.

```
void setup() {
  size(200, 200);
  star = createShape();
```
A new instance of a PShape object is created with the createShape() function.

```
  star.beginShape();
  star.fill(102);
  star.stroke(0);
  star.strokeWeight(2);
```
All the drawing functions can now be called on the PShape object itself.

```
  star.vertex(0, -50);
  star.vertex(14, -20);
  star.vertex(47, -15);
  star.vertex(23, 7);
  star.vertex(29, 40);
  star.vertex(0, 25);
  star.vertex(-29, 40);
  star.vertex(-23, 7);
  star.vertex(-47, -15);
  star.vertex(-14, -20);
  star.endShape(CLOSE);
}
```
These are all hard-coded values, but could be generated with an algorithm!

```
void draw() {
  background(255);
  translate(mouseX, mouseY);
  shape(star);
}
```
translate sets the location of the shape in the window.

shape() draws the PShape to the window.

Figure 14-32

Exercise 14-12: Rewrite Example 14-19 so that the PShape object itself is inside your own Star class that also includes x,y variables for position. Make multiple instances of the object an array. Here is some code to get you started.

```
class Star {

  // The PShape object
  PShape s;
  // The location where I will draw the shape
  float x, y;

  Star() {
    // What goes here?
  }

  void move() {
    // What goes here?
  }

  void display() {
    // What goes here?
  }
}
```

Lesson Six Project

Create a virtual ecosystem. Make a class for each "creature" in your world. Using the techniques from Chapters 13 and 14, attempt to infuse your creatures with personality. Some possibilities:

- Use Perlin noise to control the movements of creatures.
- Make the creatures look like they are breathing with oscillation.
- Design the creatures using recursion.
- Design the custom polygons using `beginShape()`.
- Use rotation in the creatures' behaviors.

Use the space provided below to sketch designs, notes, and pseudocode for your project.

Lesson Seven

Pixels Under a Microscope

Chapter 15

Chapter 16

15 Images

Politics will eventually be replaced by imagery. The politician will be only too happy to abdicate in favor of his image, because the image will be much more powerful than he could ever be.
—Marshall McLuhan

When it comes to pixels, I think I've had my fill. There are enough pixels in my fingers and brains that I probably need a few decades to digest all of them.
—John Maeda

In this chapter:
– The `PImage` class
– Displaying images
– Changing image color
– The pixels of an image
– Simple image processing
– Interactive image processing

A digital image is nothing more than data — numbers indicating variations of red, green, and blue at a particular location on a grid of pixels. Most of the time, we view these pixels as miniature rectangles sandwiched together on a computer screen. With a little creative thinking and some lower level manipulation of pixels with code, however, you can display that information in a myriad of ways. This chapter is dedicated to breaking out of simple shape drawing in Processing and using images (and their pixels) as the building blocks of Processing graphics.

15-1 Getting started with images

As you just learned in Section 14-10 on page 294, Processing has a bunch of handy classes all ready to go for your use. (Later, in Chapter 23, you will discover that you also have access to a vast library of Java classes.) While I only briefly examined `PShape` objects in Chapter 14, this chapter will be entirely dedicated to another Processing-defined class: `PImage`, a class for loading and displaying an image such as the one shown in Figure 15-1.

Figure 15-1

Example 15-1. "Hello World" images

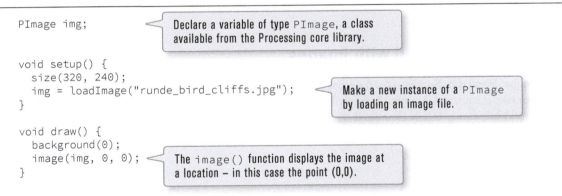

```
PImage img;                        Declare a variable of type PImage, a class
                                   available from the Processing core library.

void setup() {
  size(320, 240);
  img = loadImage("runde_bird_cliffs.jpg");     Make a new instance of a PImage
}                                                by loading an image file.

void draw() {
  background(0);
  image(img, 0, 0);       The image() function displays the image at
}                         a location – in this case the point (0,0).
```

Just as with PShape, using an instance of a PImage object is no different than using a *user-defined* class. First, a variable of type PImage, named img, is declared. Second, a new instance of a PImage object is created via the loadImage() method. loadImage() takes one argument, a String (strings of text are explored in greater detail in Chapter 17) indicating a file name, and loads that file into memory. loadImage() looks for image files stored in your Processing sketch's data folder.

The data folder: How do I get there?

Images can be added to the data folder automatically by dragging a file into your Processing window. You can also add files via:

Sketch → Add File...

or manually:

Sketch → Show Sketch Folder

This will open up the sketch folder as shown in Figure 15-2. If there is no data directory, create one. Otherwise, place your image files inside. Processing accepts the following file formats for images: GIF, JPG, TGA, and PNG. You'll want to make sure you include the file extension when referencing the file name as well, e.g., "file.jpg".

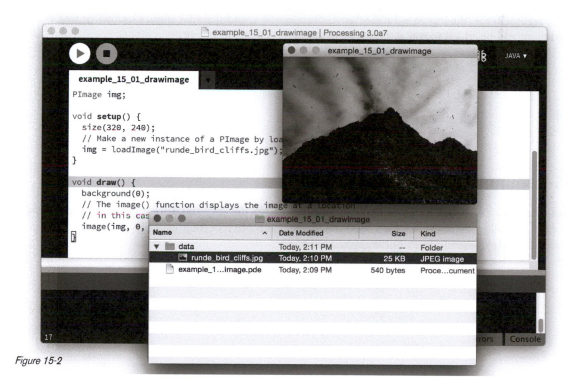

Figure 15-2

In Example 15-1, it may seem a bit peculiar that I never called a "constructor" to instantiate the PImage object, saying **new PImage()**. After all, in each of the object-related examples to date, a constructor is a must for producing an object instance.

```
Spaceship ss = new Spaceship();
Flower flr = new Flower(25);
```

And yet a `PImage` is created without `new`, using `loadImage()`:

```
PImage img = loadImage("file.jpg");
```

In fact, the `loadImage()` function performs the work of a constructor, returning a brand new instance of a `PImage` object generated from the specified filename. You can think of it as the `PImage` constructor for loading images from a file. For creating a blank image, the `createImage()` function is used.

```
// Create a blank image, 200 X 200 pixels with RGB color
PImage img = createImage(200, 200, RGB);
```

I should also note that the process of loading the image from the hard drive into memory is a slow one, and you should make sure your sketches only have to do it once, in `setup()`. Loading images in `draw()` may result in slow performance, as well as "Out of Memory" errors. You should also avoid calling `loadImage()` above `setup()` as Processing will not yet know the location of the "data" folder and will report an error.

Once the image is loaded, it's displayed with the `image()` function. The `image()` function must include three arguments — the image to be displayed, the x location, and the y location. Optionally, two arguments can be added to resize the image to a certain width and height.

```
image(img, 10, 20, 90, 60);
```

 Exercise 15-1: Load and display an image. Control the image's width and height with the mouse.

15-2 Animation with an image

From here, it's easy to see how you can use images to further develop examples from previous chapters. Note in the following example how I draw the image relative to its center using `imageMode()` which works similarly to `rectMode()` but is applied to images.

Example 15-2. Image "sprite"

```
PImage head; // A variable for the image file
float x, y;  // Variables for image location
float rot;   // A variable for image rotation

void setup() {
  size(200, 200);
  // Load image, initialize variables
  head = loadImage("face.jpg");
  x = 0;
  y = width/2;
  rot = 0;
}

void draw() {
  background(255);

  translate(x, y);
  rotate(rot);
  imageMode(CENTER);
  image(head, 0, 0);

  // Adjust variables for animation
  x += 1.0;
  rot += 0.01;
  if (x > width) {
    x = 0;
  }
}
```

Figure 15-3

> Images can be animated just like regular shapes using variables, `translate()`, `rotate()`, and so on.

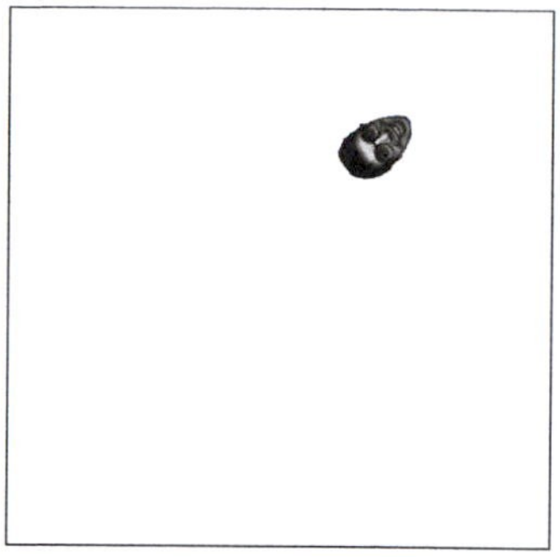

Exercise 15-2: Rewrite this example in an object-oriented fashion where the data for the image, location, size, rotation, and so on is contained in a class. Can you have the class swap images when it hits the edge of the screen?

```
class Head {

    _____ // A variable for the image file

    _____ // Variables for image location

    _____ // A variable for image rotation


    Head(String filename, _____, _____) {
      // Load image, initialize variables

      _____ = loadImage(_____);

      _____

      _____

      _____
    }

    void display() {

      _____

      _____

      _____
    }

    void move() {

      _____

      _____

      _____

      _____

      _____

      _____
    }
}
```

> The `String` class will be explored in detail in Chapter 17.

15-3 My very first image processing filter

Every now and then, when displaying an image, you might like to alter its appearance. Perhaps you would like the image to appear darker, transparent, bluish, and so on. This type of simple image filtering is achieved with Processing's `tint()` function. `tint()` is essentially the image equivalent of shape's `fill()`, setting the color and alpha transparency for displaying an image on screen. An image, nevertheless, is not usually all one color. The arguments for `tint()` simply specify how much of a given color to use for every pixel of that image, as well as how transparent those pixels should appear.

For the following examples, assume that two images (a sunflower and a dog) have been loaded and the dog is displayed as the background (which will allow me to demonstrate transparency). See Figure 15.4. For color versions of these images visit *http://www.learningprocessing.com*.

```
PImage sunflower = loadImage("sunflower.jpg");
PImage dog = loadImage("dog.jpg");
background(dog);
```

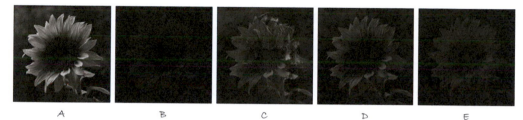

| | | | | |
| A | B | C | D | E |

Figure 15-4

If `tint()` receives one argument, only the brightness of the image is affected.

```
tint(255);
image(sunflower, 0, 0);
```
> **A**: The image retains its original state.

```
tint(100);
image(sunflower, 0, 0);
```
> **B**: The image appears darker.

A second argument will change the image's alpha transparency.

```
tint(255, 127);
image(sunflower, 0, 0);
```
> **C**: The image is at 50% opacity.

Three arguments affect the brightness of the red, green, and blue components of each color.

```
tint(0, 200, 255)
image(sunflower, 0, 0);
```
> **D**: None of it is red, most of it is green, and all of it is blue.

Finally, adding a fourth argument to the method manipulates the alpha (same as with two arguments). Incidentally, the range of values for `tint()` can be specified with `colorMode()` (see Chapter 1).

```
tint(255, 0, 0, 100);
image(sunflower, 0, 0);
```
> **E**: The image is tinted red and transparent.

Exercise 15-3: Display an image using tint(). *Use the mouse location to control the amount of red, green, and blue tint. Also try using the distance of the mouse from the corners or center.*

Exercise 15-4: Using tint(), *create a montage of blended images. What happens when you layer a large number of images, each with different alpha transparency, on top of each other? Can you make it interactive so that different images fade in and out?*

15-4 An array of images

One image is nice, a good place to start. It will not be long, however, until the temptation of using many images takes over. Yes, you could keep track of multiple images with multiple variables, but here is a magnificent opportunity to rediscover the power of the array. Let's assume I have five images and want to display a new background image each time the user clicks the mouse.

First, I'll set up an array of images, as a global variable.

```
// Image array
PImage[] images = new PImage[5];
```

Second, I'll load each image file into the appropriate location in the array. This happens in setup().

```
// Loading images into an array
images[0] = loadImage("cat.jpg");
images[1] = loadImage("mouse.jpg");
images[2] = loadImage("dog.jpg");
images[3] = loadImage("kangaroo.jpg");
images[4] = loadImage("porcupine.jpg");
```

Of course, this is somewhat awkward. Loading each image individually is not terribly elegant. With five images, sure, it's manageable, but imagine writing the above code with 100 images. One solution is to store the filenames in a String array and use a for statement to initialize all the array elements.

```
// Loading images into an array from an array of filenames
String[] filenames = {"cat.jpg", "mouse.jpg", "dog.jpg", "kangaroo.jpg",
"porcupine.jpg");
for (int i = 0; i < filenames.length; i++) {
  images[i] = loadImage(filenames[i]);
}
```

Concatenation: a new kind of addition

Usually, a plus sign (+) means, add. 2 + 2 = 4, right?

With text (as stored in a *string*, enclosed in quotes), + means *concatenate*, that is, join two strings together.

"cow" + "bell" → "cowbell"

"2" + "2" → "22"

See more about strings in Chapter 17.

Even better, if I just took a little time out of my hectic schedule to plan ahead, numbering the image files ("animal0.jpg", "animal1.jpg", "animal2.jpg", etc.), I could really simplify the code:

```
// Loading images with numbered files
for (int i = 0; i < images.length; i++) {
  images[i] = loadImage("animal" + i + ".jpg");
}
```

Once the images are loaded, it's on to `draw()`. There, I'll choose to display one particular image, picking from the array by referencing an index ("0" below).

```
image(images[0], 0, 0);
```

Of course, hard-coding the index value is foolish. I'll need a variable in order to dynamically display a different image at any given moment in time.

```
image(images[imageIndex], 0, 0);
```

The `imageIndex` variable should be declared as a global variable (of type integer). Its value can be changed throughout the course of the program. The full version is shown in Example 15-3.

Example 15-3. Swapping images

```
int maxImages = 10; // Total # of images
int imageIndex = 0; // Initial image to be displayed is the first
PImage[] images = new PImage[maxImages]; // The image array

void setup() {                          Declaring an array of images.
  size(200, 200);
  // Loading the images into the array
  // Don't forget to put the JPG files in the data folder!
  for (int i = 0; i < images.length; i++) {
    images[i] = loadImage("animal" + i + ".jpg");
  }
}                                       Loading an array of images.

void draw() {
  image(images[imageIndex], 0, 0); // Displaying one image
}
                                        Displaying one image from the array.
void mousePressed() {
  // A new image is picked randomly when the mouse is clicked
  // Note the index to the array must be an integer!
  imageIndex = int(random(images.length));
}
                                Picking a new image to display by changing the index variable!
```

To play the images in sequence as an animation, follow Example 15-4. (Only the new draw() function is included below.)

Example 15-4. Image sequence

```
void draw() {
  background(0);
  image(images[imageIndex], 0, 0);
  // Increment image index by one each cycle
  // use modulo "%" to return to 0 once the size
  // of the array is reached
  imageIndex = (imageIndex + 1) % images.length;
}
```
Remember modulus? The % sign? It allows you to cycle a counter back to 0. See Chapter 13 for a review.

Exercise 15-5: Create multiple instances of an image sequence onscreen. Have them start at different times within the sequence so that they are out of sync. Hint: Use object-oriented programming to place the image sequence in a class.

15-5 Pixels, pixels, and more pixels

If you have been diligently reading this book in precisely the prescribed order, you will notice that so far, the only offered means for drawing to the screen is through a function call. "Draw a line between these points," or "Fill an ellipse with red," or "Load this JPG image and place it on the screen here." But somewhere, somehow, someone had to write code that translates these function calls into setting the individual pixels on the screen to reflect the requested shape. A line does not appear because you say line(), it appears because all the pixels along a linear path between two points change color. Fortunately, you do not have to manage this lower-level-pixel-setting on a day-to-day basis. You have the developers of Processing (and Java) to thank for the many drawing functions that take care of this business.

Nevertheless, from time to time, you may want to break out of a mundane shape drawing existence and deal with the pixels on the screen directly. Processing provides this functionality via the `pixels` array.

You are familiar with the idea of each pixel on the screen having an (x,y) position in a two-dimensional window. However, the array `pixels` has only one dimension, storing color values in linear sequence. See Figure 15-5.

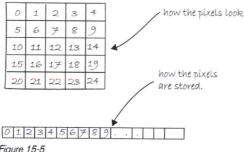

Figure 15-5

Take the following example. This sketch sets each pixel in a window to a random grayscale value. The *pixels* array is just like an other array, the only difference is that you do not have to declare it since it is a Processing built-in variable.

Example 15-5. Setting pixels

```
size(200, 200);
// Before I deal with pixels
loadPixels();

// Loop through every pixel
for (int i = 0; i < pixels.length; i++) {
```

> You can get the length of the pixels array just like with any array.

```
  // Pick a random number, 0 to 255
  float rand = random(255);
  // Create a grayscale color based on random number
  color c = color(rand);
  // Set pixel at that location to random color
  pixels[i] = c;
}
```

> You can access individual elements of the pixels array via an index, just like with any other array.

```
// When you are finished dealing with pixels
updatePixels();
```

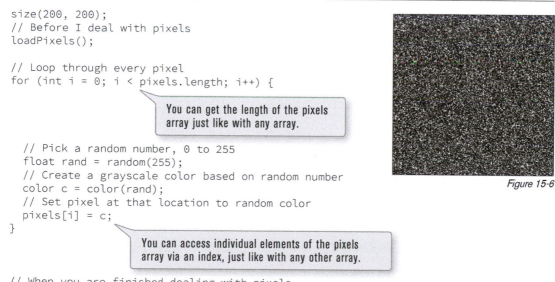

Figure 15-6

First, I should point out something important in the above example. Whenever you're accessing the pixels of a Processing window, you must alert Processing to this activity. This is accomplished with two functions:

- loadPixels() — This function is called *before* you access the pixel array, saying "load the pixels, I would like to speak with them!"

- updatePixels() — This function is called *after* you finish with the pixel array, saying "Go ahead and update the pixels, I'm all done!"

In Example 15-5, because the colors are set randomly, I did not have to worry about where the pixels are onscreen as I accessed them, since I was simply setting all the pixels with no regard to their relative location. However, in many image processing applications, the (x,y) location of the pixels themselves is crucial information. A simple example of this might be: set every even column of pixels to white and every odd to black. How could you do this with a one-dimensional pixel array? How do you know what column or row any given pixel is in?

When programming with pixels, you need to be able to think of every pixel as living in a two-dimensional world, but continue to access the data in one dimension (since that is how it's made available to us). You can do this via the following formula:

1. Assume a window or image with a given width and height.

2. You then know the pixel array has a total number of elements equaling width × height.

3. For any given (x,y) point in the window, the location in the one-dimensional pixel array is:

   pixel array location = x + (y × width);

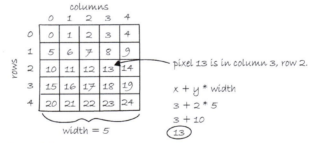

Figure 15-7

This may remind you of two-dimensional arrays in Chapter 13. In fact, you will need to use the same nested for loop technique. The difference is that, although you want to use for loops to think about the pixels in two dimensions, when you go to actually access the pixels, they live in a one-dimensional array, and you have to apply the formula from Figure 15-7.

Let's look at how it's done, completing the even/odd column problem. See Figure 15-8.

Example 15-6. Setting pixels according to their 2D location

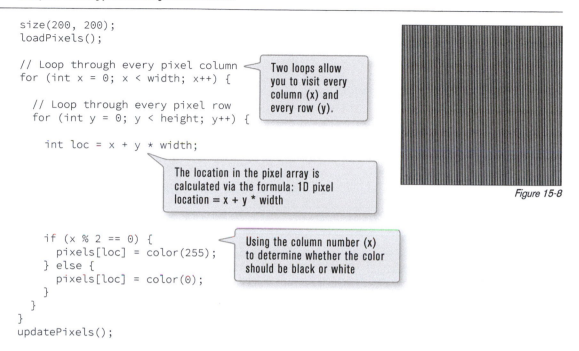

```
size(200, 200);
loadPixels();

// Loop through every pixel column
for (int x = 0; x < width; x++) {

    // Loop through every pixel row
    for (int y = 0; y < height; y++) {

        int loc = x + y * width;
```

> Two loops allow you to visit every column (x) and every row (y).

> The location in the pixel array is calculated via the formula: 1D pixel location = x + y * width

Figure 15-8

```
        if (x % 2 == 0) {
            pixels[loc] = color(255);
        } else {
            pixels[loc] = color(0);
        }
    }
}
updatePixels();
```

> Using the column number (x) to determine whether the color should be black or white

Pixel density revisited

In Section 14-2 on page 271, I briefly mentioned the `pixelDensity()` function which can be used for higher quality rendering on high pixel density displays (like the Apple "Retina"). Setting `pixelDensity(2)` actually quadruples the number of pixels used for the sketch window; the number of horizontal and vertical pixels are each doubled. When drawing shapes, everything is handled behind the scenes but in the case of working with the `pixels` array directly you have to account for the actual pixel width and height (which is now different than sketch `width` and `height`). Processing includes convenience variables `pixelWidth` and `pixelHeight` for this very scenario. For example, here's a version of Example 15-5 with `pixelDensity(2)`.

```
size(200, 200);
pixelDensity(2);
loadPixels();
for (int x = 0; x < pixelWidth x++) {
    for (int y = 0; y < pixelHeight; y++) {
        int loc = x + y * pixelWidth;
        pixels[loc] = color(random(255));
    }
}
updatePixels();
```

> The pixel density is set to 2.

> `pixelWidth` and `pixelHeight` are used instead of `width` and `height`

For the rest of this chapter, a pixel density of one will be assumed.

Exercise 15-6: Complete the code to match the corresponding screenshots.

```
size(255, 255);

_____;
for (int x = 0; x < width; x++) {
  for (int y = 0; y < height; y++) {

    int loc = _____;

    float distance = _____);

    pixels[loc] = _____;
  }
}

_____;
```

```
size(255, 255);

_____;
for (int x = 0; x < width; x++) {
  for (int y = 0; y < height; y++) {

    _____;

    if (_____) {

      _____;

    } else {

      _____;
    }
  }
}

_____;
}
```

15-6 Intro to image processing

The previous section looked at examples that set pixel values according to an arbitrary calculation. I will now look at how you might set pixels according to those found in an existing PImage object. Here is some pseudocode.

1. Load the image file into a PImage object.

2. For each pixel in the image, retrieve the pixel's color and set the display pixel to that color.

The PImage class includes some useful fields that store data related to the image — width, height, and pixels. Just as with user-defined classes, you can access these fields via the dot syntax.

```
PImage img = createImage(320, 240, RGB); // Make a PImage object
println(img.width);   // Yields 320
println(img.height);  // Yields 240
img.pixels[0] = color(255, 0, 0); // Sets the first pixel of the image to red
```

Access to these fields allows you to loop through all the pixels of an image and display them onscreen.

Example 15-7. Displaying the pixels of an image

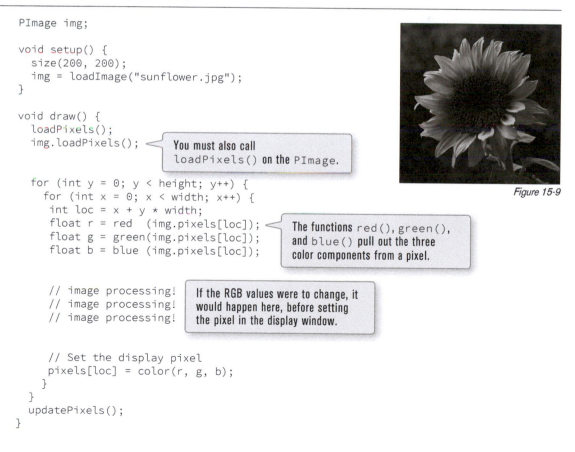

```
PImage img;

void setup() {
  size(200, 200);
  img = loadImage("sunflower.jpg");
}

void draw() {
  loadPixels();
  img.loadPixels();
```

> You must also call loadPixels() on the PImage.

Figure 15-9

```
  for (int y = 0; y < height; y++) {
    for (int x = 0; x < width; x++) {
      int loc = x + y * width;
      float r = red   (img.pixels[loc]);
      float g = green(img.pixels[loc]);
      float b = blue (img.pixels[loc]);
```

> The functions red(), green(), and blue() pull out the three color components from a pixel.

```
      // image processing!
      // image processing!
      // image processing!
```

> If the RGB values were to change, it would happen here, before setting the pixel in the display window.

```
      // Set the display pixel
      pixels[loc] = color(r, g, b);
    }
  }
  updatePixels();
}
```

Now, you could certainly come up with simplifications in order to merely display the image (e.g., the nested loop is not required, not to mention that using the image() function would allow you to skip all this pixel work entirely). However, Example 15-7 provides a basic framework for getting the red, green, and blue values for each pixel based on its spatial orientation — (x,y) location; ultimately, this will allow you to develop more advanced image processing algorithms.

Before you move on, I should stress that this example works because the display area has the same dimensions as the source image. If this were not the case, you would simply need to have two pixel location calculations, one for the source image and one for the display area.

```
int imageLoc   = x + y * img.width;
int displayLoc = x + y * width;
```

Exercise 15-7: Using Example 15-7, change the values of r, g, and b before displaying them.

15-7 A second image processing filter, making your own tint()

Just a few paragraphs ago, you were enjoying a relaxing coding session, colorizing images and adding alpha transparency with the friendly tint() method. For basic filtering, this method did the trick. The pixel by pixel method, however, will allow you to develop custom algorithms for mathematically altering the colors of an image. Consider brightness — brighter colors have higher values for their red, green, and blue components. It follows naturally that you can alter the brightness of an image by increasing or decreasing the color components of each pixel. In the next example, I will dynamically increase or decrease those values based on the mouse's horizontal location. (Note that the next two examples include only the image processing loop itself, the rest of the code is assumed.)

Example 15-8. Adjusting image brightness

```
for (int x = 0; x < img.width; x++) {
  for (int y = 0; y < img.height; y++) {
    // Calculate the 1D pixel location
    int loc = x + y * img.width;
    // Get the red, green, blue values
    float r = red   (img.pixels[loc]);
    float g = green(img.pixels[loc]);
    float b = blue (img.pixels[loc]);


    // Adjust brightness with mouseX
    float adjustBright
        = map(mouseX, 0, width, 0, 8);
    r *= adjustBright;
    g *= adjustBright;
    b *= adjustBright;

    r = constrain(r, 0, 255);
    g = constrain(g, 0, 255);
    b = constrain(b, 0, 255);

    // Make a new color
    color c = color(r, g, b);
    pixels[loc] = c;
  }
}
```

Figure 15-10

I calculate a multiplier ranging from 0.0 to 8.0 based on `mouseX` position using `map()`. That multiplier changes the RGB value of each pixel.

The RGB values are constrained between 0 and 255 before being set as a new color.

Since I am altering the image on a per pixel basis, all pixels need not be treated equally. For example, I can alter the brightness of each pixel according to its distance from the mouse.

Example 15-9. Adjusting image brightness based on pixel location

```
for (int x = 0; x < img.width; x++) {
  for (int y = 0; y < img.height; y++) {
    // Calculate the 1D pixel location
    int loc = x + y * img.width;
    // Get the red, green, blue values from pixel
    float r = red   (img.pixels[loc]);
    float g = green(img.pixels[loc]);
    float b = blue  (img.pixels[loc]);

    // Calculate an amount to change brightness
    // based on proximity to the mouse
    float distance = dist(x, y, mouseX, mouseY);
    float adjustBright = map(distance, 0, 50, 8, 0);
    r *= adjustBrightness;
    g *= adjustBrightness;
    b *= adjustBrightness;
    // Constrain RGB to between 0-255
    r = constrain(r, 0, 255);
    g = constrain(g, 0, 255);
    b = constrain(b, 0, 255);
    // Make a new color
    color c = color(r, g, b);
    pixels[loc] = c;
  }
}
```

Figure 15-11

The closer the pixel is to the mouse, the lower the value of `distance` is. I want closer pixels to be brighter, however, so I invert the `adjustBrightness` factor using `map()`. Pixels with a distance of 50 (or greater) have their brightness multiplied by 0.0 (resulting in now brightness) and brightness for pixels with a distance of 0 is multiplied by a factor of 8.

Exercise 15-8: Adjust the brightness of the red, green, and blue color components separately according to mouse interaction. For example, let mouseX *control red,* mouseY *green, distance blue, and so on.*

15-8 Writing to another PImage object's pixels

All of the image processing examples have read every pixel from a source image and written a new pixel to the Processing window directly. However, it's often more convenient to write the new pixels to a destination image (that you then display using the image() function). I will demonstrate this technique while looking at another simple pixel operation: *threshold.*

A *threshold* filter displays each pixel of an image in only one of two states, black or white. That state is set according to a particular threshold value. If the pixel's brightness is greater than the threshold, I color the pixel white, less than, black. Example 15-10 uses an arbitrary threshold of 100.

Example 15-10. Brightness threshold

```
PImage source;       // Source image
PImage destination;  // Destination image
```

> Two images are required, a source (original file) and destination (to be displayed) image.

```
void setup() {
  size(200, 200);
  source = loadImage("sunflower.jpg");
  destination = createImage(source.width,
              source.height, RGB);
}
```

> The destination image is created as a blank image the same size as the source.

```
void draw() {
  float threshold = 127;

  // The sketch is going to look at both image's pixels
  source.loadPixels();
  destination.loadPixels();

  for (int x = 0; x < source.width; x++) {
    for (int y = 0; y < source.height; y++) {
      int loc = x + y*source.width;
      // Test the brightness against the threshold
      if (brightness(source.pixels[loc]) > threshold){
        destination.pixels[loc] = color(255); // White
      } else {
        destination.pixels[loc] = color(0);    // Black
      }
    }
  }
```

> brightness() returns a value between 0 and 255, the overall brightness of the pixel's color. If it is more than 100, make it white, less than 100, make it black.

> Writing to the destination image's pixels.

```
  // The pixels in destination changed
  destination.updatePixels();
  // Display the destination
  image(destination, 0, 0);
}
```

> I have to display the destination image!

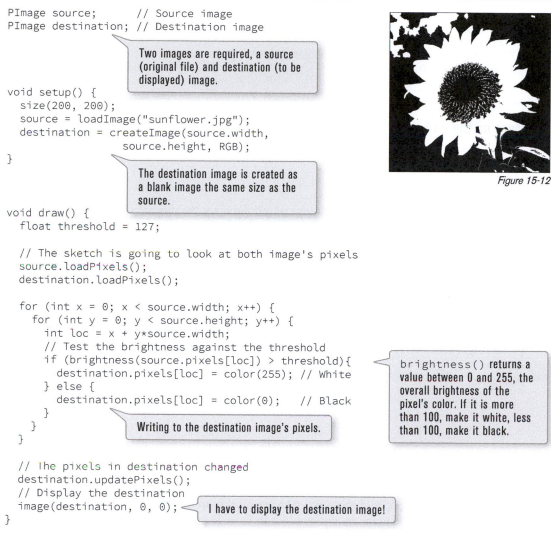

Figure 15-12

Exercise 15-9: Change the threshold according to mouseX *using* map().

This particular functionality is available without per pixel processing as part of Processing's filter() function. Understanding the lower level code, however, is crucial if you want to implement your own image processing algorithms, not available with filter().

If all you want to do is threshold, Example 15-11 is much simpler.

Example 15-11. Brightness threshold with filter

```
// Draw the image
image(img, 0, 0);
// Filter the window with a threshold effect
// 0.5 means threshold is 50% brightness
filter(THRESHOLD, 0.5);
```

More on the `filter()` function

```
filter(mode);
```

```
filter(mode, level);
```

The `filter()` function offers a set of prepackaged filters for the display window. It's not necessary to use a `PImage`, the filter will alter the look of whatever is drawn in the window at the time it is executed. Other available modes besides `THRESHOLD` are `GRAY`, `INVERT`, `POSTERIZE`, `BLUR`, `OPAQUE`, `ERODE`, and `DILATE`. See the Processing reference (*http://processing.org/reference/ filter_.html*) for examples of each.

In addition, while beyond the scope of this book, Processing also supports *shaders* via the `PShader` class. Shaders are low-level programs written in a special language called GLSL (OpenGL Shading Language) and can be used for a variety of computer graphics effects, including image processing. `PShader` is available for use with both the `P3D` and `P2D` renderers and you can learn more by reading the processing.org `PShader` tutorial by Andres Colubri (*https://processing.org/tuto rials/pshader/*).

15-9 Level II: Pixel group processing

In previous examples, you have seen a one-to-one relationship between source pixels and destination pixels. To increase an image's brightness, you take one pixel from the source image, increase the RGB values, and display one pixel in the output window. In order to perform more advanced image processing functions, however, you must move beyond the one-to-one pixel paradigm into *pixel group processing*.

Let's start by creating a new pixel out of two pixels from a source image — a pixel and its neighbor to the left.

If I know a pixel is located at (x,y):

```
int loc = x + y * img.width;
color pix = img.pixels[loc];
```

Then its left neighbor is located at (x-1,y):

```
int leftLoc = (x - 1) + y * img.width;
color leftPix = img.pixels[leftLoc];
```

I could then make a new color out of the difference between the pixel and its neighbor to the left.

```
float diff = abs(brightness(pix) - brightness(leftPix));
pixels[loc] = color(diff);
```

Example 15-12 shows the full algorithm, with the results shown in Figure 15-13.

Example 15-12. Pixel neighbor differences (edges)

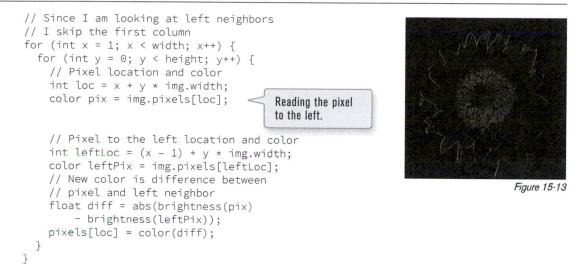

```
// Since I am looking at left neighbors
// I skip the first column
for (int x = 1; x < width; x++) {
  for (int y = 0; y < height; y++) {
    // Pixel location and color
    int loc = x + y * img.width;
    color pix = img.pixels[loc];
```

> Reading the pixel to the left.

```
    // Pixel to the left location and color
    int leftLoc = (x - 1) + y * img.width;
    color leftPix = img.pixels[leftLoc];
    // New color is difference between
    // pixel and left neighbor
    float diff = abs(brightness(pix)
        - brightness(leftPix));
    pixels[loc] = color(diff);
  }
}
```

Figure 15-13

Example 15-12 is a simple vertical edge detection algorithm. When pixels differ greatly from their neighbors, they are most likely "edge" pixels. For example, think of a picture of a white piece of paper on a black tabletop. The edges of that paper are where the colors are most different, where white meets black.

In Example 15-12, I looked at two pixels to find edges. More sophisticated algorithms, however, usually involve looking at many more neighboring pixels. After all, each pixel has eight immediate neighbors: top left, top, top right, right, bottom right, bottom, bottom left, and left. See Figure 15-14.

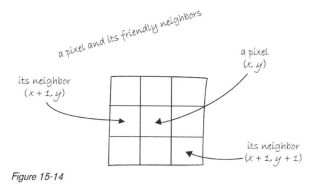

a pixel and its friendly neighbors

a pixel
(x, y)

its neighbor
(x + 1, y)

its neighbor
(x + 1, y + 1)

Figure 15-14

These image processing algorithms are often referred to as a "spatial convolution." The process uses a *weighted average* of an input pixel and its neighbors to calculate an output pixel. In other words, that new pixel is a function of an area of pixels. Neighboring areas of different sizes can be employed, such as a 3 × 3 matrix, 5 × 5, and so on.

Different combinations of weights for each pixel result in various effects. For example, an image can be *sharpened* by subtracting the neighboring pixel values and increasing the centerpoint pixel. A *blur* is achieved by taking the average of all neighboring pixels. (Note that the values in the convolution matrix add up to 1.)

For example,

```
Sharpen:
 -1 -1 -1
 -1  9 -1
 -1 -1 -1

Blur:
1/9 1/9 1/9
1/9 1/9 1/9
1/9 1/9 1/9
```

Example 15-13 performs a convolution using a 2D array (see Chapter 13 for a review of 2D arrays) to store the pixel weights of a 3 × 3 matrix. This example is probably the most advanced example you have encountered in this book so far, since it involves so many elements (nested loops, 2D arrays, pixels, etc.).

Example 15-13. Sharpen with convolution

```
PImage img;
int w = 80;

// it's possible to perform a convolution
// the image with different matrices

float[][] matrix = { { -1, -1, -1 },
                     { -1,  9, -1 },
                     { -1, -1, -1 } } ;
void setup() {
  size(200, 200);
  img = loadImage("sunflower.jpg");
}

void draw() {
  // The sketch is only going to process a portion of the image
  // so let's set the whole image as the background first
  image(img, 0, 0);

  int xstart = constrain(mouseX - w/2, 0, img.width);
  int ystart = constrain(mouseY - w/2, 0, img.height);
  int xend   = constrain(mouseX + w/2, 0, img.width);
  int yend   = constrain(mouseY + w/2, 0, img.height);
  int matrixsize = 3;
```

> The convolution matrix for a "sharpen" effect stored as a 3 × 3 two-dimensional array.

Figure 15-15

> In this example only a section of the image – an 80 × 80 rectangle around the mouse location – is processed.

```
        loadPixels();
        // Begin loops for every pixel
        for (int x = xstart; x < xend; x++) {
          for (int y = ystart; y < yend; y++) {
             color c = convolution(x, y, matrix, matrixsize, img);
             int loc = x + y*img.width;
             pixels[loc] = c;
          }
        }
        updatePixels();

        stroke(0);
        noFill();
        rect(xstart, ystart, w, w);
}
color convolution(int x, int y, float[][] matrix, int matrixsize, PImage img) {
        float rtotal = 0.0;
        float gtotal = 0.0;
        float btotal = 0.0;
        int offset = matrixsize / 2;
        // Loop through convolution matrix
        for (int i = 0; i < matrixsize; i++) {
          for (int j = 0; j < matrixsize; j++) {
             // What pixel is being examined
             int xloc = x + i - offset;
             int yloc = y + j - offset;
             int loc = xloc + img.width * yloc;

             loc = constrain(loc, 0, img.pixels.length-1);

             // Calculate the convolution
             rtotal += (red(img.pixels[loc]) * matrix[i][j]);
             gtotal += (green(img.pixels[loc]) * matrix[i][j]);
             btotal += (blue(img.pixels[loc]) * matrix[i][j]);
          }
        }
        // Make sure RGB is within range
        rtotal = constrain(rtotal, 0, 255);
        gtotal = constrain(gtotal, 0, 255);
        btotal = constrain(btotal, 0, 255);
        // Return the resulting color
        return color(rtotal, gtotal, btotal);
        }
}
```

> Each pixel location (x,y) gets passed into a function called convolution() which returns a new color value to be displayed.

> It's often good when looking at neighboring pixels to make sure you have not gone off the edge of the pixel array by accident.

> Sum all the neighboring pixels multiplied by the values in the convolution matrix.

> After the sums are constrained within a range of 0–255, a new color is made and returned.

Exercise 15-10: Try different values for the convolution matrix.

Exercise 15-11: Using the framework established by the image processing examples, create a filter that takes two images as input and generates one output image. In other words, each pixel displayed should be a function of the color values from two pixels, one from one image and one from another. For example, can you write the code to blend two images together (without using `tint()`*)?*

15-10 Creative visualization

You may be thinking: "Gosh, this is all very interesting, but seriously, when I want to blur an image or change its brightness, do I really need to write code? I mean, can't I use Photoshop?" Indeed, what I have covered here is merely an introductory understanding of what highly skilled programmers at Adobe do. The power of Processing, however, is the potential for real-time, interactive graphics applications. There is no need for you to live within the confines of "pixel point" and "pixel group" processing.

Following are two examples of algorithms for drawing Processing shapes. Instead of coloring the shapes randomly or with hard-coded values as I have in the past, I am going to select colors from the pixels of a `PImage` object. The image itself is never displayed; rather, it serves as a database of information that you can exploit for your own creative pursuits.

In this first example, for every cycle through `draw()`, I will fill one ellipse at a random location onscreen with a color taken from its corresponding location in the source image. The result is a "pointillist-like" effect. See Figure 15-16.

Example 15-14. "Pointillism"

```
PImage img;
int pointillize = 16;

void setup() {
  size(200, 200);
  img = loadImage("sunflower.jpg");
  background(0);
}

void draw() {
  // Pick a random point
  int x = int(random(img.width));
  int y = int(random(img.height));
  int loc = x + y * img.width;

  // Look up the RGB color in the source image
  img.loadPixels();
  float r = red(img.pixels[loc]);
  float g = green(img.pixels[loc]);
  float b = blue(img.pixels[loc]);

  noStroke();
  fill(r, g, b, 100);
  ellipse(x, y, pointillize, pointillize);
}
```

Figure 15-16

> Back to shapes! Instead of setting a pixel, use the color from a pixel to draw a circle.

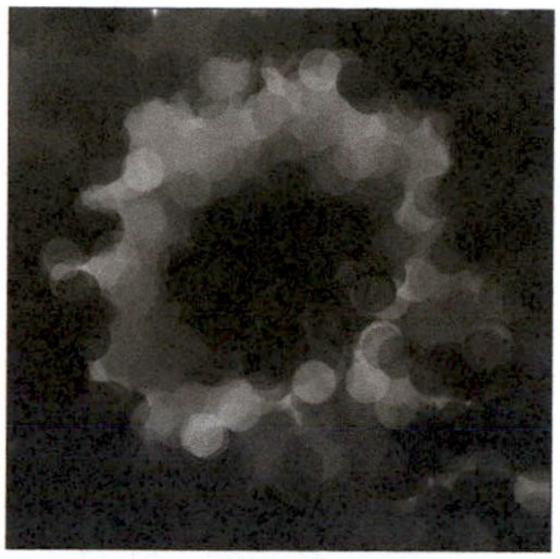

In this next example, I'll take the data from a two-dimensional image and, using the 3D translation techniques described in Chapter 14, render a rectangle for each pixel in three-dimensional space. The z position is determined by the brightness of the color. Brighter colors appear closer to the viewer and darker ones further away.

Figure 15-17

Example 15-15. 2D image mapped to 3D

```
PImage img;        // The source image
int cellsize = 2; // Dimensions of each cell in the grid
int cols, rows;    // Number of columns and rows in the system

void setup() {
  size(200, 200, P3D);
  img = loadImage("sunflower.jpg"); // Load the image
  cols = width / cellsize;              // Calculate # of columns
  rows = height / cellsize;             // Calculate # of rows
}

void draw() {
  background(255);
  img.loadPixels();
  // Begin loop for columns
  for (int i = 0; i < cols; i++) {
    // Begin loop for rows
    for (int j = 0; j < rows; j++) {
      int x = i*cellsize + cellsize/2; // x position
      int y = j*cellsize + cellsize/2; // y position
      int loc = x + y * width;         // Pixel array location
      color c = img.pixels[loc];       // Grab the color

      // Calculate a z position as a function of mouseX and pixel brightness
      float z = map(brightness(img.pixels[loc]), 0, 255, 0, mouseX);
```

> A z position is calculated by mapping pixel brightness to the mouse's x location.

```
      // Translate and draw!
      pushMatrix();
      translate(x, y, z);
      fill(c);
      noStroke();
      rectMode(CENTER);
      rect(0, 0, cellsize, cellsize);
      popMatrix();
    }
  }
}
```

Exercise 15-12: Create a sketch that uses shapes to display a pattern that covers an entire window. Load an image and color the shapes according to the pixels of that image. The following image, for example, uses triangles.

16 Video

I have no memory. It's like looking in a mirror and seeing nothing but mirror.
—Alfred Hitchcock

In this chapter:
- Displaying live video
- Displaying recorded video
- Creating a software mirror
- Computer vision basics: how to use a video camera as a sensor

16-1 Live video 101

Now that you've explored static images in Processing, you are ready to move on to moving images, specifically from a live camera (and later, from a recorded movie). I'll begin by walking through the basic steps of importing the video library and using the `Capture` class to display live video.

Step 1. Import the Processing video library.

If you skipped Chapter 12 on Processing libraries, you might want to go back and review the details. Although the video library is developed and maintained by the Processing Foundation, due to its size, it must still be downloaded separately through the contributions manager. Full instructions are provided in Section 12-3 on page 226.

Once you've got the library installed, the next step is to import the library in your code. This is done by selecting the menu option Sketch → Import Library → Video, or by typing the following line of code (which should go at the very top of your sketch):

```
import processing.video.*;
```

Using the "Import Library" menu option does nothing other than automatically insert that line into your code, so manual typing is entirely equivalent.

Step 2. Declare a `Capture` object.

You've recently seen how to create objects from classes built into the Processing language such as `PShape` and `PImage`. Both of these classes, it should be noted, are part of the *processing.core* library and, therefore, no import statement were required. The *processing.video* library has two useful classes inside of it — `Capture`, for live video, and `Movie`, for recorded video. In this step, I'll be declaring a `Capture` object.

```
Capture video;
```

Step 3. Initialize the `Capture` object.

The Capture object "video" is just like any other object. As you learned in Chapter 8, to construct an object, you use the `new` operator followed by the constructor. With a Capture object, this code typically appears in `setup()`.

```
video = new Capture();
```

The above line of code is missing the appropriate arguments for the constructor. Remember, this is not a class you wrote yourself so there is no way to know what is required between the parentheses without consulting the online reference (*http://www.processing.org/reference/libraries/video/Capture.html*).

The reference will show there are several ways to call the `Capture` constructor (see *overloading* in Chapter 23 about multiple constructors). A typical way to call the constructor is with three arguments:

```
void setup() {
  video = new Capture(this, 320, 240);
}
```

Let's walk through the arguments used in the `Capture` constructor.

- **this** — If you're confused by what `this` means, you are not alone. This is the first reference to `this` in any of the examples in this book so far. Technically speaking, `this` refers to the instance of a class in which the word `this` appears. Unfortunately, such a definition is likely to induce head spinning. A nicer way to think of it is as a self-referential statement. After all, what if you needed to refer to your Processing program within your own code? You might try to say "me" or "I." Well, these words are not available in Java, so instead you say `this`. The reason you pass `this` into the Capture object is you are telling it: "Hey listen, I want to do video capture and when the camera has a new image I want you to alert *this* sketch."
- **320** — Fortunately, the first argument, `this`, is the only confusing one. 320 refers to the width of the video captured by the camera.
- **240** — The height of the video.

There are some cases, however, where the above will not do. For example, what if you have multiple cameras attached to your computer. How do you select the one you want to capture? In addition, in some rare cases, you might also want to specify a frame rate from the camera. For these cases, Processing will give you a list of all possible camera configurations via `Capture.list()`. You can display these in your message console, for example, by saying:

```
printArray(Capture.list());
```

> When printing an array to the console, using `printArray()` rather than `println()` will format the array with line breaks and numeric indices.

You can use the text of these configurations to create a `Capture` object. On a Mac with a built-in camera, for example, this might look like:

```
video = new Capture(this, "name=FaceTime HD Camera (Built-
in),size=320x240,fps=30");
```

`Capture.list()` actually gives you an array so you can also simply refer to the index of the configuration you want.

```
video = new Capture(this, Capture.list()[0]);
```

Step 4. Start the capture process.

Once the camera is ready, it's up to you to tell Processing to start capturing images.

```
void setup() {
  video = new Capture(this, 320, 240);
  video.start();
}
```

In almost every case you want to begin capturing right in `setup()`. Nevertheless, `start()` is its own method, and you do have the option of, say, not starting capturing until some other time (such as when a button is pressed, etc.)

Step 5. Read the image from the camera.

There are two strategies for reading frames from the camera. I will briefly look at both and choose one for the remainder of the examples in this chapter. Both strategies, however, operate under the same fundamental principle: *I only want to read an image from the camera when a new frame is available to be read.*

In order to check if an image is available, you use the function `available()`, which returns true or false depending on whether something is there. If it is there, the function `read()` is called and the frame from the camera is read into memory. You can do this over and over again in the `draw()` loop, always checking to see if a new image is free to be read.

```
void draw() {
  if (video.available()) {
    video.read();
  }
}
```

The second strategy, the "event" approach, requires a function that executes any time a certain event — in this case a camera event — occurs. If you recall from Chapter 3, the function `mousePressed()` is executed whenever the mouse is pressed. With video, you have the option to implement the function `captureEvent()`, which is invoked any time a capture event occurs, that is, a new frame is available from the camera. These event functions (`mousePressed()`, `keyPressed()`, `captureEvent()`, etc.) are sometimes referred to as a "callback." And as a brief aside, if you're following closely, this is where `this` fits in. The `Capture` object, `video`, knows to notify `this` sketch by invoking `captureEvent()` because you passed it a reference to *this sketch* when creating the `Capture` object `video`.

`captureEvent()` is a function and therefore needs to live in its own block, outside of `setup()` and `draw()`.

```
void captureEvent(Capture video) {
  video.read();
}
```

You might notice something odd about `captureEvent()`. It includes an argument of type `Capture` in its definition. This might seem redundant to you; after all, in this example I already have a global variable `video`. Nevertheless in the case where you might have more than one capture device, the same event function can be used for both and the video library will make sure that the correct `Capture` object is passed in to `captureEvent()`.

To summarize, I want to call the function `read()` whenever there is something to read, and I can do so by either checking manually using `available()` within `draw()` or allowing a callback to handle it for you — `captureEvent()`. Many other libraries that I will explore in later chapters (such as Chapter 19) will work exactly the same way.

For the examples in this book, I'll use `captureEvent()`. This allows sketches to operate more efficiently by separating out the logic for reading from the camera from the main animation loop.

Step 6. Display the video image.

This is, without a doubt, the easiest part. You can think of a `Capture` object as a PImage that changes over time, and, in fact, a `Capture` object can be utilized in an identical manner as a PImage object.

```
image(video, 0, 0);
```

All of this is put together in Example 16-1.

Example 16-1. Display video

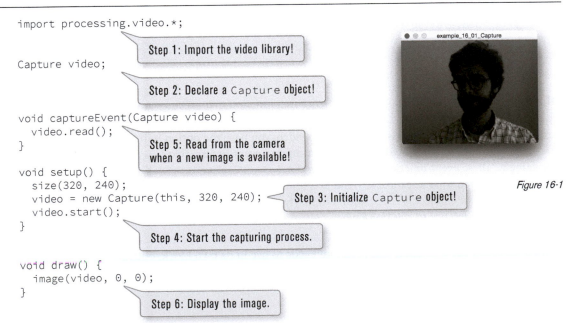

```
import processing.video.*;
```
Step 1: Import the video library!

```
Capture video;
```
Step 2: Declare a `Capture` object!

```
void captureEvent(Capture video) {
  video.read();
}
```
Step 5: Read from the camera when a new image is available!

```
void setup() {
  size(320, 240);
  video = new Capture(this, 320, 240);
  video.start();
}
```
Step 3: Initialize `Capture` object!

Step 4: Start the capturing process.

```
void draw() {
  image(video, 0, 0);
}
```
Step 6: Display the image.

Figure 16-1

Again, anything you can do with a PImage (resize, tint, move, etc.) you can do with a Capture object. As long as you read() from that object, the video image will update as you manipulate it. See Example 16-2.

Example 16-2. Manipulate video image

```
import processing.video.*;

Capture video;

void setup() {
  size(320, 240);
  video = new Capture(this, 320, 240);
  video.start();
}

void captureEvent(Capture video) {
  video.read();
}

void draw() {
  background(255);

  tint(mouseX, mouseY, 255);
  translate(width/2, height/2);
  imageMode(CENTER);
  rotate(PI/4);
  image(video, 0, 0, mouseX, mouseY);
}
```

Figure 16-2

> A video image can be tinted just like a PImage. It can also be moved, rotated, and sized just like a PImage.

Every single image example from Chapter 15 can be recreated with video. Following is the "adjusting brightness" example with a video image.

Example 16-3. Adjust video brightness

```
// Step 1. Import the video library
import processing.video.*;

// Step 2. Declare a Capture object
Capture video;

void setup() {
  size(320, 240);

  // Step 3. Initialize Capture object via Constructor
  video = new Capture(this, 320, 240);
  video.start();
}

// An event for when a new frame is available
void captureEvent(Capture video) {
  // Step 4. Read the image from the camera.
  video.read();
}
void draw() {
```

```
loadPixels();
video.loadPixels();

for (int x = 0; x < video.width; x++) {
  for (int y = 0; y < video.height; y++) {

    // Calculate the 1D location from a 2D grid
    int loc = x + y * video.width;

    // Get the red, green, blue values from a pixel
    float r = red  (video.pixels[loc]);
    float g = green(video.pixels[loc]);
    float b = blue (video.pixels[loc]);

    // Calculate an amount to change brightness based on proximity to the mouse
    float d = dist(x, y, mouseX, mouseY);
    float adjustbrightness = map(d, 0, 100, 4, 0);
    r *= adjustbrightness;
    g *= adjustbrightness;
    b *= adjustbrightness;

    // Constrain RGB to make sure they are within 0-255 color range
    r = constrain(r, 0, 255);
    g = constrain(g, 0, 255);
    b = constrain(b, 0, 255);

    // Make a new color and set pixel in the window
    color c = color(r, g, b);
    pixels[loc] = c;
  }
}
updatePixels();
}
```

Exercise 16-1: Recreate Example 15-14 (pointillism) to work with live video.

16-2 Recorded video

Displaying recorded video follows much of the same structure as live video. Processing's video library accepts most video file formats; for specifics, visit the `Movie` reference (*https://www.processing.org/refer ence/libraries/video/Movie.html*).

Step 1. Instead of a `Capture` object, declare a `Movie` object.

```
Movie movie;
```

Step 2. Initialize `Movie` object.

```
movie = new Movie(this, "testmovie.mov");
```

The only necessary arguments are `this` and the movie's filename enclosed in quotes. The movie file should be stored in the sketch's data directory.

Step 3. Start movie playing.

There are two options, `play()`, which plays the movie once, or `loop()`, which loops it continuously.

```
movie.loop();
```

Step 4. Read frame from movie.

Again, this is identical to capture. You can either check to see if a new frame is available, or use a callback function.

```
void draw() {
  if (movie.available()) {
    movie.read();
  }
}
```

Or:

```
void movieEvent(Movie movie) {
  movie.read();
}
```

Step 5. Display the movie.

```
image(movie, 0, 0);
```

Example 16-4 shows the program all put together.

Example 16-4. Display recorded movie

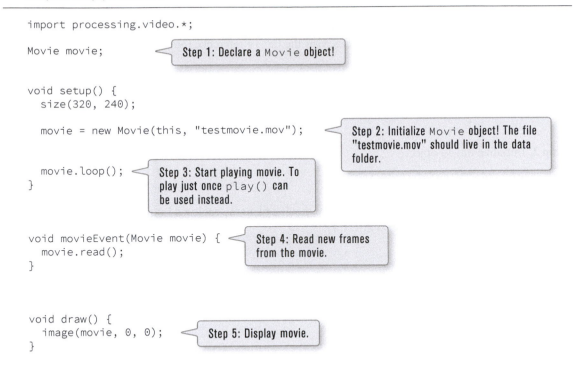

```
import processing.video.*;

Movie movie;          Step 1: Declare a Movie object!

void setup() {
  size(320, 240);

  movie = new Movie(this, "testmovie.mov");   Step 2: Initialize Movie object! The file
                                              "testmovie.mov" should live in the data
                                              folder.

  movie.loop();       Step 3: Start playing movie. To
}                     play just once play() can
                      be used instead.

void movieEvent(Movie movie) {   Step 4: Read new frames
  movie.read();                  from the movie.
}


void draw() {
  image(movie, 0, 0);   Step 5: Display movie.
}
```

Although Processing is by no means the most sophisticated environment for displaying and manipulating recorded video, there are some more advanced features available in the video library. There are functions for obtaining the duration (length measured in seconds) of a video, for speeding it up and slowing it down, and for jumping to a specific point in the video (among others). If you find that performance is sluggish and the video playback is choppy, I would suggest trying the P2D or P3D renderers as described in Section 14-2 on page 271.

Following is an example that makes use of jump() (jump to a specific point in the video) and duration() (returns the length of movie in seconds).

Example 16-5. Scrubbing forward and backward in movie

```
import processing.video.*;

Movie movie;

void setup() {
  size(200, 200);
  background(0);
  movie = new Movie(this, "testmovie.mov");
}

void movieEvent(Movie movie) {
  movie.read();
}

void draw() {
  // Ratio of mouse X over width
  float ratio = mouseX / (float) width;

  movie.jump(ratio * movie.duration());

  image(movie, 0, 0);
}
```

> In this example, if mouseX equals 0, the video jumps to the beginning. If mouseX equals width, it jumps to the end. Any other value is in between!

> The jump() function allows you to jump immediately to a point of time within the video. duration() returns the total length of the movie in seconds.

Exercise 16-2: Using the speed() *method in the* Movie *class, write a program where the user can control the playback speed of a movie with the mouse. Note* speed() *takes one argument and multiplies the movie playback rate by that value. Multiplying by 0.5 will cause the movie to play half as fast, by 2, twice as fast, by –2, twice as fast in reverse, and so on. Note that not all video formats support backward playback so reversing may only work for some video files. Details are provided in the Processing reference (https://processing.org/reference/libraries/video/Movie_speed_.html).*

16-3 Software mirrors

With small video cameras attached to more and more personal computers, developing software that manipulates an image in real-time is becoming increasingly popular. These types of applications are sometimes referred to as "mirrors," as they provide a digital reflection of a viewer's image. Processing's extensive library of functions for graphics and its ability to capture from a camera in real-time make it an excellent environment for prototyping and experimenting with software mirrors.

As I showed in this chapter, you can apply basic image processing techniques to video images, reading and replacing the pixels one by one. Taking this idea one step further, you can read the pixels and apply the colors to shapes drawn onscreen.

I will begin with an example that captures a video at 80 × 60 pixels and renders it on a 640 × 480 window. For each pixel in the video, I will draw a rectangle eight pixels wide and eight pixels tall.

Let's first write the program that displays the grid of rectangles. See Figure 16-4.

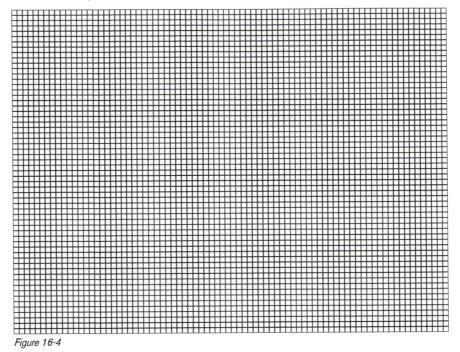

Figure 16-4

Example 16-6. Drawing a grid of 8 × 8 squares

```
// Size of each cell in the grid, ratio of window size to video size
int videoScale = 8;
// Number of columns and rows in the system
int cols, rows;

void setup() {
  size(640, 480);
  // Initialize columns and rows
  cols = width/videoScale;
  rows = height/videoScale;
}

void draw() {
  // Begin loop for columns
  for (int i = 0; i < cols; i++) {
    // Begin loop for rows
    for (int j = 0; j < rows; j++) {
      // Scaling up to draw a rectangle at (x,y)
      int x = i*videoScale;
      int y = j*videoScale;
      fill(255);
      stroke(0);
      rect(x, y, videoScale, videoScale);
    }
  }
}
```

> The `videoScale` variable stores the ratio of the window's pixel size to the grid's size.
> `80 * 8 = 640, 60 * 8 = 480`

> For every column and row, a rectangle is drawn at an (x,y) location scaled and sized by `videoScale`.

Knowing that I want to have squares eight pixels wide by eight pixels high, I can calculate the number of columns as the width divided by eight and the number of rows as the height divided by eight.

- 640/8 = 80 columns
- 480/8 = 60 rows

I can now capture a video image that is 80 × 60. This is useful because capturing a 640 × 480 video from a camera can be slow compared to 80 × 60. I only want to capture the color information at the resolution required for the sketch.

Figure 16-5

For every square at column i and row j, I look up the color at pixel (i, j) in the video image and color it accordingly. See Example 16-7 (new parts in bold).

Example 16-7. Video pixelation

```
// Size of each cell in the grid, ratio of window size to video size
int videoScale = 8;
// Number of columns and rows in the system
int cols, rows;
// Variable to hold onto Capture object
Capture video;

void setup() {
  size(640, 480);
  // Initialize columns and rows
  cols = width/videoScale;
  rows = height/videoScale;
  background(0);
  video = new Capture(this, cols, rows);
}

// Read image from the camera
void captureEvent(Capture video) {
  video.read();
}

void draw() {
video.loadPixels();
  // Begin loop for columns
  for (int i = 0; i < cols; i++) {
    // Begin loop for rows
    for (int j = 0; j < rows; j++) {
      // Where are you, pixel-wise?
      int x = i*videoScale;
      int y = j*videoScale;
      color c = video.pixels[i + j*video.width];
      fill(c);
      stroke(0);
      rect(x, y, videoScale, videoScale);
    }
  }
}
```

> The color for each square is pulled from the Capture object's pixel array.

As you can see, expanding the simple grid system to include colors from video only requires a few additions. I have to declare and initialize the Capture object, read from it, and pull colors from the pixel array.

Less literal mappings of pixel colors to shapes in the grid can also be applied. In the following example, only the colors black and white are used. Squares are larger where brighter pixels in the video appear, and smaller for darker pixels. See Figure 16-6.

Figure 16-6

Example 16-8. Brightness mirror

```
// Each pixel from the video source is drawn as
// a rectangle with size based on brightness.

import processing.video.*;

// Size of each cell in the grid
int videoScale = 10;
// Number of columns and rows in the system
int cols, rows;
// Variable for capture device
Capture video;

void setup() {
  size(640, 480);
  // Initialize columns and rows
  cols = width / videoScale;
  rows = height / videoScale;
  // Construct the Capture object
  video = new Capture(this, cols, rows);
  video.start();
}

void captureEvent(Capture video) {
  video.read();
}
void draw() {
  background(0);
```

```
video.loadPixels();
// Begin loop for columns
for (int i = 0; i < cols; i++) {
  // Begin loop for rows
  for (int j = 0; j < rows; j++) {
    // Where are you, pixel-wise?
    int x = i*videoScale;
    int y = j*videoScale;

    int loc = (video.width - i - 1) + j * video.width;
```

> In order to mirror the image, the column is reversed with the following formula: mirrored column × width – column – 1

```
    color c = video.pixels[loc];
    float sz = (brightness(c)/255) * videoScale;
```

> A rectangle's size is calculated as a function of the pixel's brightness. A bright pixel is a large rectangle, and a dark pixel is a small one.

```
    rectMode(CENTER);
    fill(255);
    noStroke();
    rect(x + videoScale/2, y + videoScale/2, sz, sz);
  }
 }
}
```

It's often useful to think of developing software mirrors in two steps. This will also help you think beyond the more obvious mapping of pixels to shapes on a grid.

Step 1. Develop an interesting pattern that covers an entire window.

Step 2. Use a video's pixels as a look-up table for coloring that pattern.

Say for Step 1, I write a program that scribbles a random line around the window. Here is my algorithm, written in pseudocode.

- Start with an (x,y) position at the center of the screen.
- Repeat forever the following:
  — Pick a new (x,y), staying within the window.
  — Draw a line from the old (x,y) to the new (x,y).
  — Save the new (x,y).

Example 16-9. The scribbler

```
// Two global variables
float x;
float y;

void setup() {
  size(320, 240);
  background(255);
  // Start x and y in the center
  x = width/2;
  y = height/2;
}


void draw() {

  float newx = constrain(x + random(-20, 20), 0, width);
  float newy = constrain(y + random(-20, 20), 0, height);

  // Line from (x,y) to the (newx,newy)
  stroke(0);
  strokeWeight(4);
  line(x, y, newx, newy);

  x = newx;
  y = newy;
}
```

Figure 16-7

> A new (x,y) location is picked as the current (x,y) plus or minus a random value. The new location is constrained within the window's pixels.

> Save the new location in (x,y) in order to start the process over again.

Now that I have finished the pattern generating sketch, I can change stroke() to set a color according to the video image. Note again the new lines of code added in bold in Example 16-10.

Example 16-10. The scribbler mirror

```
import processing.video.*;

// Two global variables
float x;
float y;

// Variable to hold onto Capture object
Capture video;

void setup() {
  size(320, 240);
  background(0);
  // Start x and y in the center
  x = width/2;
  y = height/2;
  // Start the capture process
  video = new Capture(this, width, height);
  video.start();
}

void captureEvent(Capture video) {
  // Read image from the camera
  video.read();
}

void draw() {
  video.loadPixels();

  // Pick a new x and y
  float newx = constrain(x + random(-20, 20), 0, width-1);
  float newy = constrain(y + random(-20, 20), 0, height-1);

  // Find the midpoint of the line
  int midx = int((newx + x) / 2);
  int midy = int((newy + y) / 2);
  // Pick the color from the video, reversing x
  color c = video.pixels[(width-1-midx) + midy*video.width];

  // Draw a line from (x,y) to (newx,newy)
  stroke(c);
  strokeWeight(4);
  line(x, y, newx, newy);

  // Save (newx,newy) in (x,y)
  x = newx;
  y = newy;
}
```

Figure 16-8

If the window were larger (say 800 × 600 pixels), you might want to scale the captured image down so that you do not have to capture such a high-resolution image.

The color for the scribbler is pulled from a pixel in the video image.

Exercise 16-3: Create your own software mirror using the methodology from Example 16-9 and Example 16-10. Create your system without the video first and then incorporate using the video's pixels to determine colors, behaviors, and so on.

16-4 Video as sensor, computer vision

Every example in this chapter has treated the video camera as a data source for digital imagery displayed onscreen. This section will provide a simple introduction to things you can do with a video camera when you do not display the image, that is, "computer vision." Computer vision is a scientific field of research dedicated to machines that *see*, using the camera as a sensor.

In order to better understand the inner workings of computer vision algorithms, I will write all of the code on a pixel-by-pixel level. However, to explore these topics further, you might consider downloading some of the third-party computer vision libraries that are available for Processing. Many of these libraries have advanced features beyond what will be covered in this chapter. A brief overview of the libraries will be offered at the end of this section.

Let's begin with a simple example.

The video camera is your friend because it provides a ton of information. A 320 × 240 image is 76,800 pixels! What if you were to boil down all of those pixels into one number: the overall brightness of a room? This could be accomplished with a one-dollar light sensor (or "photocell"), but as an exercise I will make a webcam do it.

You have seen in other examples that the brightness value of an individual pixel can be retrieved with the `brightness()` function, which returns a floating point number between 0 and 255. The following line of code retrieves the brightness for the first pixel in the video image.

```
float brightness = brightness(video.pixels[0]);
```

I can then compute the overall (i.e., average) brightness by adding up all the brightness values and dividing by the total number of pixels.

```
video.loadPixels();
// Start with a total of 0
float totalBrightness = 0;
// Sum the brightness of each pixel
for (int i = 0; i < video.pixels.length; i++) {
  color c = video.pixels[i];
  totalBrightness + = brightness(c);          Sum all brightness values.
}

// Compute the average
float averageBrightness = totalBrightness / video.pixels.length;
// Display the background as average brightness
background(averageBrightness);              Average brightness = total
                                            brightness / total pixels
```

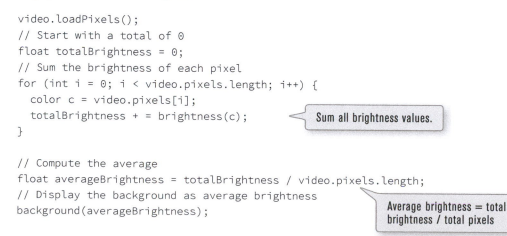

Before you start to cheer too enthusiastically from this accomplishment, while this example is an excellent demonstration of an algorithm that analyzes data provided by a video source, it does not begin to harness the power of what one can "see" with a video camera. After all, a video image is not just a collection of colors, but it is a also collection of spatially oriented colors. By developing algorithms that search through the pixels and recognize patterns, you can start to develop more advanced computer vision applications.

Tracking the brightest color is a good first step. Imagine a dark room with a single moving light source. With the techniques you will learn, that light source could replace the mouse as a form of interaction. Yes, you are on your way to playing Pong with a flashlight.

First, I will examine how to search through an image and find the (x,y) location of the brightest pixel. The strategy I will employ is to loop through all the pixels, looking for the "world record" brightest pixel (using the brightness() function). Initially, the world record will be held by the first pixel. As other pixels beat that record, they will become the world record holder. At the end of the loop, whichever pixel is the current record holder gets the "Brightest Pixel of the Image" award.

Here is the code:

```
// The world record is 0 at first
float worldRecord = 0.0;
// Which pixel will win the prize?
int xRecordHolder = 0;
int yRecordHolder = 0;

for (int x = 0; x < video.width; x++) {
  for (int y = 0; y < video.height; y++) {
    // What is current brightness
    int loc = x + y*video.width;
    float currentBrightness = brightness(video.pixels[loc]);
    if (currentBrightness > worldRecord) {
      // Set a new record
      worldRecord = currentBrightness;
      // This pixel holds the record!
      xRecordHolder = x;
      yRecordHolder = y;
    }
  }
}
```

> When you find the new brightest pixel, you must save the (x,y) location of that pixel in the array so that you can access it later.

A natural extension of this example would be to track a specific color, rather than simply the brightest. For example, I could look for the most "red" or the most "blue" in a video image. In order to perform this type of analysis, I will need to develop a methodology for comparing colors. Let's create two colors, c1 and c2.

```
color c1 = color(255, 100, 50);
color c2 = color(150, 255, 0);
```

Colors can only be compared in terms of their red, green, and blue components, so I must first separate out these values.

```
float r1 = red(c1);
float g1 = green(c1);
float b1 = blue(c1);
float r2 = red(c2);
float g2 = green(c2);
float b2 = blue(c2);
```

Now, I am ready to compare the colors. One strategy is to take the sum of the absolute value of the differences. That is a mouthful, but it's really fairly simple. Take r1 minus r2. Since I only care about the magnitude of the difference, not whether it is positive or negative, take the absolute value (the positive version of the number). Do this for green and blue, and add them all together.

```
float diff = abs(r1 - r2) + abs(g1 - g2) + abs(b1 - b2);
```

While this is perfectly adequate (and a fast calculation at that), a more accurate way to compute the difference between colors is to take the "distance" between colors. OK, so you may be thinking: "Um, seriously? How can a color be far away or close to another color?" Well, you know the distance between two points is calculated via the Pythagorean Theorem. You can think of color as a point in three-dimensional space, only instead of (x,y,z), you have (r,g,b). If two colors are near each other in this color space, they are similar; if they are far, they are different.

```
float diff = dist(r1, g1, b1, r2, g2, b2);
```

Looking for the *most red* pixel in an image, for example, is therefore looking for the color *closest* to red — (255,0,0).

By adjusting the brightness tracking code to look for the closest pixel to any given color (rather than the brightest), I can put together a color tracking sketch. In the following example, the user can click the mouse on a color in the image to be tracked. A black circle will appear at the location that most closely matches that color. See Figure 16-9.

Example 16-11. Simple color tracking

```
import processing.video.*;

// Variable for capture device
Capture video;
color trackColor;        ◁  A variable for the color
                            you are searching for.
void setup() {
  size(320, 240);
  video = new Capture(this, width, height);
  video.start();
  // Start off tracking for red
  trackColor = color(255, 0, 0);
}

void captureEvent(Capture video) {
  // Read image from the camera
```

Figure 16-9

```
    video.read();
}

void draw() {
  video.loadPixels();
  image(video, 0, 0);

  float worldRecord = 500;
  // (x,y) coordinate of closest color
  int closestX = 0;
  int closestY = 0;
  // Begin loop to walk through every pixel
  for (int x = 0; x < video.width; x++) {
    for (int y = 0; y < video.height; y++) {
      int loc = x + y * video.width;
      // What is current color
      color currentColor = video.pixels[loc];
      float r1 = red(currentColor);
      float g1 = green(currentColor);
      float b1 = blue(currentColor);
      float r2 = red(trackColor);
      float g2 = green(trackColor);
      float b2 = blue(trackColor);
      // Using euclidean distance to compare colors
      float d = dist(r1, g1, b1, r2, g2, b2);

      // If current color is more similar to tracked
      // color than closest color, save current location
      // and current difference
      if (d < worldRecord) {
        worldRecord = d;
        closestX = x;
        closestY = y;
      }
    }
  }

  if (worldRecord < 10) {
    // Draw a circle at the tracked pixel
    fill(trackColor);
    strokeWeight(4);
    stroke(0);
    ellipse(closestX, closestY, 16, 16);
  }
}

void mousePressed() {
  // Save color where the mouse is clicked in trackColor variable
  int loc = mouseX + mouseY * video.width;
  trackColor = video.pixels[loc];
}
```

> Before I begin searching, the "world record" for closest color is set to a high number that is easy for the first pixel to beat.

> I am using the dist() function to compare the current color with the color being tracked.

> I only consider the color found if its color distance is less than 10. This threshold of ten is arbitrary, and you can adjust this number depending on how accurate you require the tracking to be.

Exercise 16-4: Although more accurate, because `dist()` *involves a square root in its calculation, it's slower than the absolute value of the difference methodology. One way around this is to write your own color distance function without the square root. Rewrite Example 16-11 using the new method below. How do you need to adjust the threshold given the lack of square root?*

```
float colorDiff(float r1, float g1, float b1, _____) {
    return (r1-r2)*(r1-r2) + (g1-g2)*(g1-g2) + (b1-b2)*(b1-2);
}
```

Exercise 16-5: Take any Processing sketch you've previously created that involves mouse interaction and replace the mouse with color tracking. Create an environment for the camera that is simple and high contrast. For example, point the camera at a black (or white) tabletop with a small white (or black) object. (If you don't have a solid color tabletop, try covering with something like a white T-shirt.) Control your sketch with the object's location. The picture shown illustrates the example that controls the "snake" from Example 9-8 with a tracked bottlecap.

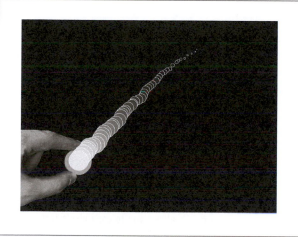

16-5 Background removal

The distance comparison for color proves useful in other computer vision algorithms as well, such as background removal. Let's say you wanted to show a video of you dancing the hula, only you did not want to be dancing in your office where you happen to be, but at the beach with waves crashing behind you. Background removal is a technique that allows you to remove the background of an image (your office) and replace it with any pixels you like (the beach), while leaving the foreground (you dancing) intact.

Here is the algorithm.

- Memorize a background image.
- Check every pixel in the current video frame. If it's very different from the corresponding pixel in the background image, it is a foreground pixel. If not, it is a background pixel. Display only foreground pixels.

To demonstrate the above algorithm, let's create a reverse green screen. The sketch will remove the background from an image and replace it with green pixels.

Step one is "memorizing" the background. The background is essentially a snapshot from the video. Since the video image changes over time, I must save a copy of a frame of video in a separate PImage object.

```
PImage backgroundImage;

void setup() {
    backgroundImage = createImage(video.width, video.height, RGB);
}
```

When backgroundImage is created, it's a blank image, with the same dimensions as the video. It's not particularly useful in this form, so I need to copy an image from the camera into the background image when I want to memorize the background. Let's do this when the mouse is pressed.

```
void mousePressed() {
    // Copying the current frame of video into the backgroundImage object
    // Note copy takes 5 arguments:
    // The source image
    // x, y, width, and height of region to be copied from the source
    // x, y, width, and height of copy destination
    backgroundImage.copy(video, 0, 0, video.width, video.height,
        0, 0, video.width,video.height);
    backgroundImage.updatePixels();
}
```

> copy() allows you to copy pixels from one image to another. Note that updatePixels() should be called after new pixels are copied!

Once I have the background image saved, I can loop through all the pixels in the current frame and compare them to the background using the distance calculation. For any given pixel (x,y), I use the following code:

```
int loc = x + y * video.width;        // Step 1: what is the 1D pixel location?
color fgColor = video.pixels[loc];              // Step 2: the foreground color
color bgColor = backgroundImage.pixels[loc]; // Step 3: the background color

// Step 4: Compare the foreground and background color
float r1 = red(fgColor); float g1 = green(fgColor); float b1 = blue(fgColor);
float r2 = red(bgColor); float g2 = green(bgColor); float b2 = blue(bgColor);
float diff = dist(r1, g1, b1, r2, g2, b2);

// Step 5: Is the foreground color different from the background color
```

```
   if (diff > threshold) {
     // If so, display the foreground color
     pixels[loc] = fgColor;
   } else {
     // If not, display green
     pixels[loc] = color(0, 255, 0);
   }
```

The above code assumes a variable named `threshold`. The lower the `threshold`, the *easier* it is for a pixel to be in the foreground. It does not have to be very different from the background pixel. Here is the full example with `threshold` as a global variable.

Example 16-12. Simple background removal

```
import processing.video.*;

// Variable for capture device
Capture video;
// Saved background
PImage backgroundImage;
// How different must a pixel be to be foreground
float threshold = 20;

void setup() {
  size(320, 240);
  video = new Capture(this, width, height);
  video.start();
  // Create an empty image the same size as the video
  backgroundImage = createImage(video.width, video.height, RGB);
}

void captureEvent(Capture video) {
  video.read();
}

void draw() {
  loadPixels();
  video.loadPixels();
  backgroundImage.loadPixels();

  // Draw the video image on the background
  image(video, 0, 0);
  // Begin loop to walk through every pixel
  for (int x = 0; x < video.width; x++) {
    for (int y = 0; y < video.height; y++) {
      int loc = x + y*video.width; // Step 1, what is the 1D pixel location
      color fgColor = video.pixels[loc]; // Step 2, what is the foreground color
      // Step 3, what is the background color
      color bgColor = backgroundImage.pixels[loc];
      // Step 4, compare the foreground and background color
      float r1 = red   (fgColor);
      float g1 = green(fgColor);
      float b1 = blue  (fgColor);
      float r2 = red   (bgColor);
      float g2 = green(bgColor);
```

Figure 16-10

> I am looking at the video's pixels, the memorized backgroundImage's pixels, as well as accessing the display pixels. `loadPixels()` for all!

```
      float b2 = blue (bgColor);
      float diff = dist(r1, g1, b1, r2, g2, b2);

      // Step 5, Is the foreground color different from the background color
      if (diff > threshold) {
        // If so, display the foreground color
        pixels[loc] = fgColor;
      } else {
        // If not, display green
        pixels[loc] = color(0, 255, 0);
      }
    }
  }
  updatePixels();
}

void mousePressed() {
  // Copying the current frame of video into the backgroundImage object
  // Note copy takes nine arguments:
  // The source image
  // x, y, width, and height of region to be copied from the source
  // x, y, width, and height of copy destination
  backgroundImage.copy(video, 0, 0, video.width, video.height,
      0, 0, video.width, video.height);
  backgroundImage.updatePixels();
}
```

> You could choose to replace the background pixels with something other than the color green!

When you get to running this example, step out of the frame, click the mouse to memorize the background without you in it, and then step back into the frame; you will see the result as seen in Figure 16-10.

If this sketch does not seem to work for you at all, check and see what "automatic" features are enabled on your camera. For example, if your camera is set to automatically adjust brightness or white balance, you have a problem. Even though the background image is memorized, once the entire image becomes brighter or changes hue, this sketch will think all the pixels have changed and are therefore part of the foreground! For best results, disable all automatic features on your camera.

Exercise 16-6: Instead of replacing the background with green pixels, replace it with another image. What values work well for threshold and what values do not work at all? Try controlling the threshold variable with the mouse.

16-6 Motion detection

Today is a happy day. Why? Because all of the work you did to learn how to remove the background from a video gets you motion detection for free. In the background removal example, I examined each pixel's relationship to a stored background image. Motion in a video image occurs when a pixel color differs greatly from what it used to be one frame earlier. In other words, motion detection is exactly the same algorithm, only instead of saving a background image once, you save the previous frame of video constantly!

The following example is identical to the background removal example with only one important change — *the previous frame of video is always saved whenever a new frame is available.*

```
void captureEvent(Capture video) {
  // Before reading the new frame, always save the previous frame for comparison!
  prevFrame.copy(video, 0, 0, video.width, video.height,
      0, 0, video.width, video.height);
  prevFrame.updatePixels();
  video.read();
}
```

(The colors displayed are also changed to black and white and some of the variable names are different, but these are trivial changes.)

Example 16-13. Simple motion detection

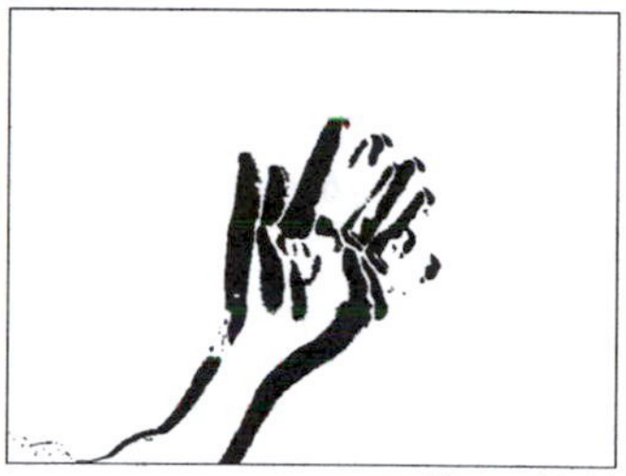

```
import processing.video.*;

// Variable for capture device
Capture video;
// Previous Frame
PImage prevFrame;
// How different must a pixel be to be a "motion" pixel
float threshold = 50;

void setup() {
  size(320, 240);
  video = new Capture(this, width, height, 30);
  video.start();
  // Create an empty image the same size as the video
  prevFrame = createImage(video.width, video.height, RGB);
}
```

Figure 16-11

```
void captureEvent(Capture video) {
  // Before reading the new frame, always save the previous frame for comparison!
  prevFrame.copy(video, 0, 0, video.width, video.height, 0,
      0, video.width, video.height);
  prevFrame.updatePixels();  // Read image from the camera
  video.read();
}

void draw() {
  loadPixels();
  video.loadPixels();
  prevFrame.loadPixels();

  // Begin loop to walk through every pixel
  for (int x = 0; x < video.width; x++) {
    for (int y = 0; y < video.height; y++) {
      int loc = x + y * video.width; // Step 1: What is the 1D pixel location?
      color current = video.pixels[loc]; // Step 2: What is the current color?
      color previous = prevFrame.pixels[loc]; // Step 3: what is the previous color?
      // Step 4, compare colors (previous vs. current)
      float r1 = red(current); float g1 = green(current); float b1 = blue(current);
```

```
      float r2 = red(previous); float g2 = green(previous);
      float b2 = blue(previous);
      float diff = dist(r1, g1, b1, r2, g2, b2);
      // Step 5, How different are the colors?
      if (diff > threshold) {
        // If motion, display black
        pixels[loc] = color(0);
      } else {
        // If not, display white
        pixels[loc] = color(255);
      }
    }
  }
  updatePixels();
}
```

> If the color at that pixel has changed, then there is "motion" at that pixel.

What if you want to know only the "overall" motion in a room? At the start of Section 16-4 on page 345, I calculated the average brightness of an image by taking the sum of each pixel's brightness and dividing it by the total number of pixels.

Average Brightness = Total Brightness / Total Number of Pixels

I can calculate the average motion the same way:

Average Motion = Total Motion / Total Number of Pixels

The following example displays a circle that changes color and size based on the average amount of motion. Note again that you do not need to *display* the video in order to analyze it!

Example 16-14. Overall motion

```
import processing.video.*;

// Variable for capture device
Capture video;
// Previous Frame
PImage prevFrame;
// How different must a pixel be to be a "motion" pixel
float threshold = 50;

void setup() {
  size(320, 240);
  // Using the default capture device
  video = new Capture(this, width, height);
  video.start();
  // Create an empty image the same size as the video
  prevFrame = createImage(video.width, video.height, RGB);
}

// New frame available from camera
void captureEvent(Capture video) {
  // Save previous frame for motion detection!!
  prevFrame.copy(video, 0, 0, video.width, video.height, 0, 0, video.width,
```

```
    video.height);
      prevFrame.updatePixels();
      video.read();
    }

    void draw() {
      background(0);

      // If you want to display the videoY
      // You don't need to display it to analyze it!
      image(video, 0, 0);

      loadPixels();
      video.loadPixels();
      prevFrame.loadPixels();

      // Begin loop to walk through every pixel
      // Start with a total of 0
      float totalMotion = 0;
      // Sum the brightness of each pixel
      for (int i = 0; i < video.pixels.length; i++) {
        color current = video.pixels[i];
        // Step 2: What is the current color?
        color previous = prevFrame.pixels[i];
        // Step 3: What is the previous color?
        // Step 4: Compare colors (previous vs. current)
        float r1 = red(current);
        float g1 = green(current);
        float b1 = blue(current);
        float r2 = red(previous);
        float g2 = green(previous);
        float b2 = blue(previous);

        float diff = dist(r1, g1, b1, r2, g2, b2);

        totalMotion += diff;
      }

      float avgMotion = totalMotion / video.pixels.length;

      // Draw a circle based on average motion
      fill(0);
      float r = avgMotion * 2;
      ellipse(width/2, height/2, r, r);
    }
```

> Motion for an individual pixel is the difference between the previous color and current color.

> totalMotion is the sum of all color differences.

> averageMotion is total motion divided by the number of pixels analyzed.

Exercise 16-7: Create a sketch that looks for the average location of motion. Can you have an ellipse follow your waving hand?

16-7 Computer vision libraries

There are several computer vision libraries already available for Processing (and there will inevitably be more). The nice thing about writing your own computer vision code is that you can control the vision algorithm at the lowest level, performing an analysis that conforms precisely to your needs. The benefit to using a third-party library is that since there has been a great deal of research in solving common computer vision problems (detecting edges, blobs, motion, tracking color, etc.), you do not need to do all of the hard work yourself! You can find a full list on the Processing website (*http://processing.org/reference/libraries/#video&vision*). Here are two I would recommend checking out.

OpenCV for Processing by Greg Borenstein (*https://github.com/atduskgreg/opencv-processing*)

OpenCV ("Open Source Computer Vision") is an open source library written in C++ and originally developed by Intel Research. It provides a broad array of computer vision and image processing capabilities from image filtering to contour finding to object detection and more.

BlobDetection by Julien "v3ga" Gachadoat (*http://www.v3ga.net/processing/BlobDetection/*)

This library, as made obvious by its name, is specifically designed for detecting blobs in an image. Blobs are defined as areas of pixels whose brightness is above or below a certain threshold. The library takes any image as input and returns an array of `Blob` objects, each of which can tell you about its edge points and bounding box.

Finally, it's also worth mentioning that recent innovations in depth sensing (most notably with the Microsoft Kinect sensor) have made many complex computer vision problems possible to implement in Processing. As all the examples in this chapter show, a traditional camera provides a grid of pixels. What if you could know the distance of each pixel from the camera? This would certainly make background subtraction much simpler for example. With a depth sensor, this is all possible. For more about depth sensing, visit the book's website for links and examples.

Lesson Seven Project

Develop a software mirror that incorporates computer vision techniques. Follow these steps.

1. Design a pattern with no color. This could be a static pattern (such as a mosaic) or a moving one (such as the "scribbler" example) or a combination.

2. Color that pattern according to pixels from an image.

3. Replace the JPG with images from a live camera (or recorded movie).

4. Using computer vision techniques, alter the behavior of the the drawn elements according to the properties of the image. For example, perhaps brighter pixels cause shapes to spin or pixels that change a lot cause shapes to fly off the screen, and so on.

Use the space provided below to sketch designs, notes, and pseudocode for your project.

Lesson Eight

The Outside World

Chapter 17

Chapter 18

Chapter 19

17 Text

I could entertain future historians by saying I think all this superstring stuff is crazy.
—Richard Feynman

In this chapter:
- Storing text in a `String` object
- Basic `String` functionality
- Creating and loading fonts
- Displaying text

17-1 Where do strings come from?

In Chapter 15, I discussed a new object data type built into the Processing environment for dealing with images — `PImage`. In this chapter, I will introduce another new data type, another class you get for free with Processing, called `String`.

The `String` class is not a completely new concept. You have dealt with strings before whenever you have printed some text to the message window or loaded an image from a file.

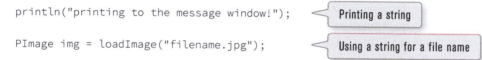

```
println("printing to the message window!");          Printing a string

PImage img = loadImage("filename.jpg");              Using a string for a file name
```

Nevertheless, although I have used a string here and there, I have yet to explore them fully and unleash their potential in this book. In order to understand the origins of the string, let's remind ourselves where classes come from. You know you can create your own classes (`Zoog`, `Car`, etc.). You can use classes built into the Processing environment, such as `PImage`. And finally, in the last chapter you learned that you could import additional Processing libraries to use certain classes such as `Capture` or `Movie`.

Nevertheless, these classes come from your life in the Processing bubble. You have yet to venture out into the great unknown, the world of thousands upon thousands of available Java classes. Before I leap over the Java API cliff (which I will do in Chapter 23), it's useful to just peek over the edge and explore one of the most basic and fundamental Java classes out there, the `String` class, which I will use to store and manipulate text.

Where do you find documentation for the `String` class?

In order to learn the details about built-in variables, functions, and classes, the Processing reference has always been your guide. Although technically a Java class, because the `String` class is so commonly used, Processing includes documentation in its reference. In addition, no import statement is required.

The Processing reference (*http://processing.org/reference/String.html*) only covers a few of the available methods of the String class. The full documentation can be found at Oracle's Java site (*http://docs.oracle.com/javase/7/docs/api/java/lang/String.html*). Also note the URL for the entire Java API. (*http://docs.oracle.com/javase/7/docs/api/*)

I am not going to cover how to use the Java documentation just yet (see Chapter 23 for more), but you can whet your appetite by visiting and perusing the above links.

17-2 What is a string?

A string, at its core, is a fancy way of storing an array of characters — if you did not have the String class, you would probably have to write some code like this:

```
char[] sometext = {'H', 'e', 'l', 'l', 'o', ' ', 'W', 'o', 'r', 'l', 'd' } ;
```

Clearly, this would be a royal pain in the Processing behind. It's much simpler to do the following and make a String object:

```
String sometext = "How do I make a String? Type characters between quotes!";
```

It appears from the above that a string is nothing more than a list of characters in between quotes. Nevertheless, this is only the data of a string. A string is an object with methods (which you can find on the reference page). This is the same as how a PImage object stored the data associated with an image as well as had functionality in the form of methods: copy(), loadPixels(), and so on. I will look more closely at String methods in Chapter 18. However, here are a few examples.

The method charAt() returns the individual character in a string at a given index. Strings are just like arrays in that the first character is index #0!

Exercise 17-1: What is the result of the following code?

```
String message = "a bunch of text here.";
char c = message.charAt(3);
println(c);

--------
```

Another useful method is length(). This is easy to confuse with the length property of an array. However, when you ask for the length of a String object, you must use the parentheses since you are calling a function called length() rather than accessing a property called length.

```
String message = "This String is 34 characters long.";
println(message.length());
```

Exercise 17-2: Loop through and print every character of a String one at a time.

```
String message = "a bunch of text here." ;
for (int i = 0; i < _____); i++) {
  char c = _____ ;
  println(c);
}
```

You can also change a String to all uppercase (or lowercase) using the toUpperCase() or toLowerCase() method.

```
String uppercase = message.toUpperCase();
println(uppercase);
```

You might notice something a bit odd here. Why didn't I simply say message.toUpperCase(); and then print the message variable? Instead, I assigned the result of message.toUpperCase() to a new variable with a different name — uppercase.

This is because a String is a special kind of object. It is *immutable*. An immutable object is one whose data can never be changed. Once you create a String object, it stays the same for life. Any time you want to change the string, you have to create a new one. So in the case of converting to uppercase, the method toUpperCase() returns a copy of the String object with all caps.

The last method I will cover in this chapter is equals(). You might first think to compare strings using the == operator.

```
String one = "hello";
String two = "hello";
println(one == two);
```

Technically speaking, when == is used with objects, it compares the memory addresses for each object. Even though each string contains the same data — "hello" — if they are different object instances, then == could result in a false comparison. The equals() function ensures that you are checking to see if two String objects contain the exact same sequence of characters, regardless of where that data is stored in the computer's memory.

```
String one = "hello";
String two = "hello";
println(one.equals(two));
```

Although both of the above methods return the correct result, it's safer to use equals(). Depending on how String objects are created in a sketch, == will not always work.

Exercise 17-3: Find the duplicates in the following array of Strings.

```
String[] words = { "I", "love", "coffee", "I", "love", "tea" } ;

for (int i = 0; i < _____; i++) {

    for (int j = _____; j < _____; j++) {

        if (_____) {

            println(_____ + " is a duplicate. ");
        }
    }
}
```

One other feature of String objects is concatenation, joining two strings together. Strings are joined with the "+" operator. The "+" operator, of course, usually means *add* in the case of numbers. When used with strings, it means *join*.

```
String helloworld = "Hello" + "World";
```

Variables can also be appended to a string using concatenation.

```
int x = 10;
String message = "The value of x is: " + x;
```

You saw an example of this in Chapter 15 when loading an array of images with numbered filenames.

Exercise 17-4: Concatenate a string from the variables given that outputs the following message.

That rectangle is 10 pixels wide, 12 pixels tall and sitting right at (100,100).

```
float w = 10;
float h = 12;
float x = 100;
float y = 100;

String message = _____;
println(message);
```

17-3 Displaying text

I will continue to explore the functions available as part of the `String` class in Chapter 18, which focuses on analyzing and manipulating text. What you have learned so far about strings is enough to get to the focus of this chapter: *rendering text*.

The easiest way to display text is to print it in the message window. This is likely something you have been doing now and then while debugging. For example, if you needed to know the horizontal mouse location, you would write:

```
println(mouseX);
```

Or if you needed to determine that a certain part of the code was executed, you might print out a descriptive message.

```
println("I got here and I'm printing out the mouse location!!!");
```

While this is valuable for debugging, it's not going to help the goal of displaying text for a user. To place text onscreen, you have to follow a series of simple steps.

1. **Declare an object of type PFont.**

   ```
   PFont f;
   ```

2. **Specify a font by referencing the font name in the function** `createFont()`. This should be done only once, usually in `setup()`. Just as with loading an image, the process of loading a font into memory is slow and would seriously affect the sketch's performance if placed inside `draw()`.

   ```
   f = createFont("Georgia", 16);
   ```

   The `createFont()` function also takes a second argument, the size of your font. While you will be able to dynamically adjust text size over the course of your Processing sketch you should pick a size that you plan to start with. For a list of available fonts (same as fonts you have installed on your system), you can use `printArray(PFont.list());`.

3. **Specify the font using** `textFont()`. `textFont()` takes one or two arguments, the font variable and the font size, which is optional. If you do not include the font size, the font will be displayed at the size originally loaded. (Note that with the P2D and P3D renderers, specifying a font size that is different from the size originally specified may result in pixelated or poor quality text.)

   ```
   textFont(f, 36);
   ```

4. **Specify a color using** `fill()`.

   ```
   fill(0);
   ```

5. **Call the** `text()` **function to display text.** (This function is just like shape or image drawing, it takes three arguments — the text to be displayed, and the x and y coordinate at which to display that text.)

   ```
   text("To be or not to be.", 10, 100);
   ```

All the steps together are shown in Example 17-1. Steps 1-3 are optional as Processing will use a default font and size should you not specify one.

Example 17-1. Simple displaying text

```
PFont f;// Step 1: Declare PFont variable

void setup() {
  size(200, 200);
  f = createFont("Georgia", 16); // Step 2: Load Font
}

void draw() {
  background(255);
  textFont(f, 16);      // Step 3: Specify font to be
used
  fill(0);              // Step 4: Specify font color

  // Step 5: Display Text
  text ("To be or note to be.", 10, 100);
}
```

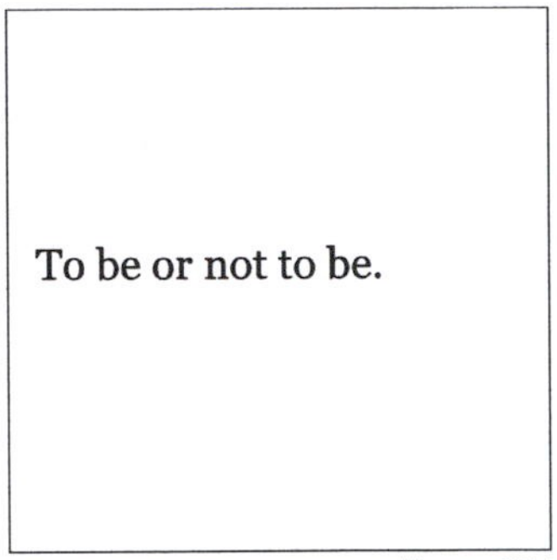

To be or not to be.

Figure 17-1

Fonts can also be created using the function `loadFont()`.

```
f = loadFont("GothamMedium-48.vlw");
```

`loadFont()` **loads from a vlw formatted font file.**

The `loadFont()` function loads a font file from the data folder. Processing uses a special font format, "vlw," that uses images to display each letter. This is useful if you want to package a specific font with your sketch and guarantee its appearance (which can vary with fonts from machine to machine.) Choose a font by selecting "Tools" → "Create Font." This will create and place the font file in your data directory. Make note of the font filename for Step 3 above. This image-based approach requires you to create the font at the size you intend to display. See Figure 17-2.

Figure 17-2

This book will use createFont() for all examples.

Exercise 17-5: Take the bouncing ball example from Chapter 5. Display the X and Y coordinates as text next to the ball.

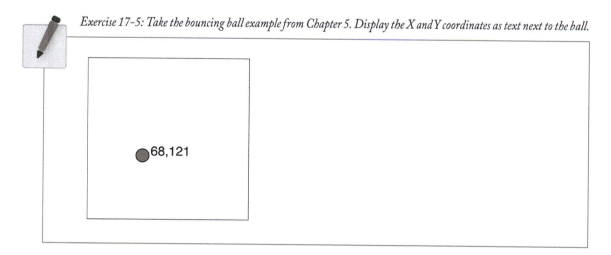

17-4 Text animation

Now that I've covered the steps required to display text, I can apply other concepts from this book to animate text in real-time.

To get started, let's look at two more useful Processing functions related to displaying text:

1. textAlign() — specifies RIGHT, LEFT, or CENTER alignment for text.

Example 17-2. Text align

```
PFont f;

void setup() {
  size(400, 200);
  f = createFont("Georgia", 16);
}

void draw() {
  background(255);

  stroke(175);
  line(width/2, 0, width/2, height);

  textFont(f);
  fill(0);

  textAlign(CENTER);
  text("This text is centered.", width/2, 60);

  textAlign(LEFT);
  text("This text is left aligned.", width/2, 100);

  textAlign(RIGHT);
  text("This text is right aligned.", width/2, 140);
}
```

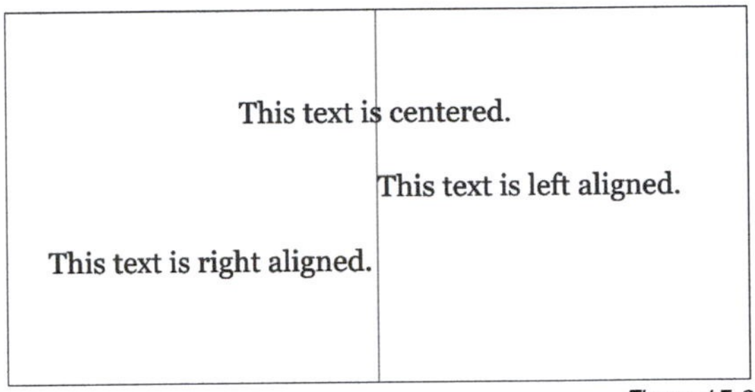

This text is centered.

This text is left aligned.

This text is right aligned.

Figure 17-3

> textAlign() sets the alignment for displaying text. It takes one argument: CENTER, LEFT, or RIGHT.

2. textWidth() — Calculates and returns the width of any character or text string.

Let's say I want to create a news ticker, where text scrolls across the bottom of the screen from left to right. When the news headline leaves the window, it reappears on the right-hand side and scrolls again. If I know the x position of the beginning of the text and I know the width of that text, I can determine when it is no longer in view (see Figure 17-4). textWidth() gives me that width.

To start, I declare variables for the text, font, and x-location of the headline, initializing them in setup().

```
// A headline
String headline = "New study shows computer programming lowers cholesterol.";
PFont f; // Global font variable
```

```
float x; // Horizontal location of headline

void setup() {
  f = createFont("Arial", 16); // Loading font
  x = width; // Initializing headline off-screen to the right
}
```

The draw() function is similar to the bouncing ball example in Chapter 5. First, I display the text at the appropriate location.

```
// Display headline at x location
textFont(f, 16);
textAlign(LEFT);
text(headline, x, 180);
```

x changes by a speed value (in this case a negative number so that the text moves to the left).

```
// Decrement x
x = x - 3;
```

Now comes the more difficult part. It was easy to test when a circle reached the left side of the screen. I would simply ask: is x less than 0? With the text, however, since it's left-aligned, when x equals zero, it's still viewable on screen. Instead, the text will be invisible when x is less than 0 minus the width of the text (see Figure 17-4). When that is the case, I reset x back to the right-hand side of the window, that is, width.

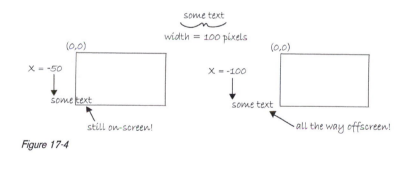

Figure 17-4

```
float w = textWidth(headline);

if (x < -w) {
  x = width;
}
```

> If x is less than the negative width, then it is completely off the screen

Example 17-3 is a full example that displays a different headline each time the previous headline leaves the screen. The headlines are stored in a String array.

Example 17-3. Scrolling headlines

```
// An array of news headlines
String[] headlines = {
  "Processing downloads break
downloading record.",
  "New study shows computer programming
lowers cholesterol.",
};

PFont f; // Global font variable
float x; // Horizontal location
int index = 0;

void setup() {
  size(400, 200);
  f = createFont("Arial", 16);
  // Initialize headline offscreen
  x = width;
}

void draw() {
  background(255);
  fill(0);

  // Display headline at x location
  textFont(f, 16);
  textAlign(LEFT);
  text(headlines[index], x, 180);

  // Decrement x
  x = x - 3;

  // If x is less than the negative width,
  // then it is off the screen
  float w = textWidth(headlines[index]);

  if (x < -w) {
    x = width;
    index = (index + 1) % headlines.length;
  }
}
```

Figure 17-5

A specific string from the array is displayed according to the value of the `index`.

`textWidth()` is used to calculate the width of the current string.

`index` is incremented when the current string has left the screen in order to display a new string.

In addition to textAlign() and textWidth(), Processing also offers the functions textLeading(), textMode(), and textSize() for additional display functionality. These functions are not necessary for the examples covered in this chapter, but you can explore them on your own in the Processing reference.

Exercise 17-6: Create a stock ticker that loops over and over. As the last stock enters the window, the first stock appears immediately to its right.

02 ZOOG 903 AAPL 60 XDSL 10 CMG 5

17-5 Text mosaic

Combining what you learned in Chapter 15 and Chapter 16 about the pixel array, you can use the pixels of an image to create a mosaic of characters. This is an extension of the video mirror code in Chapter 16. (Note that in Example 17-4, new text-related code is in bold.) See Figure 17-6.

Figure 17-6

Example 17-4. Text mirror

```
import processing.video.*;

// Size of each cell in the grid, ratio of window size to video size
int videoScale = 10;
// Number of columns and rows in the system
int cols, rows;
// Variable to hold onto capture object
Capture video;

// A String and Font
String chars = "helloworld";
PFont f;

void setup() {
  size(640, 480);
  // Set up columns and rows
  cols = width / videoScale;
  rows = height / videoScale;
  video = new Capture(this, cols, rows);
  video.start();

  // Load the font
  f = createFont("Courier", 16);
}

void captureEvent(Capture video) {
  video.read();
}

void draw() {
  background(0);
  video.loadPixels();

  // Use a variable to count through chars in a string
  int charcount = 0;

  // Begin loop for rows
  for (int j = 0; j < rows; j++) {
    // Begin loop for columns
    for (int i = 0; i < cols; i++) {
      // Where are you, pixel-wise?
      int x = i * videoScale;
      int y = j * videoScale;

      // Looking up the appropriate color in the pixel array
      color c = video.pixels[i + j* video.width];

      // Displaying an individual character from the String
      // Instead of a rectangle
      textFont(f);
      fill(c);
      text(chars.charAt(charcount), x, y);
      // Go on to the next character
      charcount = (charcount + 1) % chars.length();
    }
  }
}
```

> The source text used in the mosaic pattern. A longer string might produce more interesting results.

> Using a "fixed-width" font. In most fonts, individual characters have different widths. In a fixed-width font, all characters have the same width. This is useful here since I intend to display the letters one at a time spaced out evenly. See Section 17-7 for how to display text character by character with a non-fixed width font.

> One character from the source text is displayed colored according to the pixel location. A counter variable – "charcount" – is used to walk through the source string one character at a time.

Exercise 17-7: Create a video text mosaic where each letter is colored white, but the size of each letter is determined by a pixel's brightness. The brighter the pixel, the bigger it is. Here is a little bit of code from the inside of the pixel loop (with some blank spots) to get you started.

```
float b = brightness(video.pixels[i + j*video.width]);

float fontSize = ____ * (_____ / _____);
textSize(fontSize);
```

17-6 Rotating text

Translation and rotation (as seen in Chapter 14) can also be applied to text. For example, to rotate text around its center, translate to an origin point and use textAlign(CENTER) before displaying the text.

Example 17-5. Rotating text

```
PFont f;
String message = "this text is spinning";
float angle;

void setup() {
  size(200, 200);
  f = createFont("Arial", 20);
}


void draw() {
  background(255);
  fill(0);

  textFont(f);                      // Set the font
  translate(width/2, height/2);     // Translate to the center
  rotate(angle);                    // Rotate by angle
  textAlign(CENTER);
  text(message, 0, 0);
  theta += 0.05;
}
```

Figure 17-7

The text is center aligned and displayed at (0,0) after translating and rotating. See Chapter 14 or a review of translation and rotation.

Exercise 17-8: Display text that is centered and rotated to appear flat. Have the text scroll off into the distance.

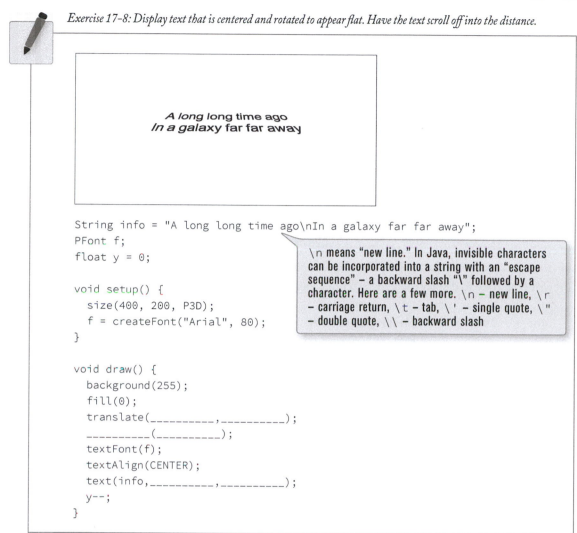

```
String info = "A long long time ago\nIn a galaxy far far away";
PFont f;
float y = 0;

void setup() {
  size(400, 200, P3D);
  f = createFont("Arial", 80);
}

void draw() {
  background(255);
  fill(0);
  translate(_____,_____);
  _____(_____);
  textFont(f);
  textAlign(CENTER);
  text(info,_____,_____);
  y--;
}
```

\n means "new line." In Java, invisible characters can be incorporated into a string with an "escape sequence" – a backward slash "\" followed by a character. Here are a few more. \n – new line, \r – carriage return, \t – tab, \' – single quote, \" – double quote, \\ – backward slash

17-7 Display text character by character

In certain graphics applications, displaying text with each character rendered individually is required. For example, if each character needs to move independently, then simply saying `text("a bunch of letters", 0, 0)` will not do.

The solution is to loop through a `String`, displaying each character one at a time.

Let's start by looking at an example that displays the text all at once. See Figure 17-8.

```
PFont f;
String txt = "Each character is not
written individually.";

void setup() {
  size(400, 200);
  f = createFont("Arial", 20);
}

void draw() {
  background(255);
  fill(0);
  textFont(f);
  text(txt, 10, height/2);
}
```

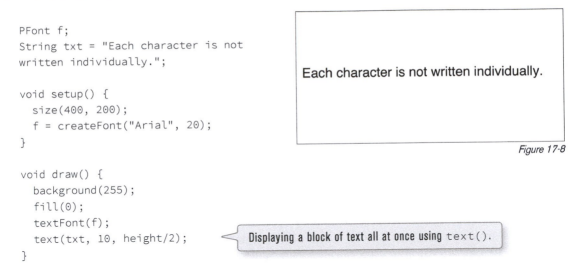

Each character is not written individually.

Figure 17-8

Displaying a block of text all at once using `text()`.

I rewrite the code to display each character in a loop, using the `charAt()` function. See Figure 17-9.

```
int x = 10;

for (int i = 0; i < txt.length(); i++) {
  text(msg.charAt(i), x, height/2);
  x += 10;
}
```

The first character is at pixel 10.

Each character is displayed one at a time with the `charAt()` function and spaced apart ten pixels.

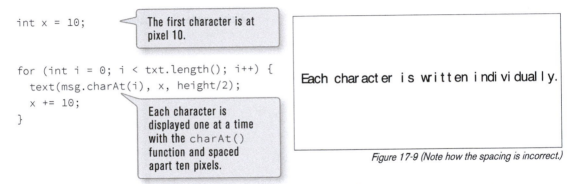

Each char act er i s wr i t t en i ndi vi dual l y.

Figure 17-9 (Note how the spacing is incorrect.)

Calling the `text()` function for each character will allow more flexibility in future examples (for coloring, sizing, and placing characters from one string individually). This example has a pretty major flaw, however. Here, the x location is increased by 10 pixels for each character. Although this is approximately correct, because each character is not exactly 10 pixels wide, the spacing is off. The proper spacing can be achieved using the `textWidth()` function as demonstrated in the following code. Note how this example achieves the proper spacing even with each character being a random size! See Figure 17-10.

```
int x = 10;
for (int i = 0; i < txt.length(); i++) {
  textSize(random(12, 36));
  text(txt.charAt(i), x, height/2);
  x += textWidth(txt.charAt(i));
}
```

`textWidth()` spaces the characters out properly.

EaCh character is written individually.

Figure 17-10 (Note how the spacing is correct!)

Exercise 17-9: Using `textWidth()`, *redo Example 17-4 (the text "mirror") to use a non-fixed-width font with proper character spacing. The following image uses Georgia.*

itwasadarkandstormynightthequickbrownfoxjumpedoverthe
lazydogitwasadarkandstormynightthequickbrownfoxjumped
overthelazydogitwasadarkandstormynightthequickbrownfox
jumpedoverthelazydogitwasadarkandstormynightthequickbr
ownfoxjumpedoverthelazydogitwasadarkandstormynightthe
quickbrownfoxjumpedoverthelazydogitwasadarkandstormyr
ightthequickbrownfoxjumpedoverthelazydogitwasadarkands
tormynightthequickbrownfoxjumpedoverthelazydogitwasada
rkandstormynightthequickbrownfoxjumpedoverthelazydogit
wasadarkandstormynightthequickbrownfoxjumpedoverthela
zydogitwasadarkandstormynightthequickbrownfoxjumpedov
erthelazydogitwasadarkandstormynightthequickbrownfoxju
pedoverthelazydogitwasadarkandstormynightthequickbrowr
foxjumpedoverthelazydogitwasadarkandstormynightthequic
kbrownfoxjumpedoverthelazydogitwasadarkandstormynight
thequickbrownfoxjumpedoverthelazydogitwasadarkandstorr
ynightthequickbrownfoxjumpedoverthelazydogitwasadarkar
dstormynightthequickbrownfoxjumpedoverthelazydogitwasa
darkandstormynightthequickbrownfoxjumpedoverthelazydc
gitwasadarkandstormynightthequickbrownfoxjumpedoverth
elazydogitwasadarkandstormynightthequickbrownfoxjumpe
overthelazydogitwasadarkandstormynightthequickbrownfox
jumpedoverthelazydogitwasadarkandstormynightthequickbr
ownfoxjumpedoverthelazydogitwasadarkandstormynightthe

This "letter-by-letter" methodology can also be applied to a sketch where characters from a string move independently of one another. The following example uses object-oriented design to make each character from the original string a `Letter` object, allowing it to both be displayed in its proper location as well as move about the screen individually.

Example 17-6. Text breaking up

```
PFont f;
String message = "click mouse to shake
it up";
// An array of Letter objects
Letter[] letters;

void setup() {
  size(260, 200);
  // Create the font
  f = createFont("Arial", 20);
  textFont(f);

  // Create the array the same size as
the String
  letters = new
Letter[message.length()];
  // Initialize Letters at the correct
x location
  int x = 16;
  for (int i = 0; i < message.length(); i++) {
    letters[i] = new Letter(x, 100, message.charAt(i));
    x += textwidth(message.charAt(i));
  }
}
void draw() {
  background(255);
  for (int i = 0; i < letters.length; i++) {
    // Display all letters
    letters[i].display();

    // If the mouse is pressed the letters shake
    // If not, they return to their original location
    if (mousePressed) {
      letters[i].shake();
    } else {
      letters[i].home();
    }
  }
}

// A class to describe a single Letter
class Letter {
  char letter;

  float homex, homey;

  // Its current location
  float x, y;

  Letter (float x_, float y_, char letter_) {
    homex = x = x_;
    homey = y = y_;
    letter = letter_;
  }

  // Display the letter
```

Figure 17-11

> Letter objects are initialized with their location within the String object as well as what character they should display.

> The object knows about its original "home" location within the string of text, as well as its current (x,y) location should it move around the screen.

```
void display() {
  fill(0);
  textAlign(LEFT);
  text(letter, x, y);
}

// Move the letter randomly
void shake() {
  x + = random(-2, 2);
  y + = random(-2, 2);
}

void home() {
  x = homex;
  y = homey;
}
```

> At any point, the current location can be set back to the home location by calling the home() function.

```
}
```

The character-by-character method also allows you to display text along a curve. Before I move on to letters, let's first look at how I would draw a series of boxes along a curve. This example makes heavy use of the trigonometric functions covered in Chapter 13.

Example 17-7. Boxes along a curve

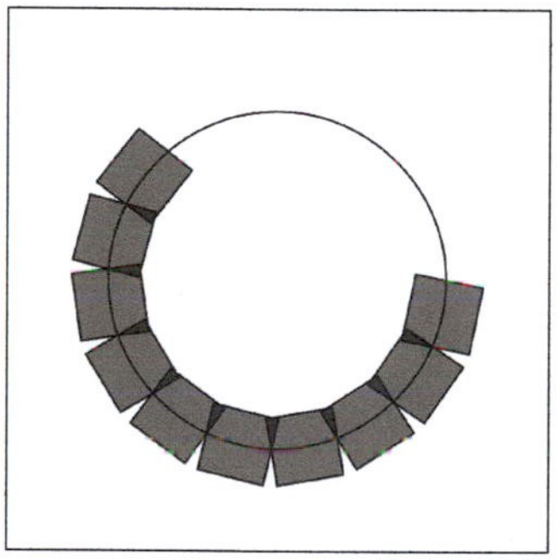

```
PFont f;
// The radius of a circle
float r = 100;
// The width and height of the boxes
float w = 40;
float h = 40;

void setup() {
  size(320, 320);
}

void draw() {
  background(255);
```

Figure 17-12

```
  // Start in the center and draw the circle
  translate(width/2, height/2);
  noFill();
  stroke(0);
  ellipse(0, 0, r*2, r*2);
```

> The curve is a circle with radius r in the center of the window.

```
  // 10 boxes along the curve
  int totalBoxes = 10;
  // I must keep track of the position along the curve
  float arclength = 0;

  // For every box
  for (int i = 0; i < totalBoxes; i++) {

    arclength += w/2;
```

> Move along the curve according to the width of the box. Each box is centered so w/2 is used.

```
    float theta = arclength / r;
```

> Angle in radians is the arclength divided by the radius.

```
pushMatrix();
// Polar to Cartesian coordinate conversion
translate(r * cos(theta), r * sin(theta));
// Rotate the box
rotate(theta);
// Display the box
fill(0, 100);
rectMode(CENTER);
rect(0, 0, w, h);
popMatrix();
// Move halfway again
arclength += w/2;
  }
}
```

Even if you find the mathematics of this example to be difficult, Figure 17-12 should reveal the next step. What I need to do is replace each box with a character from a string that fits inside the box. And since characters do not all have the same width, instead of using a variable w that stays constant, each box will have a variable width along the curve according to the textWidth() function.

Example 17-8. Characters along a curve

```
// The message to be displayed
String message = "text along a curve";

PFont f;

// The radius of a circle
float r = 100;

void setup() {
  size(320, 320);
  f = createFont("Georgia", 40, true);
  textFont(f);
  textAlign(CENTER);         The text must be centered!
}

void draw() {
  background(255);

  // Start in the center and draw the circle
  translate(width/2, height/2);
  noFill();
  stroke(0);
  ellipse(0, 0, r*2, r*2);

  // Track the position along the curve
  float arclength = 0;

  // For every box
  for (int i = 0; i < message.length(); i++) {
    // The character and its width
    char currentChar = message.charAt(i);      Instead of a constant width, I check the
    float w = textWidth(currentChar);          width of each character.

    // Each box is centered so I move half the width
```

Figure 17-13

```
  arclength + = w/2;
  // Angle in radians is the arclength divided by the radius
  // Starting on the left side of the circle by adding PI
  float theta = PI + arclength / r;

  pushMatrix();

  translate(r*cos(theta), r*sin(theta));

  // Rotate the box (offset by 90 degrees)
  rotate(theta + PI/2);
  // Display the character
  fill(0);
  text(currentChar, 0, 0);
  popMatrix();
  // Move halfway again
  arclength += w/2;
  }
}
```

> Polar-to-Cartesian conversion allows you to find the point along the curve. See Chapter 13 for a review of this concept.

Exercise 17-10: Create a sketch that starts with characters randomly scattered (and rotated). Have them slowly move back toward their "home" location. Use an object-oriented approach as seen in Example 17-6.[1]

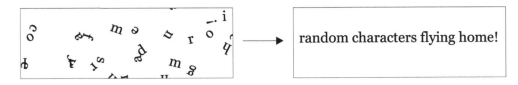

One way to solve this is to use interpolation. Interpolation refers to the process of calculating values in between two given pieces of data. In this exercise, I want to know the in-between x locations (and y locations) from the random starting point to the target location for the each letter of a string. One interpolation method is to simply take the average. Think of it as walking to a wall by always taking a step halfway.

```
x = (x + targetX) / 2;
y = (y + targetY) / 2;
```

Another possibility is to simply go 10% of the way there.

```
x = 0.9*x + 0.1*targetX;
y = 0.9*y + 0.1*targetY;
```

Processing's lerp() function will do interpolation for you. Visit the reference page (*http:// processing.org/reference/lerp_.html*) for more information.

Consider making your sketch interactive. Can you push the letters around using the mouse?

---

[1] *The origins of this exercise can be traced back to John Maeda's 1995 work* Flying Letters.

18 Data Input

A million monkeys were given a million typewriters. It's called the Internet.
—Simon Munnery

In this chapter:
– Manipulating strings
– Reading and writing text files
– Tabular data
– Word counting and text analysis
– XML and JSON data
– Threads
– Using data from APIs

This chapter will move beyond displaying text and examine how to use `String` objects as the basis for reading and writing data. I'll start by covering more sophisticated methods for manipulating strings, searching in them, chopping them up, and joining them together. Afterward, I will show how these skills allow you to use input from data sources such as text files, web pages, XML feeds, JSON data, and third party APIs, and you'll also take a step into the world of data visualization.

18-1 Manipulating strings

In Chapter 17, I touched on a few of the basic functions available in the Java `String` class, such as `charAt()`, `toUpperCase()`, `equals()`, and `length()`. These functions are documented on the Processing reference page for `String`. Nevertheless, in order to perform some more advanced data parsing techniques, you'll will need to explore some additional string manipulation functions documented on the Java website (*http://docs.oracle.com/javase/7/docs/api/java/lang/String.html*). (I'll demonstrate more about the Java API itself in Chapter 23.)

Let's take a closer look at the following two functions: `indexOf()` and `substring()`.

`indexOf()` locates a sequence of characters within a string. It takes one argument — a search string — and returns a numeric value that corresponds to the first occurrence of the search string inside of the `String` object being searched.

```
String search = "def";
String toBeSearched = "abcdefghi";
int index = toBeSearched.indexOf(search);
```
◁ The value of index in this example is 3.

Strings are just like arrays, in that the first character is index number zero and the last character is the length of the string minus one.

Exercise 18-1: Predict the result of the code below.

```
String sentence = "The quick brown fox jumps over the lazy dog.";

println(sentence.indexOf("quick"));  _____

println(sentence.indexOf("fo"));  _____

println(sentence.indexOf("The"));  _____

println(sentence.indexOf("blah blah"));  _____
```

If you're stuck on the last line of Exercise 18-1, it's because there is no way for you to know the answer without consulting the Java reference (or making an educated guess). If the search string cannot be found, indexOf() returns -1. This is a good choice because -1 is not a legitimate index value in the string itself, and therefore can indicate "not found." There are no *negative* indices in a string of characters or in an array.

After finding a search phrase within a string, you might want to separate out part of the string, saving it in a different variable. A part of a string is known as a *substring* and substrings are made with the substring() function which takes two arguments, a start index and an end index. substring() returns the substring in between the two indices.

```
String alphabet = "abcdefghi" ;
String sub = alphabet.substring(3, 6);
```
The string sub is now "def".

Note that the substring begins at the specified *start index* (the first argument) and extends to the character at *end index* (the second argument) *minus one*. I know, I know. Wouldn't it have been easier to just take the *substring* from the start index all the way to the end index? While this might initially seem true, it's actually quite convenient to stop at end index minus one. For example, if you ever want to make a substring that extends to the end of a string, you can simply go all the way to thestring.length(). In addition, with end index minus one marking the end, the length of the substring is easily calculated as *end index minus begin index.*

Exercise 18-2: Fill in the blanks to get the substring "fox jumps over the lazy dog" (without the period).

```
String sentence = "The quick brown fox jumps over the lazy dog.";

int foxIndex = sentence.indexOf(_____);
int periodIndex = sentence.indexOf(".");

String sub = _____._____(_____,_____);
```

Exercise 18-3: Write your own "substring" function that receives three arguments: a string, a starting position, and a total number of characters. The function should return the corresponding substring starting at the position and with a length matching the number. Here's some code to get you started.

```
void substring(String txt, int start, int num) {

    return _____;
}
```

18-2 Splitting and joining

In Chapter 17, you saw how strings can be joined together (referred to as "concatenation") using the "+" operator. Let's review with an example that uses concatenation to get user input from a keyboard.

Example 18-1. User input

```
PFont f;

// Variable to store text currently being typed
String typing = "";
// Variable to store saved text when return is hit
String saved = "";


void setup() {
  size(300, 200);
  f = createFont("Arial", 16);
}

void draw() {
  background(255);
  int indent = 25;

  // Set the font and fill for text
  textFont(f);
  fill(0);

  // Display everything
  text("Click in this sketch and type. \nHit return to save what you typed.",
indent, 40);
  text(typing, indent, 90);
  text(saved, indent, 130);
}

void keyPressed() {
  // If the return key is pressed, save the String and clear it
  if (key == '\n') {
    saved = typing;
    typing = "";

  // Otherwise, concatenate the String
  } else {
    typing = typing + key;
  }
}
```

> Click in this sketch and type.
> Hit return to save what you typed.
>
> 4 8 15 16 23 42

Figure 18-1

> For keyboard input, I use two variables. One will store the text as it is being typed. Another will keep a copy of the typed text once the Enter key is pressed.

> A string can be cleared by setting it equal to " ".

> Each character typed by the user is added to the end of the string.

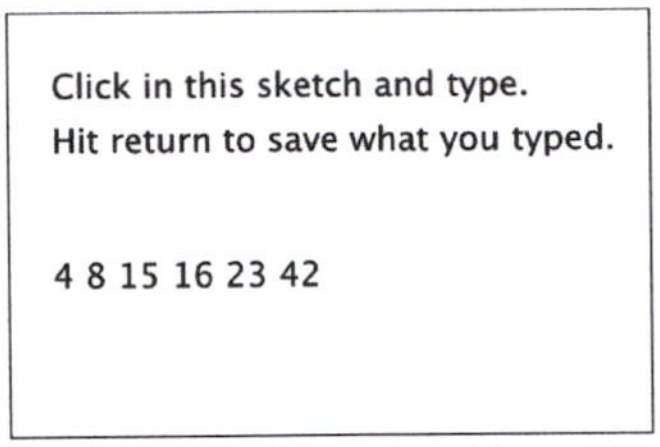

 Exercise 18-4: Create a sketch that chats with the user. For example, if a user enters "cats" the sketch might reply, "How do cats make you feel?"

Processing has two additional functions that make joining strings (or the reverse, splitting them up) easy. In sketches that involve parsing data from a file or the web, you might get hold of that data in the form of an array of strings or as one long string. Depending on what you want to accomplish, it's useful to know how to switch between these two modes of storage. This is where these two new functions, split() and join(), will come in handy.

```
"one long string or array of strings" ← → { "one", "long", "string", "or", "array",
"of", "strings" }
```

Let's take a look at the split() function. split() separates a longer string into an array of strings, based on a split character known as the *delimiter*. It takes two arguments, the String object to be split and the delimiter. (The delimiter can be a single character or a string.)

```
// Splitting a string based on spaces
String spaceswords = "The quick brown fox jumps over the lazy dog.";

String[] list = split(spaceswords, " " );

printArray(list);
```

> Note how printArray() can be used to print the contents of an array and their corresponding indices to the message console.

> This period is not set as a delimiter and therefore will be included in the last string in the array: "dog."

Here is an example using a comma as the delimiter (this time passing in a single character: ',').

```
// Splitting a string based on commas
String commaswords = "The,quick,brown,fox,jumps,over,the,lazy,dog.";
String[] list = split(commaswords, ',');
printArray(list);
```

If you want to use more than one delimiter to split up a text, you must use the Processing function splitTokens(). splitTokens() works identically as split() with one exception: any character that appears in the passed string qualifies as a delimiter.

```
// Splitting a String based on multiple delimiters
String stuff = "hats & apples, cars + phones % elephants dog.";
String[] list = splitTokens(stuff, " &,+." );
printArray(list);
```

> The period is specified as a delimiter and therefore will not be included in the last string in the array: "dog".

Exercise 18-5: Fill in what the above code will print in the Processing message window:

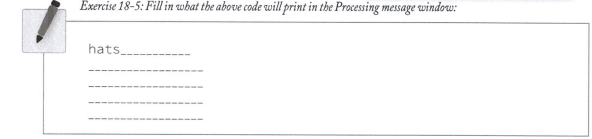

```
hats_____
_____
_____
_____
_____
```

If you are splitting numbers in a string, the resulting array can be converted into an integer array with Processing's int() function.

```
// Calculate sum of a list of numbers in a String
String numbers = "8,67,5,309";
// Converting the String array to an int array
int[] list = int(split(numbers, ','));
```

> Numbers in a string are not numbers and cannot be used in mathematical operations unless you convert them first.

```
int sum = 0;
for (int i = 0; i < list.length; i++ ) {
  sum = sum + list[i];
}
println(sum);
```

The reverse of `split()` is `join()`. `join()` takes an array of strings and joins them together into one long `String` object. The `join()` function also takes two arguments, the array to be joined and a *separator*. The separator can either be a single character or a string of characters.

Consider the following array:

```
String[] lines = {"It", "was", "a", "dark", "and", "stormy", "night."};
```

Using the "+" operator along with a `for` loop, you can join a string together as follows:

```
// Manual Concatenation
String onelongstring = "";
for (int i = 0; i < lines.length; i++) {
    onelongstring = onelongstring + lines[i] + " ";
}
```

The `join()` function, however, allows you to bypass this process, achieving the same result in only one line of code.

```
// Using Processing's join()
String onelongstring = join(lines, " ");
```

> *Exercise 18-6: Split the following string into an array of floating point numbers and calculate the average. Note that the dot should not be considered a delimiter as it's part of the floating point value itself.*

```
String floats = "5023.23:52.3:10.4:5.9, 901.3---2.3";

float[] numbers = _____(_____(_____, "_____"));
float total = 0;
for (int i = 0; i < numbers.length; i++) {
    _____ += _____;
}

float avg = _____;
```

18-3 Dealing with data

Data can come from many different places: websites, news feeds, spreadsheets, databases, and so on. Let's say you've decided to make a map of the world's flowers. After searching online you might find a PDF version of a flower encyclopedia, or a spreadsheet of flower genera, or a JSON feed of flower data, or a

REST API that provides geolocated lat/lon coordinates, or some web page someone put together with beautiful flower photos, and so on and so forth. The question inevitably arises: "I found all this data; which should I use, and how do I get it into Processing?"

If you are really lucky, you might find a Processing library (*http://processing.org/reference/libraries/*) that hands data to you directly with code. Maybe the answer is to just download this library and write some code like:

```
import flowers.*;

void setup() {
  FlowerDatabase fdb = new FlowerDatabase();
  Flower sunflower = fdb.findFlower("sunflower");
  float h = sunflower.getAverageHeight();
}
```

In this case, someone else has done all the work for you. They've gathered data about flowers and built a Processing library with a set of functions that hands you the data in an easy-to-understand format. This library, sadly, does not exist (not yet), but there are some that do. For example, YahooWeather (*http://www.onformative.com/lab/google-weather-library-for-processing*) is a library by Marcel Schwittlick that grabs weather data from Yahoo for you, allowing you to write code like `weather.getWindSpeed()` or `weather.getSunrise()` and more. There is still plenty of work to do in the case of using a library.

Let's take another scenario. Say you're looking to build a visualization of Major League Baseball statistics. You can't find a Processing library to give you the data but you do see everything you're looking for at mlb.com. If the data is online and your web browser can show it, shouldn't you be able to get the data in Processing? Passing data from one application (like a web application) to another (say, your Processing sketch) is something that comes up again and again in software engineering. A means for doing this is an API or "application programming interface": a means by which two computer programs can talk to each other. Now that you know this, you might decide to search online for "MLB API". Unfortunately, mlb.com does not provide its data via an API. In this case you would have to load the raw source of the website itself and manually search for the data you're looking for. While possible, this solution is much less desirable given the considerable time required to read through the HTML source as well as program algorithms for parsing it.

The goal of this chapter is to give you an overview of techniques, ranging from the more difficult manual parsing of data, to the parsing of standardized formats, to the use of an API designed specifically for Processing itself. Each means of getting data comes with its own set of challenges. The ease of using a Processing library is dependent on the existence of clear documentation and examples. But in just about all cases, if you can find your data in a format designed for a computer (spreadsheets, XML, JSON, etc.), you'll be able to save some time in the day for a nice walk outside.

One other note worth a mention about working with data. When developing an application that involves a data source, such as a data visualization, it's sometimes useful to develop with "dummy" or "fake" data. You don't want to be debugging your data retrieval process at the same time as solving problems related to algorithms for drawing. In keeping with my *one-step-at-a-time* mantra, once the meat of the program is completed with dummy data, you can then focus solely on how to retrieve the actual data from the real source. You can always use random or hard-coded numbers into your code when you're experimenting with a visual idea and connect the real data later.

18-4 Working with text files

Let's begin by working with the simplest means of data retrieval: reading from a text file. Text files can be used as a very simple database (you could store settings for a program, a list of high scores, numbers for a graph, etc.) or to simulate a more complex data source.

In order to create a text file, you can use any simple text editor. Windows Notepad or Mac OS X TextEdit will do; just make sure you format the file as "plain text." It is also advisable to name the text files with the ".txt" extension, to avoid any confusion. And just as with image files in Chapter 15, these text files should be placed in the sketch's "data" directory in order for them to be recognized by the Processing sketch.

Once the text file is in place, Processing's `loadStrings()` function is used to read the content of the file into a `String` array. The individual lines of text in the file (see Figure 18-2) each become an individual element in the array.

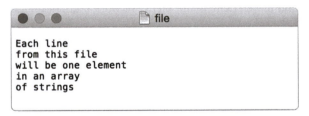

```
● ● ●                    📄 file

Each line
from this file
will be one element
in an array
of strings
```

Figure 18-2

```
String[] lines = loadStrings("file.txt");
println("There are " + lines.length + " lines.");
printArray(lines);
```
> This code will print all the lines from the source text file shown in Figure 18-2.

To run the code, create a text file called "file.txt," type a bunch of lines in that file, and place it in your sketch's data directory.

Exercise 18-7: Rewrite Example 17-3 so that it loads the headlines from a text file.

Text from a data file can be used to generate a simple visualization. Example 18-2 loads the data file shown in Figure 18-3. Note the use of the file extension ".csv" to indicate a file with *comma separated values*. The results of visualizing this data are shown in Figure 18-3.

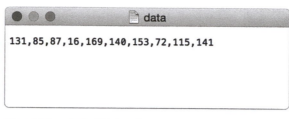

131,85,87,16,169,140,153,72,115,141

Figure 18-3 contents of "data.csv"

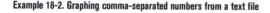

Example 18-2. Graphing comma-separated numbers from a text file

```
int[] data;

void setup() {
  size(200, 200);
  // Load text file as a String
  String[] stuff = loadStrings("data.csv");
  data = int(split(stuff[0], ','));
}
```

> The text from the file is loaded into an array. This array has one element because the file only has one line. That element is then split into an array of strings using ' , ' as a delimiter. Finally, the array is converted an array of integers using int().

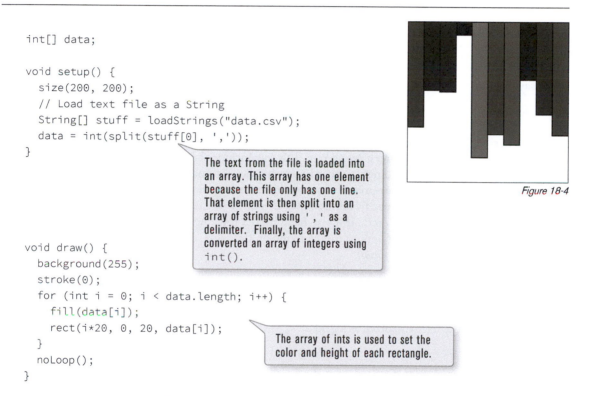

Figure 18-4

```
void draw() {
  background(255);
  stroke(0);
  for (int i = 0; i < data.length; i++) {
    fill(data[i]);
    rect(i*20, 0, 20, data[i]);
  }
  noLoop();
}
```

> The array of ints is used to set the color and height of each rectangle.

Looking at how to parse a csv file with split() was a nice learning exercise. In truth, dealing with csv files (which can easily be generated from spreadsheet software such as Google docs) is such a common activity that Processing has an entire built-in class called Table to handle the parsing for you.

18-5 Tabular data

A table consists of data arranged as a set of rows and columns, also called "tabular data." If you've ever used a spreadsheet, this is tabular data. Processing's loadTable() function takes comma-separated (csv) or tab-separated (tsv) values and automatically places the contents into a Table object storing the data in columns and rows. This is a great deal more convenient than struggling to manually parse large data files with `split()`. It was pretty simple in Example 18-2 but with larger files it can get complex quite quickly. Let's say you have a data file that looks like:

```
●  ●  ●                    data.csv
x,y,diameter,name
160,103,43.19838,Happy
372,137,52.42526,Sad
273,235,61.14072,Joyous
121,179,44.758068,Melancholy
```

Figure 18-5 Each line is a row of a table.

Instead of saying:

```
String[] stuff = loadStrings("data.csv");
```

I can say:

```
Table table = loadTable("data.csv");
```

Now I've missed an important detail. Take a look again at Figure 18-5 above. Notice how the first line of text is not the data itself, but rather a *header row*. This row includes labels that describe the data included in each subsequent row. The good news is that Processing can automatically interpret and store the headers for you, if you pass in the option `"header"` when loading the table. (In addition to `"header"`, there are other options you can specify. For example, if your file is called data.txt but is comma separated data you can pass in the option `"csv"`. If it also has a header row, then you can specifiy both options like so: `"header,csv"`). A full list of options can be found on the `loadTable()` documentation page (*http:// processing.org/reference/loadTable_.html*).

```
Table table = loadTable("data.csv", "header");
```

Now that the table is loaded, I can show how you grab individual pieces of data or iterate over the entire table. Let's look at the data visualized as a grid.

x	y	diameter	name
160	103	43.19838	Happy
372	137	52.42526	Sad
273	235	61.14072	Joyous
121	179	44.758068	Melancholy

Figure 18-6

In the above grid you can see that the data is organized in terms of rows and columns. One way to access the data, therefore, would be to request a value by its numeric row and column location (with zero being the first row or first column). This is similar to accessing a pixel color at a given (x,y) location, though in this case the y position (row) comes first. The following code requests a piece of data at a given (row, column) location.

```
int val1 = table.getInt(2, 1);
```
235

```
float val2 = table.getFloat(3, 2);
```
44.758068

```
String s = table.getString(0, 3);
```
"Happy"

While the numeric index is sometimes useful, it's generally going to be more convenient to access each piece of data by the column name. For example, I could pull out a specific row from the Table.

```
TableRow row = table.getRow(2);
```
Gets the third row (index 2)

Note in the above line of code that a Table object refers to the entire table of data while a TableRow (*http://processing.org/reference/TableRow.html*) object handles an individual row of data within the Table.

Once I have the TableRow object, I can ask for data from some or all of the columns.

```
int x = row.getInt("x");
```
273

```
int y = row.getInt("y");
```
235

```
float d = row.getFloat("diameter");
```
61.14072

```
String s = row.getString("name");
```
"Joyous"

The method getRow() (*http://processing.org/reference/Table_getRow_.html*) returns a single row from the table. If you want to grab all the rows and iterate over them you can do so in a loop with a counter accessing each row one at a time. The total number of available rows can be retrieved with getRowCount().

```
for (int i = 0; i < table.getRowCount(); i++) {

  TableRow row = table.getRow(i);
  float x = row.getFloat("x");
  float y = row.getFloat("y");
  float d = row.getFloat("diameter");
  String n = row.getString("name");


  // Do something with the data of each row

}
```

Here, I access each row of the table one at a time, in a loop.

If you want to search for a select number of rows within the table, you can do so with findRows() (*http://processing.org/reference/Table_findRows_.html*) and matchRows() (*http://processing.org/reference/Table_matchRows_.html*).

In addition to being read, `Table` objects can be altered or created on the fly while a sketch is running. Cell values can be adjusted, rows can be removed, and new rows can be added. For example, to set new values in a cell there are functions `setInt()`, `setFloat()`, and `setString()`.

```
row.setInt("x", mouseX);
```
> Update the value of column "x" to `mouseX` in a given `TableRow`.

To add a new row to a `Table`, simply call the method `addRow()` (*http://processing.org/reference/Table_addRow_.html*) and set the values of each column.

```
TableRow row = table.addRow();
```
> Create a new row.

```
row.setFloat("x", mouseX);
row.setFloat("y", mouseY);
row.setFloat("diameter", random(40, 80));
row.setString("name", "new label");
```
> Set the values of all columns in that row.

To delete a row, simply call the method `removeRow()` (*http://processing.org/reference/Table_removeR ow_.html*) and pass in the numeric index of the row you would like removed. For example, the following code removes the first row whenever the size of the table is greater than ten rows.

```
// If the table has more than 10 rows
if (table.getRowCount() > 10) {

  table.removeRow(0);
}
```
> Delete the first row (index 0).

The following example puts all of the above code together. Notice how each row of the table contains the data for a `Bubble` object.

Example 18-3. Loading and Saving Tabular Data

```
Table table;
Bubble[] bubbles;

void setup() {
  size(480, 360);
  loadData();
}

void draw() {
  background(255);
  // Display all bubbles
  for (int i = 0; i < bubbles.length; i++) {
    bubbles[i].display();
  }
}

void loadData() {
  table = loadTable("data.csv", "header");
  bubbles = new Bubble[table.getRowCount()];
```
> A `Table` object and an array of `Bubble` objects. The data from the table will fill the array.

> Load file into `table` – "header" indicates file has header row. The size of the array is then determined by the number of rows in the table.

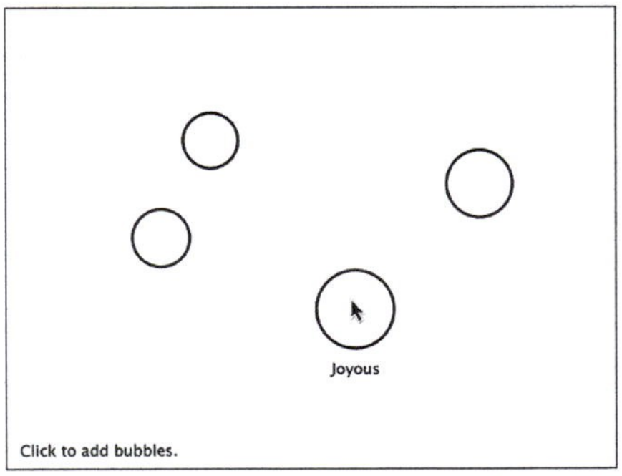

Click to add bubbles.

Joyous

Figure 18-7

```
  for (int i = 0; i < table.getRowCount(); i++) {

    TableRow row = table.getRow(i);
```

Iterate over all the rows in a table.

```
    float x = row.getFloat("x");
    float y = row.getFloat("y");
    float d = row.getFloat("diameter");
    String n = row.getString("name");
    bubbles[i] = new Bubble(x, y, d, n);
  }
}
```

Access the fields via their column name (or index).

Make a `Bubble` object out of the data from each row.

```
void mousePressed() {
  TableRow row = table.addRow();
  row.setFloat("x", mouseX);
  row.setFloat("y", mouseY);
  row.setFloat("diameter", random(40, 80));
  row.setString("name", "Blah");
```

When the mouse is pressed, create a new row and set the values for each column of that row.

```
  if (table.getRowCount() > 10) {
    table.removeRow(0);
  }
```

If the table has more than 10 rows, delete the oldest row.

```
  saveTable(table, "data/data.csv");
  loadData();
}
```

This writes the table back to the original CSV file and reload the file so that what's drawn matches.

```
class Bubble {
  float x, y;
  float diameter;
  String name;
```

This simple `Bubble` class will be used for several data examples in this chapter. It draws a circle to the window and display a text label when the mouse hovers.

```
  boolean over = false;

  // Create the Bubble
  Bubble(float tempX, float tempY, float tempD, String s) {
    x = tempX;
    y = tempY;
    diameter = tempD;
    name = s;
  }

  // Checking if mouse is over the bubble
  void rollover(float px, float py) {
    float d = dist(px, py, x, y);
    if (d < diameter/2) {
      over = true;
    } else {
      over = false;
    }
  }

  // Display the Bubble
  void display() {
    stroke(0);
```

```
        strokeWeight(2);
        noFill();
        ellipse(x, y, diameter, diameter);
        if (over) {
            fill(0);
            textAlign(CENTER);
            text(name, x, y+diameter/2+20);
        }
    }
}
```

While unrelated to the main topic of this chapter data, Example 18-3 does include a solution to the second part of Exercise 5-5 on page 77, a rollover with a circle. Here, the distance between a given point and a circle's center is compared to that circle's radius as depicted in Figure 18-8.

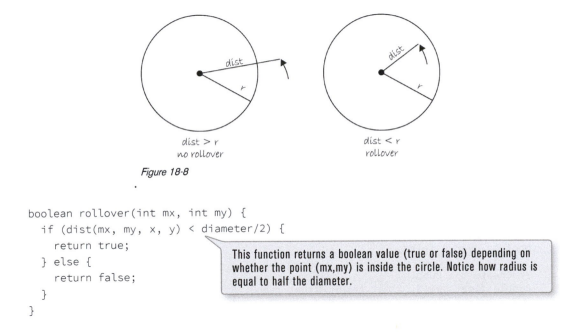

dist > r
no rollover

dist < r
rollover

Figure 18-8

```
boolean rollover(int mx, int my) {
    if (dist(mx, my, x, y) < diameter/2) {
        return true;
    } else {
        return false;
    }
}
```

This function returns a boolean value (true or false) depending on whether the point (mx,my) is inside the circle. Notice how radius is equal to half the diameter.

18-6 Data that is not in a standardized format

What if your data is not in a standard format like a table, how do you deal with it then? One of the nice features about loadStrings() is that in addition to pulling text from a file, you can also grab a URL. For example:

```
String[] lines = loadStrings("http://www.yahoo.com");
```

When you send a URL path into loadStrings(), you get back the raw HTML (Hypertext Markup Language) source of the requested web page. It's the same stuff that appears upon selecting "View Source" from a browser's menu options. You don't need to be an HTML expert to follow this section, but if you are not familiar at all with HTML, you might want to read http://en.wikipedia.org/wiki/HTML.

Unlike with the comma-delimited data from a text file that was specially formatted for use in a Processing sketch, it's not practical to have the resulting raw HTML stored in an array of strings (each element representing one line from the source). Converting the array into one long string can make things a bit simpler. As you saw earlier in the chapter, this can be achieved using `join()`.

```
String onelongstring = join(lines, " ");
```

When pulling raw HTML from a web page, it's likely you do not want all of the source, but just a small piece of it. Perhaps you're looking for weather information, a stock quote, or a news headline. You can take advantage of the text manipulation functions you learned — `indexOf()`, `substring()`, and `length()` — to find pieces of data within a large block of text. You saw an early example of this in Exercise 18-2 on page 385. Take, for example, the following `String` object:

```
String stuff = "Number of apples:62. Boy, do I like apples or what!";
```

Let's say I want to pull out the number of apples from the above text. My algorithm would be as follows:

1. Find the *end of the substring* "apples:" Call it start.
2. Find the *first period* after "apples:" Call it end.
3. Make a *substring* of the characters between start and end.
4. Convert the string to a number (if I want to use it as such).

In code, this looks like:

```
int start      = stuff.indexOf("apples:" ) + 8;   // STEP 1
int end        = stuff.indexOf(".", start);        // STEP 2
String apples  = stuff.substring(start, end);      // STEP 3
int apple_no   = int(apples);                      // STEP 4
```

> The index where a string ends can be found by searching for that string and adding its length (here, 8).

The above code will do the trick, but I should be a bit more careful to make sure I don't run into any errors if I do not find the string I am searching for. I can add some error checking and generalize the code into a function:

```
// A function that returns a substring between two substrings
String giveMeTextBetween(String s, String startTag, String endTag) {
  // Find the index of the beginning tag
  int startIndex = s.indexOf(startTag);
  // If I don't find anything
  if (startIndex == -1) {
    return "";
  }
  // Move to the end of the beginning tag
  startIndex += startTag.length();

  // Find the index of the end tag
  int endIndex = s.indexOf(endTag, startIndex);
  // If I don't find the end tag,
  if (endIndex == -1) {
    return "";
```

> A function to return a substring found between two strings. If beginning or end "tag" is not found, the function returns an empty string.

> `indexOf()` can also take a second argument, an integer. That second argument means: Find the first occurrence of the search string after this specified index. I use it here to ensure that `endIndex` follows `startIndex`.

```
  }
  // Return the text in between
  return s.substring(startIndex, endIndex);
}
```

With this technique, you are ready to connect to a website from within Processing and grab data to use in your sketches. For example, you could read the HTML source from nytimes.com and look for today's headlines, search finance.yahoo.com for stock quotes, count how many times the word "flower" appears on your favorite blog, and so on. However, HTML is an ugly, scary place with inconsistently formatted pages that are difficult to reverse engineer and parse effectively. Not to mention the fact that companies change the source code of web pages rather often, so any example that I might make while I am writing this paragraph might break by the time you read this paragraph.

For grabbing data from the web, an XML (Extensible Markup Language) or JSON (JavaScript Object Notation) feed will prove to be more reliable and easier to parse. Unlike HTML (which is designed to make content viewable by a human's eyes) XML and JSON are designed to make content viewable by a computer and facilitate the sharing of data across different systems. Most data (news, weather, and more) is available this way, and I will look at examples in Section 18-8 on page 406 and Section 18-10 on page 414. Though much less desirable, manual HTML parsing is still useful for a couple reasons. First, it never hurts to practice text manipulation techniques that reinforce key programming concepts. But more importantly, sometimes there is data you really want that is not available in an API format, and the only way to get it is with such a technique. (I should also mention that regular expressions, an incredibly powerful techinque in text pattern matching, could also be employed here. As much as I love regex, it's unfortunately beyond the scope of this book.)

An example of data only available as HTML is the Internet Movie Database (*http://imdb.com*). IMDb contains information about movies sorted by year, genre, ratings, etc. For each movie, you can find the cast and crew list, a plot summary, running time, a movie poster image, the list goes on. However, IMDb has no API and does not provide its data as XML or JSON. Pulling the data into Processing therefore requires a bit of detective work. Let's look at the page for the *Shaun the Sheep Movie*.

Figure 18-9

Looking in the HTML source from the above URL, I find a giant mess of markup.

Figure 18-10

It's up to me to pore through the raw source and find the data I am looking for. Let's say I want to know the running time of the movie and grab the movie poster image. After some digging, I find that the movie is 139 minutes long as listed in the following HTML.

```
<div class="txt-block">
  <h4 class="inline">Runtime:</h4>
    <time itemprop="duration" datetime="PT139M">139 min</time>
</div>
```

For any given movie, the running time itself will be variable, but the HTML structure of the page will stay the same. I can therefore deduce that running time will always appear in between:

```
<time itemprop="duration" datetime="PT139M">
```

and:

```
</time>
```

Knowing where the data starts and ends, I can use `giveMeTextBetween()` to pull out the running time.

```
String url = "http://www.imdb.com/title/tt0058331";
String[] lines = loadStrings(url);
// Get rid of the array in order to search the whole page
String html = join(lines, " ");
```

```
// Searching for running time
String start = "<time itemprop=\"duration\" datetime=\"PT139M\">";
```

> A quote in Java marks the beginning or end of a string. So how do you include an actual quote in a `String` object? The answer is via an "escape" sequence. (You encountered this in Exercise 17-8 on page 375.) A quote can be included using a backward slash, followed by a quote. For example: `String q = "This String has a quote \"in it";`

```
String end = "</time>";
String runningtime = giveMeTextBetween(html, start, end);
println(runningtime);
```

Example 18-4 retrieves both the running time and movie poster image from IMDb and displays it onscreen.

Example 18-4. Parsing IMDb manually

```
String runningtime;
PImage poster;

void setup() {
  size(300, 350);
  loadData();
}

void draw() {
  // Display all the stuff I want to display
  background(255);
  image(poster, 10, 10, 164, 250);
  fill(0);
  text("Shaun the Sheep", 10, 300);
  text(runningtime, 10, 320);
}
```

Shaun the Sheep
85 min

Figure 18-11

```
void loadData() {
  String url = "http://www.imdb.com/title/tt2872750/";

  String[] lines = loadStrings(url);
  String html = join(lines, "");
```

> Get the raw HTML source into an array of strings (each line is one element in the array). The next step is to turn array into one long string with `join()`.

```
  String start = "<time itemprop=\"duration\" datetime=\"PT139M\">";
  String end = "</time>";
  runningtime = giveMeTextBetween(html, start, end);
```

> Searching for running time.

```
  start = "<link rel='image_src' href=\"";
  end = "\">";
  String imgUrl = giveMeTextBetween(html, start, end);
  poster = loadImage(imgUrl);
}
```

> Searching for the URL of the poster image.

> Now, load that image!

```
String giveMeTextBetween(String s, String before, String after) {

  String found = "";
```

> This function returns a substring between two substrings (before and after). If it can't find anything it returns an empty string.

```
  // Find the index of before
  int start = s.indexOf(before);
  if (start == -1) {
    return "";
  }

  // Move to the end of the beginning tag
  // and find the index of the "after" String
  start += before.length();
  int end = s.indexOf(after, start);
  if (end == -1) {
    return "";
  }

  // Return the text in between
  return s.substring(start, end);
}
```

Exercise 18-8: Expand Example 18-4 to also search for the movie's rating on IMDb.

Exercise 18-9: Expand Example 18-4 to data related to more than one movie. Can you retrieve the list of all movies released in a given year? Consider creating a `Movie` *class that has a function for retrieving data related to itself.*

Exercise 18-10: Wikipedia (http://www.wikipedia.org/) is another site with lots of data not available via an API. Create a sketch that grabs information from a Wikipedia page.

18-7 Text analysis

Loading text from a URL need not only be an exercise in parsing out small bits of information. It's possible with Processing to analyze large amounts of text found on the web from news feeds, articles, and speeches, to entire books. A nice source is *Project Gutenberg* (*http://www.gutenberg.org/*) which makes available thousands of public domain texts. Algorithms for analyzing text merits an entire book itself, but let's look at some basic techniques.

A text concordance is an alphabetical list of words that appear in a book or body of text along with contextual information. A sophisticated concordance might keep a list of where each word appears (like an index) as well as which words appear next to which other words. In this case, I'm going to create a simple concordance, one that simply stores a list of words and their corresponding counts, i.e., how many times they appeared in the text. Concordances can be used for text analysis applications such as spam filtering or sentiment analysis. To accomplish this task, I am going to use the Processing built-in class `IntDict`.

As you learned in Chapter 9, an array is an ordered list of variables. Each element of the array is numbered and be accessed by its numeric index.

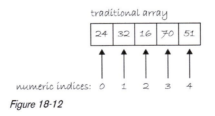

Figure 18-12

However, what if instead of numbering the elements of an array you could name them? This element is named "Sue," this one "Bob," this one "Jane," and so on and so forth. In programming, this kind of data structure is often referred to as an *associative array*, *map*, or *dictionary*. It's a collection of (key, value) pairs. Imagine you had a dictionary of people's ages. When you look up "Sue" (the key), the definition, or value, is her age, 24.

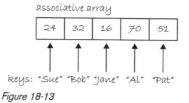

associative array

| 24 | 32 | 16 | 70 | 51 |

keys: "Sue" "Bob" "Jane" "Al" "Pat"

Figure 18-13

Associative arrays can be incredibly convenient for various applications. For example, you could keep a list of student IDs (student name, id) or a list of prices (product name, price) in a dictionary. Here a dictionary is the perfect data structure to hold the concordance. Each element of the dictionary is a word paired with its count.

While there are many classes in Java for dealing with advanced data structures like maps, Processing provides you with a set of three built-in dictionary classes that are easy to use: IntDict, FloatDict, and StringDict. In all of these classes, the key is always a string while the value is variable (an integer, floating point number, or String). For the concordance, I'll use an IntDict.

Creating an IntDict is as easy as calling an empty constructor. Let's say you want a dictionary to keep track of an inventory of supplies.

```
IntDict inventory = new IntDict();
```

Values can be paired with their keys using the set() method.

```
inventory.set("pencils", 10);
inventory.set("paper clips", 128);
inventory.set("pens, 16");
```
> set() assigns an integer to a String.

There are a variety of other methods that can be called to change the value associated with a particular key. For example, if you wanted to add five pencils, you can use add().

```
inventory.add("pencils", 5);
```
> The value of "pencils" is now 15.

A particularly convenient method for the concordance example is increment() which adds one to a key's value.

```
inventory.increment("pens");
```
> The value of "pencils" is now 16.

To retrieve a value associated with a particular key, the get() method is used.

```
int num = inventory.get("pencils");
```
> The value of num is 16.

Finally, dictionaries can be sorted by their keys (alphabetical) or values (smallest to largest or the reverse) with the methods sortKeys(), sortKeysReverse(), sortValues(), and sortValuesReverse().

The concordance now becomes a rather simple program to write. All I need to do is load in a text file, chop it into words with splitTokens() and call increment() on an IntDict for every single word found in the text. The following example does precisely this with the entire text of Shakespeare's play, *A Midsummer Night's Dream*, displaying a simple graph of the most used words.

Example 18-5. Text concordance using IntDict

```
String[] allwords;

String delimiters = " ,.?!;:[]";

IntDict concordance;
```
> Any punctuation is used as a delimiter.

```
void setup() {
  size(360, 640);

  // Load A Midsummer Night's Dream into an array of
strings
  String url = "http://www.gutenberg.org/cache/epub/
1514/pg1514.txt";
  String[] rawtext = loadStrings(url);

  // Join the big array together as one long string
  String everything = join(rawtext, "" );

  allwords = splitTokens(everything, delimiters);
```

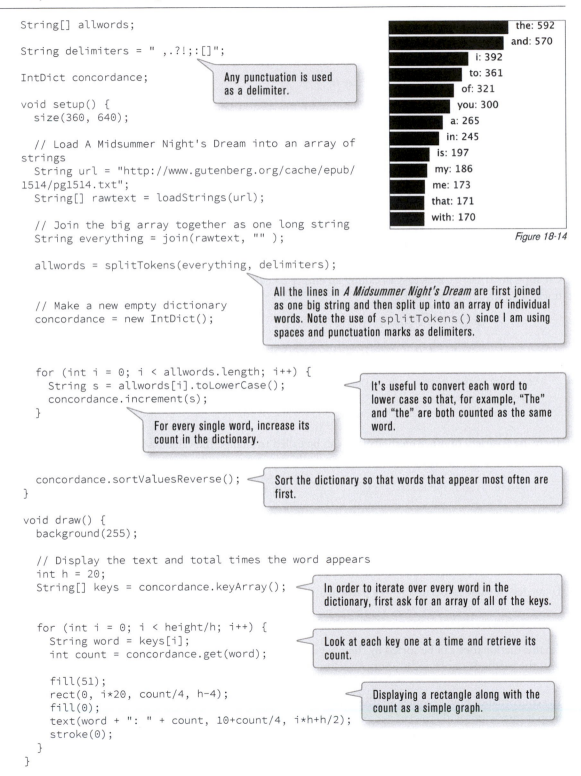

the: 592
and: 570
i: 392
to: 361
of: 321
you: 300
a: 265
in: 245
is: 197
my: 186
me: 173
that: 171
with: 170

Figure 18-14

```
  // Make a new empty dictionary
  concordance = new IntDict();
```
> All the lines in *A Midsummer Night's Dream* are first joined as one big string and then split up into an array of individual words. Note the use of splitTokens() since I am using spaces and punctuation marks as delimiters.

```
  for (int i = 0; i < allwords.length; i++) {
    String s = allwords[i].toLowerCase();
    concordance.increment(s);
  }
```
> For every single word, increase its count in the dictionary.

> It's useful to convert each word to lower case so that, for example, "The" and "the" are both counted as the same word.

```
  concordance.sortValuesReverse();
}
```
> Sort the dictionary so that words that appear most often are first.

```
void draw() {
  background(255);

  // Display the text and total times the word appears
  int h = 20;
  String[] keys = concordance.keyArray();
```
> In order to iterate over every word in the dictionary, first ask for an array of all of the keys.

```
  for (int i = 0; i < height/h; i++) {
    String word = keys[i];
    int count = concordance.get(word);
```
> Look at each key one at a time and retrieve its count.

```
    fill(51);
    rect(0, i*20, count/4, h-4);
    fill(0);
    text(word + ": " + count, 10+count/4, i*h+h/2);
    stroke(0);
  }
}
```
> Displaying a rectangle along with the count as a simple graph.

Exercise 18-11: Create a sketch that visualizes the process of generating the concordance. One example is an animation where each word is read one at a time. When a new word is found, it's added to the sketch window; when it's a word already found, the font size increases.

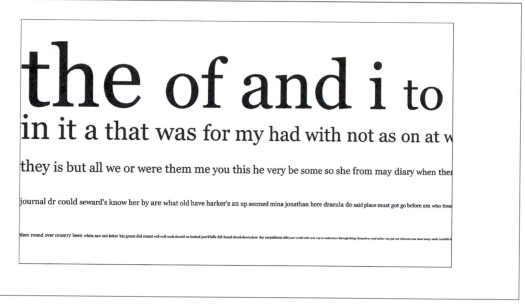

Exercise 18-12: Count the number of times each letter of the alphabet appears in a text. Here is one possibility (but you should be more creative). Note this sketch will require the use of the `charAt()` *function. How would you do this with an array or with an* `IntDict`*?*

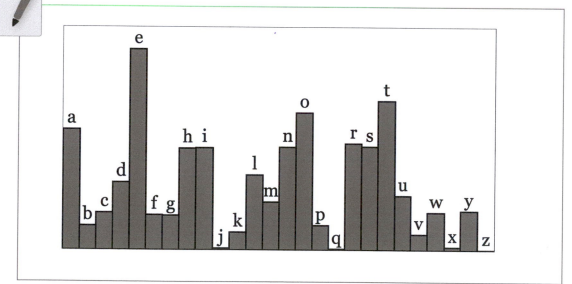

Exercise 18-13: In James W. Pennebaker's book The Secret Life of Pronouns, *Pennebaker describes his research into how the frequency of words that have little to no meaning on their own (I, you, they, a, an, the, etc.) are a window into the emotional state or personality of an author or speaker. For example, heavy use of the pronoun "I" is an indicator of "depression, stress, or insecurity". Create a Processing sketch that analyzes your use of pronouns across a body of text. For more, visit http://www.analyzewords.com/.*

Before moving on, I'll briefly mention that Processing also includes three classes for lists of numbers and strings: `IntList`, `FloatList`, and `StringList`. In other words, if you just want a list of words (without their counts) you could use a `StringList` rather than an `IntDict`. These lists will come up again in Section 23-4 on page 509.

18-8 XML

The examples in Section 18-6 on page 396 demonstrated the process of manually searching through text for individual pieces of data. If your data is available via a standardized format such as XML or JSON, however, these manual techniques are no longer required. XML is designed to facilitate the sharing of data across different systems, and you can retrieve that data using the built-in Processing XML class.

XML organizes information in a tree structure. Let's imagine a list of students. Each student has an ID number, name, address, email, and telephone number. Each student's address has a city, state, and zip code. An XML tree for this dataset might look like Figure 18-15.

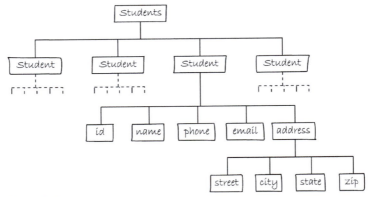

Figure 18-15

The XML source itself (with two students listed) is:

```
<?xml version = "1.0" encoding = "UTF-8 "?>
<students>
  <student>
    <id>001</id>
    <name>Daniel Shiffman</name>
    <phone>555-555-5555</phone>
    <email>daniel@shiffman.net</email>
    <address>
```

```
      <street>123 Processing Way</street>
      <city>Loops</city>
      <state>New York</state>
      <zip>01234</zip>
    </address>
  </student>
  <student>
    <id>002</id>
    <name>Zoog</name>
    <phone>555-555-5555</phone>
    <email>zoog@planetzoron.uni</email>
    <address>
      <street>45.3 Nebula 5</street>
      <city>Boolean City</city>
      <state>Booles</state>
      <zip>12358</zip>
    </address>
  </student>
</students>
```

Note the similarities to object-oriented programming. You can think of the XML tree in the following terms. The XML document represents an array of student objects. Each student object has multiple pieces of information, an ID, a name, a phone number, an email address, and a mailing address. The mailing address is also an object that has multiple pieces of data, such as street, city, state, and zip.

Exercise 18-14: Revisit the Bubble *class from Example 18-3. Design an XML tree structure for these Bubble objects. Diagram the tree and write out the XML source. (Use the empty diagram and fill in the blanks below.)*

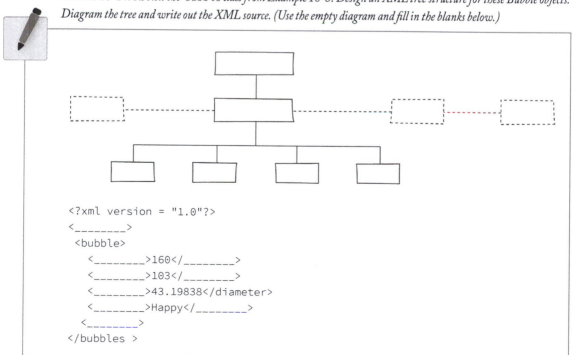

```
<?xml version = "1.0"?>
<_____>
  <bubble>
      <_____>160</_____>
      <_____>103</_____>
      <_____>43.19838</diameter>
      <_____>Happy</_____>
      <_____>
  </bubbles >
```

Let's look at some data made available from a web service such as Yahoo Weather. Here is the raw XML source. (Note I have edited it slightly for simplification purposes.)

```
<?xml version="1.0" encoding="UTF-8" standalone="yes" ?>
<rss version="2.0" xmlns:yweather="http://xml.weather.yahoo.com/ns/rss/1.0">
  <channel>
    <item>
      <title>Conditions for New York, NY at 12:49 pm EDT</title>
      <geo:lat>40.67</geo:lat>
      <geo:long>-73.94</geo:long>
      <link>http://us.rd.yahoo.com/dailynews/rss/weather/New_York__NY//link>
      <pubDate>Thu, 24 Jul 2014 12:49 pm EDT</pubDate>
      <yweather:condition text="Partly Cloudy" code="30" temp="76"/>
      <yweather:forecast day="Thu" low="65" high="82" text="Partly Cloudy"/>
    </item>
  </channel>
</rss>
```

The data is mapped in the tree stucture shown in Figure 18-16.

Figure 18-16

You may be wondering what the top level "RSS" is all about. Yahoo's XML weather data is provided in RSS format. RSS stands for "Really Simple Syndication" and is a standardized XML format for syndicating web content (such as news articles, etc.). You can read more about RSS on Wikipedia (*http://en.wikipedia.org/wiki/RSS*).

Now that you have a handle on the tree structure, let's look at the specifics inside that structure. With the exception of the first line (which simply indicates that this page is XML formatted), this XML document contains a nested list of *elements*, each with a start tag, that is, <channel>, and an end tag, that is, </channel>. Some of these elements have content between the tags:

```
<title>Conditions for New York, NY at 12:49 pm EDT</title>
```

and some have attributes (formatted by *Attribute Name* equals *Attribute Value in quotes*):

```
<yweather:forecast day="Thu" low="65" high="82" text="Partly Cloudy"/>
```

18-9 Using the Processing XML class

Since the syntax of XML is standardized, I could certainly use `split()`, `indexof()`, and `substring()` to find the pieces I want in the XML source. The point here, however, is that because XML is a standard format, I don't have to do this. Rather, I can use an XML parser. In Processing, XML can be parsed using the built-in Processing class `XML`.

```
XML xml = loadXML("http://xml.weather.yahoo.com/forecastrss?p=10003");
```

Here, instead of `loadStrings()` or `loadTable()`, I'm now calling `loadXML()` and passing in the address (URL or local file) of the XML document. An `XML` object represents one element of an XML tree. When a document is first loaded, that `XML` object is always the root element. Referring back to XML tree diagram (Figure 18-16), I find the current temperature via the following path:

1. The root of the tree is **RSS**.
2. **RSS** has a child named **channel**.
3. **Channel** has a child named **item**.
4. **Item** has a child named **yweather:condition**.
5. The temperature is stored in **yweather:condition** as the attribute **temp**.

The children of an element are accessed via the `getChild()` function.

```
XML channel = xml.getChild("channel");
```
> Accessing the "channel" child element of the root element

The content of an element itself is retrieved with one of the following methods: `getContent()`, `getIntContent()`, or `getFloatcContent()`. `getContent()` is for generic use and will always give you the content as a String. If you intend to use the content as a number, Processing will convert it for you with either `getIntContent()` or `getFloatcContent()`. Attributes can also be read as either numbers — `getInt()`, `getFloat()` — or text — `getString()`.

Following steps one through five outlined above through the XML tree, I have:

```
XML root = loadXML("http://xml.weather.yahoo.com/forecastrss?p=10003");

XML channel    = root.getChild("channel");                        Step 2    Step 1

XML item       = channel.getChild("item");                        Step 3

XML yweather   = item.getChild("yweather:condition");             Step 4

int temperature = yweather.getInt("temp");                        Step 5
```

However, this is a bit long-winded and so can be compressed down into one (or three, as below) lines of code.

```
XML root = loadXML(http://xml.weather.yahoo.com/forecastrss?p=10003);

XML forecast =
    root.getChild("channel").getChild("item").getChild("yweather:condition");
int temperature = forecast.getInt("temp");
```

> Steps 2-4

Finally, the second line of code above can be further condensed to:

```
XML forecast = xml.getChild("channel/item/yweather:condition");
```

> Steps 2-4

Following is the above code put together in an example that retrieves weather data for multiple zip codes by parsing Yahoo's XML feed.

Example 18-6. Parsing Yahoo weather XML

```
int temperature = 0;
String weather = "";
```

> Temperature is stored as a number and the description of the weather as a string.

```
Zip code: 10003
Today's high: 81
Forecast: Partly Cloudy
```

Figure 18-17

```
// The zip code
String zip = "10003";

void setup() {
  size(200, 200);

  // The URL for the XML document
  String url = "http://xml.weather.yahoo.com/
forecastrss?p=" + zip;

  // Load the XML document
  XML xml = loadXML(url);

  XML forecast = xml.getChild("channel/item/yweather:forecast");
```

> Here, I grab the XML element that I want.

```
  temperature = forecast.getInt("high");
  weather = forecast.getString("text");
}
```

> And then I pull the attributes from that XML element.

```
void draw() {
  background(255);
  fill(0);

  // Display all the stuff I want to display
  text("Zip code: " + zip, 10, 50);
  text("Today's high: " + temperature, 10, 70);
  text("Forecast: " + weather, 10, 90);
}
```

Other useful XML functions are:

- `hasChildren()` — checks whether or not an element has any children
- `getChildren()` — returns an array containing all child elements
- `getAttributeCount()` — counts the specified element's number of attributes
- `hasAttribute()` — checks whether or not an element has the specified attribute

In this example I'm accessing the child nodes by their name (i.e., "channel," "item,", etc.), however they can also be accessed numerically via an index (starting at zero, same as an array). This is convenient when looping over a list of children, much like I did with tabular data when I iterated over rows in a table.

In Example 18-3, I used a `Table` to store information related to `Bubble` objects. An XML document can also be used in the same manner. Here is a possible solution to Exercise 18-14 on page 407, an XML tree of `Bubble` objects. (Note that this solution uses element *attributes* for x and y coordinates; this was not the format provided in Exercise 18-14 on page 407 since I had not yet covered attributes.)

```xml
<?xml version="1.0" encoding="UTF-8"?>
<bubbles>
  <bubble>
    <position x="160" y="103"/>
    <diameter>43.19838</diameter>
    <label>Happy</label>
  </bubble>
  <bubble>
    <position x="372" y="137"/>
    <diameter>52.42526</diameter>
    <label>Sad</label>
  </bubble>
  <bubble>
    <position x="273" y="235"/>
    <diameter>61.14072</diameter>
    <label>Joyous</label>
  </bubble>
  <bubble>
    <position x="121" y="179"/>
    <diameter>44.758068</diameter>
    <label>Melancholy</label>
  </bubble>
</bubbles>
```

I can use `getChildren()` to retrieve the array of `<bubble>` elements and make a `Bubble` object from each one. Here is the example which uses the identical `Bubble` class from earlier (not included below). The new code is in bold.

Example 18-7. Using Processing's XML class

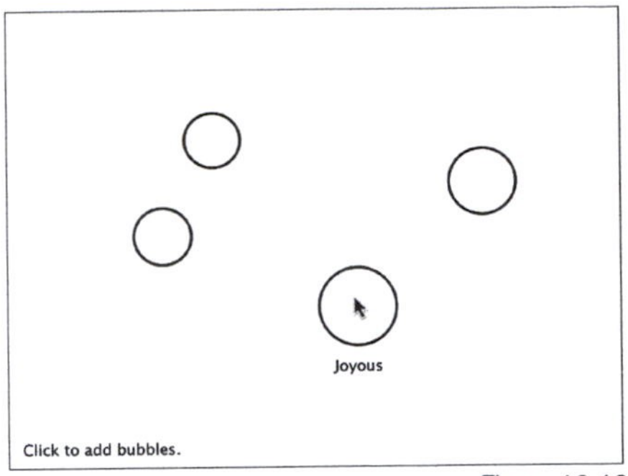

```
// An Array of Bubble objects
Bubble[] bubbles;
// An XML object
XML xml;

void setup() {
  size(480, 360);
  loadData();
}

void loadData() {
  // Load XML file
  xml = loadXML("data.xml");
  // Get all the child nodes named "bubble"
  XML[] children = xml.getChildren("bubble");

  bubbles = new Bubble[children.length];

  for (int i = 0; i < bubbles.length; i++) {

    XML positionElement = children[i].getChild("position");
    float x = positionElement.getInt("x");
    float y = positionElement.getInt("y");



    // The diameter is the content of the child named "diameter"
    XML diameterElement = children[i].getChild("diameter");
    float diameter = diameterElement.getFloatContent();



    // The label is the content of the child named "label"
    XML labelElement = children[i].getChild("label");
    String label = labelElement.getContent();

    // Make a Bubble object out of the data read
    bubbles[i] = new Bubble(x, y, diameter, label);
  }
}

void draw() {
  background(255);
  // Display all bubbles
  for (int i = 0; i < bubbles.length; i++) {
    bubbles[i].display();
    bubbles[i].rollover(mouseX, mouseY);
  }
}
```

Joyous

Click to add bubbles.

Figure 18-18

> The size of the `Bubble` array is determined by the total XML elements named "bubble."

> The position element has two attributes: "x" and "y". Attributes can be accessed as an integer or float via `getInt()` and `getFloat()`.

> Notice, however, with the content of an XML node, I retrieve via `getIntContent()` and `getFloatContent()`.

Exercise 18-15: Use the following XML document to initialize an array of objects. Design the objects to use all of the values in each XML element. (Feel free to rewrite the XML document to include more or less data.) If you do not want to retype the XML, it's available at this book's website.

```
<?xml version = "1.0"?>
<particles>
  <particle>
    <location x = "99" y = "192"/>
    <speed x = "-0.88238335 " y = "2.2704291"/>
    <size w = "38" h = "10"/>
  </particle>
  <particle>
    <location x = "97" y = "14"/>
    <speed x = "2.8775783" y = "2.9483867"/>
    <size w = "81" h = "43"/>
  </particle>
  <particle>
    <location x = "159" y = "193"/>
    <speed x = "-1.2341062" y = "0.44016743"/>
    <size w = "19" h = "95"/>
  </particle>
  <particle>
    <location x = "102" y = "53"/>
    <speed x = "0.8000488" y = "-2.2791147"/>
    <size w = "25" h = "95"/>
  </particle>
  <particle>
    <location x = "152" y = "181"/>
    <speed x = "1.9928784" y = "-2.9540048"/>
    <size w = "74" h = "19"/>
  </particle>
</particles>
```

In addition to loadXML(), Processing also includes a saveXML() function for writing XML files to your sketch folder. You can modify the XML tree itself by adding or removing elements with addChild() or removeChild(), as well as modify the content of elements or attributes with setContent(), setIntContent(), setFloatContent(), setString(), setInt(), and setFloat().

Exercise 18-16: Add the functionality of creating new bubbles on mouse clicks to Example 18-7. Here is some code to get you started.

```
void mousePressed() {

  // Create a new XML bubble element

  XML bubble = xml.addChild(_____);

  XML position = bubble.addChild(_____);

  position.setInt("x", _____);

  position.setInt(_____, _____);

  XML diameter = bubble.addChild(_____));

  diameter._____(random(40, 80));
  XML label = bubble.addChild("label");

  label._____("new label");

  saveXML(xml, "data/data.xml");
  loadData();
}
```

18-10 JSON

Another increasingly popular data exchange format is JSON (pronounced like the name Jason), which stands for JavaScript Object Notation. Its design was based on the syntax for objects in the JavaScript programming language (and is most commonly used to pass data between web applications) but has become rather ubiquitous and language-agnostic. While you don't need to know anything about JavaScript to work in Processing, it won't hurt to get a sense of some basic JavaScript syntax while learning it.

JSON is an alternative to XML and the data can be looked at in a similarly tree-like manner. All JSON data comes in the following two ways: an object or an array. Luckily, you already know about these two concepts and only need to learn a new syntax for encoding them.

Let's take a look at a JSON object first. A JSON object is like a Processing object only with no functions. It's simply a collection of variables with a name and a value (or "name/value pair"). For example, following is JSON data describing a person:

```
{
    "name":"Olympia",
    "age":3,
    "height":96.5,
    "state":"giggling"
}
```

> Each name/value pair is separated by a comma.

Notice how this maps closely to classes in Processing.

```
class Person {
    String name;
    int age;
    float height;
    String state;
}
```

There are no classes in JSON, only the object literals themselves. Also an object can contain, as part of itself, another object.

```
{
    "name":"Olympia",
    "age":3,
    "height":96.5,
    "state":"giggling",
    "brother":{
        "name":"Elias",
        "age":6
    }
}
```

> The value of "brother" is an object containing two name/value pairs.

In XML, the preceding JSON data would look like the following (for simplicity I'm avoiding the use of XML attributes).

```
<xml version="1.0" encoding="UTF-8"?>
<person>
  <name>Olympia</name>
  <age>3</age>
  <height>96.5</height>
  <state>giggling</state>
  <brother>
    <name>Elias</name>
    <age>6</age>
  </brother>
</person>
```

Multiple JSON objects can appear in the data as an array. Just like the arrays you use in Processing, a JSON array is simply a list of values (primitives or objects). The syntax, however, is different with square brackets indicating the use of an array rather than curly ones. Here is a simple JSON array of integers:

```
[1, 7, 8, 9, 10, 13, 15]
```

You might find an array as part of an object.

```
{
  "name":"Olympia",
  "favorite colors":[
    "purple",
    "blue",
    "pink"
  ]
}
```

> The value of "favorite colors" is an array of strings.

Or an array of objects themselves. For example, here is what the bubbles would look like in JSON. Notice how this JSON data is organized as a single JSON object "bubbles," which contains a JSON array of JSON objects, the bubbles. Flip back to compare to the CSV and XML versions of the same data.

```
{
  "bubbles":[
    {
      "position":{
        "x":160,
        "y":103
      },
      "diameter":43.19838,
      "label":"Happy"
    },
    {
      "position":{
        "x":372,
        "y":137
      },
      "diameter":52.42526,
      "label":"Sad"
    },
    {
      "position":{
        "x":273,
        "y":235
      },
      "diameter":61.14072,
      "label":"Joyous"
    }
  ]
}
```

Exercise 18-17: Make up the rest of this missing JSON (loosely based on a weather API).

```
{
    "cities": [
        {
            "name":"New York",
            "weather":{

                "high":_____,

                _____
            },
            "wind"_____

                _____

            }
        },
        {
            "name":_____,
            "weather":{

                "high":_____,

                _____
            },

            _____

            _____

            _____

            _____

            _____

            _____
}
```

18-11 JSONObject **and** JSONArray

Now that I've covered the syntax of JSON, I can look at using the data in Processing. One thing that can be a bit tricky about working with JSON in Processing is that I have to treat objects and arrays differently. With XML, I simply had a single XML class with all the parsing functionality I needed. With JSON, I have two classes: `JSONObject` and `JSONArray`, and I'll have to be conscientious about picking which class I am using during the parsing process.

The first step is simply loading the data with either `loadJSONObject()` or `loadJSONArray()`. But which one? I have to look and see what is at the root of the JSON file, an object or array. This can be a little tricky. Let's look at these two JSON examples:

Sample 1:

```
[
  {
    "name":"Elias"
  },
  {
    "name":"Olympia"
  }
]
```

Sample 2:

```
{
  "names":[
    {
      "name":"Elias"
    },
    {
      "name":"Olympia"
    }
  ]
}
```

Look how similar the above two samples look. They both contain exactly the same data, two names "Elias" and "Olympia." There is one, very key difference, however, to how the data is formatted: the very first character. Is it a "[" or a "{"? The answer will determine whether you're loading an array ("[") or an object("{").

```
JSONObject json = loadJSONObject("file.json");
```
JSON objects start with a curly bracket: {

```
JSONArray json = JSONArray("file.json");
```
JSON arrays start with a square bracket: [

Typically, even if the data is ultimately organized as an array of objects (such as the array of "bubble" objects), the root element of the JSON data will be an object that contains that array. Let's look at the bubble data one more time.

```
{
  "bubbles":[
    {
      "position":{
        "x":160,
        "y":103
```

```
    },
      "diameter":43.19838,
      "label":"Happy"
    },
    {
      "position":{
        "x":372,
        "y":137
      },
      "diameter":52.42526,
      "label":"Sad"

    }
  ]
}
```

With the above, I first load an object and then pull the array out of that object.

```
JSONObject json = loadJSONObject("data.json");
JSONArray bubbleData = json.getJSONArray("bubbles");
```

Load the entire JSON file as an object.

Pull the array of bubbles out of that object.

Just as with XML, the data from an element is accessed via its name, in this case "bubbles." With a JSONArray, however, each element of the array is retrieved via its numeric index.

```
for (int i = 0; i < bubbleData.size(); i++) {
  JSONObject bubble = bubbleData.getJSONObject(i);
}
```

Iterating over a JSONArray.

And when you're looking for a specific piece of data from a JSONObject, such as an integer or string, the functions are identical to those of XML attributes.

```
JSONObject position = bubble.getJSONObject("position");
```

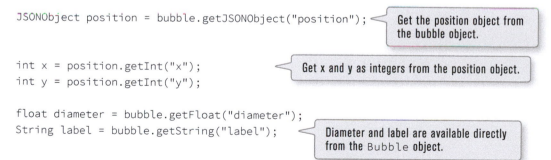

Get the position object from the bubble object.

```
int x = position.getInt("x");
int y = position.getInt("y");
```

Get x and y as integers from the position object.

```
float diameter = bubble.getFloat("diameter");
String label = bubble.getString("label");
```

Diameter and label are available directly from the Bubble object.

Putting this all together, I can now make a JSON version of the bubbles example (leaving out the draw() function and Bubble class which haven't changed.)

Example 18-8. Using Processing's JSON classes

```
// An Array of Bubble objects
Bubble[] bubbles;

void setup() {
  size(480, 360);
  loadData();
}

void loadData() {
  JSONObject json = loadJSONObject("data.json");
  JSONArray bubbleData = json.getJSONArray("bubbles");


  bubbles = new Bubble[bubbleData.size()];


  for (int i = 0; i < bubbleData.size(); i++) {

    JSONObject bubble = bubbleData.getJSONObject(i);

    // Get a position object
    JSONObject position = bubble.getJSONObject("position");
    // Get (x,y) from JSON object "position"
    int x = position.getInt("x");
    int y = position.getInt("y");

    // Get diamter and label
    float diameter = bubble.getFloat("diameter");
    String label = bubble.getString("label");

    bubbles[i] = new Bubble(x, y, diameter, label);
  }
}
```

> Load the JSON file and grab the array.

> The size of the array of Bubble objects is determined by the length of the JSON array

> Iterate through the array, grabbing each JSON object one at a time.

> Put the Bubble objects into an array.

Exercise 18-18: Retrieve the description and current temperature using the following JSON from openweathermap.org (http://openweathermap.org/current).

```
{
  "weather":[
    {
      "id":801,
      "main":"Clouds",
      "description":"few clouds",
      "icon":"02d"
    }
  ],
  "main":{
    "temp":73.45,
    "humidity":83,
    "pressure":999,
    "temp_min":70,
    "temp_max":75.99
  }
}
JSONObject json = loadJSONObject(
    "http://api.openweathermap.org/data/2.5/weather?q=New%20York");

JSONObject main = json.getJSONObject(_____);

int temp = main._____("temp");

// Grab the description (this is just one way to do it)

_____ weather = json.getJSON _____("weather");

String des = weather.getJSONObject(____)._____(_____);
```

18-12 Threads

As you have seen, the various loading functions — loadStrings(), loadTable(), loadXML(), and loadJSONObject() — can be used for retrieving data from URLs. Nonetheless, unless your sketch only needs to load the data once during setup(), you may have a problem. For example, consider a sketch that grabs the price of AAPL stock from an XML feed every five minutes. Each time loadXML() is called, the sketch will pause while waiting to receive the data. Any animation will stutter. This is because these loading functions are "blocking." In other words, the sketch will sit and wait at that line of code until loadXML() completes its task. With a local data file, this is extremely fast. Nonetheless, a request for a URL (known as an "HTTP request") in Processing is *synchronous*, meaning your sketch waits for a response from the server before continuing. Who knows how will that take? No one; you are at the mercy of the server!

The answer to this problem lies in the concept of *threads*. By now you are quite familiar with the idea of writing a program that follows a specific sequence of steps — setup() first then draw() over and over and over again! A thread is also a series of steps with a beginning, a middle, and an end. A Processing sketch is a single thread, often referred to as the *animation* thread. Other threads' sequences, however, can run independently of the main animation loop. In fact, you can launch any number of threads at one time, and they will all run concurrently.

Processing does this quite often, such as with library functions like captureEvent() and movieEvent(). These functions are triggered by a different thread running behind the scenes, and they alert Processing whenever they have something to report. This is useful when you need to perform a task that takes too long and would slow down the main animation's frame rate, such as grabbing data from the network. Here, you want to handle the request *asynchronously* in a different thread. If that thread gets stuck or has an error, the entire program won't grind to a halt, since the error only stops that individual thread and not the main animation loop.

Writing your own thread can be a complex endeavor that involves extending the Java Thread (*https:// docs.oracle.com/javase/tutorial/essential/concurrency/threads.html*) class. However, the thread() method is a quick and dirty way to implement a simple thread in Processing. By passing in a string that matches the name of a function declared elsewhere in the sketch, Processing will execute that function in a separate thread. Let's take a look at a skeleton of how this works.

```
void setup() {
  thread("someFunction");
}

void draw() {

}

void someFunction() {
  // This function will run as a thread when called via
  // thread("someFunction") as it was in setup!
}
```

The thread() function receives a string as an argument. The string should match the name of the function you want to run as a thread. In the above example it's "someFunction".

Let's look at a more practical example. For an example of data that changes often, I'll use time.jsontest.com which gives you the current time (in milliseconds). While I could retrieve this from the system clock, this works well for demonstrating continuously requesting data that changes over time. Not knowing about threads, my first instinct might be to say:

```
void draw() {
  JSONObject json = loadJSONObject("http://time.jsontest.com/");
  String time = json.getString("time");
  text(time, 40, 100);
}
```

> The code will stop here and wait to receive the data before moving on.

This would give me the current time every cycle through draw(). If I examine the frame rate, however, I'll notice that the sketch is running incredibly slowly (and all it needs to do is draw a single string!). This is where calling the parsing code as a separate thread will help a lot.

```
String time = "";

void draw() {
  thread("requestData");
  text(time, 40, 100);
}
```

> Now the code will move on to the next line while requestData() executes in a separate thread.

```
void requestData() {
  JSONObject json = loadJSONObject("http://time.jsontest.com/");
  time = json.getString("time");
}
```

The logic is identical, only I am not requesting the data directly in draw(), but executing that request as a separate thread. Notice that I am not doing any drawing in requestData(). This is key as executing drawing functions in code that runs on a separate thread can cause conflicts with the main animation thread (i.e., draw()) resulting in strange behavior and errors.

In the above example, I likely don't want to request the data sixty times per second (the default frame rate). Instead I might make use of the Timer class from Section 10-6 on page 201, and ask for the data once per second. Here is a full example that does exactly that with added animation to show that draw() never stutters.

Example 18-9. Threads

```
Timer timer = new Timer(1000);
String time = "";

void setup() {
  size(200, 200);
  thread("retrieveData");
  timer.start();
}

void draw() {
  background(255);
  if (timer.isFinished()) {
    retrieveData();

    timer.start();
  }

  fill(0);
  text(time, 40, 100);

  translate(20, 100);
  stroke(0);
  rotate(frameCount*0.04);
  for (int i = 0; i < 10; i++) {
    rotate(radians(36));
    line(5, 0, 10, 0);
  }
}

// get the data
void retrieveData() {
  JSONObject json = loadJSONObject("http://time.jsontest.com/");
  time = json.getString("time");
}
```

Start by requesting the data asynchronously in a thread.

Every one second, make a new request.

And restart the timer.

Here I draw a little animation to demonstrate that the `draw()` loop never pauses.

☀ 12:36:20 PM

Figure 18-19

Exercise 18-19: Update the weather XML or weather JSON example to request the data in a thread.

18-13 APIs

It's a bit silly for me to call this section "APIs" given that most of this chapter is about data from APIs. Still, it's worth taking a moment to pause and reflect. What makes something an API versus just some data you found, and what are some pitfalls you might run into when using an API?

As I've stated, an API (Application Programming Interface) is an interface through which one application can access the services of another. These can come in many forms. Openweathermap.org, as you saw in Exercise 18-18 on page 421, is an API that offers its data in JSON, XML, and HTML formats. The key element that makes this service an API is exactly that offer; openweathermap.org's sole purpose in life is to offer you its data. And not just offer it, but allow you to query it for specific data in a specific format. Let's look at a short list of sample queries.

http://api.openweathermap.org/data/2.5/weather?lat=35&lon=139
    A request for current weather data for a specific latitude and longitude.

http://api.openweathermap.org/data/2.5/forecast/daily?
q=London&mode=xml&units=metric&cnt=7&lang=zh_cn
    A request for a seven day London forecast in XML format with metric units and in Chinese.

http://api.openweathermap.org/data/2.5/history/station?id=5091&type=day
    A request for a historical data for a given weather station.

One thing to note about openweathermap.org is that it does not require that you tell the API any information about yourself. You simply send a request to a URL and get the data back. Other APIs, however, require you to sign up and obtain an access token. *The New York Times* API is one such example. Before you can make a request from Processing, you'll need to visit *The New York Times* Developer site (*http://developer.nytimes.com/*) and request an API key. Once you have that key, you can store it in your code as a string.

```
// This is not a real key
String apiKey = "40e2es0b3ca44563f9c62aeded4431dc:12:51913116";
```

You also need to know what the URL is for the API itself. This information is documented for you on the developer site, but here it is for simplicity:

```
String url = "http://api.nytimes.com/svc/search/v2/articlesearch.json";
```

Finally, you have to tell the API what it is you are looking for. This is done with a "query string," a sequence of name value pairs describing the parameters of the query joined with an ampersand. This functions similarly to how you pass arguments to a function in Processing. If you wanted to search for the term "processing" from a search() function you might say:

```
search("processing");
```

Here, the API acts as the function call, and you send it the arguments via the query string. Here is a simple example asking for a list of the oldest articles that contain the term "processing" (the oldest of which turns out to be May 12th, 1852).

```
String query = "?q=processing&sort=oldest";
```

> The name/value pairs that configure the API query are: (q,processing) and (sort,oldest)

This isn't just guesswork. Figuring out how to put together a query string requires reading through the API's documentation. For *The New York Times*, it's all outlined on the *Times'* developer website (*http://developer.nytimes.com/docs/read/article_search_api_v2*). Once you have your query you can join all the pieces together and pass it to loadJSONObject(). Here is a tiny example that simply displays the most recent headline.

Example 18-10. NYTimes API query

```
void setup() {
  size(200, 200);

  String apiKey = "40e2ea0b3ca44563f9c62aeded0431dc:18:51513116";
  String url = "http://api.nytimes.com/svc/search/v2/articlesearch.json";
  String query = "?q=processing&sort=newest";

  // Make the API query
  JSONObject json = loadJSONObject(url+query+"&api-key="+apiKey);
```

> Here, I format the call to the API by joining the URL with the API key with the query string.

```
  String headline = json.getJSONObject("response").getJSONArray("docs").
    getJSONObject(0).getJSONObject("headline").getString("main");
  background(255);
  fill(0);
  text(headline, 10, 10, 180, 190);
}
```

> Grabbing a single headline from the results.

Some APIs require a deeper level of authentication beyond an API access key. Twitter, for example, uses an authentication protocol known as "OAuth" to provide access to its data. Writing an OAuth application requires more than just passing a String into a request and is beyond the scope of this book. However, in these cases, if you're lucky, you can find a Processing library that handles all of the authentication for you. There are several APIs that can be used directly with Processing via a library, and you can find a list of them in the "Data / Protocols" section of the libraires reference page (*http://processing.org/reference/libra ries/index.html*) for some ideas. Temboo (*https://www.temboo.com/processing*), for example, offers a Processing library that handles OAuth for you and provides direct access to many APIs (including Twitter) in Processing. With Temboo, you can write code that looks like:

```
TembooSession session = new TembooSession("ACCOUNT_NAME", "APP_NAME", "APP_KEY");
```

> Temboo acts as a go-between you and Twitter, so first you just authenticate with Temboo.

```
Tweets tweets = new Tweets(session);
tweets.setCredential("your-twitter-name");
tweetsChoreo.setQuery("arugula");
TweetsResultSet tweetsResults = tweets.run();
```

> Then you can configure a query to send to Twitter itself and grab the results.

```
JSONObject searchResults = parseJSONObject(tweetsResults.getResponse());

JSONArray statuses = searchResults.getJSONArray("statuses");

JSONObject tweet = statuses.getJSONObject(0);
String tweetText = tweet.getString("text");
```

> Finally, you can search through the results and grab a tweet.

19 Data Streams

I'm mad as hell and I'm not going to take this anymore!
—Howard Beale, *Network*

In this chapter:
– Sockets
– Servers
– Clients
– Multi-user processing
– Serial communication

19-1 Network communication

In this chapter, I will use the Processing network library to create sketches that talk to each other in real-time. Examples of this are multi-user applications such as games, instant messenger, and chat (among other things).

In Chapter 18, I looked at how you can request the raw source of a URL using `loadStrings()`, `loadXML()`, and `loadJSON()`. You make the request, sit back, and await the results. You may have noticed that this process does not happen instantaneously. Sometimes the program may pause for seconds (or even minutes) while a document loads. This is due to the length of time required for what Processing performs behind the scenes — sending a request and retrieving the corresponding response.

Let's consider, for a moment, how you make similar "requests and responses" in your every day life. Perhaps you wake up one morning and think to yourself that a vacation, say in Tuscany, is in order. You turn on your computer, launch a web browser, type *www.google.com* in the address bar, and enter "romantic getaway Tuscany villa". You, the *client*, made a request, and it's the job of google, the *server*, to provide a response.

```
                        The Client:
  Hi. I'm a web browser, and I have a request. I was wondering if you might
  be so kind as to send me your web page about vacation villas in Tuscany?


                       [Dramatic Pause]


                        The Server:
  Sure, no problem, here is my response. It's a whole lot of bytes, but if
  you read it as html you'll see it's a nicely formatted page about Tuscany
  vacation rentals.  Enjoy! Oh, can you let me know that you received it ok?


                        The Client:
  Got it, thanks!


             [The Client and the Server shake hands.]
```

The above process is known as HTTP request and response, a bi-directional communication between a client and a server. The client sends a request to the server, which responds at its leisure, while the client sits and waits for the response. The HTTP stands for "hyper-text transfer protocol," a protocol for sending data back and forth in the world wide web. For each request, the connection between the client and server is opened and then promptly closed when completed. This methodology works well for loading web pages in a browser. However, for applications in Processing where you need near real-time communication, a connection that is opened and closed for each exchange would cause delays and lag. For these applications, a continous connection is required — a *socket* connection. .

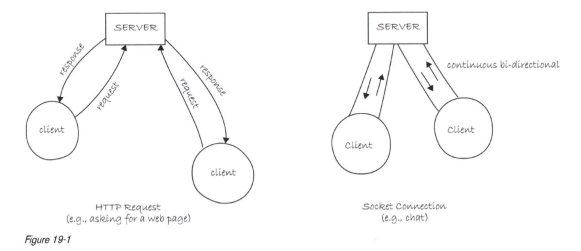

HTTP Request
(e.g., asking for a web page)

Socket Connection
(e.g., chat)

Figure 19-1

19-2 Creating a server

In order to start working with sockets, I'll first build a server; the server's job will be to open connections for clients and respond to their requests. Socket connections consist of an IP address — the numeric address of a machine on the network — and a port number — a number used to route information from one program to another. To create a server, I first need to choose that port number (I'll get to the IP address later). Any client that wants to connect to the server will need to know this number. Port numbers range from 0 to 65535 and any number is fair game, however, ports 0 through 1023 are usually reserved for common services, so it's best to avoid those. If you're unsure, a google search will turn up information on whether the port is likely used by another application. For these examples, I will use the port 5204 (this is the same port used in the Processing network library reference (*https://processing.org/reference/libra ries/net*).

To create a server, I first import the library and create an instance of a `Server` object.

```
import processing.net.* ;

Server server;
```

The server is initialized via the constructor, which takes two arguments: `this` (a reference to *this* sketch as explained in Chapter 16) and an integer value for a port number.

```
server = new Server(this, 5204);
```

The server starts and waits for connections as soon as it is created. It can be closed at any time by calling the `stop()` function.

```
server.stop();
```

You may recall from my discussion of video capturing in Chapter 16 that I used a callback function (`captureEvent()`) to handle a new frame of video available from the camera. I can find out if a new client has connected to the server with the same technique, using the callback function `serverEvent()`. `serverEvent()` requires two arguments: a server (the one generating the event) and a client (that has connected). I might use this function, for example, to retrieve the IP address of the connected client.

```
// The serverEvent function is called whenever
// A new client connects
void serverEvent(Server server, Client client) {
  println("A new client has connected: " + client.ip());
}
```

> Server events occur *only* when a new client connects.

The use of a callback also allows the network messages to be handled "asynchronously" as I discussed with threads in Section 18-12 on page 421.

When a client sends a message (after having connected), a `serverEvent()` is *not* generated. Instead, I must use the `available()` function to determine if there is a new message from any client available to be read. If there is, a reference to the client broadcasting the method is returned and I can read the content using the `readString()` method. If nothing is available, the function will return the value `null`, meaning no value (or no client object exists).

```
void draw() {
  // If there is no client, someClient will be " null "
  Client someClient = server.available();
  // The sketch should only proceed if the client is not null
  if (someClient! = null) {
    println("Client says: " + someClient.readString());
  }
}
```

The function readString() is useful in applications where text information is sent across the network. If the data should be treated differently, for instance, as a number (as you will see in future examples), other read() methods can be called.

A server can also send messages out to clients, and this is done with the write() method.

```
server.write("Great, thanks for the message!\n");
```

Depending on what you're doing, it's often a good idea to send a *newline* character at the end of your messages. In a moment, when I write the client sketch, you'll see how this is useful. The escape sequence for adding a newline character to a string is \n (for a reminder about escape characters see Chapter 18).

Putting all of the above together, I can write a simple chat server. This server replies to any message it receives with the phrase "How does 'that' make you feel?" See Example 19-1, Figure 19-2.

Example 19-1. Simple therapy server

```
// Import the net libraries
import processing.net.*;

// Declare a server
Server server;

// Used to indicate a new message has arrived
float newMessageColor = 255;

String incomingMessage = "";

void setup() {
  size(400, 200);
  // Create the Server on port 5204
  server = new Server(this, 5204);
}
```

> This sketch runs a Server on port 5204.

```
void draw() {
  background(newMessageColor);

  // newMessageColor fades to white over time
  newMessageColor = constrain(newMessageColor + 0.3, 0, 255);
  textAlign(CENTER);
  fill(255);
  text(incomingMessage, width/2, height/2);
```

> The most recent incoming message is displayed in the window.

```
  // If there is no client, client will be null
  Client client = server.available();
  // The sketch should only proceed if the client is not null
  if (client != null) {
    // Receive the message
    incomingMessage = client.readString();
    incomingMessage = incomingMessage.trim();
```

> The message is read using readString(). The trim() function is used to remove the extra line break that comes in with the message.

```
    // Print to Processing message window
    println("Client says: " + incomingMessage);
```

```
    // Write message back out (note this goes to ALL clients)
    server.write("How does " + incomingMessage + " make you feel?\n");
    // Reset newMessageColor to black
    newMessageColor = 0;
  }
}

// The serverEvent function is called whenever a new client connects.
void serverEvent(Server server, Client client) {
  incomingMessage = "A new client has connected: " + client.ip();
  println(incomingMessage);
  // Reset newMessageColor to black
  newMessageColor = 0;
}
```

> A reply is sent using `write()`.

Once the server is running, I can create a client that connects to the server. Ultimately, I will build an example where the server and client are written in Processing. However, just to demonstrate that the server is in fact working, let's look at connecting it to any network client application. Telnet is a standard protocol for remote connections and all machines generally come with built-in telnet abilities. On a Mac or Linux, launch terminal; on Windows, go to the command prompt. I also recommend using PuTTY (*http://www.chiark.greenend.org.uk/~sgtatham/putty/*), a free telnet client.

Since I am connecting to the server from the same machine that the server is running on, the address I connect to is *localhost*, meaning the local computer, port 5204. I could also use the address 127.0.0.1. This is a special address reserved for programs on a computer to speak to each other locally (i.e., on the same machine) and is the equivalent of *localhost*. If I were connecting from a different computer, I would have to know the network IP address of the machine running the server.

Figure 19-2

Telnet clients traditionally send messages to the server when the user presses the Enter key. The carriage return and line feed are included in the message, and therefore, when the server sends back the reply, you will notice that "How does processing" and "make you feel" appear on separate lines.

Exercise 19-1: Using String manipulation techniques from Chapter 15, fix Example 19-1 so that if the client sends newline characters, the server removes them before replying back to the client. You will want to alter the `incomingMessage` *variable.*

```
incomingMessage = client.readString();

incomingMessage = incomingMessage._____(_____,_____);
```

19-3 Creating a client

Once I have written a server and tested it with telnet, I can then develop my own client in Processing. I'll start off the same way I did with a server, importing the processing.net library and declaring an instance of a `Client` object.

```
import processing.net.*;

Client client;
```

The client constructor requires three arguments — `this`, referring again to *this* sketch, the IP address you want to connect to (as a `String` object), and the port number (as an `int`).

```
client = new Client(this, "127.0.0.1", 5204);
```

If the server is running on a different computer than the client, you will need to know the IP address of that server computer. In addition, if there is no server running at the specified IP and port, the Processing sketch will output the error message: *"java.net.ConnectException: Connection refused"* meaning either the server rejected the client or that there is no server.

Sending to the server is easy using the `write()` function.

```
client.write("Hello!");
```

Reading messages from the server is handled with the `read()` function. The `read()` method, however, reads from the server one byte at a time. To read the entire message as a `String`, `readString()` is used. And in this case I are going to use `readStringUntil()` in order to guarantee that I read the entire string all the way up to the line break.

Before I can even contemplate reading from the server, I must determine when it is appropriate to read new data. Just as you saw with getting new images from a camera with `captureEvent()`, the network library will trigger a `clientEvent()`. The `clientEvent()` is triggered whenever there is data available to be read.

```
void clientEvent(Client client) {
  String msg = client.readStringUntil('\n');
}
```

The value of `msg` will be `null` until the client reads all the way up to the line break.

Using the code from Example 18-1, (keyboard input), I can create a Processing client that connects and communicates with my server, sending messages entered by the user.

Example 19-2. Simple therapy client

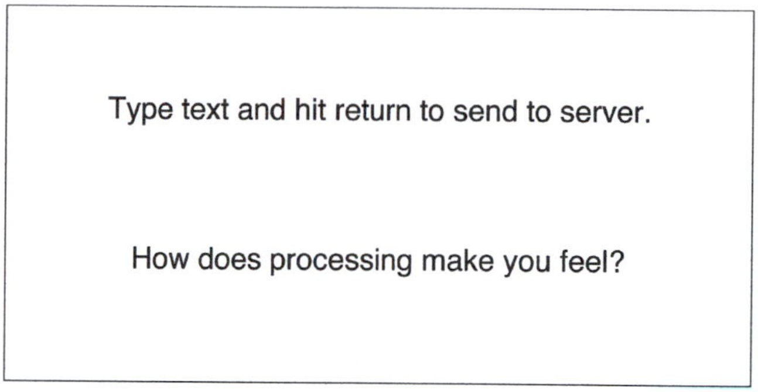

```
// Import the net libraries
import processing.net.*;

// Declare a client
Client client;

float newMessageColor =
0;          // Used to indicate a
new message
String messageFromServer =
"";    // A String to hold
whatever the server says
String typing =
"";          // A String
to hold what the user types

void setup() {
  size(400, 200);
  // Create the Client
  client = new Client(this, "127.0.0.1", 5204);
}
void draw() {
  background(255);

  // Display message from server
  fill(newMessageColor);
  textAlign(CENTER);
  text(messageFromServer, width/2, 140);
  // Fade message from server to white
  newMessageColor = constrain(newMessageColor + 1, 0, 255);



  // Display Instructions
  fill(0);
  text("Type text and press Enter to send to server.", width/2, 60);
  // Display text typed by user
  fill(0);
  text(typing, width/2, 80);
}

void clientEvent(Client client) {

  String msg = client.readStringUntil('\n');

  if (msg != null) {
    messageFromServer = msg;
    // Set brightness to 0
    newMessageColor = 0;
  }
}

// Simple user keyboard input
```

Type text and hit return to send to server.

How does processing make you feel?

Figure 19-3

Connect to server at 127.0.0.1 (localhost), port 5204

The new message fades to white by increasing the brightness.

If there is information available to read this event will be triggered

The value of msg will be null until the client reads all the way up to the line break. When a the message finally comes in, it's stored in a global variable `messageFromServer` for use in the rest of the code.

```
void keyPressed() {
  // If the return key is pressed, save the String and clear it
  if (key == '\n') {
    client.write(typing);
    typing = "";
  } else {
    typing = typing + key;
  }
}
```

When the user hits enter, `typing` is sent to the server.

Exercise 19-2: Create a client and server that talk to each other. Have the client send messages typed by the user and the server respond autonomously. For example, you could use String parsing techniques to reverse the words sent by the client. Client: "How are you?" Server: "You are how?"

Exercise 19-3: Send a server messages in the form <number> <operator> <number> (like 3 + 5) and have the server send back the result of the computation.

19-4 Broadcasting

Now that you understand the basics of how clients and servers work, you can examine more practical uses of networked communication. In the therapist client/server examples, I treated the data sent across the network as a string, but this may not always be the case. In this section, I will look at writing a server that broadcasts numeric data to clients.

How is this useful? What if you wanted to continuously broadcast the temperature outside your house or a stock quote or the amount of motion seen by a camera? You could set up a single computer running a Processing server to process and broadcast that information. Client sketches from anywhere in the world could connect to this machine to receive the information.

To demonstrate the framework for such a program, I will write a server that broadcasts a number between 0 and 255 (To keep things overly simple I'll send only one byte at a time). I will then look at clients that retrieve the data and interpret it in their own way.

Here is the server, which increments a number randomly and broadcasts it.

Example 19-3. Server broadcasting a number (0–255)

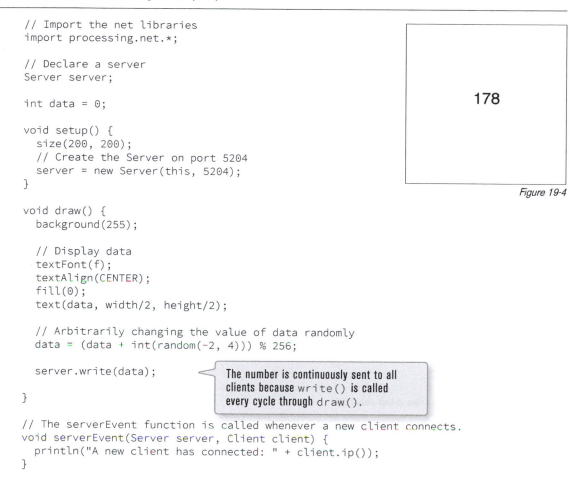

```
// Import the net libraries
import processing.net.*;

// Declare a server
Server server;

int data = 0;

void setup() {
  size(200, 200);
  // Create the Server on port 5204
  server = new Server(this, 5204);
}

void draw() {
  background(255);

  // Display data
  textFont(f);
  textAlign(CENTER);
  fill(0);
  text(data, width/2, height/2);

  // Arbitrarily changing the value of data randomly
  data = (data + int(random(-2, 4))) % 256;

  server.write(data);
```

The number is continuously sent to all clients because `write()` is called every cycle through `draw()`.

```
}

// The serverEvent function is called whenever a new client connects.
void serverEvent(Server server, Client client) {
  println("A new client has connected: " + client.ip());
}
```

Figure 19-4

Next, I'll write a client that receives the number from the server and uses it to fill a variable. The example is written with the assumption that the server and the client are running on the same computer (you can open both examples and run them together in Processing), but in a real world scenario this would likely not be the case. If you choose to run the server and clients on different computers, the machines must be networked locally (via a router or hub, ethernet or wifi) or on the internet. The IP address can be found in the network settings of your machine.

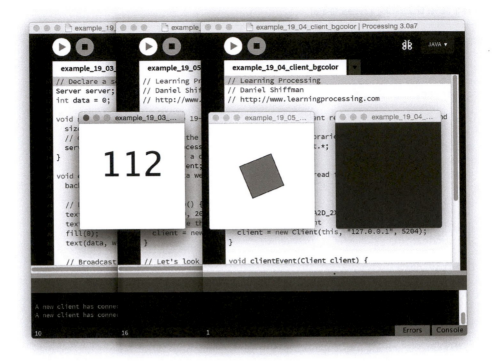

Figure 19-5 A broadcasting server running alongside two clients.

Example 19-4. Client reading values as background color

```
// Import the net libraries
import processing.net.*;

// Declare a client
Client client;

// The data to be read from the server
int data;

void setup() {
  size(200, 200);
  // Create the Client
  client = new Client(this, "127.0.0.1", 5204);
}

void clientEvent(Client client) {
  data = client.read();
}

void draw() {
  background(data);
}
```

> Here only `read()` is needed since one byte at a time works perfectly well.

> The incoming data is used to color the background.

Exercise 19-4: Write the code for the second client shown in Figure 19-5 that uses the number broadcast from the server to control the rotation of a shape.

19-5 Multi-user communication, Part 1: The server

The broadcast example demonstrates one-way communication where a server broadcasts a message and many clients receive that message. The broadcast model, however, does not allow a client to turn around and send a reply back to the server. In this section, I will cover how to create a sketch that involves communication between multiple clients facilitated by a server.

Let's explore how a chat application works. Five clients (you and four friends) connect to a server. One client types a message: "Hey everyone!" That message is sent to the server, which relays it back to all five clients. Most multi-user applications function in a similar fashion (though it's also possible for applications to communicate directly without a server, which is known as *peer-to-peer*. A multiplayer online game, for example, would likely have clients sending information related to their whereabouts and actions to a server that broadcasts that data back to all other clients playing the game.

A multi-user application can be developed in Processing using the network library. To demonstrate, I will create a networked, shared whiteboard. As a client drags its mouse around the screen, the sketch will send (x,y) coordinates to the server that passes them back to any other connected clients. Everyone connected will be able to see the drawing actions of everyone else.

In addition to learning how to communicate between multiple clients, this example will explore how to send multiple values. How can a client send two values (an x and a y coordinate) and have the server know which one is which?

The first step toward a solution involves developing a protocol for communication between the clients. In what format is the information sent and how is that information received and interpreted? Luckily for you, the time you spent learning how to create, manage, and parse `String` objects in Chapter 20 and Chapter 18 will provide all the tools you need.

Assume a client wants to send the mouse location: `mouseX` = 100 and `mouseY` = 125. I need to format that information as a string in a way that is convenient to decipher. One possibility is as follows:

> **"The first number before the comma is the x location, the second number after the comma is 125. The data ends where an newline character (\n) appears."**

In code, it would appear as follows:

```
String dataToSend = "100,125\n";
```

or, more generally:

```
String dataToSend = mouseX + "," + mouseY + "\n";
```

Here, I have developed a protocol for sending and receiving data. The integer values for mouseX and mouseY are encoded as a string during sending (number, followed by comma, followed by number, followed by newline). They will have to be decoded upon receipt, and I will get to that later. While most examples typically use a *newline* or *carriage return* to mark the end of a message (as you saw in the first section of this chapter), it is by no means required and you can design and implement any messaging protocol you so choose as long as it matches up in the client and server code.

What is really sent?

Data sent across a network is sent as a sequential list of individual bytes. Recalling the discussion of data types in Chapter 4, a byte is an 8-bit number, that is, a number made up of eight 0's and 1's or a value between 0 and 255.

Let's assume I want to send the number 42. I have two options:

```
client.write(42);    // sending the byte 42
```

In the line above, I am really sending the actual byte 42.

```
client.write("42"); // sending the String "42"
```

In the line above, I am sending a string. That string is made up of two characters, a '4' and a '2'. I am sending two bytes! Those bytes are determined via the ASCII (American Standard Code for Information Interchange) code, a standardized means for encoding characters. The character 'A' is byte 65, the character 'B' 66, and so on. The character '4' is byte 52 and '2' is 50.

When the sketch reads the data, it's up to me to know whether to interpret the bytes coming in as literal numeric values or as ASCII codes for characters. This accomplished by choosing the appropriate read() function.

```
int val = client.read();          // Matches up with client.write(42);

String s = client.readString(); // Matches up with client.write("42");
int num = int(s);                 // Convert to an integer
```

I am now ready to create a server to receive the messages from the client. It will be the client's job to format those messages with my protocol. The job of the server remains simple: (1) receive the data and (2) relay the data. This is similar to the approach I took in Section 19-2 on page 428.

Step 1. Receiving data.

```
Client client = server.available();
if (client ! = null) {
  incomingMessage = client.readStringUntil('\n');
}
```

Note how, again, the newline character ('\n') is used to mark the end of the incoming data. I am simply following the protocol established during sending. I am able to do this because I am designing both the server *and* the client.

Once that data is read, I am ready to add:

Step 2. Relaying data back out to clients.

```
Client client = server.available();
if (client != null) {
  incomingMessage = client.readStringUntil('\n');

  server.write(incomingMessage);
}
```

Writing the message back out to all clients.

Here is the full server with some bells and whistles. A message is displayed onscreen when new clients connect as well as when the server receives data.

Example 19-5. Multi-user server

```
// Import the net libraries
import processing.net.*;

// Declare a server
Server server;

String incomingMessage = "";

void setup() {
  size(400, 200);
  // Create the Server on port 5204
  server = new Server(this, 5204);
}

void draw() {
  background(255);

  // Display rectangle with new message color
  fill(0);
  textFont(f);
  textAlign(CENTER);
  text(incomingMessage, width/2, height/2);

  // If there is no client, client will be null
  Client client = server.available();
  // The sketch should only proceed if the client is not null
  if (client != null) {
    // Receive the message
    incomingMessage = client.readStringUntil('\n');
    // Print to Processing message window
    println("Client says: " + incomingMessage);
    // Write message back out (note this goes to ALL clients)
    server.write(incomingMessage);
  }
}

// The serverEvent function is called whenever a new client connects.
void serverEvent(Server server, Client client) {
  incomingMessage = "A new client has connected: " + client.ip();
  println(incomingMessage);
}
```

> All messages received from one client are immediately relayed back out to all clients with `write()`.

19-6 Multi-user communication, Part 2: The client

The client's job is three-fold:

1. **Send mouseX and mouseY coordinates to server.**

2. **Retrieve messages from server.**

3. **Display ellipses in the window based on server messages.**

For Step 1, I need to adhere to the protocol established for sending:

mouseX comma mouseY newline

```
String out = mouseX + "," + mouseY + "\n";
client.write(out);
```

The question remains: when is the appropriate time to send that information? I could choose to insert those two lines of code into the main `draw()` loop, sending mouse coordinates every frame. In the case of a whiteboard client, however, I only need to send the coordinates when the user drags the mouse around the window.

The `mouseDragged()` function is an event handling function similar to `mousePressed()`. Instead of being called when a user clicks the mouse, it's called whenever a dragging event occurs, that is, the mouse button is pressed and the mouse is moving. Note the function is called continuously as a user drags the mouse. This is where I choose to do my sending.

```
void mouseDragged() {
  String out = mouseX + "," + mouseY + "\n";
  // Send the String to the server
  client.write(out);
  // Print a message indicating data was sent
  println("Sending: " + out);
}
```

> Put the string together with the protocol: mouseX **comma** mouseY newline.

Step 2, retrieving messages from the server, works much like the therapy client and broadcast client examples.

```
// If there is information available to read from the Server
void clientEvent(Client client) {
  // Read message as a String, all messages end with a newline character
  String in = client.readStringUntil('\n');
  if (in != null) {
    // Print message received
    println( "Receiving:" + in);
  }
}
```

Once the data is placed into a `String` object, it can be interpreted with parsing techniques from Chapter 18.

First, the string is split into an array of strings using a comma as the delimiter.

```
String[] splitUp = split(in, ",");
```

The string array is then converted into an array of integers (length: 2).

```
int[] vals = int(splitUp);
```

And those integers are used to display an ellipse.

```
fill(255, 100);
noStroke();
ellipse(vals[0], vals[1], 16, 16);
```

Here is the entire client sketch:

Example 19-6. Client for multi-user whiteboard

```
// Import the net libraries
import processing.net.*;

// Declare a client
Client client;

void setup() {
  size(200, 200);
  // Create the Client
  client = new Client(this, "127.0.0.1", 5204);
  background(255);
}

// If there is information available to read from the Server
void clientEvent(Client client) {
  // Read message as a String, all messages end with a newline character
  String in = client.readStringUntil('\n');
  if (in != null) {
    // Print message received
    println( "Receiving:" + in);
    int[] vals = int(split(in, ","));

    // Render an ellipse based on those values
    fill(0, 100);
    noStroke();
    ellipse(vals[0], vals[1], 16, 16);
  }
}

void draw() {
}

// Send data whenever the user drags the mouse
void mouseDragged() {
  // Put the String together with the protocol: mouseX comma mouseY asterisk
  String out = mouseX + "," + mouseY + "*" ;
  // Send the String to the server
  client.write(out);
  // Print a message indicating data was sent
  println("Sending: " + out);
}
```

> The client reads messages from the server and parses them with `split()` according to the protocol.

> A message is sent whenever the mouse is dragged. Note that a client will receive its own messages! Nothing is drawn here!

19-7 Multi-user communication, Part 3: All together now

When running a multi-user application, the order in which the elements are launched is important. The client sketches will fail unless the server sketch is already running.

You should first (a) identify the IP address of the server, (b) choose a port and add it to the server's code, and (c) run the server.

Afterward, you can launch the clients with the correct IP address and port.

If you're working on a multi-user project, you most likely want to run the servers and clients on separate computers. After all, this is the point of creating multiuser applications in the first place. However, for testing and development purposes, it's often convenient to run all the elements from one computer. In this case, the server IP address will be "localhost" or 127.0.0.1 (note this is the IP address used in this chapter's examples).

Figure 19-6 Examples 19-5 and 19-6 running together

As will be covered in Chapter 21, Processing's "export to application" feature will allow you to export a stand-alone application for your server, which you can then run in the background while you develop your client in Processing. You can also run multiple copies of a stand-alone application to simulate an environment with more than one client. Figure 19-6 shows the server running with two client instances.

Exercise 19-5: Expand the whiteboard to allow for color. Each client should send a red, green, and blue value in addition to the (x,y) location. You will not need to make any changes to the server for this to work.

Exercise 19-6: Create a two-player game of Pong played over the network. This is a complex assignment, so build it up slowly. For instance, you should get Pong to work first without networking (if you're stuck, an example is provided at the book's website). You will also need to make changes to the server; specifically, the server will need to assign the players a paddle as they connect (left or right).

19-8 Serial communication

A nice reward for learning the ins and outs of networked communication is that it makes serial communication in Processing a breeze. Serial communication involves reading bytes from the computer's serial port. These bytes might come from a piece of hardware you purchase (a serial joystick, for example) or one that you design yourself by building a circuit and programming a microcontroller.

This book does not cover the external hardware side of serial communication. However, if you're interested in learning more about physical computing, I recommend the book *Making Things Talk: Practical Methods for Connecting Physical Objects* (Make Books) by Tom Igoe. The Arduino website (*http://www.arduino.cc/*) is also an excellent resource. Arduino is an open-source physical computing platform with a programming language modeled after Processing. I will provide some accompanying Arduino code for your reference, but the material in this book will only cover what to do once the data has already arrived in Processing.

Serial communication refers to the process of sending data in sequence, one byte at a time. The Processing serial library is designed for serial communication into the computer from a local device, most likely via a USB (Universal Serial Bus) port. The term "serial" refers to the serial port, designed to interface with modems, that is rarely found on newer computers.

The process of reading data from a serial port is virtually identical to that found in the networked client/server examples, with a few exceptions. First, instead of importing the network library, I'll import the serial library and create a `Serial` object.

```
import processing.serial.*;

Serial port = new Serial(this, "COM1", 9600);
```

The Serial constructor takes three arguments. The first one is always `this`, referring to *this* sketch (see Chapter 16). Argument two is a string representing the communications port being used. Computers label ports with a name. On a PC, these will likely be "COM1," "COM2," "COM3," and so on. On Unix-based computers (such as Mac OS X), they will be labeled "/dev/tty.something" where "something" represents a terminal device. A helpful way to sort this out is to print a list of available ports using the Serial library's `list()` function, which returns an array of strings.

```
String[] portList = Serial.list();
printArray(portList);
```

Here are two examples of what you might see in the output:

```
[0] "/dev/cu.Bluetooth-Incoming-Port"
[1] "/dev/cu.Bluetooth-Modem"
[2] "/dev/cu.usbmodem1421"

[0] "COM115"
```

Sample Mac OS X output for `Serial.list()`.

Sample Windows output for `Serial.list()`.

The first array is an example from Mac OS X with the third string (index two!) the desired port. The second is a windows example with the first and only string (index zero!) being the correct one. For the second scenario, the code would read:

```
String[] portList = Serial.list();
Serial port = new Serial(this, portList[0], 9600);
```

If you are still having trouble there are additional instructions in the online Arduino guide. (*http://www.arduino.cc/en/Guide/HomePage*).

The third argument is the rate at which the data is transmitted serially, typically 9,600 baud. Baud refers to the speed at which the information is sent, in this case the measurement is bps or "bits per second."

Bytes are sent out via the serial port using the `write()` function. The following data types can be sent: byte, char, int, byte[], and String. Remember, if you are sending a string, the actual data sent is the raw ASCII byte values for each character.

```
port.write(65); // Sending the byte 65
```

Data can be read with the same functions found in clients and servers: `read()`, `readString()`, and `readStringUntil()`. A callback function, `serialEvent()`, is triggered whenever a serial event occurs, that is, whenever there is data available to be read.

```
void serialEvent(Serial port) {
  int input = port.read();
  println("Raw Input: " + input);
}
```

The `read()` function will return a -1 if there is nothing available to read. However, assuming you're writing the code inside `serialEvent()`, there will always be available data.

Following is an example that reads data from the serial port and uses it to color the sketch's background.

Example 19-7. Reading from serial port

```
import processing.serial.*;

int val = 0; // To store data from serial port, used to color background
Serial port; // The serial port object

void setup() {
  size(200, 200);
  // In case you want to see the list of available ports
  // printArray(Serial.list());

  port = new Serial(this, Serial.list()[0], 9600);
}

void draw() {
  background(val);
}


// Called whenever there is something available to read
void serialEvent(Serial port) {
  // Read the data
  val = port.read();



  // For debugging
  // println("Raw Input: " + input);
}
```

> Initializing the `Serial` object with the first port in the list (likely different on your computer).

> The serial data is used to color the background.

> Data from the serial port is read in `serialEvent()` using the `read()` function and assigned to the global variable `val`.

For reference, if you're using Arduino, here is some corresponding code:

```
int val;

void setup() {
  Serial.begin(9600);
}

void loop() {
  val = analogRead(0);
  // Arduino's write() function sends out the raw number itself
  // We'll see examples that send as an ASCII string using print() in a moment
  Serial.write(val);
}
```

> This is not Processing code! It is Arduino code. For more, visit: http://www.arduino.cc/.

19-9 Serial communication with handshaking

It's often advantageous to add a *handshaking* component to serial communication code. If a hardware device sends bytes faster than a Processing sketch can read, for example, there can sometimes be a logjam of information, causing the sketch to lag. The sensor values may arrive late, making the interaction confusing or misleading to the user. The process of sending information only when requested, known as *handshaking*, alleviates this lag.

Example 19-8. Handshaking

```
void setup() {
  size(200, 200);

  // In case you want to see the list of available ports
  // printArray(Serial.list());

  // Using the first available port (might be different on your computer)
  port = new Serial(this, Serial.list()[0], 9600);
}
```

After the sketch finishes processing a byte inside of `serialEvent()`, it asks again for a new value.

```
// Called whenever there is something available to read
void serialEvent(Serial port) {
  // Read the data
  val = port.read();
  // For debugging
  // println("Raw Input: " + input);

  // Request a new value
  port.write(65);
}
```

> After the sketch receives a byte, it replies with the byte 65 indicating it's ready to receive the next one.

As long as the hardware device is designed to only send the sensor values when requested, any possible lag will be eliminated. Here is the revised Arduino code. This example does not care what the request byte is, only that there is a byte request. A more advanced version might have different replies for different requests.

```
int val;

void setup() {
  Serial.begin(9600);
```

> This is not Processing code! It is Arduino code. For more, visit: http://www.arduino.cc/.

```
  // Arduino speaks first sending the byte 0
  // to Processing which will then ask for data.
  Serial.write(0);
}

void loop() {
  // Only send out if something has come in
  if (Serial.available() > 0) {
    // Reading from Processing
    int input = Serial.read();
    // Sending out the sensor data
    val = analogRead(A0);
    Serial.write(val);
  }
}
```

19-10 Serial communication with strings

In cases where you need to retrieve multiple values from the serial port (or numbers greater than 255), the `readStringUntil()` function is handy. For example, let's assume you want to read from three sensors, using the values for the red, green, and blue components of your sketch's background color. Here, I will use the same protocol designed in the multi-user whiteboard example. I will ask the hardware device (where the sensors live) to send the data as follows:

Sensor Value 1 COMMA Sensor Value 2 COMMA Sensor Value 3 newline

For example:

104,5,76\n

Example 19-9. Serial communication with strings

```
import processing.serial.*;

int r, g, b;   // Used to color background
Serial port; // The serial port object

void setup() {
  size(200, 200);

  // In case you want to see the list of available ports
  // printArray(Serial.list());
  // Using the first available port (might be different on your computer)
  port = new Serial(this, Serial.list()[0], 9600);

  port.bufferUntil('\n');
}

void draw() {
  // Set the background
  background(r, g, b);
}

// Called whenever there is something available to read
void serialEvent(Serial port) {
  // Read the data
  String input = port.readString();
  if (input != null) {
    // Print message received
    println("Receiving: " + input);
    // Split up the String into an
    // array of integers
    int[] vals = int(split(input, ","));

    // Fill r,g,b variables
    r = vals[0];
    g = vals[1];
    b = vals[2];
  }
```

> I'm adding this method now that we are reading data from the Arduino as a string. A newline character (\n) indicates the message is completed and can be read with `readString()` as seen below.

> Data from the serial port is read in `serialEvent()` using the `readString()` with '\n' as the end character as specified with `bufferUntil()` above.

> The data is split into an array of strings with a comma as a delimiter and converted into an array of integers.

> Three global variables are filled using the input data.

```
    // When finished ask for values again
    port.write(65);
}
```

Corresponding Arduino code:

```
int sensor1 = 0;
int sensor2 = 0;
int sensor3 = 0;

void setup() {
  Serial.begin(9600);
  Serial.write(0);     // Starting the communication
}

void loop() {
  // Only send if requested
  if (Serial.available() > 0) {
    Serial.read();
    sensor1 = analogRead(A0);
    // This delay the analog-to-digital converter stabilize before the next read.
    delay(1);
    sensor2 = analogRead(A1);
    delay(1);
    sensor3 = analogRead(A2);
    delay(1);

    // Send the integer out as a string using print instead of write
    Serial.print(sensor1);
    // Send a comma -- ASCII code 44
    Serial.print(',');
    Serial.print(sensor2);
    Serial.print(',');
    // The last value is sent with println which adds a newline
    // character indicating the end of the string to be read.
    Serial.println(sensor3);
  }
}
```

> This is not Processing code! It is Arduino code. For more, visit: http://www.arduino.cc/.

Exercise 19-7: If you have an Arduino board, build your own interface to control a Processing sketch you have already made. (Before you attempt this, you should make sure you can successfully run the simple examples provided in this chapter.)

Lesson Eight Project

Create a data visualization by loading external information (a local file, web page, XML feed, server or serial connection) into Processing.

1. Make sure you build up the project incrementally. For example, try designing the visualization first without any real data (use random numbers or hard-coded values). If you're loading data from the web, consider using a local file while you're developing the project. Do not be afraid to *fake* the data, waiting until you're finished with aspects of the design before connecting the real data.

2. Experiment with levels of abstraction. Try displaying information literally onscreen by writing text. Build an abstract system where the input data affects the behaviors of objects (you might even use your "ecosystem" from the Lesson Six Project).

Use the space provided below to sketch designs, notes, and pseudocode for your project.

Lesson Nine

Making Noise

Chapter 20
Chapter 21

20 Sound

Check. Check. Check 1. Sibilance. Sibilance. Check. Check. Check 2. Sibilance. Sibilance.
—Barry the Roadie

In this chapter:
- Simple sound playback
- Playback with adjusting volume, pitch, and pan
- Sound synthesis
- Sound analysis

As I discussed in the introduction to this book, Processing is a programming language and development environment, rooted in Java, designed for learning to program *in a visual context*. So, if you want to develop large-scale interactive applications primarily focused on sound, the question inevitably arises "Is Processing the right programming environment for me?" This chapter will explore the possibilities of working with sound in Processing.

Integrating sound with a Processing sketch can be accomplished a number of different ways. Many Processing users choose to have Processing communicate with another programming environment such as PureData (*http://puredata.info*), Max/MSP (*http://www.cycling74.com/*), SuperCollider (*http://supercollid er.github.io/*), Ableton Live, and many more. This can be preferable given that these applications have a comprehensive set of features for sophisticated sound work. Processing can communicate with these applications via a variety of methods. One common approach is to use OSC ("open sound control"), a protocol for network communication between applications. This can be accomplished in Processing by using the network library (see the previous chapter) or with the oscP5 library (*http://www.sojamo.de/libra ries/oscP5*), by Andreas Schlegel.

This chapter will focus on three fundamental sound techniques in Processing: *playback*, *synthesis*, and *analysis*. For all of the examples, I'll use the new (as of Processing 3.0) core sound library, developed by Wilm Thoben. However, you might also want to take a look at the list of Processing libraries (*https:// processing.org/reference/libraries/*) which includes additional contributed libraries for working with sound.

20-1 Basic sound playback

The first thing you want to do is play a sound file in a Processing sketch. Just like with video in Processing, to be able to do anything with sound, you need the import statement at the top of your code.

```
import processing.sound.*;
```

Now that you have imported the library, you have the whole world (of sound) in your hands. I'll start by demonstrating how to play sound from a file. Before a sound can be played, it must be loaded into memory, much in the same way images files were loaded before they could be displayed. Here, a SoundFile object is used to store a reference to a sound from a file.

```
SoundFile song;
```

The object is initialized by passing the sound filename to the constructor, along with a reference to `this`.

```
song = new SoundFile(this, "song.mp3");
```

> The file "song.mp3" should be placed in the data directory.

Just as with images, loading the sound file from the hard drive is a slow process so the previous line of code should be placed in `setup()` so as to not hamper the speed of `draw()`.

The type of sound files compatible with Processing is limited. Possible formats are wav, aiff, and mp3. If you want to use a sound file that is not stored in a compatible format, you could download a free audio editor, such as Audacity (*http://audacity.sourceforge.net/*) and convert the file. Once the sound is loaded, playing is easy.

```
song.play();
```

> The `play()` function plays the sound once.

If you want your sound to loop forever, call `loop()` instead.

```
song.loop();
```

> The `loop()` function plays the sound sample over and over.

A sound can be stopped with `stop()` or `pause()`. Here is an example that plays a sound file (in this case, an approximately two-minute song) as soon as the Processing sketch begins and pauses (or restarts) the sound when the user clicks the mouse.

Example 20-1. Soundtrack

```
import processing.sound.*;

SoundFile song;

void setup() {
  size(640, 360);
  song = new SoundFile(this, "song.mp3");
  song.play();
}

void draw() {
}

void mousePressed() {
  if (song.isPlaying()) {
    song.pause();
  } else {
    song.play();
  }
}
```

> Note the addition of a call to `isPlaying()` to determine if the sound is playing or not. Here the mouse toggles the sound's state. If it's playing, it stops. If it's not, it plays.

Playback of sound files is also useful for short sound effects. The following example plays a doorbell sound whenever the user clicks on the circle. The `Doorbell` class implements simple button functionality (rollover and click) and just happens to be a solution for Exercise 9-8 on page 180. The code for the new concepts (related to sound playback) is shown in bold type.

Example 20-2. Doorbell

```
// Import the sound library
import processing.sound.*;

// A sound file object
SoundFile dingdong;
// A doorbell object (that will trigger the sound)
Doorbell doorbell;

void setup() {
  size(200, 200);
  // Load the sound file
  dingdong = new SoundFile(this, "dingdong.mp3");
  // Create a new doorbell
  doorbell = new Doorbell(width/2, height/2, 64);
}

void draw() {
  background(255);
  // Show the doorbell
  doorbell.display(mouseX, mouseY);
}

void mousePressed() {
  // If the user clicks on the doorbell, play the sound!
  if (doorbell.contains(mouseX, mouseY)) {
    dingdong.play();
  }
}

// A class to describe a "doorbell" (really a button)
class Doorbell {
  // Location and size
  float x;
  float y;
  float r;

  // Create the doorbell
  Doorbell(float x_, float y_, float r_) {
    x = x_;
    y = y_;
    r = r_;
  }

  // Is a point inside the doorbell? (used for mouse rollover, etc.)
  boolean contains(float mx, float my) {
    if (dist(mx, my, x, y) < r) {
      return true;
    } else {
      return false;
    }
  }

  // Show the doorbell (hardcoded colors, could be improved)
  void display(float mx, float my) {
    if (contains(mx, my)) {
      fill(100);
```

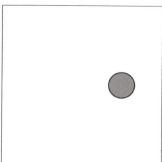

Figure 20-1

```
    } else {
      fill(175);
    }
    stroke(0);
    strokeWeight(4);
    ellipse(x, y, r, r);
  }
}
```

Exercise 20-1: Rewrite the Doorbell class to include a reference to the sound file itself. This will allow you to easily make multiple Doorbell objects that each play a different sound. Here is some code to get you started.

```
// A class to describe a "doorbell" (really a button)

class Doorbell {
  // Location and size
  float x;
  float y;
  float r;
  // A sound file object
  _____ _____;

  // Create the doorbell
  Doorbell (float x_, float y_, float r_, _____ filename) {
    x = x_;
    y = y_;
    r = r_;

    _____ = new _____(_____, _____);
  }

  void ring() {

    _____;
  }

  boolean contains(float mx, float my) {
    // same as original
  }

  void display(float mx, float my) {
    // same as original
  }
}
```

If you run the Doorbell example and click on the doorbell many times in rapid succession, you will notice that the sound restarts every time you click. It's not given a chance to finish playing. While this is not much of an issue for this straightforward example, stopping a sound from restarting can be very important in other, more complex sound sketches. The simplest way to achieve such a result is always to check and see if a sound *is playing* before you call the `play()` function. The function `isPlaying()` does exactly this, returning true or false. I used this function in the previous example to determine whether the sound should be paused or played. Here, I want to play the sound if it's *not already playing,* that is,

```
if (!dingdong.isPlaying()) {
    dingdong.play();
}
```

Remember, "!" means not!

Exercise 20–2: Create a button that toggles the pause/playing state of a sound. Can you make more than one button, each tied to its own sound?

20-2 A bit fancier sound playback

During playback, a sound sample can be manipulated in real time. Volume, pitch, and pan can all be controlled.

Let's start with volume. The technical word for volume in the world of sound is *amplitude.* A SoundFile object's volume can be set with the `amp()` function, which takes a floating point value between 0.0 and 1.0 (0.0 being silent, 1.0 being the loudest). The following snippet assumes a file named "song.mp3" and sets its volume based on `mouseX` position (by mapping it to a range between 0 and 1).

```
float volume = map(mouseX, 0, width, 0, 1);
song.amp(volume);
```

Volume ranges from 0 to 1.

Panning refers to volume of the sound in two speakers (typically a "left" and "right"). If the sound is panned all the way to the left, it will be at maximum value in the left and not heard at all in the right. Adjusting the panning in code works just as with amplitude, only the range is between -1.0 (for full pan to the left) and 1.0 (for full pan to the right).

```
float panning = map(mouseX, 0, width, -1, 1);
song.pan(panning);
```

Pan ranges from -1 to 1.

The pitch is altered by changing the rate of playback (i.e., faster playback is higher pitch, slower playback is lower pitch) using `rate()`. A rate at 1.0 is normal speed, 2.0 is twice the speed, etc. The following code uses a range from 0 (where you would not hear it at all) to 4 (a rather fast playback rate).

```
float speed = map(mouseX, 0, width, 0, 4);
song.rate(speed);
```

A reasonable range for rate (i.e., pitch) is between 0 and 4.

The following example adjusts the volume and pitch of a sound according to mouse movements. Note the use of `loop()` instead of `play()`, which loops the sound over and over rather than playing it one time.

Example 20-3. Sound manipulation

```
import processing.sound.*;

// A sound file object
SoundFile song;

void setup() {
  size(200, 200);

  // Load a sound file
  song = new SoundFile(this, "song.mp3");

  // Loop the sound forever
  // (well, at least until stop() or pause() are called)
  song.loop();
}

void draw() {
  background(255);

  float volume = map(mouseX, 0, width, 0, 1);
  song.amp(volume);

  // Set the rate to a range between 0 and 2
  // Changing the rate alters the pitch
  float speed = map(mouseY, 0, height, 0, 2)
  song.rate(speed);

  // Draw some circles to show what is going on
  stroke(0);
  fill(51, 100);
  ellipse(mouseX, 100, 48, 48);
  stroke(0);
  fill(51, 100);
  ellipse(100, mouseY, 48, 48);
}
```

Figure 20-2

> The volume is set according to the mouseX position.

> The rate is set according to the mouseY position.

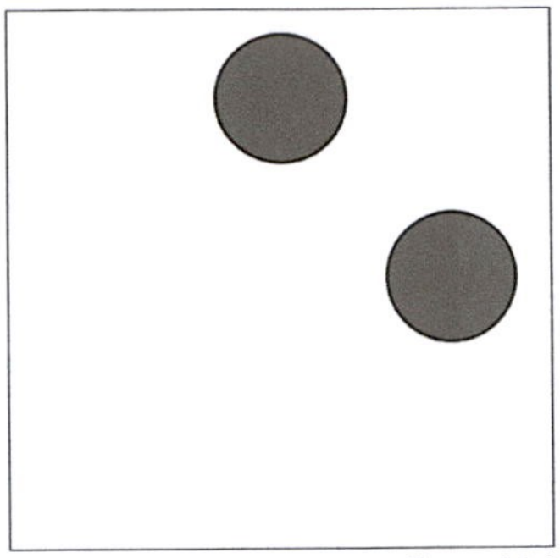

The next example uses the same sound file but pans the sound left and right.

Example 20-4. Sound manipulation

```
import processing.sound.*;

SoundFile soundFile;

void setup() {
  size(200, 200);
  soundFile = new SoundFile(this, "song.mp3");
  soundFile.loop();
}

void draw() {
  background(255);
  float panning = map(mouseX, 0, width, -1, 1);
  soundFile.pan(panning);
```

> Map `mouseX` to a panning value (between -1 and 1)

```
  // Draw a circle
  stroke(0);
  fill(51, 100);
  ellipse(mouseX, 100, 48, 48);
}
```

Exercise 20-3: In Example 20-3, flip the Y-axis so that the lower sound plays when the mouse is down rather than up.

Exercise 20-4: Using the bouncing ball sketch from Example 5-6, play a sound effect every time the ball bounces off a window's edge. Pan the effect left and right according to the x-position.

Sounds can also be manipulated by processing them with an effect, such as reverb, delay feedback, and high, low, and band pass filters. These effects require the use of a separate object to process the sound. (You'll see this same technique in more detail when I demonstrate sound analysis Section 20-4 on page 464 as well.)

A reverb filter (which occurs when a sound bounces around a room causing it to repeat, like a very fast echo) can be applied with the Reverb object.

```
Reverb reverb = new Reverb(this);
reverb.process(soundFile);
```

> This function plugs the sound file into the reverb effect

The amount of reverb can be controlled with the room() function. Think of a room built in a way that causes more or less reverb (ranging from 0 to 1.) Here's an example applying reverb.

Example 20-5. Reverb effect

```
SoundFile song;
Reverb reverb;

void setup() {
  size(200, 200);
  song = new SoundFile(this, "dragon.wav");
  song.loop();

  reverb = new Reverb(this);
  reverb.process(song);          The reverb object receives a sound to process.

}

void draw() {
  background(255);

  float room = map(mouseX, 0, width, 0, 1);
  reverb.room(room);

  stroke(0);                      The amount of reverb is controlled via the room() function and
  fill(51, 100);                  ranges between 0 and 1. You can also control the quality of the
  ellipse(mouseX, 100, 48, 48);   reverb with the damp() and wet() functions.
}
```

20-3 Sound synthesis

In addition to playing sounds that load from a file, the Processing sound library has the capability of creating sound programmatically. A deep discussion of this topic is beyond the scope of this book, but I'll introduce a few of the basic concepts. Let's begin by thinking about the physics of sound itself. Sound travels through a medium (most commonly air, but also liquids and solids) as a wave. For example, a speaker vibrates creating a wave that ripples through the air and rather quickly arrives at your ear. You encountered the concept of a wave briefly in Section 13-10 on page 250 when I demonstrated visualizing the sin() function in Processing. In fact, sound waves can be described in terms of two key properties associated with sine waves: frequency and amplitude.

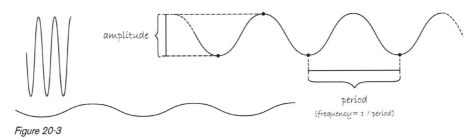

Figure 20-3

Take a look at the above diagram of waves at variable frequencies and amplitudes. The taller ones have higher amplitudes (the distance between the top and bottom of the wave) and the shorter ones lower. Amplitude is another word for volume, higher amplitudes mean louder sounds.

The frequency of a wave is related to how often it repeats (whereas the terms period and cycle refer to the inverse: how long it takes for a full cycle of the wave). A high frequency wave (or higher pitched sound) repeats often, and a lower frequency wave is stretched out and appears wider. Frequency is typically measured in hertz (Hz). One Hz is one cycle per second. Audible frequencies typically range between 20 and 20,000 Hz but what you can synthesize in Processing also highly depends on the sophistication of your speakers. In the diagram, high frequency waves are towards the top and low frequencies at the bottom.

You can specify the amplitude and frequency of a sound wave programatically in Processing with *oscillator* objects. An oscillation (a motion that repeats itself) is another term for wave. An oscillator that produces a sine wave is a SinOsc object.

```
SinOsc osc = new SinOsc(this);
```

If you want to hear the generated sound wave through the speakers, you can then call play().

```
osc.play();
```

As the program runs, you can control the frequency and amplitude of the wave. Frequency is adjusted with freq() which expects a value in Hz. Adjusting the frequency has a similar effect to rate(). To adjust the volume of the oscillation, call the amp() function as you did with sound files.

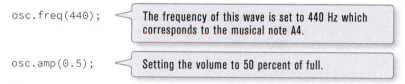

```
osc.freq(440);
```
The frequency of this wave is set to 440 Hz which corresponds to the musical note A4.

```
osc.amp(0.5);
```
Setting the volume to 50 percent of full.

Here's a quick example that controls the frequency of the sound with the mouse.

Example 20-6. Sound synthesis

```
import processing.sound.*;

SinOsc osc;

void setup() {
  size(200, 200);
  osc = new SinOsc(this);
  osc.play();
}

void draw() {
  background(255);

  float freq = map(mouseX, 0, width, 150, 880);
  osc.freq(freq);
  ellipse(mouseX, 100, 32, 32);
}
```
A good range for frequency that works reasonably well with laptop speakers is between 150 and 880 Hz.

The generated sound can also be panned from left to right (-1 to 1) using pan().

There are also other types of waves you can generate with Processing. They include a saw wave (`SawOsc`), square wave (`SqrOsc`), triangle wave (`TriOsc`), and pulse wave (`Pulse`). While each wave has a different sound quality, they can all be manipulated with the same functions as previously described.

Exercise 20-5: Create a Processing sketch that plays a melody. Can you develop algorithmic rules to generate music?

An oscillator can be used to play a musical note. The notes of a major scale, for example, correspond to the following frequencies:

Note frequencies:

Note	Frequency
C	261.63
D	293.66
E	329.63
F	349.23
G	392.00
A	440.00
B	493.88
C	523.25

A more sophisticated way to simulate a musical instrument playing a note can be accomplished with an audio envelope. An envelope controls how a note begins and ends through four parameters.

1. ***Attack Time***: this refers to the beginning of the note (like the moment you hit a key on a piano); how long it takes for the volume of the note to go from zero to its peak.
2. ***Sustain Time***: this refers to the amount of time the note plays.
3. ***Sustain Level***: this is the peak volume of the sound during its duration (from attack to release).
4. ***Release Time***: this refers to the length of time it takes for the level to decay from the sustain level to zero.

To play a note with an envelope, you need both an oscillator and an envelope.

```
TriOsc triOsc = new TriOsc(this);
Envelope env = new Envelope(this);
```

To play the note, call `play()` on both the oscillator and the envelope. For the envelope, however, you pass in four arguments: attack time, sustain time, sustain level, and release time. The times are all floating point values specifying the number of seconds, and the level is value between 0 and 1, specifying the amplitude.

```
    triOsc.play();
    env.play(triOsc, 0.1, 1, 0.5, 1);
```

In the above code, the sound takes a tenth of second (0.1) to fade in to a 50 percent (0.5) amplitude, lasts for a second (1), and fades out over a second (1).

Here is an example that plays the scale from Exercise 20-5 on page 462 using an envelope. In addition, this example uses MIDI note values. MIDI stands for Musical Instrument Digital Interface and is an audio standard for communication between digital musical devices. MIDI notes can be converted into frequencies with the following formula.

$$frequency = \left(\frac{note-69}{12}\right)^2 \times 440$$

Example 20-7. Melody with envelope

```
import processing.sound.*;

SinOsc osc;
Env envelope;

int[] scale = {
  60, 62, 64, 65, 67, 69, 71, 72          These values correspond to the notes of a
};                                        major scale. 60 is Middle C.

int note = 0;

void setup() {
  size(200, 200);
  osc = new SinOsc(this);
  envelope = new Env(this);
}

void draw() {
  background(255);

  if (frameCount % 60 == 0) {
    osc.play(translateMIDI(scale[note]), 1);
    envelope.play(osc, 0.01, 0.5, 1, 0.5);
    note = (note + 1) % scale.length;
  }
}

float translateMIDI(int note) {
  return pow(2, ((note-69)/12.0))*440;      This formula converts the midi note value to
}                                            its corresponding frequency.
```

In addition to waves, you can generate audio "noise" in Processing. In Chapter 13, I discussed distributions of random numbers and noise. In Chapter 15, I used random pixels to generate an image, and it looked a bit like static.

If you vary how a noise algorithm picks the numbers the image quality will change. Perlin noise, for example, generates a texture that looks a bit like clouds. The same can be said for audio noise. Depending on how you choose the random numbers, the result might sound harsher or smoother.

Figure 20-4

Audio noise is commonly described using colors. White noise, for example, is the term for an even distribution of random amplitudes over all frequencies. Pink noise and brown noise, however, are louder at lower frequencies and softer at higher frequences. If nothing else, the ability to generate noise in Processing may help you sleep at night. Here's a quick example that plays white noise, controlling the volume of the noise with the mouse.

Example 20-8. Audio noise

```
import processing.sound.*;

WhiteNoise noise;

void setup() {
  size(200, 200);
  noise = new WhiteNoise(this);
  noise.play();
}

void draw() {
  background(255);

  float vol = map(mouseX, 0, width, 0, 1);
  noise.amp(vol);
  ellipse(mouseX, 100, 32, 32);
}
```

20-4 Sound analysis

In Section 19-8 on page 444, I discussed at how serial communication allows a Processing sketch to respond to input from an external hardware device connected to a sensor. Analyzing the sound from a microphone is a similar pursuit. Not only can a microphone record sound, but it can determine if the sound is loud, quiet, high-pitched, low-pitched, and so on. A Processing sketch could therefore determine if it's running in a crowded room based on sound levels, or whether it's listening to a soprano or bass singer based on frequency levels. This section will cover how to use a sound's *amplitude* and *frequency* data in a sketch.

Let's begin by building a very simple example that ties the size of a circle to the volume level. To do this you first need to create an `Amplitude` object. This object's sole purpose in life is to listen to a sound and report back its amplitude (i.e., volume).

```
Amplitude analyzer = new Amplitude(this);
```

Once you have the `Amplitude` object, you next need to connect sound that you want to analyze. This is accomplished with the `input()` function. This works similarly to how I plugged a `SoundFile` into the `Reverb` object in Example 20-3. The following code loads a sound file and passes it to an analyzer. But, as you'll see in a moment, you can apply this technique to any type of sound, including input from a microphone.

```
SoundFile song = new SoundFile(this, "song.mp3");
analyzer.input(song);
```

To retrieve the volume, you then call `analyze()` which will return an amplitude value between 0 and 1.

```
float level = analyzer.analyze();
```

Here is all of the above put together in a single example, using the sound file from Example 20-3. The sound level controls the size of an ellipse. The new parts are bolded.

Example 20-9. Amplitude analysis

```
import processing.sound.*;

SoundFile song;
Amplitude analyzer;

void setup() {
  size(640, 360);
  song = new SoundFile(this, "song.mp3");
  song.loop();

  analyzer = new Amplitude(this);
  analyzer.input(song);
}

void draw() {
  background(255);

  // Get the overall volume (between 0 and 1.0)
  float volume = analyzer.analyze();

  // Draw an ellipse with size based on volume
  fill(127);
  stroke(0);
  ellipse(width/2, height/2, 10+volume*200, 10+volume*200);
}
```

> Create an `Amplitude` object to analyze the sound

> Plug the `SoundFile` object into the analyzer.

> The variable `volume` is used for the size of an ellipse.

To read the volume from a microphone, you need to plug a different input into the `Amplitude` object. To accomplish this, create an `AudioIn` object and call `start()` to begin the process of listening to the microphone.

```
AudioIn input = new AudioIn(this, 0);
input.start()
```

> The second argument here is the channel. A stereo microphone has a "left" and "right" channel. For this simple example, I'll ignore the second channel (index 1) and read from the first.

If for any reason you want to hear the microphone input come out of your speakers, you can also say `input.play()`. In this case, I don't want to cause audio feedback so I'm leaving that out. Putting it all together, I can now recreate Example 20-9 with live input.

Example 20-10. Live Microphone Input

```
import processing.sound.*;

AudioIn mic;
Amplitude analyzer;

void setup() {
  size(200, 200);

  mic = new AudioIn(this, 0);
  mic.start();

  analyzer = new Amplitude(this);
  analyzer.input(mic);
}

void draw() {
  background(255);
  float volume = analyzer.analyze();
  fill(127);
  stroke(0);
  ellipse(width/2, height/2, 10 + volume*200, 10 + volume*200);
}
```

> Create an audio input, grab the first channel, and start listening.

 Exercise 20-6: Rewrite Example 20-10 with left and right volume levels mapped to different circles.

20-5 Sound thresholding

A common sound interaction is triggering an event when a sound occurs. Consider "the clapper." Clap, the lights go on. Clap again, the lights go off. A clap can be thought of as a very loud and short sound. To program "the clapper" in Processing, I'll need to listen for volume and instigate an event when the volume is high.

In the case of clapping, you might decide that when the overall volume is greater than 0.5, the user is clapping (this is not a scientific measurement, but is good enough for now). This value of 0.5 is known as the *threshold.* Above the threshold, events are triggered, below, they are not.

```
float volume = analyzer.analyze();
if (volume > 0.5) {
  // DO SOMETHING WHEN THE VOLUME IS GREATER THAN ONE!
}
```

Example 20-11 draws rectangles in the window whenever the overall volume level is greater than 0.5. The volume level is also displayed on the left-hand side as a bar.

Example 20-11. Sound threshold

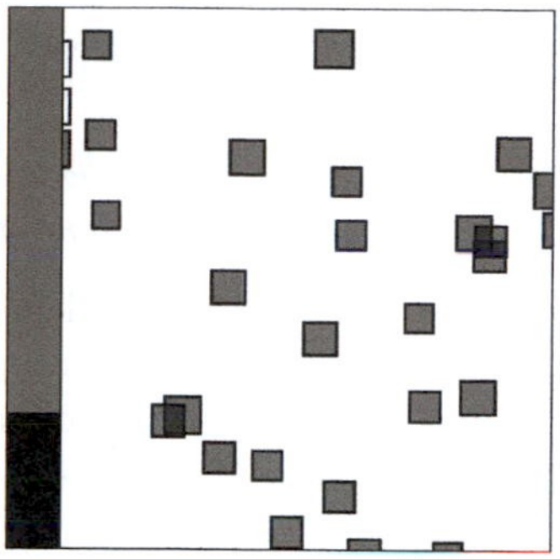

```
import processing.sound.*;

AudioIn mic;
Amplitude analyzer;

void setup() {
  size(200, 200);
  background(255);

  // Start listening to the microphone
  // Create an audio input and grab the first channel
  mic = new AudioIn(this, 0);

  // Start the Audio Input
  mic.start();

  // Create a new amplitude analyzer
  analyzer = new Amplitude(this);

  // Patch the input to the analyzer
  analyzer.input(mic);
}

void draw() {
  // Get the overall volume (between 0 and 1.0)
  float volume = analyzer.analyze();

  float threshold = 0.5;
  if (volume > threshold) {
    stroke(0);
    fill(0, 100);
    rect(random(40, width), random(height), 20, 20);
  }

  // Graph the overall volume and show threshold
  float y = map(volume, 0, 1, height, 0);
  float ythreshold = map(threshold, 0, 1, height, 0);

  noStroke();
  fill(175);
  rect(0, 0, 20, height);
  // Then draw a rectangle size according to volume
  fill(0);
  rect(0, y, 20, y);
  stroke(0);
  line(0, ythreshold, 19, ythreshold);
}
```

> If the volume is greater than 0.5 a rectangle is drawn at a random location in the window.

Figure 20-5

This application works fairly well, but does not truly emulate the *clapper*. Notice how each clap results in several rectangles drawn to the window. This is because the sound, although seemingly instantaneous to human ears, occurs over a period of time. It may be a very short period of time, but it's enough to sustain a volume level over 0.5 for several cycles through `draw()`.

In order to have a clap trigger an event one and only one time, I'll need to rethink the logic of this program. In plain English, this is what I'm trying to achieve:

- *If the sound level is above 0.5, then you are clapping and trigger the event. However, do not trigger the event if you just did a moment ago!*

The key here is how you define "a moment ago." One solution would be to implement a timer, that is, only trigger the event once and then wait one second before you are allowed to trigger the event again. This is a perfectly OK solution. Nonetheless, with sound, a timer is totally unnecessary since the sound itself will tell you when you have finished clapping!

- *If the sound level is less than 0.25, then it is quiet and you have finished clapping.*

OK, with these two pieces of logic, you are ready to program this "double-thresholded" algorithm. There are two thresholds, one to determine if you have started clapping, and one to determine if you have finished. You will need a boolean variable to tell you whether you are currently clapping or not.

Assume *clapping* equals *false* to start.

- *If the sound level is above 0.5, and you are not already clapping, trigger the event and set clapping = true.*
- *If you are clapping and the sound level is less than 0.25, then it is quiet and set clapping = false.*

In code, this translates to:

```
// If the volume is greater than one, and I am not clapping, draw a rectangle
if (vol > 0.5 && !clapping) {
  // Trigger event!
  clapping = true; // I am now clapping!
} else if (clapping && vol < 0.25) { // If I am finished clapping
  clapping = false;
}
```

Here is the full example where one and only one rectangle appears per clap.

Example 20-12. Sound events (double threshold)

Figure 20-6

```
import processing.sound.*;

AudioIn mic;
Amplitude analyzer;

float clapLevel = 0.5;   // How loud is a clap
float threshold = 0.25; // How quiet is silence
boolean clapping = false;

void setup() {
  size(200, 200);
  background(255);

  // Create an audio input and grab the first channel
  mic = new AudioIn(this, 0);

  // Start the audio Input
  mic.start();

  // Create a new amplitude analyzer
  analyzer = new Amplitude(this);

  // Patch the input to the analyzer
  analyzer.input(mic);
}

void draw() {
  // Get the overall volume (between 0 and 1.0)
  float volume = analyzer.analyze();

  if (volume > clapLevel && !clapping) {
    stroke(0);
    fill(0, 100);
    rect(random(40, width), random(height), 20, 20);
    clapping = true; // I am now clapping!
  } else if (clapping && volume < threshold) {
    clapping = false;
  }

  // Graph the overall volume
  // First draw a background strip
  noStroke();
  fill(200);
  rect(0, 0, 20, height);

  float y = map(vol, 0, 1, height, 0);
  float ybottom = map(threshold, 0, 1, height, 0);
  float ytop = map(clapLevel, 0, 1, height, 0);


  // Then draw a rectangle size according to volume
  fill(100);
  rect(0, y, 20, y);

  // Draw lines at the threshold levels
  stroke(0);
```

> If the volume is greater than 1.0, and I was not previously clapping, then I am clapping!

> Otherwise, if I was just clapping and the volume level has gone down below 0.25, then I am no longer clapping!

```
    line(0, ybottom, 19, ybottom);
    line(0, ytop, 19, ytop);
}
```

Exercise 20-7: Trigger the event from Example 20-12 after a sequence of two claps. Here is some code to get you started that assumes the existence of a variable named clapCount.

```
    if (volume > clapLevel && !clapping) {

        clapCount_____;

        if (_____) {

            _____;

            _____;

            _____;
        }

        _____;
    } else if (clapping && vol < 0.5) {
        clapping = false;
    }
```

Exercise 20-8: Create a simple game that is controlled with volume. Suggestion: First make the game work with the mouse, then replace the mouse with live input. Some examples are Pong, where the paddle's position is tied to volume, or a simple jumping game, where a character jumps each time you clap.

20-6 Spectrum analysis

Analyzing the volume of a sound in Processing is only the beginning of sound analysis. For more advanced applications, you might want to know the volume of a sound at various frequencies? Is this a high-frequency or a low-frequency sound?

The process of spectrum analysis takes a sound signal (a wave) and decodes it into a series of frequency bands. You can think of these bands like the "resolution" of the analysis. With many bands you can more precisely pinpoint the amplitude of a given frequency. With fewer bands, you are looking for the volume of a sound over a wider range of frequencies.

To do this analysis, you first need an FFT object. The FFT object serves the same purpose as the previous example's Amplitude. This time, however, it will provide an array of amplitude values (one for each band) rather than a single overall volume level. FFT stands for "Fast Fourier Transform" (named for the French mathematician Joseph Fourier) and refers to the algorithm that transforms the waveform to an array of frequency amplitudes.

```
FFT fft = new FFT(this, 512);
```

Notice how the FFT constructor requires a second argument: an integer. This value specifies the number of frequency bands in the spectrum you want to produce; a good default is 512 but it can really be any number you want. One band, incidentally, is the equivalent of just making an Amplitude analyzer object.

The next step, just as with amplitude, is to plug in the audio (whether from a file, generated sound, or microphone) into the FFT object.

```
SoundFile song = new SoundFile(this, "song.mp3");
fft.input(song);
```

Again, just as with amplitude, the next step is to call analyze().

```
fft.analyze();
```

Here, though, I am simply telling the analyzer to run the FFT algorithm. To look at the actual results, I have to examine the FFT object's spectrum array. This array holds the amplitude values (between 0 and 1) for all of the frequency bands. The length of the array is equal to the number of bands requested in the FFT constructor (512 in this case). I can loop through this array, as follows:

```
for (int i = 0; i < fft.size(); i++) {
   float amp = fft.spectrum[i];
}
```

> You can retrieve the number of frequency bands via size()

Here is all the above code put together into an example. It draws each frequency band as a line with height tied to the particular amplitude of that frequency.

Example 20-13. Spectrum analysis

```
import processing.sound.*;

// A sound file object
SoundFile song;

FFT fft;
int bands = 512;


void setup() {
  size(512, 360);

  // Play the sound
  song = new SoundFile(this, "dragon.wav");
  song.loop();

  fft = new FFT(this, bands);

  fft.input(song);
}
void draw() {
  background(255);

  fft.analyze();
  for (int i = 0; i < fft.size(); i++) {
    stroke(0);
    float y = map(fft.spectrum[i], 0, 1, height * 0.75, 0);
    line(i, height * 0.75, i, y);
  }
}
```

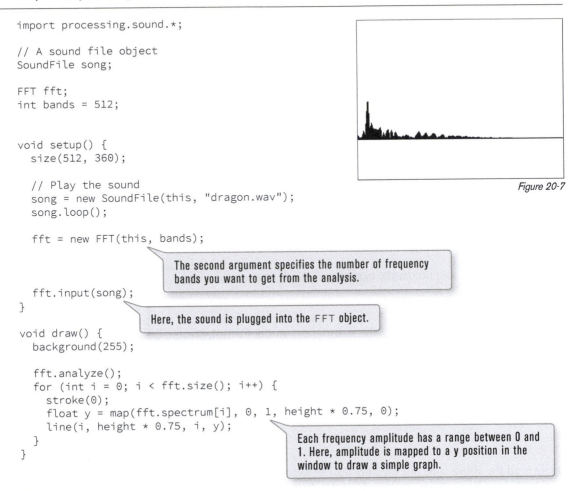

Figure 20-7

> The second argument specifies the number of frequency bands you want to get from the analysis.

> Here, the sound is plugged into the FFT object.

> Each frequency amplitude has a range between 0 and 1. Here, amplitude is mapped to a y position in the window to draw a simple graph.

Exercise 20-9: Perform the same spectrum analysis of a signal from microphone input.

Exercise 20-10: Using a smaller number of bands, create a visualization of the spectrum with a "graphic equalizer" look. See the image below for an example.

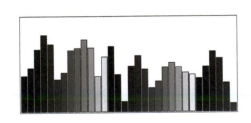

21 Exporting

Wait a minute. I thought that Art wanted to give up the exporting.
—Seinfeld

In this chapter:
- Web and JavaScript
- Stand-alone applications
- High resolution PDFs
- Images and image sequences
- Video recording

I have focused the energy in this book on learning to program. Nevertheless, eventually your code babies will grow up and want to find their way out in the world. This chapter is dedicated to a discussion of the various publishing options available to Processing sketches.

21-1 Exporting to web

Casey Reas and Ben Fry started Processing in 2001 when Java ruled the web. If you wanted to share real-time graphics or animation in a browser, embedding a Java "applet" was the primary mechanism for doing so. While Java applets still do work, it's an outdated technology not easily supported by modern day browsers. In 2012, the Processing Foundation, a not-for-profit 501(c)(3) organization, was created to support and maintain multiple environments empowering people of all backgrounds to program. The philosophy and approach to learning and creating is the core mission of the foundation rather than a focus on any particular language. Currently the Foundation maintains and supports three environments.

Processing (http://processing.org)
The environment this book is primarily about, and the continuation of the original 2001 version built on top of Java

Processing.py (http://py.processing.org)
A Python version of the project

p5.js (http://p5js.org)
A modern-day re-interpretation of Processing for the web using JavaScript, HTML, and CSS. This is the one to use if the browser is your platform of choice.

While it may seem overwhelming to learn an entire new language just to get your sketches to run online, this is the path I would recommend if you're interested in creating work for the web. In fact, p5.js is used by this book at its website for the examples running online (and where you can find p5.js versions of this book's examples). To get started I would suggest reading the Processing transition tutorial at p5js.org (*https://github.com/processing/p5.js/wiki/Processing-transition*). You'll discover that while there are some quirks and syntax differences with JavaScript, all of the fundamental concepts of computation (variables, conditionals, loops, objects, arrays) are the same. In addition all of the drawing functions you've learned here are implemented in p5.js. Finally, as a bonus, you'll discover a slew of new functions related to HTML and CSS.

I should also briefly mention the processing.js (*http://processingjs.org*) project as well. Processing.js, often confused with p5.js, is a port of Processing to JavaScript that automatically translates your Processing Java code to JavaScript. The idea here is to be able to run Processing sketches in the browser without any additional work. This is magical when it works, however, there are loads of reasons why this can go wrong. For example, any sketch using a third party library will fail. In addition, a lot of the new functionality from Processing 2.0+ is not supported. For quick and dirty publishing of simple sketches, Processing.js is a nice solution, however, if you have a larger project you're building for the web I would recommend working natively in JavaScript with p5.js.

21-2 Stand-alone applications

A great feature of Processing is that sketches can be published as stand-alone applications, meaning double-clickable programs that can run without the Processing development environment being installed.

This feature is useful if you want to distribute a downloadable version of your sketch for non-Processing users. In addition, if you're creating a program for an installation or kiosk environment, you can set an exported application to launch automatically when a machine boots up. Finally exported applications are also useful if you need to run multiple copies of a sketch at the same time (such as in the case of the client/server examples in Chapter 19).

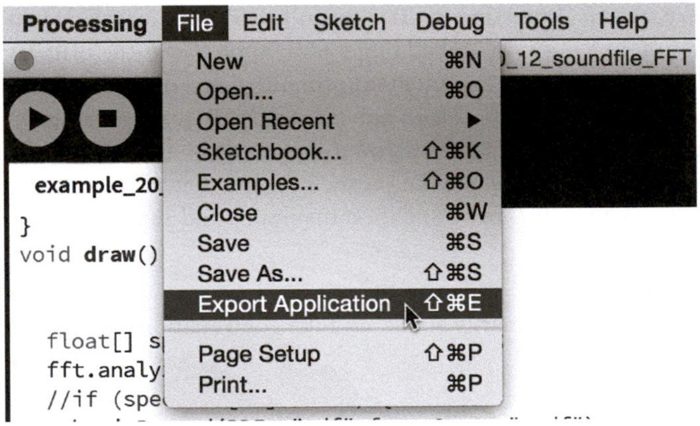

Figure 21-1

To export as an application, go to: File → Export Application (see Figure 21-1).

You'll then be presented with some options. You can select the operating systems you want to generate the application for, set the application to run in fullscreen, as well as optionally embed Java in application file itself. Embedding Java can be useful since the user of your application will need Java installed on his or her computer in order for the application to run properly. Nevertheless, the trade-off here is that this option will balloon the size of the application file itself.

While Processing can build applications for multiple operating systems all at once: Mac OS X, Windows, Linux, it's generally recommended to build the application for the same operating system you are using on a particular machine as there can often be issues otherwise.

After exporting, you will notice that a new folder appears containing the files you need, as depicted in Figure 21-2.

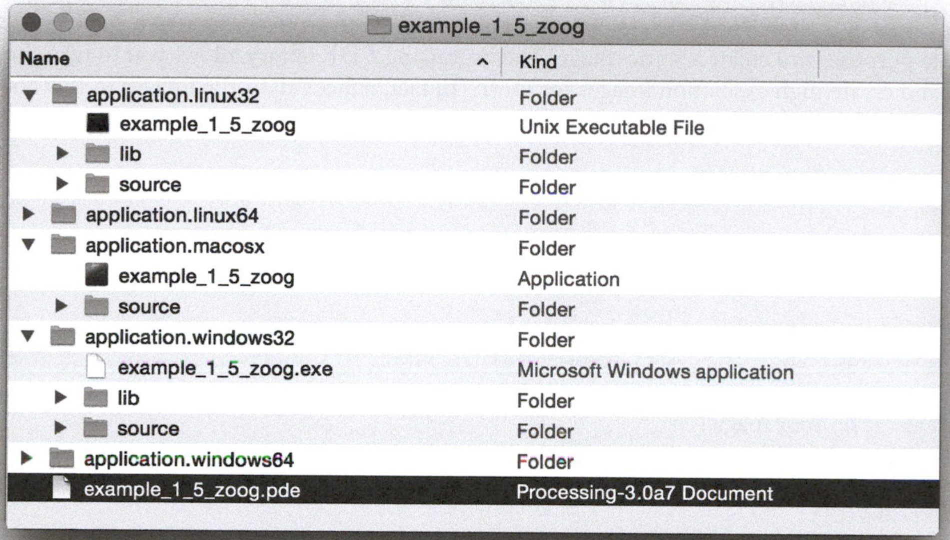

Name	^	Kind
▼ 📁 application.linux32		Folder
⬛ example_1_5_zoog		Unix Executable File
▶ 📁 lib		Folder
▶ 📁 source		Folder
▶ 📁 application.linux64		Folder
▼ 📁 application.macosx		Folder
⬛ example_1_5_zoog		Application
▶ 📁 source		Folder
▼ 📁 application.windows32		Folder
📄 example_1_5_zoog.exe		Microsoft Windows application
▶ 📁 lib		Folder
▶ 📁 source		Folder
▶ 📁 application.windows64		Folder
📄 example_1_5_zoog.pde		Processing-3.0a7 Document

Figure 21-2

- **sketchName.exe** (or named simply **sketchName** on Mac and Linux). This file is the double-clickable application.
- **"source" directory**. The application folder will include a directory containing the source files for your program. This folder is not required to run the application.
- **"lib"**. This folder only appears for Windows and Linux and contains required library files. It will always contain **core.jar**, the core processing library, as well as any others you import. On Mac OS X, the library files are visible by control-clicking the application file and selecting "Show Package Contents."

There are a few tricks related to the **Export Application** feature. You can adjust the application's icon as well as the text in the title bar, for example. For tips, take a look at the export info wiki (*https://github.com/processing/processing/wiki/Export-Info-and-Tips*).

Exercise 21-1: Export a stand-alone application for any Processing sketch you have made or any example in this book.

21-3 High-resolution PDFs

You have been using Processing primarily as a means for creating graphics programs that run on a computer screen. In fact, if you recall Chapter 3, I spent a great deal of time discussing how the flow of a program works over time. Nevertheless, now is a good time to return to the idea of a static program, one whose sole purpose is to create a static image. The Processing PDF library allows you to take these static sketches and create high-resolution images for print. (In fact, almost all of the images in this book were produced with this method.)

Following are the required steps for using the PDF library.

1. Import the library.
   ```
   import processing.pdf.*;
   ```

2. In setup(), use the size() function with the PDF renderer and a filename.
   ```
   size(400, 400, PDF, "filename.pdf");
   ```

3. In draw(), do your magic!
   ```
   background(255);
   fill(175);
   stroke(0);
   ellipse(width/2, height/2, 160, 160);
   ```

4. Call the function exit(). This is very important. Calling exit() causes the PDF to finish rendering. Without it, the file will not open properly.
   ```
   exit(); // Required!
   ```

Here is how the program looks all together:

Example 21-1. Basic PDF

```
// Import the library
import processing.pdf.*;

// Using "PDF" mode, 4th argument is the name of the file
size(400, 400, PDF, "filename.pdf");
// Draw some stuff!
background(255);
fill(175);
stroke(0);
ellipse(width/2, height/2, 160, 160);

// All finished
exit();
```

If you run this example, you will notice that no window appears. Once you have set the Processing renderer to PDF, the sketch window will no longer appear.

However, it's possible to see the Processing sketch window while rendering a PDF using the functions beginRecord() and endRecord(). This runs slower than the first example, but allows you to see what is being saved.

Example 21-2. PDF using *beginRecord()*

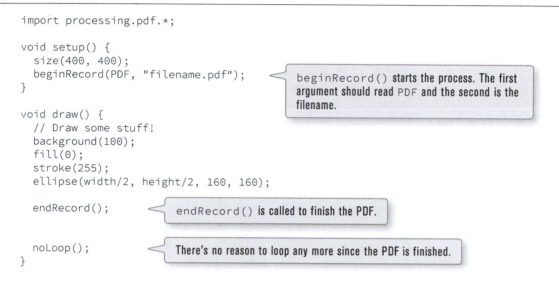

```
import processing.pdf.*;

void setup() {
  size(400, 400);
  beginRecord(PDF, "filename.pdf");
}
```
> beginRecord() starts the process. The first argument should read PDF and the second is the filename.

```
void draw() {
  // Draw some stuff!
  background(100);
  fill(0);
  stroke(255);
  ellipse(width/2, height/2, 160, 160);

  endRecord();
```
> endRecord() is called to finish the PDF.

```
  noLoop();
}
```
> There's no reason to loop any more since the PDF is finished.

The endRecord() function does not have to be called on the first frame rendered, and therefore this mode can be used to generate a PDF compiled from multiple cycles through draw(). The following example takes the "Scribbler" program from Chapter 16 and renders the result to a PDF. Here the colors are not taken from a video stream, but are picked based on a counter variable. See Figure 21-3 for a sample output.

Example 21-3. Multiple frames into one PDF

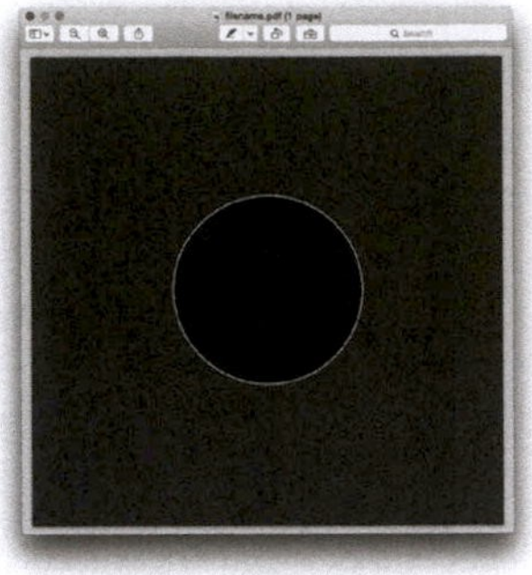

```
import processing.pdf.*;

float x = 0;
float y = 0;

void setup() {
  size(400, 400);

  beginRecord(PDF, "scribbler.pdf");
  background(255);
}
```

> background() **should be in** setup(). **If** background() **is placed in** draw() **the PDF would accumulate a lot of graphics elements only to erase them over and over again.**

Figure 21-3

```
void draw() {

  // Pick a new x and y
  float newx = constrain(x + random(-20, 20), 0, width);
  float newy = constrain(y + random(-20, 20), 0, height);

  // Draw a line from (x,y) to (newx,newy)
  stroke(frameCount%255, frameCount*3%255, frameCount*11%255, 100);
  strokeWeight(4);
  line(x, y, newx, newy);

  // Save (newx,newy) in (x,y)
  x = newx;
  y = newy;

}

// When the mouse is pressed, finish the PDF
void mousePressed() {
  endRecord();
  // Tell Processing to open the PDF
  open(sketchPath("scribbler.pdf"));
  noLoop();
}
```

> **In this example, the user chooses when to finish rendering the PDF by clicking the mouse.**

If you're rendering 3D shapes (using P3D), you will want to use beginRaw() and endRaw() instead of beginRecord() and endRecord(). This example also uses a boolean variable recordPDF to trigger the recording process.

Example 21-4. PDF and P3D

```
// Using P3D
import processing.opengl.*;
import processing.pdf.*;

// Cube rotation
float yTheta = 0.0;
float xTheta = 0.0;

// To trigger recording the PDF
boolean recordPDF = false;

void setup() {
  size(400, 400, P3D);
}

void draw() {
  // Begin making the PDF
  if (recordPDF) {
    beginRaw(PDF, "3D.pdf");
  }
  background(255);
  stroke(0);
  noFill();
  translate(width/2, height/2);
  rotateX(xTheta);
  rotateY(yTheta);
  box(100);
  xTheta + = 0.02;
  yTheta + = 0.03;

  // End making the PDF
  if (recordPDF) {
    endRaw();
    recordPDF = false;
  }
}

// Make the PDF when the mouse is pressed
void mousePressed() {
  recordPDF = true;
}
```

A boolean variable that when set to true causes a PDF to be made.

Figure 21-4

P3D mode requires the use of beginRaw() and endRaw() instead of beginRecord() and endRecord().

If you include "####" in the filename – "3D-####.pdf" – separate, numbered PDFs will be made for each frame that is rendered.

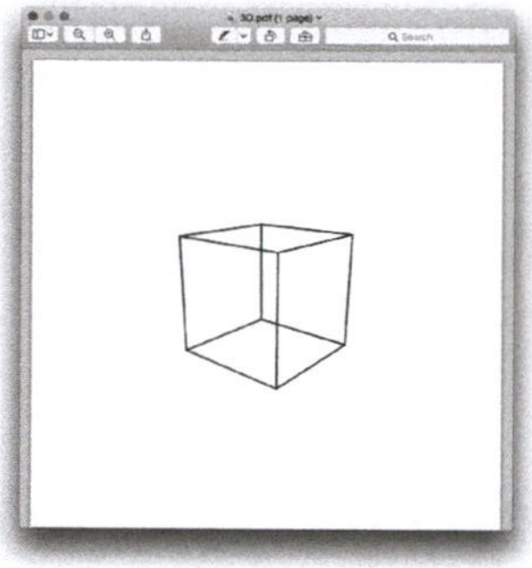

Two important notes about the **PDF** library.

- **Images** — If you're displaying images in the PDF, these will not necessarily look good after export. A 320 × 240 pixel image is still a 320 × 240 pixel image whether rendered into a high-resolution PDF or not.

- **Text** — If you're displaying text in the PDF, you will have to have the font installed in order to view the PDF properly. One way around this is to include textMode(SHAPE); after size(). This will render the text as a shape to the PDF and not require the font installed.

For full documentation of the **PDF** library, visit the Processing reference page (*http://processing.org/refer ence/libraries/pdf/*). While the PDF library will take care of many of your needs related to high-resolution generation, there are other contributed libraries that might be of interest. One is *P8gGraphicsSVG* by Philippe Lhoste for exporting files in the SVG ("Scalable Vector Graphics") format.

 Exercise 21-2: Create a PDF from any Processing sketch you have made or any example in this book.

21-4 Images and `saveFrame()`

High-resolution PDFs are useful for printing; however, you can also save the contents of the Processing window as an image file (with the same resolution as the pixel size of the window itself). This is accomplished with `save()` or `saveFrame()`.

`save()` takes one argument, the filename for the image you want to save. `save()` will generate image files with the following formats: JPG, TIF, TGA, or PNG, indicated by the file extension you include in the filename. If no extension is included, Processing will default to the TIF format.

```
background(255, 0, 0);
save("file.png");
```

21-5 Recording video

If you call `save()` multiple times with the same filename, it will overwrite the previous image. However, if you want to save a sequence of images, the `saveFrame()` function will auto-number the files. Processing will look for the *String "####"* in the filename and replace it with a numbered sequence of images. See Figure 21-5.

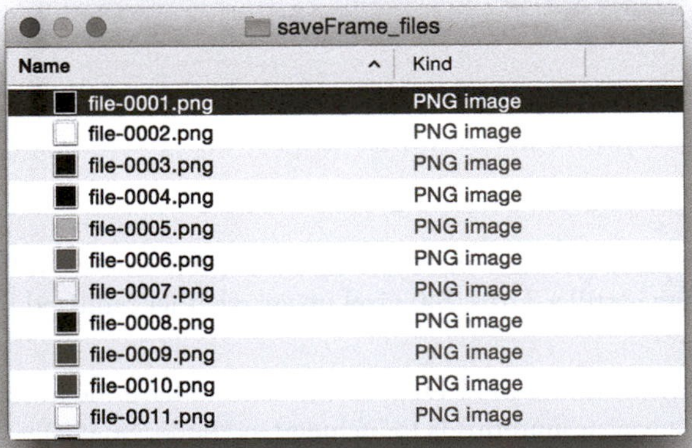

● ● ●	saveFrame_files	
Name	^	Kind
☐ file-0001.png		PNG image
☐ file-0002.png		PNG image
■ file-0003.png		PNG image
■ file-0004.png		PNG image
☐ file-0005.png		PNG image
■ file-0006.png		PNG image
☐ file-0007.png		PNG image
■ file-0008.png		PNG image
■ file-0009.png		PNG image
■ file-0010.png		PNG image
☐ file-0011.png		PNG image

Figure 21-5

```
void draw() {
  background(random(255));
  saveFrame("file-####.png");
}
```

This technique is commonly used to saved a numbered sequence of images that can be stitched together into a movie using video editing software or Processing's Movie Maker tool. Let's create a short example that adds a few features like starting and stopping recording.

The first thing I might like to add is a boolean variable to track whether the sketch is recording frames or not.

```
boolean recording = false;
```

In the main `draw()` loop I can then check the current state and save frames if recording is true.

```
if (recording) {
  saveFrame("output/frames####.png");
}
```

it's useful to specify a directory for the output since a large number of files will be generated.

Finally I can toggle the state of recording between true to false with user interaction, in this case pressing the `'r'` key on a keyboard.

```
void keyPressed() {
  if (key == 'r' || key == 'R') {
    recording = !recording;
  }
}
```

Here, a lower or upper case 'r' is valid.

Setting a boolean to not itself toggles false to true or true to false.

Another nice trick involves the placement of the call to `saveFrame()` in `draw()`. Processing only writes the current pixels to the rendered image file so any calls after `saveFrame()` won't be recorded. This is useful if you want to add some visual elements that indicate whether the sketch is recording or not. In the example below, a red circle is drawn when recording.

Example 21-5. Saving image sequence

```
boolean recording = false;

void setup() {
  size(640, 360);
}

void draw() {
  background(0);

  for (float a = 0; a < TWO_PI; a+= 0.2) {
    pushMatrix();
    translate(width/2, height/2);
    rotate(a+sin(frameCount*0.004*a));
    stroke(255);
    line(-100, 0, 100, 0);
    popMatrix();
  }

  if (recording) {
    saveFrame("output/frames####.png");
  }

  textAlign(CENTER);
  fill(255);
  if (!recording) {
    text("Press r to start recording.", width/2, height-24);
  } else {
    text("Press r to stop recording.", width/2, height-24);
  }

  stroke(255);
  if (recording) {
    fill(255, 0, 0);
  } else {
    noFill();
  }
  ellipse(width/2, height-48, 16, 16);
}

void keyPressed() {
  if (key == 'r' || key == 'R') {
    recording = !recording;
  }
}
```

A boolean to track whether the sketch is recording or not

Just drawing an arbitrary design so there is something to record.

If `recording` is true, call `saveFrame()` and auto-number the files.

Let's draw some stuff to indicate what is happening. It's important to note that none of this will show up in the rendered files because it's drawn **after** `saveFrame()`.

A red dot for when the sketch is recording.

If the user presses `'r'`, start or stop recording!

To convert the image sequence into a movie file, there are a number of options such as MPEG StreamClip for Mac and Windows (*http://www.squared5.com/*) or any commercial video editing software like Adobe Premiere or Final Cut. Processing also includes a "Movie Maker" tool (found under the file menu "Tools") which you can use by dragging in the directory of images.

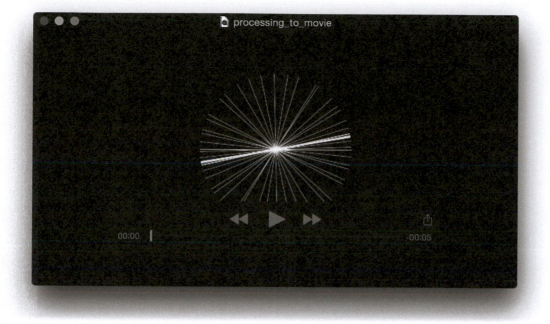

Figure 21-6 Output of Example 21-5 using the Movie Maker tool.

Exercise 21-3: Create a movie from any Processing sketch you have made or any example in this book. Try adding visual elements that do not get recorded like a display of the count of the number of recorded frames.

Lesson Nine Project

Choose one or both!

1. Incorporate sound into a Processing sketch, either by adding sound effects or by controlling the sketch with live input.

2. Use Processing to generate an output other than real-time graphics. Make a print (using PDF). Make a video, and so on.

Use the space provided below to sketch designs, notes, and pseudocode for your project.

Lesson Ten

Beyond Processing

Chapter 22
Chapter 23

22 Advanced Object-Oriented Programming

Do you ever think about things that you do think about?
—Henry Drummond, *Inherit the Wind*

In this chapter:
– Encapsulation
– Inheritance
– Polymorphism
– Overloading

In Chapter 8, I introduced *object-oriented programming* ("OOP"). The driving principle of the chapter was the pairing of data and functionality into one single idea, a *class*. A *class* is a template and from that template I made *instances* of *objects* and stored them in variables and arrays. Although you learned how to write classes and make objects, I did not delve very deeply into the core principles of OOP and explore its advanced features. Now that you are nearing the end of the book (and about to leap into the world of Java in the next chapter), it's a good time to reflect on the past and take steps toward the future.

Object-oriented programming in Processing and Java is defined by three fundamental concepts: *encapsulation, inheritance,* and *polymorphism.* You are familiar with *encapsulation* already; you just have not formalized your understanding of the concept and used the terminology. Inheritance and polymorphism are completely new concepts I will cover in this chapter. (At the end of this chapter, I will also take a quick look at *method overloading*, which allows objects to have more than one way of calling the constructor.)

22-1 Encapsulation

To understand encapsulation, let's return to the example of a Car class. And let's take that example out into the world and think about a real-life Car object, operated by a real-life driver: *you.* It's a nice summer day and you're tired of programming and opt to head to the beach for the weekend. Traffic permitting, you're hoping for a nice drive where you will turn the steering wheel a bunch of times, press on the gas and brakes, and fiddle with dial on the radio.

This car that you're driving is *encapsulated.* All you have to do to drive is operate the functions: steer(), gas(), brake(), and radio(). Do you know what is under the hood? How the catalytic converter connects to the engine or how the engine connects to the intercooler? What valves and wires and gears and belts do what? Sure, if you're an experienced auto mechanic you might be able to answer these questions, but the point is you *don't have to* in order to drive the car. This is *encapsulation.*

Encapsulation is defined as hiding the inner workings of an object from the user of that object.

In terms of object-oriented programming, the "inner workings" of an object are the data (variables of that object) and functions. The "user" of the object is you, the programmer, who is making object instances and using them throughout your code.

Now, why is this a good idea? Chapter 8 (and all of the OOP examples throughout the book) emphasized the principles of modularity and reusability. Meaning, if you already figured out how to program a car, why do it over and over again each time you have to make a car? Just organize it all into the Car class, and you have saved yourself a lot of headaches.

Encapsulation goes a step further. OOP does not just help you organize your code, it *protects you from making mistakes*. If you do not mess with the wiring of the car while you're driving it, you're less likely to break the car. Of course, sometimes a car breaks down and you need to fix it, but this requires opening the hood and looking at the code inside the class itself.

Take the following example. Let's say you're writing a BankAccount class which has a floating point variable for the bank account balance.

```
BankAccount account = new BankAccount(1000);
```

> A bank account object with a starting balance of $1,000.

You will want to encapsulate that balance and keep it hidden. Why? Let's say you need to withdraw money from that account. So you subtract $100 from that account.

```
account.balance = account.balance - 100.
```

> Withdrawing $100 by accessing the balance variable directly.

But what if there is a fee to withdraw money? Say, $1.25? You are going to get fired from that bank programming job pretty quickly, having left this detail out. With encapsulation, you would keep your job, having written the following code instead.

```
account.withdraw(100);
```

> Withdrawing $100 by calling a method!

If the withdraw() function is written correctly, the software will never forget the fee, since it will happen every single time the method is called.

```
void withdraw(float amount) {
    float fee = 1.25;
    account -= (amount + fee);
}
```

> This function ensures that a fee is also deducted whenever the money is withdrawn.

Another benefit of this strategy is that if the bank decides to raise the fee to $1.50, it can simply adjust the fee variable inside the BankAccount class and everything will keep working!

Technically speaking, in order to follow the principles of encapsulation, variables inside of a class should *never* be accessed directly and can only be retrieved with a method. This is why you will often see programmers use a lot of functions known as *getters* and *setters*, functions that retrieve or change the value of variables. Here is an example of a Point class with two variables (x and y) that are accessed with getters and setters.

```
class Point {
  float x, y;

  Point(float tempX, float tempY) {
    x = tempX;
    y = tempY;
  }

  // Getters
  float getX() {
    return x;
  }

  float getY() {
    return y;
  }

  // Setters
  float setX(float val) {
    x = val;
  }

  float setY(float val) {
    if (val > height) {
      val = height;
    }
    y = val;
  }
}
```

> The variables x and y are accessed with getter and setter functions.

> Getters and setters protect the value of variables. For example, here the value of y can never be set to greater than the sketch's height.

If I had a Point object p and I wanted to increment the y value, I would have to do it this way:

```
p.setY(p.getY() + 1);
```

> Instead of: p.y = p.y + 1;

Although the syntax above is awkward, the advantage here is that you cannot set the y-coordinate greater than the height because of the test in p.setY(), whereas p.y = p.y + 1; doesn't check that for you. If you wanted to enforce this requirement Java allows you to mark a variable as "private" to make it illegal to access directly (in other words, if you try to, the program will not even run).

```
class Point {
  private float x;
  private float y;
}
```

> Although rarely seen in Processing examples, variables can be set as private, meaning only accessible inside the class itself. By default all variables and functions in Processing are "public."

While formal encapsulation is a core principle of object-oriented programming and can be important when designing large-scale applications programmed by a team of developers, sticking to the letter of the law (as with incrementing the y value of the Point object above) is often rather inconvenient and almost silly for a simple Processing sketch. So, it's not the end of the world if you make a Point class and access the x and y variables directly. I have done this several times in the examples found in this book.

However, understanding the principle of *encapsulation* should be a driving force in how you design your objects and manage your code. Any time you start to expose the inner workings of an object outside of the class itself, you should ask yourself: Is this necessary? Could this code go inside a function inside the class? In the end, you will be a happier programmer and keep that job at the bank.

22-2 Inheritance

Inheritance, the second in my list of three fundamental object-oriented programming concepts, allows you to create new classes that are based on existing classes.

Let's take a look at the world of animals: dogs, cats, monkeys, pandas, wombats, and sea nettles. Arbitrarily, let's begin by programming a Dog class. A Dog object will have an age variable (an integer), as well as eat(), sleep(), and bark() functions.

```
class Dog {
  int age;

  Dog() {
    age = 0;
  }

  void eat() {
    // eating code goes here
  }

  void sleep() {
    // sleeping code goes here
  }

  void bark() {
    println("Woof!");
  }
}
```

> Notice how dogs and cats have the same variables (age) and functions (eat, sleep). However, they also have a unique function for barking or meowing.

> Only dogs bark!

Finished with dogs, I can now move on to cats.

```
class Cat {
  int age;

  Cat() {
    age = 0;
  }

  void eat() {
    // eating code goes here
  }
}
```

```
    void sleep() {
        // sleeping code goes here
    }

    void meow() {
        println("Meow!");
    }
}
```

> Only cats meow!

Sadly, as I move onto fish, horses, koala bears, and lemurs, this process will become rather tedious as I rewrite the same code over and over again. What if, instead, I could develop a generic Animal class to describe any type of animal? After all, all animals eat and sleep. I could then say the following:

- A dog is an animal and has all the properties of animals and can do all the things animals can do. In addition, a dog can bark.

- A cat is an animal and has all the properties of animals and can do all the things animals can do. In addition, a cat can meow.

Inheritance allows me to program just this. With inheritance, classes can inherit properties (variables) and functionality (methods) from other classes. The Dog class is a child (a.k.a. a *subclass*) of the Animal class. Children inherit all variables and functions automatically from their parent (a.k.a. *superclass*). Children can also include additional variables and functions not found in the parent. Inheritance follows a tree-structure (much like a phylogenetic "tree of life"). Dogs can inherit from mammals which inherit from animals, and so on. See Figure 22-1.

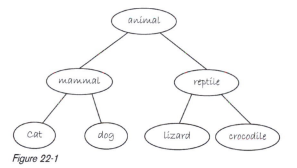

Figure 22-1

Here is how the syntax works with inheritance.

```
class Animal {
    int age;

    Animal() {
        age = 0;
    }

    void eat() {
        // eating code goes here
    }
```

> The Animal class is the parent (or super) class.

> The variable age is inherited by Dog and Cat.

> The functions eat() and sleep() are inherited by Dog and Cat.

```
  void sleep() {
    // sleeping code goes here
  }
}
```

```
class Dog extends Animal {
```

> The `Dog` class is the child (or sub) class. This is indicated with the code `extends Animal`

```
  Dog() {
    super();
  }
```

> `super()` means execute code found in the parent class.

```
  void bark() {
    println("Woof!");
  }
}
```

> Since `bark()` is not part of the parent class, it has to be defined in the child class.

```
class Cat extends Animal {

  Cat() {
    super();
  }

  void meow() {
    println("Meow!");
  }
}
```

The following new terms have been introduced:

- `extends` — This keyword is used to indicate a parent class for the class being defined. Note that classes can only extend *one* class. However, classes can extend classes that extend other classes, that is, `Dog` extends `Animal`, `Terrier` extends `Dog`. Everything is inherited all the way down the line.

- `super()` — Super calls the constructor in the parent class. In other words, whatever you do in the parent constructor, do so in the child constructor as well. Processing will call `super()` for you in most cases, however, I typically leave it in the code to be more clear about what is happening. Other code can be written into the constructor in addition to `super()`, but `super()` must come first.

A subclass can be expanded to include additional functions and properties beyond what is contained in the superclass. For example, let's assume that a `Dog` object has a `haircolor` variable in addition to `age`, which is set randomly in the constructor. The class would now look like so:

```
class Dog extends Animal {
  color haircolor;
```

> A child class can introduce new variables not included in the parent.

```
  Dog() {
    super();
    haircolor = color(random(255));
  }
```

```
  void bark() {
    println("Woof!");
  }
}
```

Note how the parent constructor is called via `super()`, setting the age to 0, but the haircolor is set inside the `Dog` constructor itself. Suppose a `Dog` object eats differently than a generic `Animal` object. Parent functions can be *overridden* by rewriting the function inside the subclass.

```
class Dog extends Animal {
  color haircolor;

  Dog() {
    super();
    haircolor = color(random(255));
  }

  void eat() {
    // Code for how a dog specifically eats
  }

  void bark() {
    println("Woof!");
  }
}
```

> A child can override a parent function if necessary.

But what if a dog should eat the same way an animal does, but with some additional functionality? A subclass can both run the code from a parent class and incorporate some custom code.

```
class Dog extends Animal {
  color haircolor;

  Dog() {
    super();
    haircolor = color(random(255));
  }

  void eat() {
    // Call eat() from Animal
    super.eat();

    // Add some additional code
    // for how a dog specifically eats
    println("Yum!!!");
  }

  void bark() {
    println("Woof!");
```

> A child can execute a function from the parent while adding its own code as well.

```
    }
  }
```

Exercise 22-1: Continuing with the car example from my discussion of encapsulation, how would you design a system of classes for vehicles (that is, cars, trucks, buses, and motorcycles)? What variables and functions would you include in a parent class? And what would be added or overridden in the child classes? What if you wanted to include planes, trains, and boats in this example as well? Diagram it, modeled after Figure 22-1.

22-3 An inheritance example: shapes

Now that you have had an introduction to the theory of inheritance and its syntax, I can develop a working example in Processing.

A typical example of inheritance involves shapes. Although a bit of a cliché, it's useful because of its simplicity. I will create a generic Shape class where all Shape objects have an (x,y) location as well as a size, and a function for display. Shapes move around the screen by jiggling randomly.

```
class Shape {
  float x;
  float y;
  float r;

  Shape(float x_, float y_, float r_) {
    x = x_;
    y = y_;
    r = r_;
  }

  void jiggle() {
    x += random(-1, 1);
    y += random(-1, 1);
  }

  void display() {
    // This method deliberately left empty
  }
}
```

> A generic shape does not really know how to be displayed. This will be overridden in the child classes.

Next, I create a subclass from Shape (let's call it Square). It will inherit all the instance variables and methods from Shape. I'll write a new constructor with the name Square and execute the code from the parent class by calling super().

```
class Square extends Shape {
  // Variables for only Square are added here if neeeded.

  Square(float x_, float y_, float r_) {          Variables are inherited from the parent.
    super(x_,y_,r_);
  }
                          If the parent constructor takes
                          arguments then super() needs to
                          pass in those arguments.

  // Inherits jiggle() from parent

  // Add a display method
  void display() {              Aha, the square overrides its parent for display.
    rectMode(CENTER);
    fill(175);
    stroke(0);
    rect(x,y,r,r);
  }
}
```

Notice that if I call the parent constructor with super(), I must include the required arguments. Also, because I want to display the square onscreen, I override display(). Even though I want the square to jiggle, I do not need to write the jiggle() function since it is inherited.

What if I want a subclass of Shape to include additional functionality? Following is an example of a Circle class that, in addition to extending Shape, contains an instance variable to keep track of color. (Note this is purely to demonstrate this feature of inheritance; it would be more logical to place a color variable in the parent Shape class.) It also expands the jiggle() function to adjust size and incorporates a new function to change color.

```
class Circle extends Shape {

  // Inherits all instance variables from parent + adding one
  color c;

  Circle(float x_, float y_, float r_, color c_) {
    super(x_, y_, r_); // Call the parent constructor
    c = c_;            // Also deal with this new instance variable
  }

  // Call the parent jiggle, but do some more stuff too
  void jiggle() {
    super.jiggle();
    r += random(-1, 1);          The circle jiggles its size as well as its (x,y) location.
    r = constrain(r, 0, 100);
```

```
    }

    void changeColor() {
      c = color(random(255));
    }
```

> The changeColor() function is unique to circles.

```
    void display() {
      ellipseMode(CENTER);
      fill(c);
      stroke(0);
      ellipse(x, y, r, r);
    }
  }
```

To demonstrate that inheritance is working, here is a program that makes one Square object and one Circle object. The Shape, Square, and Circle classes are not included again, but are identical to the ones above. See Example 22-1.

Example 22-1. Inheritance

```
Square s;
Circle c;
```

> This sketch includes one Circle object and one Square object. No Shape object is made. The Shape class exists only as part of the inheritance tree!

```
void setup() {
  size(200, 200);

  // A square and circle
  s = new Square(75, 75, 10);
  c = new Circle(125, 125, 20, color(175));
}

void draw() {
  background(255);

  c.jiggle();
  s.jiggle();

  c.display();
  s.display();
}
```

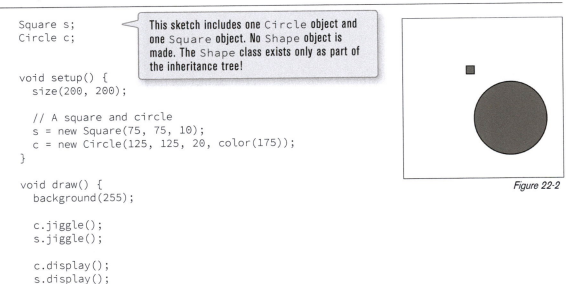

Figure 22-2

Exercise 22-2: Write a Line *class that extends* Shape *and has variables for the two points of the line. When the line jiggles, move both points. You will not need* r *for anything in the* Line *class.*

```
class Line _____ {
    float x2, y2;

    Line(_____,_____,_____,_____) {
        super(_____);
        x2 = _____;
        y2 = _____;
    }

    void jiggle() {
        _____
        _____
        _____
    }

    void display() {
        stroke(255);
        line(_____);
    }
}
```

Exercise 22-3: Do any of the sketches you have created merit the use of inheritance? Try to find one and revise it.

22-4 Polymorphism

Armed with the concepts of inheritance, I can program a diverse animal kingdom with arrays of dogs, cats, turtles, and kiwis frolicking about.

```
Dog[] dogs = new Dog[100];
Cat[] cats = new Cat[101];
Turtle[] turtles = new Turtle[23];
Kiwi[] kiwis = new Kiwi[6];
for (int i = 0; i < dogs.length; i++) {
    dogs[i] = new Dog();
}
for (int i = 0; i < cats.length; i++) {
    cats[i] = new Cat();
}
for (int i = 0; i < turtles.length; i++) {
    turtle[i] = new Turtle();
```

> 100 dogs. 101 cats. 23 turtles. 6 kiwis.

> Because the arrays are different sizes, a separate loop is needed for each array.

```
}
for (int i = 0; i < kiwis.length; i++) {
  kiwis[i] = new Kiwi();
}
```

As the day begins, the animals are all pretty hungry and are looking to eat. So it's off to looping time.

```
for (int i = 0; i < dogs.length; i++) {
  dogs[i].eat();
}
for (int i = 0; i < cats.length; i++) {
  cats[i].eat();
}
for (int i = 0; i < turtles.length; i++) {
  turtles[i].eat();
}
for (int i = 0; i < kiwis.length; i++) {
  kiwis[i].eat();
}
```

This works great, but as my world expands to include many more animal species, I am going to get stuck writing a lot of individual loops. Isn't this unnecessary? After all, the creatures are all animals, and they all like to eat. Why not just have one array of Animal objects and fill it with all different kinds of animals?

```
Animal[] kingdom = new Animal[1000];
```

> The array is defined with type Animal, but specific animal subtypes can be inserted.

```
for (int i = 0; i < kingdom.length; i++) {
  if (i < 100) {
    kingdom[i] = new Dog();
  } else if (i < 400) {
    kingdom[i] = new Cat();
  } else if (i < 900) {
    kingdom[i] = new Turtle();
  } else {
    kingdom[i] = new Kiwi();
  }
}
for (int i = 0; i < kingdom.length; i++) {
  kingdom[i].eat();
}
```

> Dogs, cats, turtles, and kiwis are all in the same array.

> When it is time for all the animals to eat, I can just loop through that one big array.

The ability to treat a Dog object as either a member of the Dog class or the Animal class (its parent) is known as *polymorphism*, the third tenet of object-oriented programming.

Polymorphism (from the Greek, *polymorphos*, meaning many forms) refers to the treatment of a single object instance in multiple forms. A dog is certainly a Dog, but since Dog *extends* Animal, it can also be considered an Animal. In code, I can refer to it both ways.

```
Dog rover = new Dog();
Animal spot = new Dog();
```

> Normally, the type on the left must match the type on the right. With polymorphism, it's OK if they don't as long as the type on the right is a child of the type on the left.

Although the second line of code might initially seem to violate syntax rules, both ways of declaring a Dog object are legal. Even though I declare spot as an Animal, I am really making a Dog object and storing it in the spot variable. And I can safely call all of the Animal methods on spot because the rules of inheritance dictate that a dog can do anything an animal can.

What if the Dog class, however, overrides the eat() function in the Animal class? Even if spot is declared as an Animal, Java will determine that its true identity is that of a Dog and run the appropriate version of the eat() function.

This is particularly useful when you have an array.

Let's rewrite the shape example from the previous section to include many Circle objects and many Square objects.

```
// Many Squares and many Circles
Square[] s = new Square[10];
Circle[] c = new Circle[20];
```

> The old "non-polymorphism" way with multiple arrays.

```
void setup() {
  size(200, 200);

  // Initialize the arrays
  for (int i = 0; i < s.length; i++) {
    s[i] = new Square(100, 100, 10);
  }
  for (int i = 0; i < c.length; i++) {
    c[i] = new Circle(100, 100, 10, color(random(255), 100));
  }
}

void draw() {
  background(100);

  // Jiggle and display all squares
  for (int i = 0; i < s.length; i++) {
    s[i].jiggle();
    s[i].display();
  }

  // Jiggle and display all circles
  for (int i = 0; i < c.length; i++) {
    c[i].jiggle();
    c[i].display();
```

```
        }
    }
```

Polymorphism allows me to simplify the above by just making one array of Shape objects that contains both Circle objects and Square objects. I do not have to worry about which are which, this will all be taken care of for me! (Also, note that the code for the classes has not changed, so I'm not including it here.) See Example 22.2.

Example 22-2. Polymorphism

```
// One array of Shapes
Shape[] shapes = new Shape[30];


void setup() {
  size(200, 200);
```

> The new polymorphism way with one array that has different types of objects that extend Shape.

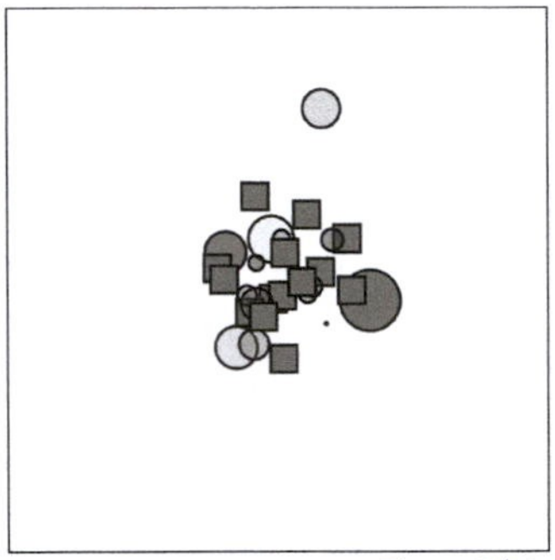

```

  for (int i = 0; i < shapes.length; i++) {
    int r = int(random(2));
    // Randomly choose a circle or square
    if (r == 0) {
      color c = color(random(255), 100);
      shapes[i] = new Circle(100, 100, 10, c);
    } else {
      shapes[i] = new Square(100, 100, 10);
    }
  }
}

void draw() {
  background(100);
  // Jiggle and display all shapes
  for (int i = 0; i < shapes.length; i++) {
    shapes[i].jiggle();
    shapes[i].display();
  }
}
```

Figure 22-3

Exercise 22-4: Add the Line class you created in Exercise 22-2 on page 497 to Example 22-2. Randomly put circles, squares, and lines in the array. Notice how you barely have to change any code (you should only have to edit setup() above).

Exercise 22-5: Implement polymorphism in the sketch you made for Exercise 22-3 on page 497.

22-5 Overloading

In Chapter 16, you learned how to create a `Capture` object in order to read live images from a video camera. If you looked at the Processing reference page (*http://www.processing.org/reference/libraries/video/Capture.html*), you may have noticed that the `Capture` constructor can be called with three, four, or five arguments:

```
Capture(parent, config)
Capture(parent, width, height)
Capture(parent, width, height, fps)
Capture(parent, width, height, name)
Capture(parent, width, height, name, fps)
```

Functions that can take varying numbers of arguments are actually something you saw all the way back in Chapter 1! `fill()`, for example, can be called with one number (for grayscale), three (for RGB color), or four (to include alpha transparency).

```
fill(255);
fill(255, 0, 255);
fill(0, 0, 255, 150);
```

The ability to define functions with the same name (but different arguments) is known as *overloading*. With `fill()`, for example, Processing does not get confused about which definition of `fill()` to look up; it simply finds the one where the arguments match. A function's name in combination with its arguments is known as the function's *signature* — it's what makes that function definition unique. Let's look at an example that demonstrates how overloading can be useful.

Let's say I have a `Fish` class. Each `Fish` object has a location: x and y.

```
class Fish {
   float x;
   float y;
```

What if, when I make a `Fish` object, I sometimes want to make one with a random location and sometimes with a specific location. To make this possible, I could write two different constructors:

```
Fish() {
   x = random(0, width);
   y = random(0, height);
}
```

> Overloading allows me to define two constructors for the same object (as long as these constructors take different arguments).

```
Fish(float tempX, float tempY) {
   x = tempX;
   y = tempY;
}
}
```

When you create a `Fish` object in the main program, you can do so with either constructor:

```
Fish fish1 = new Fish();
Fish fish2 = new Fish(100, 200);
```

> If two constructors are defined, an object can be initialized using either one.

In the discussion above, I've focused on the number of arguments (along with its name) as what defines a function. However, the argument's type is also fundamental to its signature. You could, for example, write a third `Fish` constructor with only two arguments if one of those arguments were, say, a string.

23 Java

I love coffee, I love tea, I love the Java Jive and it loves me.
—Ben Oakland and Milton Drake

In this chapter:
- Processing is really Java
- If you did not have Processing what would your code look like?
- Exploring the Java API
- Some useful Java classes: ArrayList and Rectangle
- Exception (error) handling – try and catch
- Beyond Processing?

23-1 Revealing the wizard

What is Processing exactly? Is it a programming language? It may seem a bit odd to ask this question at the very last chapter of this book. After all, I've dedicated 22 chapters to Processing. Shouldn't you know what it is by now? The truth, however, is that you have been living under something of a convenient fiction thinking that you are learning Processing. While yes, this is the title of the book, you've actually been learning a specific programming language: Java. Processing is really a piece of software with which you write code and a library of functions (ellipse, line, fill, stroke, etc.) for drawing and more. It's not a language. The language, in fact, is Java, and by pulling back the curtain of Processing, what you will discover is that you have been learning Java all along. For example, in Java, you:

- Declare, initialize, and use variables the same way.
- Declare, initialize, and use arrays the same way.
- Employ conditional and loop statements the same way.
- Define and call functions the same way.
- Create classes the same way.
- Instantiate objects the same way.

Processing, of course, gives you some extra stuff for free (and simplifies some stuff here and there), and this is why it is a great tool for learning and for developing interactive graphics projects. Here is a list of some of what Processing offers that is not as easily available with just plain Java.

- A set of functions for drawing shapes.
- A set of functions for loading and displaying text, images, and video.
- A set of functions for 3D transformations.
- A set of functions for mouse and keyboard interaction.
- A simple development environment to write your code.
- A friendly online community of artists, designers, and programmers!

23-2 If you did not have Processing, what would your code look like?

In Chapter 2, I discussed the compilation and execution process — this is what happens when you press the play button and turn your code into a window with graphics. Step 1 of this process involves "translating" your Processing code into Java. In fact, when you export to application, this same process occurs and you will notice in the source folder that along with the file "SketchName.pde," a new file will appear named "SketchName.java." This is your "translated" code, only *translation* is somewhat of a misnomer since very little changes. Let's look at an example:

```
// Randomly Growing Square
float w = 30.0; // Variable to keep track of size of rect

void setup() {
  size(640, 360);
}
```

> What you are used to seeing, your regular old Processing code.

```
void draw() {
  background(100);
  rectMode(CENTER);
  fill(255);
  noStroke();
  rect(mouseX, mouseY, w, w);   // Draw a rect at mouse location
  w + = random(-1, 1);          // Randomly adjust size variable
}
```

Exporting the sketch, you can open up the Java file and look at the Java source.

```
// Randomly Growing Square with Java Stuff
import processing.core.*;
import processing.data.*;
import processing.event.*;
import processing.opengl.*;
```

> The translated Java code has some new stuff at the top, but everything else stays the same.

```
import java.util.HashMap;
import java.util.ArrayList;
import java.io.File;
import java.io.BufferedReader;
import java.io.PrintWriter;
import java.io.InputStream;
import java.io.OutputStream;
import java.io.IOException;


// Randomly Growing Square
public class JavaExample extends PApplet {

  // Variable to keep track of size of rect
  float w = 30.0f;
```

> Numbers have an 'f' next to them to indicate floating point.

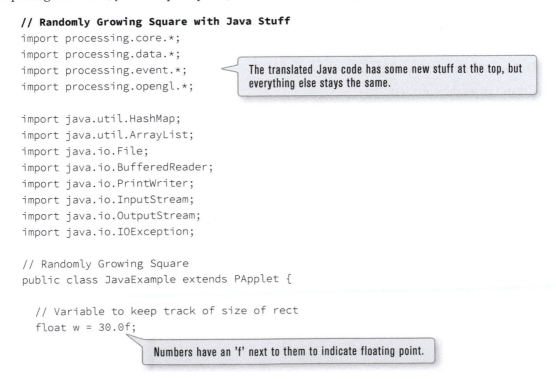

```
public void setup() {
  size(640, 360);
}
```

> Functions are defined as `public`.

```
public void draw() {
  background(100);
  rectMode(CENTER);
  fill(255);
  noStroke();
  rect(mouseX, mouseY, w, w);   // Draw a rect at mouse location
  w += random(-1, 1);           // Randomly adjust size variable
}

static public void main(String[] passedArgs) {
  String[] appletArgs = new String[] { "JavaExample" };
  if (passedArgs != null) {
    PApplet.main(concat(appletArgs, passedArgs));
  } else {
    PApplet.main(appletArgs);
  }
}
}
```

> There's a new function called main.

It's clear that little has changed; rather, some code has been added before and after the usual `setup()` and `draw()` functions.

- **Import Statements** — At the top, there are a set of import statements allowing access to certain libraries. You have seen this before when using Processing libraries. If you were using regular Java instead of Processing, specifying all libraries would always be required. Processing, however, assumes a base set of libraries from Java (e.g., `java.io.File*`) and from Processing (e.g., `processing.core.*`), which is why you do not see these in every sketch.

- **public** — In Java, variables, functions, and classes can be `public` or `private`. This designation indicates what level of access should be granted to a particular piece of code. It's not something you have to worry much about in the simpler Processing environment, but it becomes an important consideration when moving on to larger Java programs. As an individual programmer, you're most often granting or denying access to yourself, as a means for protecting against errors. You encountered some examples of this in Chapter 22's discussion about encapsulation.

- **class JavaExample** — Sound somewhat familiar? Java, it turns out, is a true object-oriented language. Everything written in Java is part of a class! You are used to the idea of the `Zoog` class, `Car` class, `PImage` class, and so on, but it is important to note that the sketch as a whole is a class, too! Processing fills this stuff in for you so you do not have to worry about classes when you are first learning to program.

- **extends PApplet** — Well, after reading Chapter 22, you should be quite comfortable with what this means. This is just another example of inheritance. Here, the class `JavaExample` is a *child* of the class `PApplet` (or, equivalently, `PApplet` is the *parent* of `JavaExample`). `PApplet` is a class developed by the creators of Processing and by *extending* it, the sketch has access to all of the Processing goodies —

`setup()`, `draw()`, `mouseX`, `mouseY`, and so on. This little bit of code is the secret behind how almost everything works in a Processing sketch.

Processing has served you so well because it eliminates the need to worry about the above four elements, all the while providing access to the benefits of the Java programming language. The rest of this chapter will show how you can begin to make use of access to the full Java API. (You briefly began this journey when you worked with string parsing in Chapter 17 and Chapter 18.)

23-3 Exploring the Java API

The Processing reference quickly became your best friend forever while learning to program. The Java API will start off more as an acquaintance you bump into from time to time. That acquaintance might turn into a really excellent friend someday, but for now, small doses will be just fine.

You can explore the full Java documentation by visiting:

http://www.oracle.com/technetwork/java/index.html

There, you can click over to API specifications:

http://www.oracle.com/technetwork/java/api-141528.html

and find a selection of versions of Java. While most machines will likely have a version of Java installed, Processing includes Java in the application itself (at the time of this writing, Java version 1.8.0_31). While there are differences between versions of Java, for your purposes they will not be terribly relevant, and you can look at the API for Java 1.8. See Figure 23-1.

And so, very quickly, you will find yourself completely lost. And that is OK. The Java API is huge. Humongous. It's not really meant to be read or even *perused*. It's really purely a reference, for looking up specific classes that you know you need to look up.

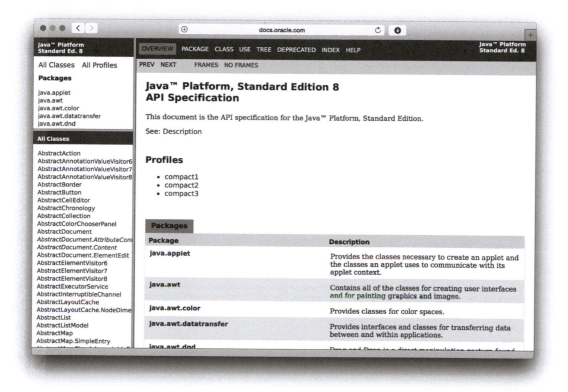

Figure 23-1 http://docs.oracle.com/javase/8/docs/api/

For example, you might be working on a program that requires sophisticated random number generation beyond what `random()` can do, and you overheard a conversation about the class `Random` and thought "Hey, maybe I should check that out!" The reference page for a specific class can be found by scrolling down the "All Classes" list, or else by selecting the right *package* (in this case the package **java.util**). A package, much like a library, is a collection of classes (the API organizes them by topic). The easiest way to find a class, though, is to just type the name of the class and Java (i.e., "Java Random") into google. The documentation page is just about always the first result. See Figure 23-2.

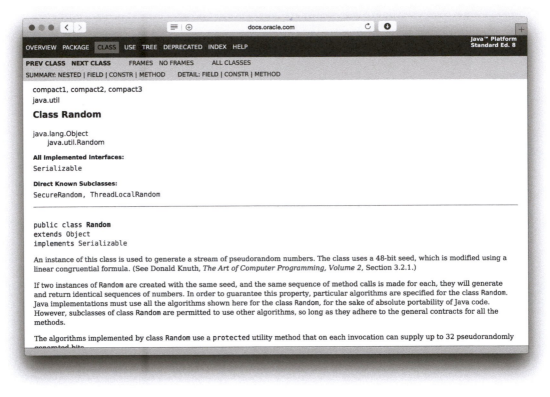

Figure 23-2

Just as with the Processing reference, the Java page includes an explanation of what the class does, the constructors for creating an object instance, and available fields (variables) and methods (functions). Since Random is not imported already, Processing imports by assumption, you do not need to explicitly write an import statement referencing the java.util package to use it.

Here is some code that makes a Random object and calls the function nextBoolean() on it to get a random true or false.

Example 23-1. Using java.util.Random instead of *random()*

```
import java.util.Random;

Random r;

void setup() {
  size(640, 360);
  r = new Random();

}
void draw() {
  boolean trueorfalse = r.nextBoolean();
  if (trueorfalse) {
    background(0);
  } else {
    background(255);
  }
}
```

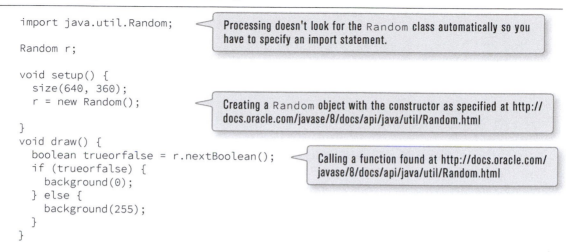

Processing doesn't look for the `Random` class automatically so you have to specify an import statement.

Creating a `Random` object with the constructor as specified at http://docs.oracle.com/javase/8/docs/api/java/util/Random.html

Calling a function found at http://docs.oracle.com/javase/8/docs/api/java/util/Random.html

Exercise 23-1: Visit the Java reference page for Random *and use it to get a random integer between 0 and 9. http://docs.oracle.com/javase/8/docs/api/java/util/Random.html.*

23-4 Other useful Java classes: `ArrayList`

In Chapter 6, you learned how to use an array to keep track of ordered lists of information. You created an array of *N* objects and used a `for` loop to access each element in the array. The size of that array was fixed — you were limited to having *N* and only *N* elements.

There are alternatives. One option is to use a very large array and use a variable to track how much of the array to use at any given time (see Chapter 10's rain catcher example). Processing also offers `expand()`, `contract()`, `subset()`, `splice()` and other methods for resizing arrays. It would be great, however, to have a class that implements a flexibly sized array, allowing items to be added or removed from the beginning, middle, and end of that array.

This is exactly what the Java class `ArrayList` (also found in the java.util package) does.

The reference page is here: http://docs.oracle.com/javase/8/docs/api/java/util/ArrayList.html.

Using an `ArrayList` is conceptually similar to a standard array, but the syntax is different. Here is some code (that assumes the existence of a class `Particle`) demonstrating identical results, first with an array, and second with an `ArrayList`. All of the methods used in this example are documented on the JavaDoc reference page.

```
// The array way
// Declaring the array
Particle[] parray = new Particle[10];
```

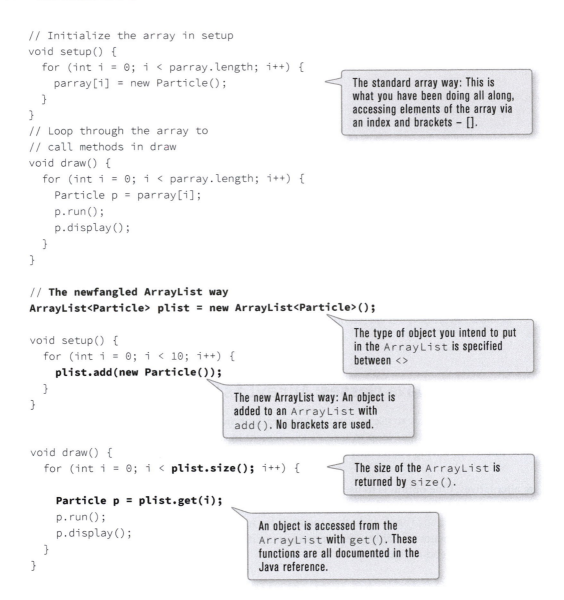

```
// Initialize the array in setup
void setup() {
  for (int i = 0; i < parray.length; i++) {
    parray[i] = new Particle();
  }
}
// Loop through the array to
// call methods in draw
void draw() {
  for (int i = 0; i < parray.length; i++) {
    Particle p = parray[i];
    p.run();
    p.display();
  }
}
```

The standard array way: This is what you have been doing all along, accessing elements of the array via an index and brackets – [].

```
// The newfangled ArrayList way
ArrayList<Particle> plist = new ArrayList<Particle>();

void setup() {
  for (int i = 0; i < 10; i++) {
    plist.add(new Particle());
  }
}
```

The type of object you intend to put in the ArrayList is specified between <>

The new ArrayList way: An object is added to an ArrayList with add(). No brackets are used.

```
void draw() {
  for (int i = 0; i < plist.size(); i++) {

    Particle p = plist.get(i);
    p.run();
    p.display();
  }
}
```

The size of the ArrayList is returned by size().

An object is accessed from the ArrayList with get(). These functions are all documented in the Java reference.

Perhaps the strangest new syntax here is the declaration of the ArrayList itself. Typically when you declare an object (like PImage) you say simply the data type and the variable name:

```
PImage img;
```

With an ArrayList, however, you can say both the data type of the thing itself (ArrayList) and the data type of what you will store inside!

```
ArrayList<PImage> images;
```

A list of PImage objects!

While it's not technically required to specify the data type of what you intend to put in the ArrayList in advance, doing so simplifies the code you'll write later when using the ArrayList. For example, it opens up the possibility of an "enhanced loop."

```
for (Particle p : particles) {
    p.run();
}
```

Let's translate that. Say "for each" instead of "for" and say "in" instead of ":". Now you have:

"For each Particle p in particles, run that Particle p!"

This style of loop (sometimes referred to as "for each") is a feature of many programming languages and arrived in Java version 1.5. This type of loop can also be used with regular arrays and only recently starting appearing in Processing examples. For simplicity I did not introduce this style of loop in Chapter 9, but now is a good time to go back and revisit.

 Exercise 23-2: Rewrite any of the Chapter 9 examples using an enhanced loop.

What I've done so far by simply using a fixed size of 10 has not unlocked the power of the ArrayList. The Following is a better example that adds one new particle to the ArrayList with each cycle through draw(). I also make sure the ArrayList never gets larger than 100 particles. See Figure 23-3.

> The term "particle system" was coined in 1983 by William T. Reeves as he developed the "Genesis" effect for the end of the movie, *Star Trek II: The Wrath of Khan.*
>
> A particle system is typically a collection of independent objects, usually represented by a simple shape or dot. It can be used to model types of natural phenomena, such as explosions, fire, smoke, sparks, waterfalls, clouds, fog, petals, grass, bubbles, and so on.

Example 23-2. Simple particle system with ArrayList

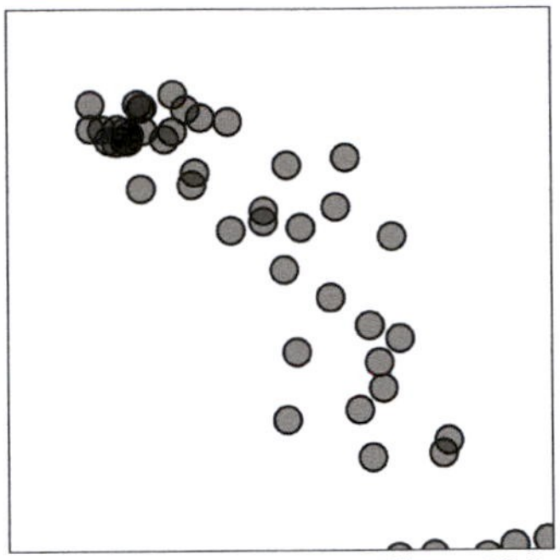

```
ArrayList<Particle> particles;

void setup() {
  size(200, 200);
  particles = new ArrayList<Particle>();
}

void draw() {

  particles.add(new Particle());


  background(255);
```

> A new `Particle` object is added to the `ArrayList` every cycle through `draw()`.

Figure 23-3

```
  // Iterate through the ArrayList and get each Particle

  for (Particle p : particles) {
    p.run();
    p.gravity();
    p.display();
  }
```

> Using an enhanced loop to iterate through all `Particle` objects.

```
  if (particles.size() > 100) {
    particles.remove(0);
  }
}
```

> If the `ArrayList` has more than 100 elements in it, delete the first element, using `remove()`.

```
// A simple Particle class
class Particle {
  float x;
  float y;
  float xspeed;
  float yspeed;


  Particle() {
    x = mouseX;
    y = mouseY;
    xspeed = random(-1, 1);
    yspeed = random(-2, 0);
  }

  void run() {
    x = x + xspeed;
    y = y + yspeed;
  }

  void gravity() {
    yspeed + = 0.1;
  }

  void display() {
    stroke(0);
```

```
        fill(0, 75);
        ellipse(x, y, 10, 10);
    }
}
```

Exercise 23-3: Rewrite Example 23-2 so that particles are removed from the list whenever they leave the window (i.e., their y location is greater than height). Note that you cannot use the enhanced loop syntax when modifying an ArrayList *inside the loop.*

Hint: Add a function that returns a boolean in the Particle *class when the particle leaves the window.*

```
_____ offScreen() {

    if (_____) {

        return _____;
    } else {
        return false;
    }
}
```

Hint: In order for this to work properly, you must iterate through elements of the ArrayList *backward! Why? Because when an element is removed, all subsequent elements are shifted to the left (see Figure 23-4).*

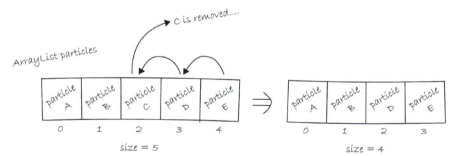

Figure 23-4

```
for (int i = _____; i _____; i_____) {
    Particle p = particles.get(i);
    p.run();
    p.gravity();
    p.render();
    if (_____) {

        _____;
    }
}
```

Before you move on I'd like to look at one other scenario where the `ArrayList` class is useful. In Example 9-8, I looked at how to store a history of mouse locations using two arrays, one for x-values and one for y-values.

```
int[] xpos = new int[50];
int[] ypos = new int[50];
```

I made this example before looking at arrays of objects, but with all that you now know I can make a couple of key improvements. The first one is that I can simplify and use a single array. After all, if I had a `Point` class that stored an x and y then all I need is an array of `Point` objects.

```
class Point {
    float x;
    float y;
}

Point[] positions = new Point[50];
```

In fact, to implement this I don't even need to create a `Point` class. This sort of scenario comes up so often that Processing includes a built-in class for this very purpose: `PVector`. To make a `PVector` object I simply pass an x and y into the constructor.

```
PVector mouse = new PVector(mouseX, mouseY);
```

> A `PVector` object stores an x and a y together (and, optionally, a z if you're working in three dimensions.

I can then access the invididual x and y components of a `PVector` using the dot syntax.

```
ellipse(mouse.x, mouse.y, 16, 16);
```

In terms of the scope of this book, I'm going to stop here in the discussion of vectors and the `PVector` class. A full explanation and discussion of vectors and their various applications can be found in The Nature of Code (*http://natureofcode.com*) book which is freely avaialable online.

For us, the key here is that once I have an object to store an (x,y) position, I can then use an `ArrayList` to store a history of those positions.

```
ArrayList<PVector> history = new ArrayList<PVector>();
```

> An `ArrayList` of `PVector` objects.

I can add a mouse position to the `ArrayList`.

```
PVector mouse = new PVector(mouseX, mouseY);
history.add(mouse);
```

> Every time through draw, add a new `PVector` to the list.

And I can also remove old entries if the list gets too big.

```
if (history.size() > 50) {
    history.remove(0);
}
```

> New objects are added to the end of an `ArrayList` so the object at index 0 is the oldest one in the list.

Here's how the full Snake example now looks using an `ArrayList` of `PVector` objects.

Example 23-3. Store the mouse history as ArrayList of PVector objects

```
ArrayList<PVector> history = new ArrayList<PVector>();

void setup() {
  size(640, 360);
}

void draw() {
  background(255);

  // New mouse position
  PVector mouse = new PVector(mouseX, mouseY);
  history.add(mouse);

  // Remove old ones
  if (history.size() > 50) {
    history.remove(0);
  }

  // Draw everything
  for (int i = 0; i < history.size(); i++ ) {
    noStroke();
    fill(255-i*5);
    // Grab the current PVector
    PVector position = history.get(i);
    // Look at the x and y of each PVector
    ellipse(position.x, position.y, i, i);
  }
}
```

Figure 23-5

> Looping through the `ArrayList` according to its current size.

Exercise 23-4: Revise the particle system example so that each particle stores a history of its locations in an `ArrayList` *of* PVector *objects. What kinds of trails can you draw given this addition? (You might also consider storing each particle's position and speed as vectors also. For more about how this works, take a look at Chapter 1 of the Nature of Code book (http://natureofcode.com/book/chapter-1-vectors).)*

Here's one last tidbit about resizable arrays before I move on. You might have noticed that none of my ArrayList examples use a list of integers, floats, or strings. While I could use an ArrayList to keep track of these data types, Processing includes three additional classes that I briefly mentioned in Chapter 18. IntList, FloatList, and StringList precisely for this purpose. These lists are internally more efficient than an ArrayList and a bit easier to deal with since you don't have to worry about maintaining the data type. They also let you sort the lists (ascending/descending) without having to dive into the Java Collections class. I would suggest that any time you'd want to use ArrayList for numbers or text, you're better off with Processing's lists.

23-5 Other useful Java classes: `Rectangle`

The second helpful Java class I will examine is the `Rectangle` class:

http://docs.oracle.com/javase/8/docs/api/java/awt/Rectangle.html.

A Java `Rectangle` specifies an area in a coordinate space that is enclosed by the `Rectangle` object's top-left point (x,y), its width, and its height. Sound familiar? Of course, the Processing function `rect()` draws a rectangle with precisely the same parameters. The `Rectangle` class encapsulates the idea of a rectangle into an object.

The Java `Rectangle` class includes useful methods, for instance, `contains()`. `contains()` offers a simple way of checking if a point or rectangle is located inside that rectangle, by receiving an x and a y and returning true or false, based on whether that (x,y) point is inside the rectangle or not.

Here is a simple rollover implemented with a `Rectangle` object and `contains()`. See Example 23-4.

Example 23-4. Using a java.awt.Rectangle object

```
import java.awt.Rectangle;          Import from the java.awt package

Rectangle rect1, rect2;

void setup() {
  size(640, 360);
  rect1 = new Rectangle(100, 75, 50, 50);
  rect2 = new Rectangle(300, 150, 150, 75);
}
```

This sketch uses two Rectangle objects. The arguments for the constructor are: `x`, `y`, `width`, `height`.

Figure 23-6

```
void draw() {
  background(255);
  stroke(0);

  if (rect1.contains(mouseX, mouseY)) {
    fill(200);
  } else {
    fill(100);
  }
```

The `contains()` function is used to determine if the mouse is located inside the rectangle.

```
  rect(rect1.x, rect1.y, rect1.width, rect1.height);

  // Repeat for the second Rectangle
  // (of course, I could use an array or ArrayList here!)
  if (rect2.contains(mouseX, mouseY)) {
    fill(200);
  } else {
    fill(100);
  }
  rect(rect2.x, rect2.y, rect2.width, rect2.height);
}
```

A `Rectangle` object only knows about the data associated with a rectangle. It cannot draw itself. So I still use Processing's `rect()` in combination.

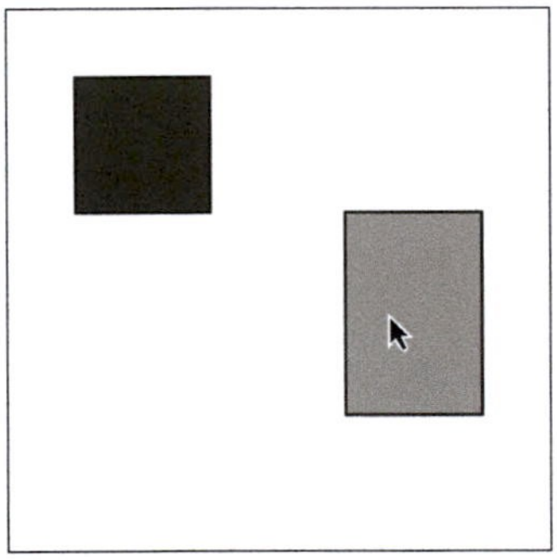

Let's have some fun and combine the particle system example with the rollover. In Example 23-5, particles are made every frame and pulled down by gravity toward the bottom of the window. If they run into a rectangle, however, they are caught. The particles are stored in an `ArrayList` and a `Rectangle` object determines if they have been caught or not. (This example contains answers to Exercise 23-3 on page 513.)

Example 23-5. Super fancy ArrayList and rectangle particle system

```
// Java Rectangle class is not automatically imported
import java.awt.Rectangle;

// Declaring a global variable of type ArrayList
ArrayList<Particle> particles;
// A "Rectangle" will suck up particles
Rectangle blackhole;

void setup() {
  size(640, 360);
  blackhole = new Rectangle(200, 200, 150, 75);
  particles = new ArrayList<Particle>();
}

void draw() {
  background(255);

  // Displaying the Rectangle
  stroke(0);
  fill(175);
  rect(blackhole.x, blackhole.y, blackhole.width, blackhole.height);

  // Add a new particle at mouse location
  particles.add(new Particle(mouseX, mouseY));

  // Loop through all Particles
  for (int i = particles.size()-1; i >= 0; i--) {
    Particle p = particles.get(i);
    p.run();
    p.gravity();
    p.display();
    if (blackhole.contains(p.x, p.y)) {
      p.stop();
    }
    if (p.finished()) {
      particles.remove(i);
    }
  }
}

// A simple Particle Class
class Particle {
  float x;
  float y;
  float xspeed;
  float yspeed;
  float life;
```

Figure 23-7

> If the `Rectangle` object contains the location of the particle, stop the particle from moving.

```
// Make the Particle
Particle(float tempX, float tempY) {
  x = tempX;
  y = tempY;
  xspeed = random(-1, 1);
  yspeed = random(-2, 0);
  life = 255;
}

// Move
void run() {
  x = x + xspeed;
  y = y + yspeed;
}

// Fall down
void gravity() {
  yspeed + = 0.1;
}

// Stop moving
void stop() {
  xspeed = 0;
  yspeed = 0;
}

// Ready for deletion
boolean finished() {
  life -= 2.0;
  if (life < 0) {
    return true;
  } else {
    return false;
  }
}

// Show
void display() {
  stroke(0);
  fill(0, life);
  ellipse(x, y, 10, 10);
}
}
```

> The particle has a `life` variable which decreases. When it goes below 0 the particle can be removed from the `ArrayList`.

23-6 Exception (error) handling

In addition to a very large library of useful classes, the Java programming language includes some features beyond what I have covered in this book. I will explore one of those features now: *exception handling*.

Programming mistakes happen. We have all seen them.

```
java.lang.ArrayIndexOutOfBoundsException
```

```
java.io.IOException: openStream() could not open file.jpg
```

```
java.lang.NullPointerException
```

It's sad when these errors occur. Really, it is. The error message prints out and the program sputters to a halt, never to continue running again. Perhaps you have developed some techniques for protecting against these error messages. For example:

```
if (index < somearray.length) {
   somearray[index] = random(0, 100);
}
```

The above is a form of "error checking." The code uses a conditional to check that the index is valid before an element at that index is accessed. The above code is quite conscientious and we should all aspire to be so careful.

Not all situations are as simple to avoid, however, and this is where *exception handling* comes into play. Exception handling refers to the process of handling *exceptions*, out of the ordinary events (i.e., errors) that occur during the execution of a program.

The code structure for exception handling in Java is known as *try catch*. In other words, "*Try* to run some code. If you run into a problem, however, *catch* the error and run some other code." If an error is caught using try catch, the program is allowed to continue. Let's look at how I might rewrite the array index error checking code try catch style.

```
try {
   somearray[index] = 200;
} catch (Exception e) {
   println("Hey, that's not a valid index!");
}
```

> The code that might produce an error goes within the "try" section. The code that should happen if an error occurs goes in the "catch" section.

The above code catches any possible exception that might occur. The type of error caught is the generic Exception. However, if you want to execute certain code based on a specific exception, you can, as the following code demonstrates.

```
try {
   somearray[index] = 200;
} catch (ArrayIndexOutOfBoundsException e) {
   println("Hey, " + index + " is not a valid index!");
} catch (NullPointerException e) {
   println("I think you forgot to create the array!");
} catch (Exception e) {
   println("Hmmm, I dunno, something weird happened");
   e.printStackTrace();
}
```

> Different "catch" sections catch different types of exceptions. In addition, each exception is an object and can therefore have methods called on it. For example:`e.printStackTrace();` displays more detailed information about the exception.

The above code, nevertheless, does nothing more than print out custom error messages. There are situations where I want more than just an explanation. For example, take the examples from Chapter 18 where I loaded data from a URL path. What if the sketch had failed to connect to the URL? It would have crashed and quit. With exception handling, I can catch that error and fill an XML object manually so that the sketch can continue running.

```
XML data;
String url = "http://lovelyapi.com/lovely.xml";
try {
  data = loadXML(url);
} catch (Exception e) {
  data = parseXML("<mood>joyful</mood>");
}

println(data);
```

> If a problem occurs connecting to the URL, fill the XML object with dummy data so that the sketch can still run.

23-7 Java outside of Processing

Here I am, the very last section of this book. You can take a break now if you want. Maybe go outside and have a walk. A little jog around the block even. It will be good for you.

OK, back now? Great, let's go on.

As I close out this chapter and the book, I will cover one final topic: what to do if and when you decide you want to start coding outside of Processing.

But why would you ever want to do this?

One instance that would merit another programming environment is in the case of making an application that does not involve any graphics! Perhaps you need to write a program that takes all of your financial info from spreadsheets and logs it in a database. Or a chat server that runs in the background on your computer. While both of these could be written in the Processing environment, they do not necessarily need any of the features of Processing to run.

In the case of developing larger and larger projects that involve many classes, the Processing environment can become a bit difficult to use. For example, what if your project involves, say, 20 classes. Creating a Processing sketch with 20 tabs (and what if it were 40? or 100?) can be hard to manage, let alone fit on the screen. In this case, a development environment designed for large-scale Java projects would be better. Since Processing is Java, you can still use all of the functions available in Processing in other development environments by importing the core libraries.

So, what do you do? First, I would say do not rush. Enjoy Processing and take the time to feel comfortable with your own coding process and style before getting yourself wrapped up in the myriad of issues and questions that come along with programming in Java.

If you feel ready, a good first step is to just take some time browsing the Java website (*http://java.sun.com/*) and start with one of the tutorials (*http://docs.oracle.com/javase/tutorial/*). The tutorials will cover the same material found in this book, but from a pure Java perspective.

The next step would be to just try compiling and running a "Hello World" Java program.

```java
public class HelloWorld {

  public static void main(String[] args) {
    System.out.println("Hello World. I miss you, Processing.");
  }
}
```

The Java site has tutorials which explain all the elements in a Hello World program, as well as provide instructions on how to compile and run it on the "command line."

http://docs.oracle.com/javase/tutorial/getStarted/application/index.html

Finally, if you are feeling ambitious, go and download Eclipse:

http://www.eclipse.org/

Eclipse is a development environment for Java with many advanced features. Some of those features will give you a headache and some will make you wonder how you ever programmed without Eclipse. Just remember, when you started with Processing in Chapter 2, you were probably up and running with your first sketch in less than five minutes. With something like Eclipse, you could need a much longer time to get started. See Figure 23-8.

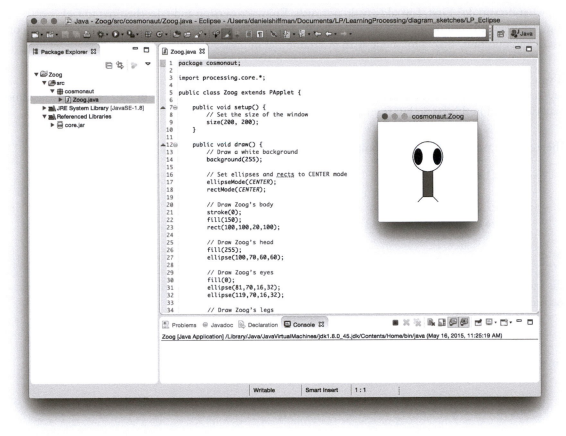

Figure 23-8 A Processing sketch in Eclipse

Visit this book's web site for links and tutorials about how to run a Processing sketch within the Eclipse environment.

Thanks for reading. Feedback is encouraged and appreciated, so come on down to *http://learningprocessing.com* and sound off!

Appendix A: Common Errors

This appendix offers a brief overview of common errors that occur in Processing, what those errors mean and why they occur. Whenever possible, Processing attempts to rephrase an error message to be clear and friendly, however the language of error messages is still often cryptic and confusing, mostly due to their origins in the Java programming language.

For these error messages, I will use the following conventions:

- Variables in the error messages will be named `myVar`.
- Arrays in the error messages will be named `myArray`.
- If the error is related to a class, the class will be named `Thing`.
- If the error is specifically related to an object variable, the variable will instead be named `myThing`.
- If the error is related to a function, the function will be named `myFunction`.

There is also another important distinction to be made regarding errors. Some errors are syntax errors and stop the program from starting. These are shown with a red squiggly line under text in the editor window as well as listed in the error console at the bottom. These errors are often called "compile-time" errors since they are caught at the moment Processing attempts to compile the code.

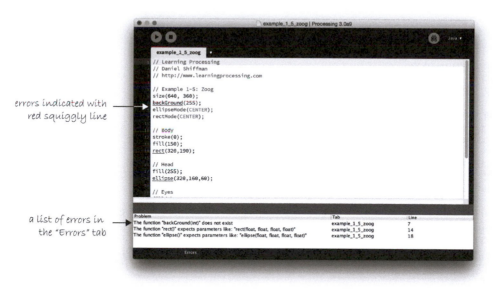

errors indicated with red squiggly line

a list of errors in the "Errors" tab

Figure A-1 compile-time errors (before you press run)

Another category is "runtime" errors. These are errors that are not caught before the code is run but rather occur due to a flaw or bug in the program itself. These are often harder to pinpoint though some tips are offered in Chapter 11. In Java these errors are *exceptions* as covered in Section 23-6 on page 518.

line highlighted when error occurs
while sketch is running

type of error indicated here

Figure A-2 runtime errors (after you press run)

Compile-time errors

Error	Page number
Missing a semi-colon ";"	525
Missing left parentheses "("	525
Missing right curly bracket "}"	526
The variable "myVar" doesn't exist.	526
The local variable "myVar" may not have been initialized.	527
The class "Thing" doesn't exist.	528
The function "myFunction()" expects parameters like this: myFunction(type, type, type, …)	529
The method "myFunction(type, type, type, …)" does not exist.	529
Error on "___"	530

Runtime errors

Error	Page number
java.lang.NullPointerException	530
java.lang.ArrayIndexOutOfBoundsException	532

A-1 Compile-time errors

Missing a semi-colon ";"

This error means exactly what it says! You have a line of code that requires a semi-colon but one is missing.

Here are some examples (with correction bolded):

Error	Corrected
`int val = 5`	`int val = 5;`

`for (int i = 0; i < 10 i++) {`
 	
`}`
	`for (int i = 0; i < 10; i++) {`
	
	`}`

Missing left parentheses "("

This error means exactly what it says! You have a conditonal statement, function call, or some other line of code that requires parenthesis and you are missing one of them. Processing will tell you whether it's left or right.

Here are some examples (same convention, bolded correction):

Error	Corrected

`if x < 5) {`
`  background(0);`
`}`
	`if (x < 5) {`
	`  background(0);`
	`}`

`background0);`	`background(0);`

Missing right curly bracket "}"

You forgot to close a block of code, such as an if statement, a loop, a function, a class, and so on.

Any time you have an opening (a.k.a. left) curly bracket in your code ("{"), you must have a matching closing (a.k.a right) curly bracket ("}"). And since blocks of code are often nested inside each other, it's easy to forget one by accident, resulting in this error. Processing will typically let you know whether you are missing a left or right curly bracket but in some cases when it's confused it may just say "Error on }".

Error	Corrected
```void setup() { for (int i = 0; i < 10; i++) { if (i > 5) { line(0, i, i, 0); } } ```	```void setup() { for (int i = 0; i < 10; i++) { if (i > 5) { line(0, i, i, 0); } } } ```

> Missing a right curly bracket!

> }

The variable "myVar" doesn't exist.

You are using a variable called "myVar" but it was never declared anywhere I can see.

This error will happen if you do not declare a variable. Remember, you can't use a variable until you have said what type it should be. You will get the error if you write:

```
myVar = 10;
```

instead of:

```
int myVar = 10;
```

Of course, you should only declare the variable once, otherwise you can run into trouble. So this is perfectly OK:

```
int myVar = 10;
myVar = 20;
```

> OK! The variable was declared.

This error can also occur if you try to use a local variable outside of the block of code where it was declared. For example:

```
if (mousePressed) {
   int myVar = 10;
}
ellipse(myVar, 10, 10, 10);
```

> Error! myVar is local to the if statement so it cannot be accessed here.

Here is a corrected version:

```
int myVar = 0;
if (mousePressed) {
  myVar = 10;
}

ellipse(myVar, 10, 10, 10);
```
> OK! The variable is declared outside of the if statement.

Or if you have declared a variable in setup(), but try to use it in draw().

```
void setup() {
  int myVar = 10;
}

void draw() {
  ellipse(myVar, 10, 10, 10);
}
```
> Error! myVar is local to the setup() so it cannot be accessed here.

Corrected:

```
int myVar = 0;

void setup() {
  myVar = 10;
}

void draw() {
  ellipse(myVar, 10, 10, 10);
}
```
> OK! The variable is global.

The same error will occur if you use an array in any of the above scenarios.

```
myArray[0] = 10;
```
> Error! No array was declared.

The local variable "myVar" may not have been initialized.

You declared the variable "myVar", but you did not initialize it. You should give it a value first.

This is a pretty simple error to fix. Most likely, you just forgot to give your variable its default starting value. This error only occurs for local variables (with global variables Processing will either not care, and assume the value is zero, or else throw a NullPointerException).

```
int myVar;
line(0, myVar, 0, 0);
```
> Error! myVar does not have a value.

```
int myVar = 10;
line(0, myVar, 0, 0);
```
> OK! myVar equals ten.

This error can also occur if you try to use an array before allocating its size properly.

```
int[] myArray;
myArray[0] = 10;
```
> Error! myArray was not created properly.

```
int[] myArray = new int[3];
myArray[0] = 10;
```
> OK! myArray is an array of three integers.

The class "Thing" doesn't exist.

You are trying to declare a variable of type Thing, but there is no data type Thing. Maybe you meant to make a class called Thing?

This error occurs because you either (a) forgot to define a class called Thing or (b) made a typo in the variable type.

A typo is pretty common:

```
intt myVar = 10;
```
> Error! You probably meant to type int not intt.

Or maybe you want to create an object of type Thing, but forgot to define the thing class.

```
Thing myThing = new Thing();
```
> Error! If you did not define a class called Thing.

This will work, of course, if you write:

```
Thing myThing;

void setup() {
  myThing = new Thing();
}
```
> OK! You did declare a class called Thing.

```
class Thing {
  Thing() { }
}
```

Finally, the error will also occur if you try to use an object from a library, but forget to import the library.

```
Capture video;

void setup() {
  video = new Capture(this, 320, 240);
}
```
> Error! You forgot to import the video library.

In this case, if Processing can, it will provide a suggestion for which library to import.

Corrected:

```
import processing.video.*;

Capture video;

void setup() {
  video = new Capture(this, 320, 240);       OK! You imported the library.
}
```

When possible Processing will offer import suggestions and you can click on them to automatically add the correct import statement to your code.

The function "myFunction()" expects parameters like this: myFunction(type, type, type, ...)

You are calling a function incorrectly, and you need these arguments to call it correctly.

This error occurs most often when you call a function with the incorrect number of arguments. For example, to draw an ellipse, you need an x location, y location, width, and height. But if you write:

```
ellipse(100, 100, 50);       Error! ellipse() requires four arguments.
```

You will get the error: "The function "ellipse()" expects parameters like this: ellipse(float, float, float, float)" The error provides the function signature, indicating you need four arguments, all floating point. The same error will also occur if you have the right number of arguments, but the wrong type.

```
ellipse(100, 100, 50, "wrong type of argument");       Error! ellipse() cannot take a string!
```

The method "function(type, type, type, ...)" doesn't exist.

You are calling a function that I have never heard of. I have no idea what you are talking about!

This is a similar error and occurs when have the wrong name for a function even if you have the correct arguments.

```
elipse(100, 100, 50, 50);       Error! You have the right number of arguments, but you spelled "ellipse" incorrectly.

functionCompletelyMadeUp(200);       Error! Unless you have defined this function, Processing has no way of knowing what it is.
```

Same goes for a function that is called on an object.

```
Capture video = new Capture(this, 320, 240, 30);

video.turnPurple();
```

> Error! There is no function called
> turnPurple() in the Capture class.

Error on "_____"

I have no idea what this error is! But here's the character that I think is causing the problem.

When Processing cannot give you a detailed error message it just points out the line of code and character where it thinks the error is occuring. It usually gets it right, but you may want to check the line above and below just in case too. The most common cause of this error message is a stray character that is invalid.

```
float x = 0;

void draw() {
  x = x + 1:
}
```

> Error! Most likely you simply typed the ':'
> symbol by accident. It's fairly obvious a semi-
> colon was intended, but Processing is not able
> to guess here!

A-2 Runtime errors

java.lang.NullPointerException

I have encountered a variable whose value is null. I can't work with this.

The NullPointerException error can be one of the most difficult errors to fix. It's most commonly caused by forgetting to initialize an object. As mentioned in Chapter 8, when you declare a variable that is an object, it's first given the value of null, meaning nothing. (This does not apply to primitives, such as integers and floats.) If you attempt to then use that variable without having initialized it (by calling the constructor), this error will occur. Here are a few examples (that assume the existence of a class called Thing).

```
Thing thing;

void setup() {
  size(200, 200);
}

void draw() {
  thing.display();
}
```

> Error! thing was never initialized and
> therefore has the value null.

Corrected:

```
Thing thing;

void setup() {
   thing = new Thing();
}

void draw() {
   thing.display();
}
```

OK! `thing` is not `null` because it was initialized with the constructor.

OK! `thing` is not `null` because it was initialized with the constructor.

Sometimes, the same error can occur if you do initialize the object, but as a local variable by accident.

```
Thing thing;

void setup() {
   Thing thing = new Thing();
}

void draw() {
   thing.display();
}
```

Error! This line of code declares and initializes a different `thing` variable (even though it has the same name). It's a local variable for only `setup()`. The global `thing` is still null!

The same goes for an array as well. If you forget to initialize the elements, you will get this error.

```
Thing[] things = new Thing[10];

for (int i = 0; i < things.length; i++) {
   things[i].display();
}
```

Error! All the elements in the array are `null`!

Corrected:

```
Thing[] things = new Thing[10];

for (int i = 0; i < things.length; i++) {
   things[i] = new Thing();
}

for (int i = 0; i < things.length; i++) {
   things[i].display();
}
```

OK! The first loop initialized the elements of the array.

Finally, if you forget to allocate space for an array, you can also end up with this error.

```
int[] myArray;

void setup() {
```

```
    myArray[0] = 5;
}
```

> Error! myArray is null because you never created it and gave it a size.

Corrected:

```
int[] myArray = new int[3];

void setup() {
  myArray[0] = 5;
}
```

> OK! myArray is an array of three integers.

java.lang.ArrayIndexOutOfBoundsException:

You tried to access an element of an array that does not exist. (Instead of "##", the error message will include the invalid index value.)

This error will happen when the index value of any array is invalid. For example, if your array is of length 10, the only valid indices are zero through nine. Anything less than zero or greater than nine will produce this error.

```
int[] myArray = new int[10];

myArray[-1] = 0
```

> Error! -1 is not a valid index.

```
myArray[0] = 0;
myArray[5] = 0;
```

> OK! 0 and 5 are valid indices.

```
myArray[10] = 0;
myArray[20] = 0;
```

> Error! 10 and 20 are not valid indices.

This error can be a bit harder to debug when you are using a variable for the index.

```
int[] myArray = new int[100];
myArray[mouseX] = 0;
```

> Error! mouseX may be bigger than 99.

```
int index = constrain(mouseX, 0, myArray.length-1);
myArray[index] = 0;
```

> OK! mouseX is constrained between 0 and 99 first.

A loop can also be the source of the problem.

```
for (int i = 0; i < 200; i++) {
  myArray[i] = 0;
}
```

> Error! i loops past 99.

```
for (int i = 0; i < myArray.length; i++) {
```

> OK! Using the length property of the array as the exit condition for the loop.

```
    myArray[i] = 0;
}

for (int i = 0; i < 200; i++) {
  if (i < myArray.length) {
    myArray[i] = 0;
  }
}
```

OK! If your loop really needs to go to 200, then you could incorporate an `if` statement inside the loop.

Index

Symbols

2D rotation, 277
3D rotation
    around different axes, 280-282
    Processing solar system example, 292
3D shapes, custom, 275
3D translation
    and transformation matrix, 285-291
    and Z-axis, 265-271
    P3D for, 271
    Processing solar system example, 292
    rotation around different axes, 280-282

A

abs() function, 60
Adobe Premiere, 482
agreements, 4
algorithms, 189
    and breaking down ideas into parts, 192
    basics, 190
    defined, 20
    for intersection functionality, 195
    for large projects, 189
    Rain Game example, 192
alpha channel, 14
alpha values, 14
amp() function, 457
amplitude, sound, 464
analysis, sound, 464
angles, 246, 247
animation
    of text, 368-370
    with images, 304
APIs (Application Programming Interfaces)
    and data input, 424-426
    Java, 506
Apple, Fiona, 67
Arduino, 444
arguments
    parameters vs., 127
    with functions, 124-128
array references, 51
array(s), 163-185
    about, 166

declaring and creating, 167-169
    initializing, 169
    interactive objects, 178
    of images, 308
    of objects, 175
    operations, 167, 170
    Processing functions, 181
    snake application, 173-174
    two-dimensional, 257-260
    uses for, 163-165
    Zoog application, 182
ArrayList class, 509-515
assignment operations, 54
asynchronous data streams, 427
available() function, 331, 429

B

background() function, 11
background(s), removing, 349-352
beginRecord() function, 477
beginShape() function, 273
BlobDetection (Gachadoat), 356
blobs, 356
Bobrow, Daniel G., 13
Boole, George, 67
boolean expressions, 67
boolean variables, 79-81
Borenstein, Greg, 356
brightness, 16, 316
broadcasting, 434
built-in libraries, 226
built-in variables, 58
buttons, 79-81

C

call(s), 123
callback function, 429
capture arguments, 330
capture class, 330
captureEvent() function, 331
CENTER mode, 6
charAt() function, 362
class data, 143
class name, 143

class(es), 140
  as data types, 155
  elements of, 143
  objects vs., 140
  tabs for, 147-150
  writing, 143
clicks, mouse, 42-43
client
  broadcasting to, 434
  creating, 432
  multi-user communication, 440
clientEvent() function, 432
coding, Processing, 23-25
color
  custom ranges, 15-17
  grayscale, 10
  RGB, 12
color transparency, 14
colorMode() function, 15
comma-separated values (CSVs), 391
commands, 4
complex data types, 146
computer vision, 345-347, 356
concatenation
  and data input, 385-388
  with Strings, 309, 364
conditionals, 67-90
  boolean expressions, 67
  boolean variables, 79-81
  bouncing ball example, 83-88
  for gravity simulation, 89-90
  if, else, else if, 68-71
  in sketch, 72
  logical operators, 75
  rollover(s), 78, 396
constrain() function, 73
constructor arguments, 151-152
constructor(s), 143, 146
contains() function, 516
contributed libraries, 226
control structure, 95
CORNER mode, 6
cosine, 247
createFont() function, 365
creative visualization, 324
custom 3D shapes, 275
custom color ranges, 15-17
custom tinting algorithms, 316

D
data folder, loading images to, 303
data input, 383-426
  and APIs, 424-426
  dealing with differing varieties of data, 388
  from data in nonstandard format, 396-400
  from XML, 406-408
  manipulating strings for, 383
  string concatenation for, 385-388
  tabular data for, 391-394
  text analysis for, 402-406
  text files for, 390
  with JSON, 414-416
  with JSONArray, 417-419
  with JSONObject, 417-419
  with Processing XML class, 409-413
  with threads, 421-423
data streams, 427-450
  broadcasting, 434
  creating a client, 432
  creating a server, 428-431
  multi-user communication (client and server), 443
  multi-user communication (client), 440
  multi-user communication (server), 437-439
  serial communication, 444-446
  serial communication with handshaking, 446
  serial communication with strings, 448
  synchronous vs. asynchronous, 427
data types
  objects as, 155
  PShape, 294
data, fake, 389
debugging, 219-224
  and simplifying your code, 220-222
  defined, 19
  functions and, 124
  getting others involved with, 220
  println() for, 222-224
  strategies for, 219-224
  taking a break before, 220
declaration
  of array, 167-169
  of object variable, 146
  of variables, 51-52
definitions, function, 123
degrees, 246
Design By Numbers, 13
Disney, Walt, 33

display() function, 123, 271
displayHeight variable, 58
displayWidth variable, 58
dist() function, 133
do-while loop, 95
draw() function, 34-41, 43, 104
drawCircle() function, 255
Drummond, Henry, 487

E

Eclipse, 521
eclipse() function, 7
edge detection/edge pixels, 321
else (boolean expression), 68-71
else if (boolean expression), 68-71
Emerson, Ralph Waldo, 33
encapsulation, 487-490
endRecord() function, 477
endShape() function, 273
equals() function, 363
error handling (Java), 518
error tracking, 25
error(s), common, 518
event probability, 237
exception (error) handling, 518
exit conditions
    for loops, 98-100
    for recursive functions, 255
export to application, 443
exporting, 473-484
    high-resolution PDFs, 476-480
    images/saveFrame(), 480
    recording video for, 480-482
    stand-alone applications, 474
    to web, 473
extends (keyword), 492

F

factorials, 253
fake data, 389
Feurzeig, Wally, 13
Feynman, Richard, 361
filter() function, 319
filter(s), 307
Final Cut, 482
flip() function, 10
FloatList class, 515
flow, interaction and, 33

fonts, 365
for loop, 100
fractals, 253
frameCount variable, 58
frameRate variable, 58
frameRate() function, 43
frequency, sound, 464
Fry, Benjamin, 13, 19, 473
fullScreen() function, 21, 23
function(s), 117-135
    alternate names for, 118
    and arguments, 124-128
    and coding, 4
    and return type, 132-134
    and simple modularity, 121-124
    array, 181
    benefits of, 121-124
    defining a, 119
    passing by copy to, 129
    reasons for writing your own, 117
    reorganizing Zoog with, 135
    user-defined, 119
functionality, 143
    adding with variables, 62
    class, 143
    intersection, 195

G

Gachadoat, Julien, 356
getter functions, 488
global variables, local variables vs., 104
graph paper, 3
gravity simulation, 89-90
grayscale color, 10

H

handshaking, 446
height variable, 58
high-resolution PDFs, 476-480
Hitchcock, Alfred, 329
Hopper, Grace Murray, 19
hour() function, 201
HSB values, 16
HTTP request and response, 428
hue, 16

I

if (boolean expression), 68-71

Igoe, Tom, 444
image() function, 304
image(s), 301-325
    animation with, 304
    arrays of, 308
    basics, 301-304
    creative visualization, 324
    custom tinting algorithms for, 316
    displaying in PDFs, 479
    filters for, 307
    introduction to processing of, 315
    loading to data folder, 303
    pixel group processing, 320-322
    pixel manipulation, 310-312
    saveFrame() for exporting, 480
imageMode() function, 304
immutable objects, 363
import statements, 505
incremental development, philosophy of, 18-20, 60
index, array elements, 166
indexOf() function, 383
infinite loops, 98-100
inheritance, 490-496
initialization
    of arrays, 169
    of objects, 146
    of variables, 51-52
installation, Processing, 20
int() function, 61
interaction, 33-45
    and flow, 33
    and key presses, 42-43
    and mouse clicks, 42-43
    and mouse location, 37-41
    arrays of interactive objects, 178
    draw() for, 34-36
    setup() for, 34-36
interactive objects, 178
interpolation, 382
intersect() function, 195-213
intersection functionality, 195-213
IntList class, 515
IP addresses, 443
isPlaying() function, 457
iteration, 93-95

J

Java, 503-522

API for, 506
ArrayList class, 509-515
exception (error) handling, 518
Processing and, 14
Processing as expansion of, 503
Processing code translated into, 504-506
Rectangle class, 516
when Processing is unnecessary, 520
Java applets, 15
Java programming language, 25
Java String class, 383
JavaExample class, 505
JSON, 414-416
JSON feed, 398
JSONArray, 417-419
JSONObject, 417-419

K

Kernighan, Brian, 12
key press(es), 42-43
key variable, 58
keyCode variable, 58
keyPressed variable, 58
keyPressed() function, 42
Kierkegaard, Soren, 93

L

length() function, 362
lerp() function, 382
libraries, 225-230
    about, 225
    built-in, 226
    computer vision, 356
    contributed, 226
    manual installation of, 227-230
line() function, 119
live video, 329-333
loadFont() method, 366
loadImage() method, 302
local variables, global variables vs., 104
localhost, 431
logical operators, 75
Logo (programming language), 13
loops, 93-113, 95
    and iteration, 93-95
    exit conditions, 98-100
    for adding arms to Zoog, 109
    for loop, 100

inside the main loop, 107-109
variable scope, 104
while loop, 95-97

M

Maeda, John, 13, 301
Making Things Talk (Igoe), 444
Mandelbrot, Benoit, 253
map() function, 244
mapping, 244
mathematics, 233-260
   and programming, 233
   angles, 246
   event probability in code, 237
   map() function, 244
   modulus, 234
   oscillation, 250-251
   Perlin noise, 240-242
   probability, 237
   random numbers, 236
   recursion, 253-256
   trigonometry, 247
   two-dimensional arrays, 257-260
McLuhan, Marshall, 301
methods, functions vs., 118
millis() function, 201
mirrors, software, 337-343
MIT Media Lab, 19
modularity, functions and, 121-124
modulo operator, 234
modulus, 234
mosaic(s), 371
motion, video detection of, 352
mouse
   clicks, 42-43
   location, 37-39
   rollover(s), 78, 396
mouseButton variable, 58
mouseDragged() function, 441
mousePressed variable, 58
mousePressed() function, 42
movie class, 330
MPEG StreamClip, 482
multi-user communication
   client, 440
   client and server, 443
   server, 437-439
multiple rollovers, 78

N

network libraries, 226
network socket(s), 428
new PImage() function, 303
newline character, 430
noise() function, 241
noiseDetail() function, 241
nonstandardized data, input from, 396-400
null value, 146

O

object references, 51
object(s), 139-159
   advantages of using, 141
   arrays of, 175
   arrays of interactive, 178
   as data types, 155
   conceptual discussion of, 139
   constructor arguments for, 151-152
   declaring variable for, 146
   initializing, 146
   interactive, 178
   making a Zoog class, 156
   tabs for, 147-150
   using, 145-147
   writing template for, 143
object-oriented programming
   advanced, 487-502
   encapsulation, 487-490
   inheritance, 490-496
   overloading, 501
   polymorphism, 497-500
objects, 4, 140
opacity, color, 14
OpenCV for Processing (Borenstein), 356
operation, array, 170
oscillation, 250-251
oscillator objects, 461
overloading, 501

P

P3D, 271
p5.js, 473
Papert, Seymour, 13
PApplet, 505
parameters
   arguments vs., 127
   defined, 125

with functions, 124-128
Parker, Dorothy, 163
particle system, 511
passing arguments, 127
passing by copy (passing by value), 129, 156
PDF files, high-resolution, 476-480
PDF libraries, 226
Perlin noise, 240-242, 244
Perlin, Ken, 240
philosophy of incremental development, 18-20, 60
physics (gravity simulation), 89-90
pi (π), 247
PImage class, 301, 315
pixel group processing, 320-322
pixel(s), 3-17
    and color transparency, 14
    and grayscale color, 10
    and RGB color, 12
    and simple shapes, 5-8
    custom color ranges, 15-17
    graph paper example, 3
    group processing, 320-322
    manipulating in images, 310-312
    writing to destination PImage, 318-320
playback, sound
    basic, 453-457
    for sound effects, 454
    real-time manipulation of, 457-459
polar coordinates, 248
polymorphism, 497-500
popMatrix() function, 285-291
port numbers, 428
primitive values, 51, 146
println() function, 24, 222-224
probability
    event probability in code, 237
    review of basics, 237
Processing
    and Run button, 29
    and sketches, 22
    as expansion of Java, 503
    basics of, 11-14
    coding in, 23-25
    downloading and installing, 20
    error tracking, 25
    Java and, 14
    origins of, 13, 473
    preparing to use, 19-30

reasons to use, 19
reference for, 27
testing before using, 20-22
translation of code into Java, 504-506
web incompatibility of, 15
when Java is preferable to, 520
Zoog sketch example, 29
Processing Foundation, 473
processing.js, 474
Processing.py, 473
programming, mathematics and, 233
pseudo-random numbers, 236
PShape, 294
public designation, 505
pushMatrix() function, 285-291
PVector class, 514
Python Mode, 25

R
radians, 246
radians() function, 247
Rain Game (algorithm example), 192
    breaking down description into parts, 192
    catcher for, 193
    integration of elements, 209
    intersection functionality, 195-213
    raindrops for, 204-208
    timer for, 201
random (term), 240
random class, 507
random numbers, 236
    and event probability in code, 237
    and Perlin noise, 240-242
random() function, 60-61, 132, 236, 237
ranges, custom color, 15-17
read() function, 432
readString() function, 429
readStringUntil() function, 448
Reas, Casey, 13, 19, 473
rect() function, 7, 27
Rectangle class, 516
recursion, 253-256
Reeves, William T., 511
refactoring, 156
reference, Processing, 27
return statement, 133
return type, 132-134
RGB color, 12

rollover() function, 178
rollover(s)
    circle, 396
    multiple, 78, 396
    rectangle, 78
rotation
    around different axes, 280-282
    Processing solar system example, 292
    simple, 277
    text, 373
Run button, 29

S

Sagan, Carl, 49
saturation, 16
save() function, 480
saveFrame() function, 480
scale() function, 284
scope, 104
screen, placing text on, 365
second() function, 201
sensor, video as, 345-347
serial communication, 444-446
    with handshaking, 446
    with strings, 448
serial libraries, 226
server
    broadcasting from, 434
    creating, 428-431
    multi-user communication, 437-439, 443
serverEvent() function, 429
setter functions, 488
setup() function, 34-36, 104, 143
shapes
    custom 3D, 275
    PShape for storing, 294
    simple, 5-8
    vertex, 272
simple modularity, 121-124
simple rotation, 277
simple shapes, 5-8
sine, 247
size() function, 23, 271
sketches, 22
    conditionals in, 72
    exporting, 473-484
    first example, 29
    publishing as stand-alone applications, 474

socket(s), 428
software mirrors, 337-343
sound, 453-471
    analysis, 464
    basic playback, 453-457
    manipulating during playback, 457-459
    spectrum analysis, 470
    synthesis, 460-464
    thresholding, 466-468
sound libraries, 226
spatial convolution, 322
spectrum analysis, 470
stand-alone applications, exporting, 474
Star Trek II: The Wrath of Khan (film), 511
String class
    defined, 362-364
    text and, 361
string objects, 383
string(s)
    concatenation for data input, 385-388
    manipulating for data input, 383
    serial communication with, 448
StringList class, 515
stroke() function, 10
substring() function, 384
super() function, 492
synchronous data streams, 427
synthesis, sound, 460-464
system variables, 58

T

tab-separated values (TSVs), 391
tables, 391-394
tabs, creating, 147-150
tabular data, 391-394
tangent, 247
telnet, 431
temporary arguments, 152
text, 361-382
    and String class, 361
    animation, 368-370
    displaying, 365-367
    displaying character by character, 375-382
    displaying in PDFs, 479
    mosaic, 371
    placing on screen, 365
    rotating, 373
    String, defined, 362-364

text analysis, 402-406
text editing software, 20
text files, 390
textAlign() function, 368
textFont() function, 365
textWidth() function, 368, 376
third-party (contributed) libraries, 226
this argument, 330
thread() function, 422
thread(s), 421-423
threshold filter, 318
thresholding, sound, 466-468
timer(s), 201
tint() function, 307
    custom tinting algorithms, 316
    for images, 307
toLowerCase() function, 363
Tomlin, Lily, 225
toUpperCase() function, 363
transformation matrix, 285-291
translate() function, 267
translation, 265-293
    and custom 3D shapes, 275
    and scale() function, 284
    and transformation matrix, 285-291
    and vertex shapes, 272
    and Z-axis, 265-271
    P3D for, 271
    Processing solar system example, 292
    rotation around different axes, 280-282
    simple rotation, 277
    text rotation, 373
transparency, color, 14
triangles, 247
trigonometric functions, 250-251
trigonometry, 247
try catch, 519
Twain, Mark, 219
two-dimensional arrays, 257-260

V

variable scope, 104
variables, 49-62
    and random() function, 60-61
    array as list of, 166
    boolean, 79-81
    declaration, 146
    declaration and initialization, 51-52
    defined, 49
    for adding functionality, 62
    global vs. local, 104
    system, 58
    using, 53-56
    using multiple, 57
verbs, 4
vertex shapes, 272
vertex() function, 275
video, 329-357
    as sensor, 345-347
    background removal, 349-352
    computer vision libraries, 356
    exporting, 480-482
    for computer vision, 345-347
    live, 329-333
    motion detection, 352
    recorded, 335
    software mirrors, 337-343
video libraries, 226
vision, computer, 345-347, 356
visualization, creative, 324

W

web
    exporting to, 473
    Processing incompatibility, 15
while loop, 95-97, 171
width variable, 58
Wilde, Oscar, 139

X

XML feed, 398
XML, data input from, 406-413

Z

Z-axis, 265-271
Zoog (application example), 16
    adding functionality with variables, 62
    and translate() function, 270
    conditionals for animation, 83-88
    dynamic sketch, 35-36
    mouse interaction, 43
    multiplying with arrays, 182
    reorganizing with functions, 135
    static sketch, 29
    using loops to add arms, 109
    with object-oriented programming, 156